WITHDRAWN
HARVARD LIBRARY
WITHDRAWN

PHILOSOPHY AND THE CIVILIZING ARTS:
ESSAYS PRESENTED TO HERBERT W. SCHNEIDER
ON HIS EIGHTIETH BIRTHDAY

HERBERT W. SCHNEIDER

PHILOSOPHY

AND THE CIVILIZING ARTS

Essays Presented to

Herbert W. Schneider

Edited by

Craig Walton and John P. Anton

OHIO UNIVERSITY PRESS / ATHENS

Copyright © 1974 by Craig Walton and John P. Anton
Library of Congress Catalog Number LC 73 — 92907
ISBN 8214-0145-9
Manufactured in the United States of America by
Oberlin Printing Co., Inc.
Design by Hal Stevens
All Rights Reserved

CONTENTS

I. Editors' Preface, with *Tabula congratulatoria* vii
II. Biographical Sketch of Herbert W. Schneider xi
III. Studies in Ancient Philosophy
    1. "Tragic Vision and Philosophic Theoria in Classical Greece," by John P. Anton 1
    2. "Poliscraft," by Max Fisch 24
    3. "Dialogue and Dialectic," by Victorino Tejera ... 49
    4. "A Key to Plato's Early Dialogues," by Theodore Waldman 60
IV. Studies in Modern Philosophy
    5. "On Hobbes's Humanism," by Bertram Morris .. 89
    6. "Hume and Jefferson on the Uses of History," by Craig Walton 103
    7. "The Philosophical Bases of Modern Racism," by Richard H. Popkin 126
    8. "Science and Social Progress," by Joseph L. Blau 166
    9. "Naturalism in American Philosophy," by Paul Kurtz 178
    10. "Philosophical Puns," by George Kline 213
    11. "Kant's Ethics as a Part of Metaphysics: A Possible Development of Newtonianism," by Giorgio Tonelli 236

Contents

- V. Studies in Social Theory
  - 12. "Promise and Peril in Pragmatic Historical Thought," by Whitaker T. Deininger 264
  - 13. "Institutions and the Alienated Man," by Darnell Rucker 283
  - 14. "The Experience of Value," by Ralph Ross 316
- VI. Studies in Problems of Education
  - 15. "Educating the Person," by James L. Jarrett .. 345
  - 16. "Advice to the New Philosophy Teacher," by Lewis Hahn 356
  - 17. "The Moral Responsibilities of Teachers of Philosophy," by J. Glenn Gray 370
  - 18. "Religion Among the Liberal Arts," by John A. Hutchison 378
  - 19. " 'New Heavens, New Earth' — The Landscape of Contemporary Apocalypse," by Nathan Scott 389
- VII. Papers by Herbert W. Schneider
  - 20. "The American Establishment, The Civilizing Arts, and Philosophy" 433
  - 21. "Radical Empiricism and Religion" 446
  - 22. "Philosophy Will Never Be a Science" 467
  - 23. "Reasonable Rationalism: The Heritage of the Enlightenment" 474
  - 24. "Community, Communication and Communion" 487
- VIII. Bibliography of Published Works of Herbert W. Schneider 495
- IX. Brief Biographical Notes on Contributors 505

PHILOSOPHY AND THE CIVILIZING ARTS:
Essays in Honor of Herbert W. Schneider

I. Editors' Preface

WITH FEW EXCEPTIONS, THE PAPERS IN THIS VOLUME WERE presented to Herbert Schneider at a surprise party held on March 25, 1972, at the Faculty Club of the University of California at Berkeley. Speeches of tribute were offered by Edward Strong, Bertram Morris, John Anton, Beatrice Yamasaki, Richard Popkin, Joseph Blau and Craig Walton. Others attending were:

Morton Beckner	James Groves
John Cambus	Jean Harrell
Jane Cauvel	Kathleen Harrington
Mr. and Mrs. Stanley Daugert	James Jarrett
Whitaker Deininger	William Kerr
William Dennis	George Kline
James Doyle	Mrs. Bertram Morris
Stephen Erikson	Stephen Pepper†
John Fisher	Ralph Ross
Marjorie Grene	Darnell Rucker
	Mary Welsley

To the regret of all who knew her or benefited from her

Editor's Preface

inspiration, Adrienne Koch passed away shortly before the celebration took place. She had planned to participate and pay a personal tribute to her "beloved mentor." The following colleagues and friends of Herbert Schneider asked to be counted as present in spirit though unable to attend:

Justus Buchler
Frederick Burkhardt
William Callaghan
Shepard B. Clough
Stanley Creon
Paul Edwards
Wm. F. Edwards
Charles Frankel
Horace Friess
Edwin Garlan
George Geiger
Stanley Grean
Harold Hantz
W. T. Jones
Donald F. Koch
Paul Oskar Kristeller

Sterling Lamprecht†
Harold Larrabee
John Malcolm
Benson Mates
Eugene Mayers
Emmanuel Mesthene
J. Brooke Mosley
David F. Norton
P. T. Raju
John Herman Randall, Jr.
Cyril Richardson
Patrick Romanell
Frederick Sontag
Janet L. Travis
Eric Weil
W. H. Werkmeister
Daniel Day Williams

Papers for this occasion were invited without restrictions as to theme. Herbert Schneider's personal example as teacher and writer, philosopher and scholar, has touched the lives of Americans over a wide range of interests and six decades thus far, so that the editors' project could not be readily confinable to one school of thought or academic discipline. It was believed that once the papers arrived, they would fall into an order of their own. Fortunately such a grouping emerged, as our table of contents indicates. If there is some deeper theme connecting these essays, it is above all a spirit of investigation, born of love of human wisdom and sustained by the enduring and initial amazement at the panorama of human follies and nobilities taken in the flesh and studied for whatever they may offer. The variety of inspirations and themes, of critique and intuition here offered reflect the range and depth of response to Professor Schneider's appeal to the American scholar, here published for the

Preface

first time under the title, "The American Establishment, the Civilizing Arts and Philosophy." To assist in making this affinity more palpable, we have chosen to include four papers by Herbert Schneider previously published but presently hard to find, as especially exemplary of his wit, balance and humanity.

The editors wish especially to thank Mr. Jon Parks for his labors in preparing an early version of the bibliography, and Professor James Jarrett for his tireless efforts to arrange for the banquet. The typing assistance of the secretarial staff at the Departments of Philosophy of Northern Illinois University and the University of Nevada, Las Vegas, is gratefully acknowledged. The biographical sketch which follows owes much to the valuable suggestions and information supplied by Professors H. Larrabee, J. Blau and R. Popkin. It must be added that the basic ideas for the editorial arrangement of these papers came from Professor Schneider himself, who was kind enough to suggest where the joints lay. Finally, without the kindness and support of an anonymous donor, the Associated Colleges in Claremont, Calif., and Mr. Oskar Piest, publication would not have been possible. To Ms. Patricia Fitch and her staff at the Ohio University Press at Athens we owe a special debt for the encouragement we received and the care with which the printing of this volume was accomplished.

Craig Walton
John P. Anton

HERBERT WALLACE SCHNEIDER
A Biographical Sketch

HERBERT SCHNEIDER LIVES IN A WELL-WINDOWED, AIRY and spacious, though small house partly hidden by old trees and bushes, in Claremont, California. A visitor may be asked to join in a walk through the small college town whose doctoral program in philosophy was brought into this world by his host. It is a town of many trees, mostly houses and permanent families, students and faculty who have enjoyed and prized Schneider's gentle influence and subtle example over the years. Returning to his home, the visitor cannot help but notice the daily details of the life of one of America's well-known "helpers" — letters, projects, phone calls, all manner of communications from men and women in many areas of study, affairs and the arts sharing their activities because they treasure his responses and gentle comment (the point of which it is often a long and heartwarming labor to find). Many countries, many disciplines, many points of view come together at his desk where he continues to reply, nourish, guide and bring together young and old from many concerns, each of them finding a larger, more varied and far richer world for their efforts.

If the visitor were to ask, and persist when first turned from the subject toward something less personal, he might find out some of the personal story Herbert Schneider rarely

Biographical Sketch of Herbert W. Schneider

tells, and then only in pieces — but it is a story the more remarkable for being so hard to gather together. In this volume brought together by a few of his pupils and friends as a partial honor to his scholarly achievement and interpersonal genius, some introduction must be attempted in spite of the genuine modesty of its object. In a country where European settlers have not yet been here 400 years, Herbert Schneider has been not only here but also giving to and lending scholarly insight into its culture for the greater part of over 80 years. The fullness of his contribution to this country and to the international community of scholars will never be fully assessed, but on this occasion some beginnings in that direction are surely justified — though thankfully his work continues at a more brisk pace than any bibliographer could match.

Professor Schneider was born in Berea, Ohio on March 16, 1892. His father, Frederick William Schneider, was a Methodist minister and also vice-president and a professor of German at Wallace College (later Baldwin-Wallace). When about 19, he and his parents moved to Brooklyn in order to obtain the best quality education the parents could find — and thus began Herbert Schneider's 60-odd year contact with Columbia University, his first meeting with Frederick J. E. Woodbridge, John Dewey, John Coss and W. T. Bush, and soon the assembling of what became Columbia's golden age in philosophy and America's strongest, most influential group of gifted and open philosophers active in one place. Schneider completed the B. A. at Columbia in 1915, and by 1917 had worked under John Dewey to complete his doctoral dissertation titled, "Ethics as the Science of Social Progress."

In his 80-plus years thus far, Herbert Schneider's playfulness and work have not been confined to scholarship and philosophical reflection, but have entered into several "careers" at once — in addition to scholarship and reflection, there are long and fruitful stories of Professor Schneider as a builder and maintainer of programs or institutionalizations of cherished insights; as internationalist who has opened many Americans to the rest of the world, and many

Biographical Sketch of Herbert W. Schneider

Asians and Europeans to America; and finally as teacher and friend to many whose lives are altered by his inspiration and solid support. In what follows, we shall begin with some pieces of the story of his scholarship and philosophical reflection, then proceed to his other careers — as builder, internationalist, and colleague.

By 1930, the theory of relativity had hit the learned world with an unavoidable bombshell, assimilation of which is not yet complete. Trying to reach back from the United States of that time to the earliest beginnings of the Puritan movement in the early 1600's, Professor Schneider's *Puritan Mind* began with one of the most stimulating and sensible comments on the scholar's work to be seen in recent times: the present and past interpret each other, in us; we measure bodies from points themselves in motion, in the mental as well as the physical dimensions. We learn that nothing is *itself* intelligible, but that things make each other intelligible. Perhaps science and society evolve continuously, but the fine arts — philosophy, religion, music, poetry, etc. — wander wherever "the spirit listeth"; they are not "surplus products" but the very essence of life. "The skeleton of an idea may be examined by the logician after its death; ... as an incident in the study of life, [his autopsy] is useful, but as a substitute for it, it is philosophic fanaticism."

About 1920, John Coss suggested that Professor Schneider consider a history of American philosophy; in 1946 the work was completed (and dedicated to Coss). Schneider's wide reading and genuine respect for the efforts, well- or poorly-done, of long-dead men and women to come to grips with themselves and their world yielded just the opposite of what was then being called "history" of philosophy. That is, instead of finding one *Volksgeist* running silent and deep beneath the surface of only-apparent variety, he found no one "Americanism" at all, but a remarkably rich and (to this day) unrejected legacy of foreign inspirations, native accomodations and responses, civic and religious construction and academic jargon, an inferiority that we feel "intellectually colonial" but also a vitality and re-interpretation

Biographical Sketch of Herbert W. Schneider

of European influence into American idiom and realities which, one might add, is not too frequent a sight in some of the intellectually imperial capitals of Europe. In the 17th and 18th centuries, philosophy flourished though it was not taught — because it was the motivating core of arts and sciences, not a separate "body" of doctrines. When interest shifted, in the 19th century, from inquiry and construction to systems and "orthodoxy," philosophy become a "subject" which developed its own "professors." Whether Schneider heard such a view from Dewey, or *vice versa* (Schneider was Dewey's assistant from 1920 till 1935, colleague till Dewey's death in 1952), Dewey did express the view, recorded in Schneider's *History,* that philosophy is a general *theory* of education, where the several civilizing arts (teaching, governing, music, painting, literature, family, devotion, etc.) were the *practice* of that theory. The wedding of theory to practice then becomes the job of introducing *into* the activities of all who work, some educational process by which they can tie their works in to each other and to life as they all have it in common in that time and place. *Then* schools would be closer to the culture, and the actions of life enlightened. Professor Schneider's most recent edition of his *History* appends the story of critical realism as it was emerging just before and then during his own years at Columbia, a story of the fashioning of a logic, a psychology and a theory of act whereby the haunting and sterile dualisms of subject/object, internal/external, noumenal/phenomenal, fact/value, individual/ communal, mind/body and so many more were attacked, undermined and demolished to lay clear the ground for "reconstruction" such as began to emerge in the works of Dewey, Mead, later Lamprecht, Buchler, Randall, and so many others (including, though never mentioned in his *History,* the "constructive" works of Professor Schneider himself).

One of the first of these works in book form was *Three Dimensions of Public Morality* (1956), part of which grew out of Schneider's assisting Dewey 1920-1935 in seminars such as Moral and Political Philosophy. Other contributions to this work came from interdisciplinary courses and several

Biographical Sketch of Herbert W. Schneider

years as head of UNESCO's Division of International Cultural Cooperation in Paris. Man's ability to listen, learn, work or devote himself so as to make something "else" his "own," to "appropriate" a world, is the basis for his ability to respond to others and from response-ability arise his dignity and freedom as worked outcomes (not innate gifts).

"The moral schizophrenia which most needs diagnosis and cure is the inner, intellectual corruption that we have undergone as persons allowing ourselves to be carried away by diverging ideals. Our consciences are in peril when we pay lip service to three incompatible ideals. Liberty is in danger of going toward what Hobbes described as its inevitable culmination, 'the war of all against all.' Equality is in danger of sanctioning tyranny and cruelty, while fraternity is apt to cloak bigotry. The three ancient specters — war, tyranny, fanaticism — which have haunted the growth of civilization for ages have now returned to oppress us more savagely than ever." This book, then, is Professor Schneider's effort philosophically to clarify liberty, equality and fraternity in order to be able to evaluate and labor toward them as converging and compatible. Liberty means the gaining recognition of rights claimed; equality adds to this public recognition an acceptance of each person's *needs*. We cannot ask others to make us happy, but we must ask each other to make us all secure, and to give public attention to each one's needs. Finally, fraternity is that dimension of public morality by which we encourage and cultivate personal standards — not so much brotherly love as the moral discipline of brotherhood: living in peace and aiding each other when needed.

We learn of evil through daily experience; of good, only gradually and as principles. These principles are basic, yet they come late and cannot be inherited. In his 1960 *Morals for Mankind,* Professor Schneider tackles the question of a possible global moral frame for our fast-developing global activities. In one sense, transcultural contacts *are* fertilizing shared values; but there is no global value-set at present. At this time, any human value-creations must be esteemed as contributory to the human effort to improve global condi-

Biographical Sketch of Herbert W. Schneider

tions of life. How "improve" life without one set of values to define the terms? There is no known beginning *or* end of civilization, but improvement of it is not a "value" so much as a process of interplay and cooperating. We are "at sea" and "in fairly deep water"; we require a "traveler's code" for keeping the human race together through all sorts of weather. What bonds exist now, as a network for common interests? Professor Schneider develops three suggestions: common needs (the shared *means* to particular ends such as life, health, work, play, home, liberty); reciprocal obligations (e.g. refrain from inhumanity and terrorism); and finally liberal exchanges (not for friendship so much as for neighborliness, the sharing of experience, differences and resources). "A universal neighborliness does not imply a 'love' of all mankind nor even a respect for the dignity of every man. Love and respect are later developments. Concerns, duties, and neighborliness come first, and the first of these three is neighborliness. Love begins at home, but conscience should not be so exclusive. Morality is seriously defective until it includes mankind, not only on scientific principle but also in actual behavior."

After some fifty years of reading, trying out and interpreting various philosophers' ontologies, Professor Schneider accepted the offer to give a series of lectures in honor of his teacher Woodbridge, lectures published as *Ways of Being* (1962). His aim was not to claim that there "is" one Whole System unifying all that is — on that issue he gently foregoes the privilege — but to try to begin where we are, and explore the "fields". Unlike Aristotle who sought the *what* via the four *aitiai,* Professor Schneider seeks *how* things are, with four areas of questions: (1) identification (who? which?); (2) definition or classification (what?); (3) correlation (wherefor? where-to? why?); and (4) orientation (where-in? field or residence). Each of these questionings is an operation, the first and fourth being most important, second and third operations being secondary. He then explores three ways of being — natural, cultural, and formal. Natural being is the area of interaction and processes; its fields are space/time, electromagnetics, natural history, selectivity and finality.

Biographical Sketch of Herbert W. Schneider

Cultural being is the area of transaction and procedures, its four elements being the funding of memory, the vesting of interests, organizing of ideas and the vitality of imagination. Its four categories are historical being, moral being, co-existence and communion. Formal being is the area of order and systems, their logics and instrumentalities; here the five contexts of ideas-in-systems are in relationship to (1) nature, (2) culture, (3) systems of symbolism, (4) systems of implication, and (5) systems of evidence. Some concrete "chaos" must already be given if the theoretician of order is to bring order out of it; no merely theoretical chaos will do, as far as ontologists are concerned. Therefore here we would do well "to refrain from saying much about the order of orders or the structure of the world of all possible formulations. There are those who imagine universal order to be the best of all possible worlds, but, being a world of endless dictionaries, it is obviously no place to live." We can explore the fields which are about us, as to how they are, and we do find togetherness of some beings and dimensions of being with others, in several ways discussed here as "fitnesses" or "harmonies," objectively found, so that the demands of situational structures upon the ontologist lead finally to an objective relativism. Finally:

> "Reality is the subject-given as well as the object-to-be-known of ontological analysis, and to imagine that there is a wide gulf between the world whence our questioning arises and the reality which we learn to know is to make an assumption designed to be frustrating. In other words, the concepts of the unconditional and of the immediate are both abstractions. Reality is not a succession of pure immediacies held in chains by the all-encompassing world, nor is it a final, superworldly resting place for minds at their wits' end. If reality is real it must be identical with the world in which both bodies and minds work together. But the truth about this world is less real, for it exists only in fragments and varying perspectives; in its ideal form or perfection it does not exist at all."

Dewey wrote Schneider a letter about how he might alter his own *Experience and Nature* some years after its publication. The letter, pages 42f. of *Ways of Being,* deserves some study

Biographical Sketch of Herbert W. Schneider

as to the close relationship and intriguing differences between Dewey and Schneider. These few brief comments on a few of Herbert Schneider's philosophical works can only suggest their breadth and depth, or the work for which they make a beginning. Professor Schneider's building labors have not been confined to original research and philosophical reflection. In the early 1920's he worked with John Coss and Irwin Edman to replace introductory philosophy "textbooks" with reading of original sources. Woodbridge, Dewey, W. T. Bush and John Coss undertook building their department by adding Schneider, Edman, then John Herman Randall, Jr., James Gutmann, Horace Friess and Ernest Nagel. Soon after the change in the introductory philosophy course, Schneider was one of the chief organizing talents behind construction of a two year Contemporary Civilization course, taught by members of the philosophy, history and social science faculties (including Randall, Friess, Edman, Tugwell, and Karmen). The staff had to assemble their own readings in that pre-paperback age, and their "syllabus" became an original-sources study of the development of Western culture since the Renaissance, crossing economic and political with philosophic and artistic developments to lay a foundation for students' coming to terms with their times. It became a model, soon to be copied (at Harvard and elsewhere) or "rebutted" (at Chicago). Professors Schneider, Edman and Friess also initiated Columbia's first philosophy of religion course about 1926, and in 1936, Schneider founded what became an international journal for the scholarly study of man's religions, *The Review of Religion* (which shut down in 1958). In 1943, Schneider worked with an interdepartmental committee to create a Ph.D. curriculum in the Study of Religion, which later gave rise to the present Department of Religion and was of incalculable influence as a precedent that man's religions could be seriously studied to the student's enlightenment without preachment, provincialism or church/state collusion.

Not even the compiling of the appended bibliography of

Biographical Sketch of Herbert W. Schneider

Professor Schneider's published works could possibly locate the hundreds of studies, translations and treatises dedicated to him as their source of inspiration. Some note can be made, however, of his efforts to sustain and strengthen Woodbridge and Bush's *Journal of Philosophy*. Professor Schneider began lending editorial labors of every sort in the early 1920's, was first named on the masthead in July of 1924. His name appeared there next to Woodbridge and Bush until their deaths, so close one upon the other, in June of 1940 and February of 1941 (respectively). At that point Schneider was joined by Professors Randall and Nagel, the three being listed in that order until 1961, after which all three were to yield to the younger Columbia colleagues now editing the *Journal*. But "youth" is hardly easily defined, for at the same time he was withdrawing from work on the *Journal of Philosophy,* Professor Schneider was meeting with Professors Edward Strong, John Goheen and Richard H. Popkin to discuss founding a new journal, the first issue of which appeared in 1963 as the *Journal of the History of Philosophy*. Today, some ten years later, that journal is respected internationally and has set a high standard of scholarship both here and abroad. What is not so well known is the organizational and promotional, financial and interpersonal genius which brought it forth and nourished it so richly in vital ways — the genius, all hands attest, of Herbert Schneider. Mention was made earlier of his bringing Claremont Graduate School's Ph.D. program into the world — with vitally needed financial aids somehow located as well. In addition the Blaisdell Institute for the Study of Religions and Cultures counted him as its Director (1957-1962) and owes its considerable contribution of convening the International Association for the History of Religions meeting in Claremont (Spring, 1966) to the scholarly-entrepreneurial magic of Professor Schneider. Those who have succeeded, and those who have failed at bringing about scholarly and personal interchange even on temporary bases must marvel at this partial recounting of one man's philosophical enterprise.

Closely related to his building of institutions within the United States are Professor Schneider's projects to bring

Biographical Sketch of Herbert W. Schneider

Americans to Europe and Asia, and Europeans and Asians to America in person and by their writings. The bibliography of this volume is some indicator of the reach of his travels and participation abroad; in a short space we can only mention facets of his internationalism. In 1926 he traveled to the new fascist state of Italy to study its emergence and meet its leaders, a work which resulted in this country's first scholarly treatment of the *fascisti*. His travels to India and work on the East-West Philosophers' Conferences are noted by their published outcomes, but the strength of ties then created and by which Asian scholars have been drawn to explore and share with Occidentals can hardly be praised enough or appraised at all at this early date in the global interchanges constituting "the Republic of Letters." Professor Schneider served many years on the American Philosophical Association's Committee on International Cooperation, which he chaired for several years and which has served to fertilize "liberal exchanges." In addition to the internationality of projects already discussed, finally notice must be taken of UNESCO's invitation to Professor Schneider to serve (1953-1956) as head of its Division of International Cultural Cooperation. Needless to say, uncounted scholars later came to the United States or from the United States to Europe and Asia because of his efforts at that time — only some of the names are a matter of record. The International Bibliography of Philosophy was undertaken at that time due to his efforts, as was the founding of the International Association for the History of Religions. It is a further measure of the man that the author of the most richly researched volume on the history of American philosophers, great and small, is also one of the most active links between American scholars and those of Europe and Asia.

Our present purpose was only to attempt a sketch. The drama and detail of so much of Herbert Schneider's gift to American and international life and learning must wait for full treatment elsewhere. But something of Herbert Schneider, the teacher and colleague, must be somehow mentioned even though the deeper interpersonal relationships perforce

Biographical Sketch of Herbert W. Schneider

tie the tongues of the eloquent. Professor Blau recounts a luncheon some thirty years ago during which Herbert Schneider somewhat off-handedly remarked that, "The first verse of Genesis ought to be translated, 'Now, to begin our story, God created the heaven and the earth'." He knew some small bits of Hebrew, and had studied some texts, but as a philosopher he was bothered by "in the beginning," and as a gifted writer he transformed the historical absoluteness of "in the beginning" to the mythic quality of our story's beginning. Though today's newest translations are not literally his version, they are remarkably closer to mythic utterance than absolute history. Students, correspondents and colleagues in all walks of life would draw a similar moral from their own similar experiences, namely that Herbert Schneider has casually tossed off more one-line insights than most of us will garner in an entire life of labor. Professor Klein has been so struck by these as to undertake a study of "philosophical puns," printed below, examining one of Professor Schneider's most typical instruments (for example, from his most recent book, *Civilized Religion:* "Being devout without being devoted brings religious observance into ill repute and hypocrisy.").

Some fourteen years ago, one of the editors of this volume first sat in a philosophy classroom—a course offered by Herbert Schneider on Ancient Greek and Roman Philosophy. After some weeks had passed, each day finding at least some students both prepared by having read assignments yet unprepared for the treasures so casually and gently turned up from between the lines, time came for an assignment: we were to write our "reflections" on the *Euthyphro, Apology, Crito* and *Phaedo*. After class, students gathered around, utterly baffled. "What do you mean, 'reflections'? What are we supposed to do?" Yes, the word had been "reflections"; how does one reflect? We departed, flattered and deeply puzzled — flattered that even we might be capable of something interesting as a response after 2300 years of students' responses, yet puzzled as to what we were "supposed to do." There was some grumbling that it was an impossible assignment. But for others, it was the beginning of a most strange

Biographical Sketch of Herbert W. Schneider

possibility become actual — that the learned might listen to fools, that the older ones might want to hear the younger ones, that even though philosophers have labored over many centuries there might be something yet ahead to be found even in oneself, if the interest of such a gentle but learned scholar were any mark. We know of hundreds whose lives in American learning began in something much like this event; there may be thousands. Herbert Schneider expresses his questions and shares his responses so that others respond from the best they can muster, and often learn from him of the work they themselves have (even unwittingly) already begun. His genuine interest and respect for the widest range of persons, from an almost-equally wide range of studies, seem to work upon those persons not only as support but as inspiration and challenge all at once. Philosophers and their philosophies are so-engendered. But that is not wholly unprecedented. In "Philosophy Will Never Be a Science" (reprinted below), Herbert Schneider wrote:

"...the philosopher is a Socratic man, wisely seeking truth among men. Philosophical truth is found only in the context of human life and hence the philosophical mind must have a genuine love for human affairs and a readiness to remain in human fellowship. Both the pursuit of truth and the pursuit of wisdom may be endless, but they are endless in different ways. Truth remains eventual; it comes at the end. But wisdom is more analagous to happiness; the pursuit of wisdom and happiness requires that these goals be conceived not as end-products, but as qualifications of the pursuit, exhibiting themselves along the way. Wisdom and happiness are not objects; they are ways of being human."

Craig Walton
John P. Anton

1

TRAGIC VISION AND PHILOSOPHIC *THEORIA* IN CLASSICAL GREECE*

John P. Anton

INTRODUCTION

*With the kind permission of Prof. Schneider, this paper is published simultaneously in the Greek journal *Diotima* (I, 1973), pp. 11-31.

THE ANCIENT GREEKS WERE FULLY AWARE OF THE AFFINITY between tragic poetry and philosophic thinking. Although the relationships between these two basic pursuits of the classical mind are far too intricate to be discussed within the limits of a brief essay, at least certain essential aspects that help us understand the points of convergence between tragic vision and philosophic theoria can be explored with some hope of success. The thesis of this paper is that there was a unified and integrated set of ideals expressed through the works of artists, poets, orators, lawgivers, statesmen and philosophers of Greece. More specifically, the purpose here is to understand in what ways philosopher and tragedian ultimately addressed themselves

Tragic Vision and Philosophic Theoria

to the same lofty concern and served the same goal: to illumine the condition of man and set the limits of man's aspiration to perfection. The universe of the poets and that of the philosophers, despite their rhetorical differences and ways of approaching the wonders and splendors of man and nature, were one and the same cosmos. Emotional thought and rational passion both were considered gateways leading directly to the citadel of wisdom, to understanding "being" and "becoming." As enterprises with special educational claims, tragic poetry and philosophic prose were alike pursuing the quest for harmony in the powers of man's soul. The assumed harmony of the celestial spheres, the order of the intelligible cosmos, is essentially akin to man's nature.[1] The ideal of *harmonia* as the high point of conduct and aspiration was believed to be communicated through the effects of poetry and the discourses of philosophy. When Plato taught that human beings can reproduce the divine order only by knowing it he was repeating and extending a deep conviction shared by poets and sages of long before his time. He said in the *Republic* that "familiarity with the divine and orderly makes the philosopher divine and orderly as far as man may be" (500C); and again in the *Timaeus*: "By learning to know them and acquiring the power to compute them rightly according to nature, we may reproduce the necessary revolutions of the universe and reduce to settled order the wandering motions in ourselves" (47C).

Tragic vision is most difficult to define. It stands for what the tragedian himself has seen and understood to be the spectacle of life and what he wants us to see once we have reached the threshold of catharsis. The tragic feelings of pity and terror, brought about through action cast in poetic *logos*, lead to an experience beyond themselves. Catharsis is only the prelude to a dramatic kind of understanding. Here, the emotions brought to a peak suddenly fold upon

---

1. See also F. M. Cornford, *The Unwritten Philosophy and Other Essays* (Cambridge: University Press, 1950), especially the essay "The Harmony of the Spheres," pp. 20 ff.

John P. Anton

themselves and without losing their qualitative intensity lead to a profound insight into the unexpected possibilities of the human situation fraught as they are with ambiguity and uncertainty. The difficulty with defining philosophic vision is comparable. Ever since the speculations of the pre-Socratics, Greek thought was a continuous and unbroken effort on the part of its leading practitioners to stretch the powers of the mind to their ultimate, the purpose of which remained unchanging throughout the ancient era: to see man and nature and to view both wholly and steadily. But philosophic *logos* for the Greeks was more than a passion for inquiry and flawless thinking. It was directed toward the noble goals of the good life, both individual and collective. The theoria, the vision of man and nature in which philosophers sought to find fulfillment, was always meant to have a public as well as a private dimension. The perspicacity of the philosophic statement was tied to an educational and persuasive concern. The philosophers were citizens as much as the tragedians. Both addressed their *logoi* to the problems of man.[2]

My main objective in this paper is to discuss the background and the principles that kept together these two kinds of vision of human life: the philosophic and the tragic. The two visions are actually aspects of one and the same outlook, two sides of the same coin. Both were meant to serve the same end: to assist individual citizens bring to perfection the wholeness of their humanity. The driving force of these visions was the passion for the enrichment of the Greek *ethos*. To say that the objective is the same for poet and philosopher is not to imply that the Greeks failed to perceive the differences that make art and ethics separate enterprises, but only that they were convinced of the functional convergence between the two, even when these were spoken of as rivals. This adherence to the natural wholeness of man and the co-operative character of his cultural

---

2. W. Jaeger, *Paideia* (New York: Oxford University Press, 1960) I, "Introduction," p. xxii, where he emphasizes the way in which the *theoria* of Greek philosophy was deeply connected with Greek art and poetry.

enterprises in the pursuit of total fulfillment provided a conception of life with an immunity against inner disintegration and fragmentation in the *ethos*, at least from the philosophical point of view.

II

Greek anthropocentrism and the social context of conduct

It is virtually impossible for the intelligent student of classical Greek culture to examine the documents and monuments it left behind and not notice that the Greeks made the concern for man the pivotal point of their reflective and practical activities. On the whole, they conceived of their deities in anthropomorphic terms, placing them within nature and endowing them with limited power. The divinities were also notably preoccupied with tasks which had recognizable human relevance. It is significant that Greek art, sculpture in particular, found it delightful to work with the human form, so that when the gods were made visible in stone and marble no better way could be found than that of the idealized human body. Art was not the only activity that moved from the divine to the human and through the latter to restate the divine. Philosophy as the quest for wisdom enriched its reflective course by making increasingly explicit the scope of its investigations into the cosmos when it gave primacy to the problems of men. Tragedy, whatever its origins in religious rites and legends, settled for nothing less than the fate and fortunes of man. The essential characteristic, therefore, of the cultural development of classical Greece is its anthropocentric attitude, its humanistic consciousness. As Werner Jaeger has aptly said, "... other nations made gods, kings, spirits: the Greeks alone made men."[3]

When Aristotle defined *ousia* (substance) as designating a concrete and whole individual, he was summarizing in the neutral language of the newly formalized principles of the

---

3. *Ibid.* I, xxiii.

logic of nature what was all along the dominant classical conception of man, to wit a unified and integrated being, one of the many types of natural beings, but with his own set of distinctive features. For the Greeks all specific human processes and cultural enterprises, political, social, ethical, artistic, scientific, philosophical and religious, and all resulting systems of values and practices sanctioned through institutionalized conduct, refer and pertain to the total man as a concrete individual, whose nature is to be at once logical and political. This, I take it, is the core of the classical Greek anthropocentrism or humanism.

Clearly, then, there are four basic ingredients in this anthropocentrism from the point of view of ontology: (i) human beings *qua* individuals exemplify one kind of substance in the spectrum of living things; they are one kind of natural wholes or *onta physika*. (ii) Taken together all the kinds of wholes constitute a system of interrelated and interdependent entities providing the maximum natural environment for any given individual or group within the total collection of kinds of animate and inanimate beings. (iii) Each concrete individual as a whole is itself a unified thing possessing a plurality of powers, exhibiting activities and capable of undergoing sufferings. (iv) The human individual in particular appears to be the most complex entity of all the naturally unified beings the Greeks ever came to discover.

This Greek anthropocentrism was circumscribed by a philosophical naturalism with built-in criteria for fixing the boundaries for human fulfillment. The process whereby this fulfillment of the human potentialities was brought about called for conscious design, deliberation and discipline. Since it involved choice and an element of adventure, the Greeks soon found out that this activity was an art, not a science in the strict sense of the word, although as their men of wisdom kept reminding their fellow citizens, the activity could hardly advance its cause without the knowledge that science and experience give. As art it turned out to be a very unusual one. It became the art of the good life and was expected to culminate in cultural excellence. Its task

Tragic Vision and Philosophic Theoria

was to enhance the human potential such as it happened to be in each case and heighten the quality of life through transformations of nature in accordance with ideal ends. It called for candid evaluation of means and open debate about ends until nothing but the best could serve as the distinctly human good. Experience, failure as well as success, taught a good many Greeks the consequences of self-deception. Their intellectual record shows that they knew why it was that ignorance of the ways of nature — and of the gods — led to distorted views of the ways of man just as the unexamined choices led to perverted pursuits in politics and ethics. To live and live well demanded a calling for *energeia*, putting to work the powers and aspirations denoted by the idea of man. This sort of life demands that the goals set forth be pursued with all the force of intelligence. In fact, intelligence itself must co-ordinately reach its own excellence. This is *techne ariste*, the highest of the arts, culture and education at their best.[4]

Since the early days of their civilization the Greeks had learned that man has no choice over the factuality of his existence and the nature that sustains him. Both realms are regulated by *nomos*. If men, whether as individuals or communities, try to ignore the materials of existence, *Dike*, justice, will seek them out. Herodotus speaks of the *pthonos* (envy) the gods feel against any man who boasts of his being more than usually successful. Pindar (fr.169 DC) states that "Law is the king of all, of mortals and immortals alike, it carries all, judging the most violent deed with victorious hand." The philosophers reasoned that the scheme of all beings depends on universal balance and all nature obeys an obligating and regulating necessity. Any disturbance in this balance was intolerable and had to be set aright. As Anaximander said: "For things make reparation and satis-

---

4. *Ibid*. I, 274: "Culture was for the Greeks the original creation and original experience of a process of deliberate guidance and formation of human character. Understanding that, we shall also understand the power of such an ideal to inspire the imagination of a great poet. It was a moment unique in the history of the world when poetry and culture came together to create an ideal."

faction to one another according to the appointed time ..."
(fr. 1 DC); and Heraclitus: "The sun will not overstep his measure; if he does the Erinyes, the handmaids of Justice, will find them out" (fr. 94 DC).[5] Fortunately for the Greeks, all this thinking and talking about *nomos* and *physis*, law and nature, did not trap them to go into the arid problems of determinism. Being still fresh and excitable knowers they took the more rewarding path of finding out what freedom can mean when it stands for choosing to do something and work with the possibilities of nature and human nature. What impressed them most, evidently, was the discovery that they had the capacity to turn the totality of human endowment into a harmony of excellences, the sort of thing Plato came to mean by his idea of justice. But they also discovered that this task demanded not only a great deal of constant work but that it had to be a co-operative enterprise. The job had to be done in the *polis*, in the organized communities of men.[6]

The binding force of this conviction led to making the collective work of men a social and political excellence to which each citizen was expected to contribute and to emulate. It fell upon the genius of Plato to articulate with in-

---

5. The Orphic saga and pre-Socratic thinking spoke of the necessity of nature, the obligatory character of *Nomos*, which sets the limits of all process and hence makes prediction possible. The link between natural necessity and the principles of human justice was seen as the basis for condemning force and caprice in human affairs. Even in the heyday of sophistic thought when the demythologizing of Being and the sharp distinction between nature and convention were carrying the day, a radical sophist like Callicles (?) found it necessary to appeal to the nature of man to support his extreme position (Plato's *Gorgias*). Antiphon could speak of "laws implanted by nature" (fr. 44) which are being trampled on by artificial legal systems. Socrates, Plato, and Aristotle paid special attention to the grave problems generated by the sophistic separation of human nature from human laws which rendered the latter variable, capricious, and non-universal.

6. *See* W. Jaeger, *op. cit.*, xxv-xxvi, for the social foundations of the Greek ideals. "Any future humanism must be built on the fundamental fact of all Greek education — the fact that for the Greeks humanity always implied the essential quality of a human being, his political character ..." (xxvi).

Tragic Vision and Philosophic Theoria

clusiveness and precision the philosophical foundations of the social aspects of excellence. In his *Republic* he came to call it Justice, the harmony of excellences and ideal values, pictured vividly in the model Socrates essayed so laboriously to put forth only to see it fall a bit short of the idea of Justice itself. Nevertheless, he proposed it as a human best with all the pains and sacrifices it can exact from those who may decide to take seriously the business of implementing it as social policy. Regardless of the degree of dialectical purity the model enjoys in the *Republic*, it clearly demands that all human capacities and attainments be able to exhibit with recognizable finality a pattern of cultural unity. The concrete embodiment of this pattern remains the same; ultimately, it is the individual man as citizen. That is why the *Republic* ends where it does and not before the myth of Er is introduced in the last book.

III

The concept of justice: the link between the two visions of life

We must now turn to the concept of justice in man and the *polis*. We hope to show that here can be found the link that unites the tasks of poet and philosopher and therefore co-ordinates their respective visions: the tragic and the theoretical.

To understand Greek society and its institutions requires viewing it in the context of the city-state, the *polis*. Not only were the city-states many and diverse, but most of them presented a character of their own that gave a special emphasis to the plurality of institutions, social differentiations, degree of civic awareness, division of labor, modes of distribution of political power and forms of consecration of cultural values. As in the case of cosmic order where *Dike* oversees the balance in the forces of nature, so it was with civic order where man's system of laws, the *Nomos*, keeps in check the diverse human interests, ambitions and drives. Institutionalized conduct was tuned only secondarily

John P. Anton

to the rules governing special professions and the acceptable ways of making a living, and primarily to the good of men as individuals and citizens of the *polis*. At least such was the ideal the wise men and venerated lawgivers had in mind. The forces and tasks of human life the Greeks sought to institutionalize can be understood in two complementary ways. From the psychological point of view, they take us back to the traits of human existence, to the powers of the soul, the natural endowment of mankind, the drives, the appetites, the emotions, volitional capabilities and the reflective faculties, as they constitute together the functional whole, the *psychē*. From the cultural point of view, they take the concrete form of public roles and functions which the citizens perform as members of a *polis*, the community.

The idea of justice, in theory at least, demanded the unbreakable alliance between the two. The best achievements of the Greeks reflect this conviction about the continuity between human nature and culture, which may well be regarded the backbone of their theoria of life. Their failures, and there were many, can be attributed to the emergence of views and interests that tended to drive a wedge between the endowment of the *psychē* and the cultural crystallization of values; that is, failures are related to the intellectual and political crises that caused deep distortions and infected good judgment about the *psychē* or the culture or both. But the pattern of their ideals and values, their cultural ethos, was such that it demanded a unification of roles and personal conduct; furthermore it exercised through its sanctions considerable control over noxious tendencies that could lead to what we have come to call in modern times phenomena of alienation and fragmentation.

As long as the Greeks were able to think clearly and maintain the bond between nature and convention their visions enjoyed an inclusive authenticity and gave their lives an air of celebration. After the age of the sophists, the death of Socrates in 399 B.C. proved to be the turning point in the life of Greece. The Greeks, especially Athens, never really recovered from the crisis in statesmanship. Neither Plato or Aristotle, with all their profound analyses

Tragic Vision and Philosophic Theoria

and their wisdom, could cure the malaise. Exhaustion overtook the modes of public conduct. The gap between the ways of talking about the *psychē* and the ways of talking about culture grew increasingly disparate. This disparity explains why the fourth century discussed the problem of virtue with such passion.

Yet the fifth century remains the crown and glory of the classical conception of the whole and integrated man. Commitment to it was every citizen's concern. Excellence and the performance of public roles were expected to converge. The individual citizen, whether sculptor or philosopher, statesman or historian, tragedian or admiral, contributed to the harmonious interdependence of institutions. Some evidently succeeded more than others. Some men, like Cleisthenes, Aeschylus, Pericles, excelled in many ways, while others did so only in what they could do best. But what brought supreme honor to the citizen was not impressive specialization but wholesomeness of personality and wisdom made public. However, not all public roles were held in equal esteem. In this regard, the Greeks were in fact partisans of a distinctive hierarchical ordering of institutions. Let me explain. The Greeks admired excellence no matter who, or what, possessed it: ship or state, statue or athlete, speech or spear. Yet, excellent as these may be, they take an appropriate place in the scale of values. Given this scale nothing surpasses man in excellence when he has become *kalos kagathos*. But on the other hand, the Greeks also taught, at least Plato did, the *isonomia* of ideal values: the true, the good, the beautiful, the pious, the just are significantly enough on a par. The hierarchy of excellent things is a wonderful *taxis,* an arrangement; the isonomic order of ideal values is a dialectic *cosmos*. In a just society the creation of excellence in *taxis* is sustained by philosophic devotion to the *cosmos* of ideals. That is why Plato insisted on a government by philosopher-kings.

To do justice to one's own *psychē*, one's natural endowment, and also co-operate with other citizens to promote justice in society is precisely what the great tragic visions of the poets and the ethical theories of Plato and Aristotle sought to defend. This double aspect of *the just* as an end was made available to all citizens in the grand days of the Athenian democracy. When Plato came to spell it out in detail it became abundantly clear why justice as the co-ordinating excellence of other excellences could serve as the common ground for the visions of man the tragedians and the philosophers shared. Moreover, it provided the context for understanding and evaluating professional roles, particular functions and specialized work. Above and beyond the artist, the knower, the statesman, and the like, was the whole being that each man was expected to become as *politēs*.

The tragic poets no less than the philosophers did their utmost to support the same view and cast themselves in the role of teachers in this superb sense. Aristophanes has Aeschylus say in the *Frogs*, "We poets are the teachers of men." Sophocles knew well how ignorance breeds self-deception and becomes one's own worst enemy when he said: "The hardest evil to wrestle with is ignorance" (fr. 238 N, 924 P). Yet, the tragedian did not distribute to the spectators handbooks on ethics; his task was to evoke justice dramatically either as a celebration of life or as a hair-raising spectacle of grand failure. The techniques were many, the vision was one.

The rise and development of Greek tragedy can be seen as a sustained and cumulative effort to state in a new medium the drama of the total Greek ethos. In this sense tragedy is one among other parallel expressions of the same ethos, one more way of articulating its rich contents. If the tragedians as artists have a philosophy, so to speak, it didn't have to come to them from the philosophers, nor did they in turn have to lend it to the historians. Their philosophy is rooted in the Greek ethos, in the wisdom that comes from trying to be fully human. It was theirs to bring to the citizens the drama of existence, help them see more, and also to show them how to remain speechless before the spectacle of man and his possibilities.[7] Philosophy, no

---

7. *Ibid.*, I, 251.

Tragic Vision and Philosophic Theoria

less than tragedy, aimed at ideal human transformations, but somehow the philosophical failures of Socrates' interlocutors do not quite excite passion as do the deeds of Sophocles' tragic personages. The point here is that regardless of the different ways in which tragedy and philosophy appeal to us, they both pursue the same ultimate end and both serve in the broader sense political functions. What makes the co-ordination and convergence possible is the idea of justice, to use Plato's words. Aristotle aptly remarks that the characters of early tragedy spoke politically, not rhetorically.[8] Aeschylus, in the closing words of the *Eumenides*[9], "revealed the essential political character of his poetry. That was the basis of its educational force, a force at once moral, religious and purely human; for morality, religion and all human life were now aspects of the all-embracing life of the polis."[10] The ethical vision in tragic poetry is not meant to convey or support a particular moralistic code. The tragic poet is profoundly ethical in the sense that he alerts us to the ethos of excellence in the life of the *polis*. It is noteworthy that the *Oresteia* ends in a special vision. Orestes sees more clearly and is restored to sanity. But so does Sophocles' Oedipus see more after the pitiful act of self-blinding, and in his own way, Creon sees more clearly in the *Antigone*. These tragic personages face different situations but they see the same spectacle: what happens in life when the pressure of passions and acts of *hubris* and ignorance force man to lose sight of the desiderated harmony of human wholeness. The vision, effected on the stage

---

8. *Poetics*, vi, 1450b 7.
9. "Again let the wine be poured
   By the glare of the crackling pine;
   Now great, all-seeing Zeus
   Guards the city of Pallas;
   Thus God and Fate are reconciled.
   Then let every voice
   Crown our song with a shout of joy!"
From the *Eumenides*, tr. Philip Velacott, *The Oresteian Trilogy* (Penguin Books, 1959).
10. *Paideia* I, 239.

and communicated to the citizens, is the fruit of purification, of understanding predicaments. The lofty goal of human fulfillment in excellence, if this be happiness, is what all men desire by nature, to speak with Aristotle. The political *ethos* is everyone's concern: it is what the art of the good life seeks to sustain.

IV

The philosophical reorientation of mimesis and catharsis

The rivalry between poetry and philosophy has a historical basis, to be sure, but is best understood in the light of the issues and circumstances to which it was tied. The contest served a genuine purpose which both antagonists felt they could meet adequately: to educate the citizens of Hellas and help them rise to the lofty ideal of excellence. We must not conclude from the spirit of this competition either that the two educational agents were speaking at cross purposes or that the contest was cast in the way Plato sharpened the issues by dividing the rivals in the celebrated passages in his *Republic*. Plato's enthusiasm for cultural reform is one thing, the historical developments leading up to the collision as Plato saw it, quite another. The point I hope to make clear is that tragedy and philosophy were not separated by some unbridgeable chasm either by way of function or with regard to means. If that were the case then the convergence of their respective visions of life would be impossible and the unity of the cultural quality of Hellas only a pious dream of Hellenists.

While tragedy was a distinctive Athenian achievement, philosophy was an importation from Ionia and other progressive city states. Chronologically their apogees overlap to some extent but do not coincide. Tragedy dominates the intellectual and artistic affairs of Athens almost throughout the fifth century. Philosophy doesn't come into its own until the end of the fifth, and then mainly as living *dialogos*, and flourishes as written logos in the fourth century. In his attack on tragic poetry, Plato brought together certain crucial questions about the nature of education and statesmanship and extended the application of Socrates' thought. He declared his teacher's way of doing philosophy superior to any other method for examining the problems of man. By the same criterion, the function of poetry had to be reconsidered. By the time Plato unleashed his attacks against the poets and made tragic poetry the target of his moral and political dissatisfactions, the last of the great tragedians of Athens had died more than a generation ago. It makes more sense, then, to say that Plato's attack was intended against the popularity which the presentation of tragedies enjoyed during the fourth century and more specifically against the new crop of poets and the thousands of plays written at that time. Harkening back from the time the *Apology* was written we hear of a judgment about Socrates uttered by Socrates himself in 399 B.C. but pronounced by Apollo's priestess at some earlier date: "Sophocles is wise, Euripides is wiser, but Socrates is the wisest of all men." The comparisons no doubt served a purpose at that time but do not necessarily convey the antagonisms Plato spoke of in his sustained analyses of the place of poetry in public education. It does not strengthen our argument to add here that Plato, as the legend has it, tried his hand in tragic poetry but forsook all such thoughts after he met Socrates. Just the same, his dialogues are living testimonies to the fact that the lessons of tragic thought were not wasted on Plato. What he attacked then was not the era that produced the visions of Aeschylus, Sophocles and Euripides but the decline of the art and its loss of educational force. Yet Plato, the Athenian thinker, inherited and deepened the basic concerns of tragic poetry, retained its fundamental objectives and used the philosopher's way to theoria to illumine man's fate and perfection in excellence.

In a serious sense Plato became convinced that philosophy could supplant tragedy not only by taking over its sweeping themes and treating human action in greater depth but also by showing how mimesis and catharsis — concepts that Aristotle will place at the heart of the analysis of tragedy — take on greater significance when treated in the light of the new method, the dialectic. The interesting thing to note, therefore, is not what Plato rejected but what he absorbed and extended. It would not be off the mark to say that the true inheritor of fifth century tragic poetry in Athens was not the run-of-the-mill playwright in the fourth century, but the practitioner of a newly discovered mode of philosophy. However, it is difficult to see this continuity when we isolate Plato's indictment of tragic poetry from the general climate of opinion of his time; but by missing the continuity one loses the deeper affinity between these two creative expressions of Athens. The fact remains that the tragedians were as much interested in educating the emotions as Plato was. His lifelong cultivation of eros, also understood as one of Socrates' distinguishing features, requires no special comment at this point. But Plato did set out to illumine the human situation and the springs of action by declaring the superiority of the new approach. The great debate seems to have been about the adequacy of method rather than the nature of the goals. But with the switch in method there inevitably came a change in the conceptualization of the basic ideas with which tragedy had worked.

The Athenian citizen, from the point of view that interests us in this paper, underwent a somewhat drastic change when the fourth century came into its own. With respect to his relation to tragedy, the Athenian of the fifth century was mainly a celebrant, even if a vicarious participant in the dramatic rites, but his counterpart in the fourth century took the more distant attitude of the spectator. By this time, "the thyrsus-bearers were many but few were the mystics," to twist Plato's own phrase to fit the situation (*Phaedo* 69d). The vision of the tragic celebrant gives way to the philosopher's rational synopsis of life. Mimesis and catharsis undergo a scrutiny in the fourth century to find a fresh place in the emerging modes of intellectual comprehension of excellence.

Plato found it necessary to recast the meanings of mimesis and catharsis on the basis of a new educational scheme clarified with the aid of his dialectic. He came to

Tragic Vision and Philosophic Theoria

the conclusion that the education of the passions, including the ones appropriate to tragedy, belongs ultimately to *philosophikos logos*, not to *dramatikos logos*. However, this implies a reserved criticism and not a rejection of the tragic worldview of the poets.[11] It carries with it the thesis that in the light of the dialectic, as method and ontology, the tragic vision is limited in scope and in many cases misleading as educational policy; furthermore, judged as a case of knowledge, tragic poetry is considerably inadequate since as mimesis it imitates corruptible, changing objects. Tragedy, being inferior as a grade of cognition, is unqualified to lead to the correct vision of the changeless and eternal forms, to the standards of excellence so basic to public and private life. Plato, no doubt, spoke with the authority of the ex-poet as well as with the excitement the new discovery brought. Even if we want to hold Plato literally to his most severe moments of censorship, we must acknowledge him as the first philosopher to raise the question of the adequacy of the tragic vision and its claim to wisdom. After Plato, it will never be sound practice to defend the claims of dramatic or any other poetic genre as cognitive disclosure without giving an account of the nature and function of its *logos* on ethical, or ontological, or epistemological grounds, or on all three.

When Aristotle appeared on the scene the furor of the battle was over. He looked at the controversy far more dispassionately than his teacher did, and worked out in considerable depth an attempt to reinstate the *logos* of the tragic vision. In contrast to Plato, he assigned to the concepts of mimesis and catharsis a role in dramatic art closer to what the tragedians would have approved. In essence, he restored the truth claims and ethical relevance of both these

---

11. R. P. Winnington-Ingram takes the view that Plato rejected tragedy because he was against the tragic world-view of the poets. The point is too strong; it neglects, for instance, the fact that Plato absorbed many aspects of the tragedians, including concepts and techniques. Compare Winnington-Ingram's essay "Greek and Modern Tragedy," esp. pp. 102-3, in *The Living Heritage of Greek Antiquity* (Paris and La Haye, 1967), pp. 96-113.

concepts by making them theoretically respectable. We read in the *Poetics* (1451 b 6-11): "Poetry, therefore, is a more philosophical and a higher thing than history: for poetry tends to express the universal, history the particular. By the universal I mean how a person of a certain type will on occasion speak or act, according to the law of probability or necessity; and it is this universality at which poetry aims in the names she attaches to the personages" (Bywater).

There is still another way of identifying philosophical aspects in poetry. Aside from expressing the universal, tragic poetry, through the vision it discloses, brings to the open another element, ethical in its texture. It belongs to the function of catharsis to make this clear. But catharsis, as Aristotle understood the term, is not primarily what Lessing took it to be, i.e., to help the spectator become familiar with the passions of pity and fear, or what Weil and Bernays thought about it as being an outburst and spilling over of the passions. It makes good sense to relate the function of catharsis to the nature of human entelechy. What is needed then is to view the effects of catharsis as special acts of illumination, of intellectual enlightenment, of understanding conduct in the context of certain emotions. Catharsis is best understood as a case of fulfillment when viewed within the general framework of the educational process leading to *eudaimonia* through the moral and intellectual excellences. Insofar as the presentation of tragedies was never in the class of sheer entertainment for the Greeks, we must regard the function of dramatic poetry to fall within the orbit of the educational means by which it was possible to bring about the desirable *harmonia* in the powers of the soul.

It is not too difficult to see why Plato did not want to take any chances with educational curricula when the ethical and political stakes were high. He was making a good point when he insisted that only citizens who were sufficiently exposed to the theoretical disciplines and familiar with the dark forces of the soul are immune to the strong emotions of tragic poetry. He was equally aware of the fact that he had no power to legislate and impose his educational policies on his fellow Athenians. What he did instead was to open a school to train the philosophical statesmen of the future and place at the heart of the curriculum a doctrine of inquiry and conception of life that offered an alternative to the catharsis and mimesis of the tragic vision: the dialectic and theoria of the lover of wisdom.

Aristotle not only came to the defense of the constructive role of tragic poetry but found his teacher's injunctions unnecessarily restrictive. He went back to the dramatic plays to find there what was needed to resolve the conflict between tragic vision and philosophic theoria which Plato's critique had generated. His definition of tragedy[12] contains new ingredients for the understanding of mimesis in tragedy and it also suggests a different approach to the way in which catharsis functions within the inclusive goal of *eudaimonia*. Actually, neither Plato and certainly not Aristotle ever came to propose the condemnation and dismissal of the tragic emotions. But once the problem of two different ways of handling these emotions for the sake of effecting excellence came up, the issue had to be faced. Plato's solutions proved to be more partisan and tougher. Aristotle's way was far closer to the nature of the facts and therefore more just. He gave the poet his ethical due and the philosopher the visionary scope that Plato was so reluctant to share with the dramatists.

V

Concluding Remarks

Tragic catharsis and philosophic wisdom are ends, completions, fulfillments of enterprises rooted in the Greek experience. By way of ends, the enterprises converge. Soc-

---

12. *Poetics*, vi, 2. "A tragedy, then is the imitation of an action that is serious and also, as having magnitude, complete in itself; in language with pleasurable accessories, each kind brought in separately in the parts of the work; in a dramatic, not in a narrative form; with incidents arousing pity and fear, wherewith to accomplish its catharsis of such emotions, ..." (Bywater).

rates was proclaimed at Delphi the wisest of all men, yet the ones to whom he was compared were tragic poets. The continuity was clearly recognized. Given the general trust of the Greek *paideia* in the love of excellence, the pursuit of the good life called for the involvement of all the powers and aspects of the human personality, as Plato persuasively argued. This way of understanding the vocation of man precluded sharp divisions in the structure of the culture. Furthermore, it advised against the professionalizing of talent to be distributed between, say, art and science, literature and philosophy, the theoretical and the practical, the contemplative and the productive. To be sure, dramatists and philosophers, and generally poets as well as knowers, sought to prevent the separation of the ideal of the good life from the task of illumining the causes of human failure.

The Greeks believed that the desire to pursue the good life was best communicated through the power of personal example. The directness of personal witnessing worked more effectively than either theory or abstract talking. The magnetic personalities of Pericles, Socrates and other great men of Athens left lasting memories in the minds of their contemporaries. Somehow the immediate appeal and the sensuous excitement of the arts as vehicles for communication and education were not only perfectly known to the Greeks but were fully exploited for cultural purposes. There is a parallel between the power of the living example and that of the work of art. We learn what a beautiful statue is when we see one, just as we begin to understand what promise the good life holds for us when we encounter a good man. True, the excellent man needs no manual of ethics; no theoretical system of ethics can make him more virtuous than he already is. But the main concern of education is to impart excellence to those who do not possess it. Most men belong to the category of pupils, not teachers. Socrates throughout his mature years and down to the day of his death confessed his ignorance and declared himself a lover of wisdom, not a wise man. He remained a pupil, and if others regarded him as a teacher it was only because he was a more educable pupil.

Tragic Vision and Philosophic Theoria

It is most difficult to remain a pupil and by doing so, never cease to aspire to goodness. This realization comes with the aid of instruction as an awakening of our desire to rise to excellence; but it can be quickened through a sudden shock, a blunt encounter, as it were, with the drama of misfortune. People are shocked into the possibilities of existence not so much because of some systematic training or what promises to come with the exercise of perfected intelligence, but through the awesome consequences of self-deception, pains and evils that befall men in the absence of excellence. The tragedians, to be sure, offered no formalized systems of morality (or, if they did, we have no record of such products.) What they shared with their fellow citizens was their vision, their seeing, their imaginative apprehension of the woes and weals of humanity. They communicated their insights dramatically. They aimed at invoking virtue existentially, by showing what happens to men and women when judgment breaks down and justice fails to maintain balance and harmony.

The catharsis which the tragic vision effects and the inculcation of *hexis* or habit which philosophic ethics offers, are functionally alike. They complement each other to produce a clearer view of the possibilities of human life. Aristotle's incontinent man, Sophocles' Creon or Euripides' Theseus, are not total strangers to each other. Any seemingly good man with an *hamartia*, a serious deficiency, when placed in a challenging situation will sooner or later enter a course of suffering if not destruction. There is nothing fatal about such reversals in the affairs of men, nor such a thing as mysterious fate operating on its own as a separate power among the elements of the cosmos. Oedipus or Creon, endowed with special powers of judgment to overcome the down-pull of *hamartia* — that is, if permitted to see and foresee correctly — cease being tragic personages. But now we are no longer in the realm of tragedy. The determination to see wholly and steadily the wide range of human vices and virtues, and act on this basis, paves the way to the heights of excellence. But this is the way of the philosopher, not the tragic hero.

John P. Anton

The fundamental difference between tragic vision and philosophic *theoria* of ethical conduct is not one of function but of means and ways. To summarize the issues: (1) Tragedy intimates the road to ethical excellence through its dramatic advocacy for the negation and removal of the *hamartia* or flaw that brings disorder in judgment and catastrophe in fortune; (2) Philosophy seeks to articulate and defend priorities of ends in human conduct, and specify the means for the attainment of the good life.

Tragedy, as Aristotle informs us, functions to effect catharsis through pity and fear. Philosophy promises to disclose the ends of life in a *theoria*. Both help us see: the former through dramatic negation and resolution, the latter through discursive and explicit affirmation. Consider Aeschylus' *Oresteia* and place it next to Plato's *Republic*. The first moves from the portentous news of Agamemnon's return to his murder, to the avenging of Orestes, the relentless pursuit of the Furies, the terrible torment of Orestes, down to the reconstruction of social justice in Athens and the transformation of the Erinyes to Eumenides. The *Republic* moves from Book I, the refutation of Thrasymachus' theory of justice, to the step-by-step construction of the paradigm of a just city so that Socrates may instruct Glaucon and Adeimantus and convey the new view of what it is to be a just man.

Tragedy must persuade dramatically before it can point the way to excellence. After the citizen has seen enough, a change of attitude and a transformation of habit may begin to set in and hopefully effect that wonderful feeling of the sprouting of the soul's wings, as Plato expresses it in the *Phaedrus*. Philosophy, in order to instruct, must engage men in *dialogos*. Once certain conceptual gains are made, there emerges an expectation, a promise that a *hexis* will really take hold and lead to the realization of self-knowledge. Aristotle called it the fulfillment of human *entelechy*. The teacher may, and often does, fail to communicate his ideal of excellence, but the pupil does not have to face the same horrors which follow the tragic hero's failure. Euthyphro fails to learn from Socrates; but when the dialogue

Tragic Vision and Philosophic Theoria

bearing his name closes, we ponder the issues, not the dramatic consequences of Euthyphro's demeanor. In the *Symposium,* Socrates' concern for excellence and love becomes far more challenging than Alcibiades' excesses.

Tragic art presupposes the quest for excellence and assumes as its proper context the concept of the whole person. Philosophic ethics articulates this idea in theoria. What the tragic poets, at least the great ones, evoke dramatically, Socrates, the philosopher, compels us to see logically. Because of his radical understanding of human limitations, Socrates offered a new conception of a theoria of man, an extended and novel awareness of the dangers and the pitfalls of another sort of *hubris,* of excess intellectual pride. This discovery makes Socrates profoundly continuous with the tragic poets.[13] Like them, he offers no system of ethics, no handbook on excellence. The complete articulation of the good life will come with the thinkers of the fourth century: Plato, Aristotle and the Stoics. The tragedians and Socrates presented the case for the pursuit of justice and the good life mainly by way of personal example, or through the *dramatis personae* in their tragedies. After you have seen a good tragedy or heard Socrates conduct a dialogue with a fellow Athenian who claimed to know, you somehow become aware of what you must not do, what courses of action lead to *hubris,* what unbridled emotion can do to the power of judgment. After a good tragedy has unfolded the spectacle of human failure, one feels the need to remain speechless. Silence seems to follow on the footsteps of catharsis. The tragic vision has done its work. Philosophy, however, compels you to proceed with inquiry. Plato's advice in the *Seventh Epistle* (344 B) is: "The study of virtue and vice must be accompanied by an inquiry into what is false and true of existence in general and must be carried on by constant practice through a long period." Failure to question is willingness to acquiesce in the dubious comforts of a new kind of *hubris.*

---

13. *See* my "The Ultimate Theme of the *Phaedo,*" *Arethusa,* I (1968), 1, pp. 94-102.

John P. Anton

Tragic *hubris*, we are told, can cause the fall of royal houses. Philosophic *hubris* can do something worse: it can bring down whole cultures and lay them in ignoble ruins. Such are the horrors of self-deception, whether of the passions or of the mind.

2

THE POLISCRAFT
A Dialogue
By Max H. Fisch

PERSONS:
Pol, of political science, who teaches the history of political theory and has her students read Plato's *Republic* and Aristotle's *Politics* in the first quarter; Machiavelli's *Prince,* Hobbes's *Leviathan,* and Rousseau's *Social Contract* in the second; etc. ("My parents named me Mary. My friends called me Polly. When I went into political science they shortened it to Pol.")

Phil, of philosophy, who teaches a sequence in ethics in which the students read Aristotle's *Nicomachean Ethics,* Hume's *Inquiry concerning the Principles of Morals,* Kant's *Metaphysic of Morals,* Mill's *Utilitarianism,* etc.

Clay, of classics, who teaches ancient history for the history department.

PLACE AND TIMES:
Clay's office on an afternoon in May and an afternoon in September.

(References in parentheses are to pages of Loeb Classical Library editions; unless the context indicates otherwise, to those of its edition of the *Nicomachean Ethics*.)

Max Fisch

I. *May*

Pol. Phil and I have chatted now and then about the rough time our students gave us with Aristotle last fall. Some of them knew enough Greek to make things out for themselves, but others were taking your ancient history, and our guess is they were getting ideas from you. Anyway, whether the questions come from you or not, we want to be readier for them next fall, and we'd like you to help us.
Clay. What were some of the questions?
Pol. Well, my students didn't mind Aristotle's being wrong — say, about Plato, or about slavery, or women, or usury. What they minded was my being wrong — say, about the *Politics* being politics. I played up those 158 constitutions in the Lyceum Library, reviewed *The Athenian Constitution,* and showed how in the *Politics,* especially in books IV-VI, Aristotle used such empirical data. The students said, fine, but how about the constitutions of Rome, Macedon, Egypt, Judea, Syria, Persia, and points east? It isn't as if he hadn't heard of them. There were probably few things he knew better than the constitution of Macedon. And it isn't as if he hadn't got round to them, or held his conclusions tentatively until evidence from India and China came in. It's rather as if all that were ruled out in advance as irrelevant. But it isn't irrelevant to politics. So how can it have been politics he was doing?
Clay. And your students, Phil?
Phil. They were willing to let Aristotle have his doctrine of the mean, his magnificence as a moral virtue, his intellectual virtues; but they wouldn't let me call what he was doing ethics, or describe the end of Book X as a transition from ethics to politics. I grant you, I said, that what philosophers now call ethics, if it is a science at all, is a theoretical one, more accurately if a bit pedantically called metaethics, while for Aristotle ethics was a practical science; and I illustrated his distinction between theoretical and practical syllogism. But I gave them a list of ten passages in which he talks like an Oxford analyst, and I said if they understood those passages

Poliscraft

they would pass the Aristotle exam. They asked, where does Aristotle call ethics a practical science, or any kind of science, or anything at all? And why take those ten passages out of context as ethics if in context they are something else? So I put the question to you that I put to them: isn't "Ethics" in the title of the *Nicomachean Ethics* the name of a science or discipline at work in that treatise?

Clay. No more than "Politics" is in the title of the *Politics*. There is only one science at work in both the *Ethics* and the *Politics*, and it is not named in either title. Its name is *hê politikê*, with *technê*, art or craft, or *epistêmê*, science or know-how, understood. *Hê politikê* is not "politics" or "political science" or "political theory" in any sense those terms now bear. Little as I like linguistic hybrids, I can think of no better rendering for it than "the poliscraft"; that is, the art or craft of creating a polis, keeping it going, guiding it into change for the better, guarding it from change for the worse.

Pol. But surely the polis is a state, the one the Greeks know best, and they are generalizing from what they know to what they don't, as we all do. So why not call it "statecraft"? That has the advantage that the stink of hybridity has nearly worn off it.

Clay. The Greeks generalize less than the translations make them seem to. Here's the way I put it to my students. The state is one thing the Greeks don't have a name for, and their polis is one thing we don't have a name for. The translators render it sometimes "city," sometimes "state," sometimes "city-state," sometimes even "society." All four are wrong, and there is no other rendering that is right. The nearest Greek word for society is *koinônia*, which must serve also for community and partnership. The polis is a species of *koinônia;* so is the family and the village; but leagues, federations, nations, and empires are not, though a league is sometimes called *to koinon*. The nearest Greek word for "city" is *astu*. A polis is not an *astu*, nor is it an *astu* that is also a state, nor is it any other species of state, because the Greeks altogether lack that conception. So if we care about accuracy there is nothing for it but to take over the Greek word itself and put polis for *polis*. Which brings us to "the poliscraft" for *hê politikê*. But that is not the title of the *Politics*.

Pol. Then what is the title of the *Politics*, and what does it mean?

Phil. And what about "Ethics" in the title of the *Nicomachean Ethics?*

Clay. Now you are pulling my leg. You both know enough Greek to make that out for yourselves. But it may be easier if you bear in mind an English muddle that must have struck you. Our names for arts and sciences — the largest single group of them — end in *-ics*. Mathematics, physics, mechanics, economics, politics, ethics, aesthetics, poetics, semiotics — you could make up a list of fifty of them from our catalogue of courses. They are plural in form though singular in use. Nearly all of them are Greek, and the rest are modeled on Greek. But in Greek they are singular in form as well as in use, ending in the feminine singular *-ikê*, like *hê politikê,* the poliscraft. In German they are still singular, ending in *-ik;* and in French too, ending in *-ique,* with one exception, *les mathématiques*. They used to be singular in English, and the plurals were reserved, as in Greek, for their objects of study. Politic was the science, and politics were what it studied. But the only surviving singulars I can think of are logic, rhetoric, and music.

Phil. If we go outside the catalogue, there's magic.

Clay. Now what sense, I ask you, does a plural make as the name of an art or science? I can see as little reason for physics or semiotics as for logics, rhetorics, musics, or magics.

Pol. It's enough to give you the *-ic*-ups.

Phil. I think it was back in 1892 that Bosanquet could still give a book the title *History of Aesthetic*.

Clay. But now, in the smog of the English plurals, when something is said about aesthetics or politics, you often can't tell whether it is being said about the sciences or about the objects they study. And the confusion is worse when the plurals occur as titles.

Pol. If Bosanquet were choosing his title now, and struggling out of the smog, I suppose he would resort to something like *History of Aesthetic Thought*.

Poliscraft

Phil. Whewell said "the fundamental antithesis of philosophy" was that of thought and things, and he built his philosophy of science on it.

Clay. Then maybe it's no accident that Greek is the native language of philosophy, because the distinction of thinker, thought and thing is sun-clear in Greek. The scientist or artist is masculine singular — *ho politikos,* the poliscraftsman. Male chauvinism, Pol. But, as offset, the art or science is feminine singular— *hê politikê,* the poliscraft. The objects it studies or makes, or with or on which it works, are neuter plural — *ta politika,* with *pragmata* understood, the things or affairs of the polis: institutions and constitutions, codes of law, magistracies, assemblies, juries, elections, trials, market-places, gymnasiums, schools, police, armies, fleets, wars, peaces, treaties, alliances — the whole works.

Pol. If the sorting had still to be done, and a Greek genius were setting himself the task, he could hardly hit upon a simpler means than the differences between *-ikos, -ikê,* and *-ika,* already built into his language. But didn't the remuddling begin long before the English smog?

Clay. Right you are. It began in late Latin and grew in medieval. By that time there was something called in Greek *hê êthikê,* which studied the *pragmata* that Aristotle had been the first to call *ta êthika.* If there had been such a freak as an ethicist, he would have been called *ho êthikos.* That would have gone into Latin as *ethicus.* Fortunately, there was no such rascal, so those names don't occur. But both *hê êthikê,* the science, and *ta êthika,* its objects, went into Latin as *ethica,* since Latin lacks the definite article and spells the feminine singular and the neuter plural alike. So if you wrote in Latin and wanted to avoid confusion, you romanized the Greek singular as the name of the science, and declined it as Greek, not Latin: *ethice, ethices,* etc.; *politice, politices,* etc. But few Latin writers were ever so meticulous as that.

Phil. The *Ethica* of Spinoza is singular, though you wouldn't know from the title; and White in his translation of about 1883 rendered it *Ethic,* I suppose because he noticed that in the subtitles of the five parts Spinoza uses the romanized Greek genitive singular, *Ethices.* But in the present English smog everybody makes it plural.

Clay. To come back now to your questions, if you will look at the Greek titles of the *Rhetoric, Poetics, Nicomachean Ethics and Politics,* what will jump out at you is that in the Greek titles rhetoric and poetic are singular and are names of sciences, but ethics and politics are plural and so can't be names of sciences. At this point I confess Greek clarity fails because they are genitive plurals, and the genitive plural of adjectives like these is the same in all three genders. But these must be masculine or neuter. I take them as masculine, and so as rough descriptions of two sets of *logoi* or discourses delivered by the one science of poliscraft, or by Aristotle in the one capacity of poliscraftsman. But they may be taken as neuter, and so as rough descriptions of two sets of objects, *ta êthika pragmata* and *ta politika pragmata,* studied by the one science of poliscraft.

Phil. Why "rough" descriptions?

Clay. On the side of the *logoi,* because what is strictly "ethical" about those collected in the *Nicomachean Ethics* is only the theory of the *aretai êthikai,* the "ethical" excellences, the "moral virtues." On the side of the objects, because the two sets are not mutually exclusive, but each in an extended sense includes the other.

Pol. But aren't there several references in the *Politics* to the *Ethics* as if to another work, presumably the work of another science?

Clay. So the translators render them, but if you will look at the Greek you will see that there is no significant difference between references to the "ethical" *logoi* and references to other *logoi* which have been collected in the *Politics* itself.

Phil. Doesn't Aristotle say in Book I of the *Metaphysics* (42) that Socrates turned from physics to ethics?

Clay. No, from nature as a whole to *ta êthika.* And in Book XIII (194) he is said to have dealt with the moral virtues and in that connection to have been the first to search for universal definitions. But the only passage in which the Socratic turn is described as from the study of nature to a different science is in the *Parts of Animals* (76-78), and the science named there is *hê politikê,* the poliscraft.

Phil. Doesn't Aristotle in the *Posterior Analytics* (170), after contrasting knowledge and opinion, say that the question how the operations of thought are to be assigned to the several intellectual virtues belongs partly to physics and partly to ethics?

Clay. More exactly, is a matter partly for physical, partly for ethical consideration. It does in fact receive such consideration in *On the Soul* and in Book VI of the *Nicomachean Ethics*. In the former case it is physics that does the considering; in the latter, the poliscraft.

Pol. Phil and I have certainly been remiss about these niceties, and we want you to push us toward precision; but the importance you attach to this particular precision doesn't yet come through to me.

Clay. Not to fall back on Whewell, I remark simply that a man may practice two or more arts or sciences; an art or science may study two or more distinguishable sets of objects; a set of objects may be studied by two or more arts or sciences. *Ta êthika pragmata,* for example, are studied by physics, the poliscraft, and rhetoric. There is no one-to-one correspondence between scientist, science, and set of objects. So one may recognize *ta êthika* as a distinguishable set of objects of study without supposing that there is or ought to be a science confined to the study of those objects and called therefore *hê êthikê,* or a scientist specializing in the study of them and called therefore *ho êthikos.* Aristotle recognizes *ta êthika* but neither *hê êthikê* nor *ho êthikos.*

Phil. But even if he doesn't recognize them in any surviving text, may he not have done so in conversation or in lost lectures, or might he not have done so if the question had arisen?

Clay. You philosophers are so sure ethics must be as old as philosophy that I can see I'll have a hard time persuading you that there was no art, science, study, discipline, inquiry, or branch of philosophy called ethics until after Aristotle. The adjective *êthikos, ê, on* doesn't occur before Aristotle and was almost certainly coined by him. But he uses it so freely and in such a wide range of contexts that if there had come down to him a nameless or misnamed science for which *hê êthikê* was a fitting name, or if he had created such a science himself, he would surely have called it by that name, and the name would turn up somewhere in the *logoi* dealing with *ta êthika,* if not in their titles.

Phil. Considering how few pre-Aristotelian texts have survived, mightn't that adjective chance not to occur in any of them and yet have been frequent in texts that have not survived?

Clay. Just ask yourself on how many surviving pages of Plato and of Xenophon some form of the adjective would have slipped from their pens if it had been in Socrates's vocabulary or in theirs.

Phil. Well, then, if Aristotle coined it, but not to name a science, what did he coin it for?

Clay. My guess is, for the bottom use that he makes of it. He needs to distinguish two kinds of *hexeis,* habits or skills. One kind we acquire by being taught. For them the adjective *dianoêtikai,* intellectual, is available. The other kind we acquire by being trained. There is no adjective for them. There is a verb *ethidzein* for training, accustoming, habituating; a noun *ethos* for a custom or habit so acquired, and a noun *êthos* for a total character composed of such customs or habits. What Aristotle does is to form the adjective *êthikos* from the noun *êthos.* He can then describe the *hexeis* acquired in this way as *êthikai,* and the excellences or virtues among them he can then call *aretai êthikai,* to mark them off from the *aretai dianoêtikai,* the intellectual virtues. Here's the way I diagram it for my students:

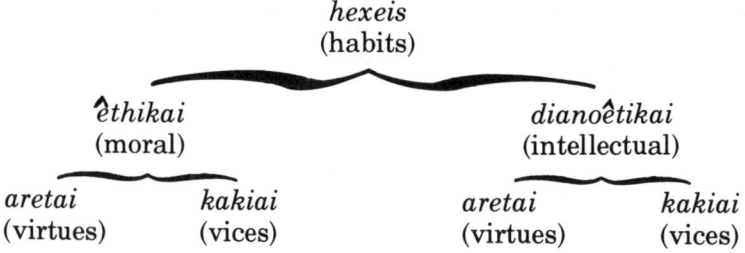

The exact phrases *hexeis êthikai* and *hexeis dianoêtikai* I haven't found in the corpus, but the singular *êthikê hexis*

Poliscraft

occurs at least once (328). The generic notion is certainly *hexis,* and I don't see any other route by which a taxonomist could get from it to *aretai êthikai,* the bottom use that Aristotle makes of the adjective he coined. My guess is that he coined it for that use. In any case, it is the poliscraft that distinguishes the two sets of virtues, determines their relations to each other, and provides for the acquiring of both by the members of the polis.

Phil. Aristotle seems to have recognized executive and judicial subcrafts within the poliscraft (348). Imagine, then, if you can, that he had distinguished an ethical subcraft and had called it *hê êthikê.* What would he have meant by the name?

Clay. On that inadmissible assumption, he would have meant by it the subcraft that defines the skills that call for training, the character skills; that plans and provides for the training; and that conducts it.

Pol. Why is the assumption inadmissible?

Clay. Because the character, the *êthos,* of the polis is so central, so focal for the poliscraft that Aristotle cannot have thought of deputing the theory of the excellences of character to a subcraft.

Pol. Give up, Phil?

Clay. After Aristotle, after the death of the polis, there may have been what passed for an autonomous ethics, a nonpolitical, even an anti-political ethics. And eventually there would be ethicists who would say that Aristotle had at least opened the way for such an autonomous ethics by separating his ethics from his politics, by making ethics a preface, an introduction, a prerequisite to politics — as though the *Nicomachean Ethics* were a sort of *Prolegomena to All Future Politics.* But I suspect that whatever puts itself forward as pure ethics is simply politics in disguise, and most of it partisan politics.

Pol. How will it do, Clay, if Phil and I take it as your hypothesis that the *Nicomachean Ethics* is straight undisguised poliscraft, reread it and the *Politics* this summer to try out the hypothesis, and meet with you early in the fall to discuss our results?

Clay. Fine — on one condition. That is, that you don't rely on any translation, or on any number of translations and commentaries checked against each other. You both know enough Greek to use the Loeb Classical Library bilingual editions, and keep looking across from the translation to the Greek text. There are no reliable translations. The great merit of the Loeb ones is that they don't pretend to be reliable — to be equivalent to, or substitutable for, the Greek originals. They don't pretend to say what the Greek says. They are just ponies or trots to carry you alongside the Greek and help you make out for yourself what it so untranslatably says. The Loebs of the particular texts that concern us have the further advantage that they were done by the same man, Rackham. He also did the *Eudemian Ethics* and the *Athenian Constitution.* If only he had done the *Magna Moralia* or *Great Ethics* too! Anyway, have a look at those works also. What you will find is that all the translations, including the Loebs, are loaded against the hypothesis, though not all of them at every point or in the same way. Even Rackham's English Aristotle speaks of an ethics of which the Greek one was innocent (77). To test the hypothesis, therefore, you must test it against the Greek texts, either directly or by way of testing the translations against them. Even if you find me wrong, I can promise you that neither the *Nicomachean Ethics* nor the *Politics* will ever look the same again.

Pol. Loebs it is.

Phil. See you in September.

II. *September*

Clay. Well, how has it gone? I see you've brought your Loebs.

Pol. I begin this fall as usual with Plato's *Republic,* so I've been using Shorey's Loeb edition of that as well as Rackham's of the *Politics.* Two things have specially struck me in the *Republic.* One is the conceptualizing of the polis-craft by the separation from it of other arts that may happen

Poliscraft

to be practised also by the poliscraftsman, such as the art of making money. The other is the conceptualizing of justice in the individual as the result of internalizing the constitution of the just polis. I see now that the title *Politeia* means not republic but polity or constitution, and that it applies to the polity of an individual soul as well as, and by way of, the polity of a polis. A worse translation than "Republic" could hardly have been devised. I notice, too, that both Plato and Aristotle speak as freely of the *êthos* or character of the polity of a polis as of that of an individual.

Clay. That's part of what I meant last May when I said that *ta êthika pragmata* include *ta politika pragmata,* and vice versa.

Phil. What you say about internalizing, Pol, reminds me that Plato in the *Theaetetus* (178) and *Sophist* (440) describes thinking as internalized dialogue. The analogy seems to be from polis to individual, not the other way round. Thinking is an interiorizing of the discussions that go on in the polis over questions of public policy, rather than public discussion being an exteriorizing of thought, in spite of the fact that I often "think things over" by trying them silently on myself before saying them aloud to others.

Pol. The really big thing, though, that the summer did for me was to convince me that you are right, Clay, about the Greeks lacking the concept of the state. Like nearly everyone else, I had always credited Machiavelli with making it the central concept of modern European political theory. He was led to it, I thought, by there being in the Italy of his day so many different kinds of state, and by the fact that among them, after a lapse of nearly two millennia, there were polises once more. But I thought he was just throwing the spotlight on a concept the Greeks already had but made less of than he did. My only evidence for this was that the translations of the *Republic* and *Politics* used the word "state" so freely. I now see that in every case it is a mistranslation, and in nearly every case a mistranslation of *polis*. So I now agree with you, Clay, not only that *polis* should not be translated, but also that *hê politikê,* if it is to be translated at all, should be rendered "the poliscraft." My trouble now is that

I'm thrown off course, almost at the beginning, on my way from Plato and Aristotle through Machiavelli and Hobbes to Hegel's *"Es ist der Gang Gottes in der Welt, dass der Staat ist."*

Clay. Durchgang strengstens verboten!

Pol. Even if I reject Knox's dreadful boner, "The march of God in the world, that is what the state is," and adopt the innocent rendering, "It's God's way in the world that there should be the state"?

Clay. Even if.

Phil. The big thing for me this summer was discovering in the *Ethics* a completely articulated theory of human good as the end of the poliscraft. What stood in the way of my seeing it before is that the terms in which it is put together are all technical and that the recent translators agree only in abhorring technicalities. The key term is *hexis,* as your diagram showed us in May. It was regularly rendered *habitus* in Latin, and English translators at least as late as Thomas Taylor rendered it "habit." That is the only possible technical rendering, but the recent translators have all discarded it. The worst offender is Ross. By my count, he renders it "state" 46 times, "state of character" 43 times, "state of mind" 6 times, "disposition" 4 times, "state of being" twice, and "formed state," "permanent state," "state of health," "character," "practised faculty" and "habit of body" once each. Not once does he render it simply "habit." If he had done so all 107 times, I would have understood the theory long ago as I do now, and been saved hours of embarrassment before my students.

Clay. The single step that would most improve our grasp of Greek philosophy is eliminating "state" as a rendering of *polis* or of *hexis* or of any other Greek noun in any of its senses. The translators may plead that if "habit" is to be technical for *hexis,* they will be left with nothing but "custom" for *ethos.* But, far from being a hardship, that is nearly as it should be. Every *ethos* is a *hexis,* but not every *hexis* is an *ethos.* Every intellectual virtue is a *hexis;* no intellectual virtue is an *ethos.* Every moral virtue is both an *ethos* and a *hexis.* But a moral virtue is called an *ethos* retrospectively, looking back to the way it has been acquired; and it is called a *hexis* prospectively, looking forward to its exercise on future occasions. "Custom" and "habit" fit the distinction pretty well. If "custom" is not quite so good for *ethos* as "habit" is for *hexis,* we are reconciled by the fact that *hexis* is more technical and far more important than *ethos.*

Phil. "Disposition" has become so fashionable in philosophy that I was tempted at first to use it for *hexis.* Certainly it is the least objectionable of Ross's eleven different renderings.

Clay. There are two counts against that. It would cut us off to no purpose from the two thousand years of *habitus* and habit. And we should keep "disposition" for *diathesis.*

Pol. To come back to the *Politics,* I have one remaining difficulty about taking *polis* and *politikê* in the restricted senses you have urged on us. If Aristotle meant them to be so taken, why does he call the social animals *politika* and thus make the difference between bee and man one of degree? He says merely that man, by virtue of his speech, is an animal MORE *politikon* than any bee or any other gregarious animal (10).

Clay. We mustn't be misled by the fact that *we* call them social and that "social" on our lips is weaker than "political," weaker even than "gregarious." Aristotle's meaning is that among gregarious animals some species live in organized communities of limited size with division of labor toward common ends, more nearly analogous to the polis than to any other human community. But among polis-dwelling animals in that extended sense, man is marked off by speech and all that it makes possible, so that he is pre-eminently the polisdweller.

Pol. Then the way seems open for taking in the strongest sense the propositions that the polis is natural and that man is by nature a polisdweller (8).

Clay. The sense, namely, that man is an animal that becomes man in the polis, not short of it in the family or village or tribe, not beyond it in the nation or empire.

Pol. Or world-state, shall we imagine Aristotle adding?

Clay. Let's do. So we shall reject all translations that water those propositions down into making man a merely social or in our sense a political animal.

Phil. I can imagine some young squirt in the Lyceum saying: "Get with it, Ari! The polis is dead, and Alexander's tutor should be the first to know it. It's nations and empires from here on in."

Clay. And I can imagine Ari replying: "The polis is not dead, and if it dies it will rise again. There is as much call for poliscraftsmen today as there ever was. If the polis is to be swallowed up tomorrow in nations and empires, and if arts of nation- and empire-building are to be forged, they will not be able to claim human good as their end in the way the poliscraft does, because it will be too evident that they do not raise our humanity to new heights but debase it. So they will be reduced to claiming to protect or restore the polis. That will be a fraudulent claim, but it will be the tribute that lying arts must pay to the truth that man is a polis-dwelling animal."

Phil. Oh come now, Clay. Why make Aristotle so remote and irrelevant? I can't imagine his taking such a high disdainful moral line. If not to the young squirt, at least to us I think he would say: "To be sure your metropolises and megalopolises are not polises, but of all your arts the least remote from the poliscraft is your 'city planning'; and Plato and I will be honored if you find our poliscraft worth studying and are able to transpose some part of it into the terms of city planning."

Pol. The polis looks to us like a local phenomenon, both in place and in time. But upon that historical accident Aristotle erects the two fundamental propositions of what we might call his philosophical anthropology.

Clay. I prefer to go on calling it his poliscraft, because . . . .

Phil. Mind if I break in with one of the difficulties that still keep me from going all the way with you about the relation between the *Ethics* and the *Politics?* I confess that the notion I previously had was the one that Robert Williams tacked on at the end of the translation of the *Ethics* which he dedicated to Jowett in 1869, at a time when Jowett was beginning his translation of the *Politics*. The last sentence of the *Ethics,* which Rackham renders plainly "Let us then begin our discussion," is puffed by Williams into: "Here, then, we abandon Ethics, and commence the consideration of Politics." With your help, my Loeb summer has got me well past that view. But there is a sentence a bit before the end in which Aristotle speaks of going on to constitutions and legislation "in order to complete as far as possible the philosophy concerning human affairs" (642). Doesn't that suggest a more comprehensive discipline, not divided into mutually exclusive parts, but beginning in what we call ethics and issuing in what Aristotle calls poliscraft? I was going to join Pol in calling it philosophical anthropology, but I gather you object.

Clay. I object very strongly. In the first place, because ethics doesn't yet exist, and the philosophy concerning human affairs is not a more comprehensive discipline uniting ethics and poliscraft, however intimately. It is poliscraft throughout. And in the second place, because to call it philosophical anthropology would be to make it a theoretical instead of a practical science. We forget that the poliscraft was not something that Plato and Aristotle dreamed up. It was a going art, and there was a demand for men who had been trained in it. The questions Plato and Aristotle ask and answer, including those we call ethical, arise out of the practice of that art. Aristotle's hearers come from the polises of the Hellenic world, and they will practice the art in those polises. We do not deliberate about affairs in India, he says somewhere in the *Eudemian Ethics* (290), because those affairs are not up to us. To a detached and speculative intelligence they may be as full of interest as those of the polis are to us, but they are none of our business.

Pol. Unless an Alexander makes them so.

Phil. Let's back up now from the end to the beginning. With minor variations, the translators start off: "Every art and every inquiry, and likewise every act and every choice, seems to aim at some good. Hence it has been well said that the good is that at which all things aim." Doesn't that sound more like ethics than like poliscraft?

Clay. An accurate translation doesn't exist. Rackham's is better than most. They are all too general in one respect, and not general enough in another. Aristotle's four nouns are *technê, methodos, praxis,* and *proairesis.* In rendering them we must be guided by the synonyms and the examples he goes on to give. The synonyms are *epistêmê, dynamis,* and *gnôsis.* The examples are medicine, shipbuilding, military strategy, estate management, rhetoric, gymnastics, and the poliscraft. What he is talking about is the arts and crafts as they are practised in the polis; nothing more general than that. *Technê, methodos, epistêmê* and *gnôsis* emphasize their more theoretical aspects; *praxis, proairesis,* and *dynamis* their more practical aspects. It is when they come to *praxis* and *proairesis* that the translators go astray. No translator of any Greek text has ever done justice to the generality of the three cognates: the verb *prattein,* to do regularly; the noun *pragma,* what is regularly done, or the regular thing to do; and the noun *praxis,* the regular doing of it. The same goes for *proairesis* and its cognates. When Socrates is asked what he does, he understands that he is being asked what his vocation, his calling, his profession, his business, is. And one of his answers, as phrased in the *Gorgias* (514), is that he is one of the few Athenians, not to say the only one, who has taken up the true poliscraft, and the only one alive who is devoting himself to the practice of it.

Phil. Do you mean that Aristotle is not talking about single acts and decisions of private individuals on private occasions? That *praxis* is not act but practice? The practice of medicine for example?

Pol. So nothing in the *Ethics* is addressed to the *idiôtês,* the private person? And Aristotle's teleology does not endorse the notion that every single idiotic act aims at some good?

Clay. Exactly. It is only the arts and crafts as institutionalized in the polis that are in question, and the argument moves toward the conclusion that the poliscraft is the architectonic art to which all the rest are subordinate, and that their several ends are subsidiary directly or indirectly to its end, the architectonic end, which is human good, the good for man. So the sense of the opening words is: *Every* art and *every* science, and likewise *every* practice and *every* profession, is taken to aim at *some* good; so it has been well said that the good is what is aimed at in *all* such cases. *But*—and then the distinctions begin.

Phil. I'll come back to *praxis* and *pragma* later. My next difficulty is this. Aristotle says farther on (6) that even if human good is the same for individual and polis, that of the polis is greater and more perfect both to attain and to preserve. To secure it for one person only is better than nothing, but to secure it for people and polises is nobler and more divine. Isn't there an opening here for Pol and me to ask, if the poliscraft aims at human good for the polis, may there not be another art that aims at it for a people like the Macedonians who haven't yet reached the polis stage, and still another and prior art, ethics perhaps, that aims at it for the single individual?

Clay. Your translation is the best yet, and it helps me to close the opening. This is the only occurrence of *ethnos* in the *Ethics*. It has technical meanings in the *Politics*. In the plural it often means the non-Hellenic peoples, races, or nations. But here it is singular, and its singularity is emphasized by the plurality of polises. I think it means the Hellenic people. Aristotle assumes that since his hearers will be serving as poliscraftsmen in the polises of the Hellenic people, the inquiry on which he and they are entering will make toward the good life for those polises and so for that people. But the living of the good life will of course be done by the members of each polis each living his own life. There are not three arts in question, but only one, and that one is the poliscraft.

Phil. But Aristotle goes on in the next sentence, as most translators construe it: "These are the ends at which our inquiry aims, since it is in a sense a political one." Doesn't that suggest that Aristotle is aware that it is straining a point to call what goes on in the *Ethics* a poliscraft inquiry?

Max Fisch

Clay. I don't deny that the *tis* in the phrase *politikê tis ousa,* taken out of context, might conceivably mean "in a sense." But it is simply the indefinite pronoun, and all the phrase means is "being a poliscraft one." Aristotle's poliscraft will of course go on to other inquiries, but this one is about its aims. Our inquiry addresses itself to *these* matters, he says (that is, to human good for our people, our polises, and their members), since it is the poliscraft and not, say, medicine or shipbuilding that is now defining its end. There is no hint that there is another sense of poliscraft in which it is not a poliscraft inquiry, or that there is another craft in some sense of whose name it is more properly called by the name of *that* craft.

Phil. But doesn't the *Great Ethics* begin a similar inquiry by saying in effect that a treatise concerning *ta êthê* and *ta êthika pragmata,* though it might be called *êthikê,* is more justly called *politikê,* not only because it belongs to the poliscraft to conduct such an inquiry, but because that is its first order of business, its very *archê?*

Clay. Yes, but there is no hint that if we did describe it by the adjective *êthikê* we would be assigning it to an art or science or discipline bearing the name *hê êthikê,* whose business it also is. Still less is there any hint that we would be denying that it is any of the poliscraft's business. On the usual view that the *Great Ethics* is post-Aristotelian, it is evidence therefore that for some time after Aristotle there is still no science called *hê êthikê.* Or, if you prefer, that the only science of "ethics" is still the poliscraft.

Phil. How about the *Eudemian Ethics?* It is usually assumed since Jaeger to be considerably earlier than the *Nicomachean.* It does not announce itself as poliscraft to begin with, nor does it lead into the *Politics* at the end, nor is there any declaration in between that it is the poliscraft speaking. Doesn't that suggest that pulling ethics out of the poliscraft's hat was a trick Aristotle learned later?

Clay. I observe first that is is nowhere said that it is *hê êthikê* that speaks. On the contrary, it is several times assumed that the hearers are students of the poliscraft. For example, it is argued that the philosophic method being fol-

Poliscraft

lowed is not superfluous even for the poliscraftsman (218); that Plato's Good is of no use to the poliscraft (230); that promoting friendship is supposed to be the special task of the poliscraft (358); that the absolutely good is absolutely desirable, but for each individual his own, and these must agree; that virtue brings about this agreement, and the poliscraft exists to make them agree for those for whom as yet they do not (374-376). And I remind you in the second place that the *Eudemian Ethics* has three books in common with the *Nicomachean*. Between III and VII of the *Eudemian* read V-VII of the *Nicomachean* and you will begin to feel the omnipresence of the poliscraft. But of course I concede that what the *Nicomachean* is explicit and emphatic about the *Eudemian* takes mostly for granted.

Phil. My last textual difficulty, at least for the present, is with a passage in one of the common books, at the beginning of chapter 8 of Book VI of the *Nicomachean* (346). Aristotle says that *phronêsis,* prudence, is the same *hexis* as *hê politikê,* the poliscraft, but they have not the same *to einai;* or, as the translators render it, that they differ in essence. I make no sense of the poliscraft differing from prudence in essence though not as habit. However, Aristotle goes on to say that it is the same intellectual virtue, the same virtuous habit, namely prudence, that is variously exercised in the conduct of one's own affairs, in the management of an estate, and in the legislative, executive and judicial functions of the polis; but that, while each of its other exercises has the name of a craft or a subcraft, its exercise in the conduct of one's own affairs is commonly called by the name of the virtuous habit that is generic to them all, — as though taking care of oneself were the primary exercise of prudence, needing no special name, and all the other exercises were secondary, needing special names to distinguish them. Now my question is, if Aristotle had been asked to propose a name for that primary exercise, would he not have proposed *hê ethikê,* and would we not, in our English fog, have to render it "ethics"?

Clay. "Essence," both here and in the parallel passage about justice (260), suggests something more recondite than Aristotle intends. The initial point is simply, as you say, that it is one and the same habit that has so many and such diverse exercises. The further point is that we should not dignify by the name of the virtue its short-sighted exercise in the direct pursuit of one's individual welfare, if indeed it is the virtue that is so exercised. Perhaps what is commonly called prudence is really imprudence. It is probably not possible to obtain human good for oneself otherwise than by seeking it for one's family and one's polis. That is not so much because family and polis are instrumental to a good life for oneself, as because the good life consists in activity of soul in accordance with virtue, including the virtue of prudence, and because domestic economy and poliscraft are the higher exercises of prudence. And of course its highest exercise is in the orders it issues not to, but in behalf of, the contemplative life that consists in the exercise of the still higher intellectual virtues (372).

Phil. So an enlightened ethics would include the poliscraft?

Clay. I find no ethics on the premises. It is true that there is a tradition going back to antiquity, according to which Aristotle recognized three practical sciences concerned with the three spheres of action open to man: ethics, aiming at human good for the individual; economics, for the family; politics, for the state. But I find no such doctrine here or elsewhere in the corpus. Nor do I find any other doctrine concerning relations between the three. As your students protested last fall, *hê êthikê* is nowhere called a practical science, or an art or science of any kind, or anything at all. It is not even mentioned. The explanation of this is that it did not yet exist.

Phil. I'll go over all the passages again with your comments in mind. But, assuming for the present that you have been right throughout, I want to raise three further questions and then return to *praxis* and *pragma*. First question. Suppose physiology were taught only in medical schools, only by physicians, only to would-be physicians, and only with a view to improving the practice of medicine. Suppose it were taught not as a pre-medical or preparatory course, but as the first business of the medical art itself, its very *archê*. Let it even be called "Principles of Medicine" or "Healthcraft 100." Whatever we called it, wouldn't it still be physiology?

Pol. What's in a name? That which we call ethics, by any other name would smell .... ?

Clay. I should say it wouldn't *yet* be physiology; perhaps not quite medicine either; more likely the rudiments of something of the order of homeopathy or acupuncture. But is the analogy to your purpose in the first place? Physiology, after all, is a theoretical science, and was already so in Aristotle's time. And a theoretical science does not become practical by lending premises to a practical one, nor does the practical one become theoretical by borrowing them. In the *Ethics* premises are borrowed from the theoretical sciences of metaphysics and physics, including physiology and psychology; but it is a practical science that does the borrowing, and the practical science that does it is the poliscraft. Whereas your difficulty, I thought, hinged rather on the relation between two practical sciences, ethics and the poliscraft.

Pol. Your attempted analogy between physiology and ethics reminds me, Phil, that Aristotle's own standing analogy, like Plato's, is between medicine and the poliscraft. It is the poliscraft, not ethics, that stands to the soul in the relation in which medicine stands to the body (60 ff.). And just as medicine draws directly on physics as including anatomy and physiology, so the poliscraft draws directly on physics as including psychology. In neither case is there any need or room for an intervening practical science of ethics.

Clay. And Aristotle's analogy goes a step farther. The poliscraft, like medicine, is a *dynamis,* you remember (2, 4). And in the *Metaphysics* (248 ff.) a *dynamis* is a faculty or power in one thing to bring about change in another, or in itself *qua* other. The last clause is added to cover the special and exceptional case for which Aristotle's example is the physician who is one of his own patients (250). The analogous special and exceptional case would be that of the poliscraftsman who applies his skill to the guidance of his own private conduct. So if ethics had existed, and if it had been a practical science, and if, as the tradition I mentioned further assumes, it had been the practical science or art by which the conduct of the *idiôtês,* the private individual, should be guided, then, in Aristotle's view at least, instead of the poliscraft being a special and exceptional application of ethics, ethics would have been a special and exceptional application of the poliscraft.

Pol. And Aristotle remarks in the *Politics* (266) that a wise physician when ill does not treat himself but calls in another physician.

Clay. Well, we've had to look closely to see that there is no room in Aristotle's scheme for ethics as an autonomous practical science, prior to the poliscraft. But we can see at a glance that there is no room whatever for ethics as a theoretical science.

Phil. That brings me to my second question. If there was no autonomous science of ethics, whether practical or theoretical, until after Aristotle, when did it arise and who were its founders?

Clay. We don't know. The history of ethics is still to be written. The research for it has not even begun. The books on the subject are nearly worthless, because their authors have not asked themselves the right questions. Meanwhile, a better history of ethics than any called by that name is Sabine's *History of Political Theory.*

Pol. Cheers for Sabine.

Phil. Third question. John Passmore wrote a book called *Hume's Intentions.* Pol and I would be glad if you would write one on Aristotle's intentions. It would have much still to teach us. That is one way to approach the great philosophers. But for centuries now ethicists have been reading Aristotle as if he were a great ethicist, perhaps the greatest, and in their own sense of ethics as an autonomous philosophical discipline: almost, in fact, as if he were a contemporary with whom they might discuss the issues that concern them. Is not that also a legitimate approach to the study of a great philosopher? If our thinking is enriched and clarified by such encounters, if they result in better answers to our own questions, what does it matter if our questions were not his? May not an autonomous ethics draw good nourishment from the *Nicomachean Ethics,* even if Aristotle did not intend an autonomous ethics or so much as contemplate it as a possibility?

Clay. I see no general objection to learning from Aristotle on one's own terms. I only say that learning from him on his terms, or coming to terms with him, is sometimes better, and that this is one of those times. The greatness of Aristotle lies in the fact that what your ethicists have found in him is not there, and that something better is there. What is there is the tentative rationale of a going local art. What is not there is an autonomous ethics.

Pol. So the best place for ethics is between the same covers with politics, as in Hobbes's *Leviathan* and Bentham's *Principles of Morals and Legislation* and Hegel's *Philosophy of Right*?

Phil. But that sort of ethics has gone out of fashion. For a couple of generations it's been analytic or meta-ethics. The people who do it almost never do politics also. Ethically and politically neutral ethics, you might call it. Logical analysis of the way the language of morals operates.

Clay. What you mean is the way the English language of morals operates, as though that were the universal language of morals, or were about to be. As though whatever has been said in all the mutually untranslatable languages of morals there have been could be said in English, and had better be if it wants a hearing. Linguistic imperialism, I call it. It's what's left of the British empire. I'm suspicious of all claims to universality in ethics, as well as of all claims to neutrality, and doubly so when the two claims are made in the same breath. The worst thing about a professedly autonomous ethics is the premature claim to universality it carries with it. It will be time enough for a universal ethics when we have universal institutions.

Pol. The owl of Minerva?

Phil. Now, Clay, complaining as you do about the English smog, you should welcome whatever desmogging and tidying up gets done, and be ready to forgive the unconscious linguistic chauvinism of the people who are doing it. But may I come back now to *praxis* and *pragma?* You know I've worked at American pragmatism, particularly that of Peirce. I give a seminar on him now and then. It came over me during the summer that I had somehow been keeping Aristotle and Peirce in separate compartments, in spite of Peirce's admiration of Aristotle. I recalled his placing Socrates and Aristotle in the pedigree of pragmatism, and recommending the *Politics* as a specimen of Aristotle at his best. Earlier this afternoon it dawned on me that Peirce's pragmatism differed from James's in emphasizing not the particularity of sensations but the very generality of institutionalized habits of action that you find in Aristotle's *prattein, praxis,* and *pragma.* I recalled, too, that Peirce thought the pragmatic tinge of Aristotle's thought came from Socrates. Now Peirce, like Aristotle, was a natural scientist. He did not understand the Socratic turn from nature as a whole to *ta êthika pragmata* and to the poliscraft as a turn away from nature. He retained Aristotle's distinction between theoretical and practical science, but provided for two-way traffic between them. It was for theory's sake that he found the meanings of scientific hypotheses in conceived habits of action, and that he made the most elaborate study ever of the practical sciences.

Pol. So Peirce's pragmatism is what one comes to farther down the Socratic turn, on past Aristotle?

Phil. And the doubts you raise, Clay, about ethics as a practical science remind me that Peirce, after long conceiving ethics as exclusively a practical science, and then finding a place for parts of it (and even of politics) under the theoretical science of sociology, late in life made the normative part of ethics a theoretical science in its own right — the mid one of a normative trio: aesthetics, ethics, and logic.

Clay. I can only repeat that an autonomous theoretical science of ethics would be premature and pretentious, and add that an autonomous practical science of ethics is morally revolting. So I take great comfort in finding neither in Aristotle.

Poliscraft

Phil. Then you may take a little comfort in Peirce's not making it quite autonomous, but dependent on aesthetics and on the prior sciences of mathematics and phenomenology. And I may now confess that I find this much comfort in your view of Aristotle, that it goes far to account for the absence from the *Ethics* of so much that an autonomous science of ethics would have had to take account of, and the bare mention of so much else that it would have had to deal with at length.

Pol. Well, I must be Loebing along. If you can spare the time, Clay, we'd like to meet with you every week for a while. So far we've been occupied with matters of orientation and approach. We haven't come to grips yet with the substance either of the *Ethics* or of the *Politics*.

Clay. Gladly. Same time, same place. And I'll expect to be learning more and more from you both as we go along. I'm not wearing my infallibility cap in these sessions. And of course I haven't reached my present views unaided. I owe a great deal, for example, to the researches of Stanford Cashdollar for his 1969 Illinois thesis, *An Inquiry into Aristotle's Ethics and Politics.** And like everybody else I have learned from the translations and commentaries — especially from those I have disagreed with most often.

Phil. Suppose for next week we try the definition of happiness, what it uses from the physics and psychology, how the rest of the *Ethics* unpacks it, and how it is applied in the *Politics*. Then the week after that we might try the doctrine of the mean — what the mean is, how it is determined, how the doctrine applies to justice, where it breaks down, and so on.

Clay. I'll be expecting you.

Pol. See you then. Armed with Loebs.

---

*His own principal conclusions have since been presented in "Aristotle's Politics of Morals," *Journal of the History of Philosophy* 11: 145-160, 1973.

3

DIALOGUE AND DIALECTIC
V. Tejera

Philosophies may die of too much method. But doxography is a killer of philosophy itself.

ARISTOTLE'S *TOPICS* CAN BE CALLED "DIALECTICAL" BEcause it is a work about reasoning, persuasion, and the producing of conviction: but it is still innocent of the principle of the syllogism. The *Topics* was written before the *Analytics*. The principle of the syllogism, discovered and displayed in the *Analytics*, constitutes Aristotle's conception of deductive reasoning. The *Prior Analytics* are what we would call his strictly logical work. So, in the first place, we seem to have a contrast in Aristotle between "dialectics" and "analytics," in which dialectics (the art of persuasive reasoning to produce conviction) is not limited to, but is wider than logical or strictly syllogistic demonstration.

But we also find, in the second place, that there is some contrast in Aristotle between *logikōs* and *analytikōs*. In *Posterior Analytics* I.22.84a8, for instance, *logikōs* is used as synonymous with reasoning-in-general, but *analytikōs* is restricted to strictly syllogistic (or demonstrative) reasoning. So, here we have "logical" and "dialectical" on one side, distinguished from "analytical" on the other side. This will remind us that it is only in the last fifty years or so (out of twenty-five hundred) that "logical" has meant "purely logical" or strictly deductive or formal. But neither are notions of deductivity themselves unchanging and eternally fixed. However, our problem is not with "logical" but with "dialectical."

In Aristotle, then, the difference between syllogistic reasoning and dialectical reasoning (see *Topics*, Bk. I) is that the first is apodeictic because it proceeds from premises that are "true and primary," but dialectic reasons from premises that are only "generally accepted" (ἔνδοχα). This makes dialectical reasoning what we would call hypothetical or "iffy" reasoning. In any case, finally, dialectic is here only a part of the "organon" or instrumentation of the search for knowledge, not knowledge itself.

Eleatic Method

Now, Aristotle called Zeno of Elea (fl.460 B.C.) the founder of dialectic (according to *Diog. Laert*.8.2.57(3) and Sext. Empir. *Adv. Log*.I.6-7) because, in the paradoxes that made Zeno famous, he did not claim to be arguing from premises he knew to be true but from premises admitted by his adversaries. Between the life times of Parmenides and Aristotle, then, it was clear to all involved (from Eleatics and Sophists to Socrates, from Protagoras to Plato) that dialectical reasoning was hypothetical and not demonstrative or apodeictic.

It is also ultimately to Zeno that the Greek founders of geometry owed the method of disproof known as the *reductio ad absurdum*. Thus, the geometric mode of reasoning was, in its origins, deeply involved with the dialectical or hypothetical method of reasoning. Because this has been obscured by Scholastic logic and Cartesian mathematicism, we need to recover and emphasize, as a fact in Plato's background, that if Plato was as much influenced by geometry as so many historians like to state,[1] then the geometers' reductios, or dialectical habits, must have been as present to his mind, and as operative in his *Dialogues*, as their demonstrative endeavors. Of course, the kinds of problem that Zeno and the geometers were solving did not easily allow of practising the dialectical method by means of

---

[1] From, for example, Hermann and Stallbaum to J. H. Randall.

oral questioning and answering. Perhaps they worked graphically, and were among the first theorists to do so.

Plato's Protagoras as a Dissòs Lógos, or Protagoras Protagorized

So now, if we look for a dialectician among the practitioners of the art of *oral* disputation, we find the outstanding one to be the Sophist Protagoras. Protagoras (as we all know) was famous for his antilogies, or *dissoì lógoi*, which were sets of arguments first on one side of a given claim and then on the other. Protagoras' procedure seems to have consisted in taking a pair of contradictory assertions, and then giving arguments in favor of both — thus constructing what we call an antinomy. Because Zeno had repeatedly (perhaps systematically) deduced contradictory conclusions from his adversaries' assertions (thus rendering them not only hypothetical but untrue too), it seems that Protagoras inferred, or tended to infer, that it is always possible to construct an antinomy on any question.

In any case, we see that the *doctrinal* relativism imputed to Protagoras by the speakers in the *Theaetetus* has a *methodological* counterpart in Protagoras' manual on the art of disputation (or eristic or agonistic). It is safe to assume, therefore, that Plato's methodological sophistication took fuller cognizance of this fact than we who are noticing it now. We can conclude, then, that inasmuch as Zeno's concern to refute Parmenides' doctrinal opponents really minimized the dogmatic side of Eleaticism while maximizing its methodology, Plato's consciousness of Eleaticism must certainly have featured its famous methodology quite as much as (or more than) its difficult doctrines. Socrates' words in the *Phaedrus* (261D) make explicit the connection, in Plato's reflection, between Eleaticism and method: "Do we not know that the Eleatic Palamedes [i.e., Zeno] has such an *art of speaking* that the same things appear to his hearers to be alike and unlike, one and many, stationary and in motion?"

Correspondingly we can also conclude, in relation to Protagoras, that Plato was at least as aware of his skillful and methodic technique as he was of his doctrines. It is indeed not his doctrines that are discussed in the dialogue which Plato honors with his name. It would seem, rather, that the *Protagoras* is an extended dramatic application of (and tribute to) the method of the *Dissoì Lógoi* in which we find both of the master disputants each taking, in turn, both sides of the same question (i.e., reversing themselves on it)! The *Protagoras* I would say, was Plato's two-fold argument to end all twofold arguments! Indeed on the question itself, whether human excellence can be taught only if there is an idea of it, we notice also that the different possible positions all get the support, in successive anastrophes, of both Socrates and Protagoras. As far as Plato, the author, is concerned this is neither scepticism nor eclecticism but rather *the dramatic dialogue as critical inquiry* into alternative solutions to a given problem.

Is Plato's "Parmenides" an Eleaticized Protagoras, or Parmenides Zenonized?

In the *Parmenides* Plato's youthful Socrates complacently clears up (to his own naive satisfaction) a paradox of Zeno's by invoking the theory of ideas. He is then confronted by the fictional Parmenides with a series of real difficulties in his theory and he, Socrates, cannot solve the difficulties. Parmenides' intent, however, was not refutative or elenctic but kindly and educational (as we see from Stephanus pp. 135, 136). He tells the youthful Socrates that his impulse towards reasoning (ἐπὶ τοὺς λόγους) is beautiful and sacred, but he needs more training (γυμνασία). "What, then, is the method of training?" the youth asks. "That which you heard Zeno practising," Parmenides answers. The older man then commends Socrates for dealing with his problem in terms of what is graspable by reason more than anything else (i.e., for dealing with his problem in what we would call mainly conceptual terms), and goes on to urge that he acquire practice in the elaboration of *antilogies*. "You must do something more than that" (i.e., than think mainly in conceptual terms); "you must consider not only what happens if a given hypothesis is true, but also what happens if it is not true." Asked by Socrates to frame a hypothesis and illustrate the method, so as to help him understand it, Zeno declines the request but adds that "without a far-ranging (πλάνης) circuit (διεξόδον) of the mind through all things it cannot attain the truth." So, recapitulating, the training which is being recommended to the young Socrates has here been said to have the following characteristics: (i) it is training in handling what is especially graspable by reason, (ii) it is training in the construction of antilogies, (iii) it is training in looking at the consequences of asserting and denying hypotheses, and (iv) it is systematic or, at least, very thorough *search*.

It is the old philosopher, our father Parmenides himself, who consents to illustrate the training method and conduct a full-scale dialectical exercise. The hypothesis he takes up is "whether the one is or is not" (εἴτε ἓν ἔστιν εἴτε μὴ ἕν); and he is made to say by the author of the dialogue that it is his own hypothesis. Without taking up the question of whether in fact this was the exact starting point of the philosophy of the historical Parmenides, we can agree that the exercise which Parmenides conducts appears to meet all the conditions specified earlier for the dialectical training method. It follows that any discussion of detail that is not to violate the integrity of this work of Plato's, must be based on an effective recognition of the dialectic structure which both arises within, and is generative of the greater part of, the architectonic of the dialogue.

Any reader who has thought about the influence of the historical Zeno or the significance of the historical Protagoras, will — when he comes to Plato's *Parmenides* — be both pleased and challenged by the pervasive mixture of Zenonian and Protagorean traits in the logical behavior of the father of philosophy in the dialogue which honors him with its name. Zeno had applied his dialectical method to Parmenides' doctrinal opponents: Plato now applied Zeno's method to (what is said to be) Parmenides' own doctrine. This is one irony. And it is another irony that the whole performance (in part two of the dialogue) looks, as to form, like a monumental Protagorean *dissòs logós*. Antinomies I to IV (137C-160B) rehearse the paradoxical consequences of the hypothesis that the one is, while antinomies V to VIII (160B-166C) elaborate the paradoxes that arise if this hypothesis is denied. There can be no doubt that Plato is a past master of the dialectic *method* of argumentation both as it had been practised down to his time and as it came to be characterized by Aristotle.

But does our emphasis on Plato's "acceptance" of, and fun with, Eleatic method require us to conclude that he was much less interested in Eleatic doctrine? Of course he was also interested in the doctrine — but found himself obliged to criticize it. And he chose to criticize it by turning Eleatic method against Eleatic doctrine. But this destructive criticism works both ways in the *Parmenides*: if you take the method seriously you must reject the doctrine, but if you take the doctrine seriously you must reject the method. Here is a third irony in the dialogue, and it is an irony that positively tells us something (i.e., without need of interpretative inference). It tells us that we cannot consistently agree with *both* Parmenides *and* Zeno.

Plato would also seem to be *showing* us that we are not to take either member of the Eleatic school literally. On one hand, Zeno's method, literally applied, destroys all assertion including his master's. On the other hand Parmenides' statements, taken out of the context of his poem and asserted as categorical truth-claims, would be refutable by Zeno's method and first of all (in Plato's fiction) by Parmenides himself. But this is still not the whole of the philosophic joke, or the end of the structural ironies in the dialogue. For, by dramatizing in the first part of the dialogue the serious difficulties in the theory of ideas, Plato is (i) forcing us to be nonliteral about doctrines being discussed in the bosom of his own Academy and has (ii) exhibited as operative a pragmatistic view of "theory" according to which that theory is best which has fewest paradoxical consequences.

Now these are not strange things for Plato to be doing or implying. On the contrary we must understand that the whole of Plato's philosophical activity, as constituted by the *Dialogues*, was nondogmatic (like his master Socrates') and that the dialogue-form is itself designed to avoid that mode of philosophizing that argues about doctrines literally asserted and inescapably falls into doctrinal assertion itself.[2] The system-seeking and doxographical kinds of reading that Plato's dialogues have mostly been subjected to in their history, are also the kinds of reading that have done most violence to the integrity of the philosophical dialogue-form that Plato developed. One of the great unnoticed things that Plato did for philosophy was to show, this early in its career, the wrong-headedness of philosophical doxography before the doxographers had fairly gotten started on their systematically misleading, dogmalisting labors.

We have witnessed the ironic manner in which Plato, the author, uses the dialectic as part of the dialogue structure of the *Protagoras* and the *Parmenides,* and we have emphasized the "hypothetical" nature of the dialectic technique. Now we must face the question that arises when we find Socrates, the ubiquitous character in Plato's dramatic constructions, claiming that there is "a portion of the intelligible ... which reasoning itself grasps by the power of dialectics, treating its hypotheses ... as springboards to enable it to rise to that which requires no assumption and is the starting point of all" (τμῆμα του νοητοῦ ... οὗ αὐτὸς ὁ λόγος ἅπτεται τῇ τοῦ διαλέγεσθαι δυνάμει, τὰς ὑποθέσεις ποιούμενος ... οἷον ἐπιβάσεις τε καὶ ὁρμάς, ἵναμέχρι τοῦ ἀνυποθέτου ἐπὶ τὴν τοῦ παντὸς ἀρχὴν ἰών

Socrates is suggesting (here and farther on in *Republic VII* that there is a knowledge which transcends the conditional nature of the hypotheses of the special sciences, which is achievable by means of pure reasoning (διὰ τοῦ λόγου ... ἀνευπασῶν τῶν αἰσθήσεων) by the well-trained man with synoptic (συνοπτικός) power, and which — since it relates all the ideas of the arts and sciences (τέχναι) to the idea of the good as their first principle — provides both a secure anchoring for scientific knowledge and a terminal for the knowledge

---

2. This claim is argued for in "Plato: the Open Mind," Ch. V of the author's *Modes of Greek Thought* (New York: Appleton-Century-Crofts, 1971).

seeker. This is the goal of intelligence (ἐπ'αὐτῷ γίγνεται τῷ τοῦ νοητοῦ τέλει) and the completion, or end, of the dialectic. What shall we say to this claim of the fictional Socrates that there is a knowledge (νόησις or διάνοια) which is not hypothetical (ἀνυπόθετον)?

Well, the claim is not challenged or criticized any farther on in the *Republic*; so, in that sense, it can be said to be an unquestioned postulate of Socrates. But neither is it developed in any further detail by Socrates himself. It can be said, perhaps, to be presupposed in the later discussion of the intellectual or positive pleasures. And we can recognize that the aesthetic motive is very near the surface when this sort of unconditional knowledge or understanding is desiderated by Socrates (because otherwise the knowledge process would have no end that *felt* like one, and no beginning that was *not arbitrary*). But the huge development which later philosophy has given to the notion that there must be a knowledge which is absolute cannot be charged to Plato, the creator and manager of the fictional Socrates. For, in the very discussion of the special sciences which leads him to the notion, Socrates categorizes all of these as conditional (510B-511E). And, secondly, because there is irony in the very situation from which the notion arises. If I have rightly sensed the spirit in which it is desiderated, the corresponding verbalization or metadescription of that spirit would, quite simply, run something like this: *If* there is to be a resting place from questioning for comprehensive theorizing, and *if* there is to be a kind of understanding that is not conditional, i.e., *if* there is to be a surcease from the destruction of assertion by the dialectic, *then* there must be something which is both noetic and unquestioned. But this is all, itself, conditional.

The Underlying Design of the Dialogues

Even if we accept as categorical Socrates' postulation of unconditional knowledge we cannot avoid the fact that this postulation is inextricably embedded, and advanced, within the framework of a conceptual experiment in constitution-making and within a socially critical and satirical literary construction. By conceptual experiment I mean, in Plato's case, a design or format which underlies all the dialogues and which frees the author from the burden of over-all doctrinal consistency (from dialogue to dialogue) by holding all claims in a state of dramatic or conversational suspension and putting them in the mouths of likely speakers other than Plato himself. It is a design which exempts attempted solutions to philosophic problems from sounding, or having to claim to be, definitive. This is because it is a design which allows the "solutions" to be both explicitly criticized at the discursive or dialectical level, and implicitly related to the world or tests of action — even while these "solutions" are being elaborated. The dialogue form makes all system-seeking paraphrases of the dialogues as illegitimate as the paraphrasing of good poetry. So that, when a metadescription is given (as above) of something that has *happened* in a dialogue, what is being given is not a paraphrase of anything which I claim Plato *said*, but a verbalization of the structure of the reader's response.

The determinacy, the openness, and the direction in our responses to the dialogues are, of course, the product of Plato's art and they bear on both the need for action and the need for thought. The dialogues are not knowledge, in the theoretical sense, so much as they are *openings towards knowledge*, in the sense that knowledge is something we can act on or something that clarifies human action. In this respect, what the *Dialogues* give us is very much like what we get from Greek drama, namely, a clarification of the condition of man — the talkative, political animal — from a perspective of humanity. What we get from the characters *in* the *Dialogues* are presumptions, mistakes, clever moves, assertions and evasions, very much as in tragedy and comedy. From Plato's Socrates we also get some deliberative ethical conduct. But what we get from his author is great art.

Plato's Use of the Dialectic in the Dialogues

Returning to the arena of disputation and categorical claims we can, in retrospect, now sum up the history of the dialectic as clarified by Plato's use of it in the *Dialogues*. In Zeno the dialectic was an elenctic (or refutative) process which, Plato was quick to see, was destructive of all categorical assertion, and could produce only negative conviction. This is exhibited to us in the *Protagoras* and the *Parmenides*. But in Aristotle's very early *Topics* the dialectic is tacitly a persuasive process which can produce positive conviction. (Aristotle will, later, say that demonstrative proof is the most convincing, *Rhetoric I.i,* but is not always allowed by the subject matter or effective with an audience. Hence the need for dialectic and rhetoric).[3] Thus, in the sense that Plato's *Dialogues* produce (i) dramatic clarification of the knowledge process and (ii) a stimulus to more thoughtful or deliberate action, we find in these *Dialogues* a synthesis of both the rhetorical conception of dialectic and the Zenonian, or refutative, conception. It is a synthesis which just about exhausted, for philosophy and for its time, the creative possibilities in either view of the dialectic.

Aristotle Again

Perhaps we should remember that the texts we have of Aristotle were only his so-called "lecture notes" for use in the live situation of "classroom" discussion. It may be that we go too far in taking them as the parts of a categorical system of philosophical doctrine. I am not claiming that Aristotle was not (or was) systematic in his teaching, only that we perhaps should distinguish more than we do between Aristotle's talent for system and the system of his editors. For Aristotle himself, in any case, the texts, his sharing and developing of them, were both a means to and constitutive of the humanly full and good life. It is no accident that Aristotle's published works were dialogues. We can put it (continuing our speculation) like this: in his art of dialectical inquiry the living, historical Socrates avoided the categorical assertion or imposition of doctrine; but he felt no need to write. As his disciple Plato, likewise, had to avoid assertion; but Plato liked to write. The dialogue form solves the problem of practising philosophy in writing, while avoiding indoctrination of the listener or reader. So, if Aristotle is to be thought of as a disciple of Plato in the way

---

3. See *Aristotle Again*.

Victorino Tejera

Plato was a disciple of Socrates, then Aristotle's systematic or categorical writings (as opposed to his dialogues) could not have been intended doctrinally or for use outside of the context of co-operative dialectical inquiry, i.e., of inquiry mediated by rational or theoretical discussion or conversation. A true disciple of Plato's, if I am right about the nature of Plato's philosophical activity, *could* have *published* only dialogues.

4

A KEY TO PLATO'S EARLY DIALOGUES
Theodore Waldman

IN THIS ESSAY, I WISH TO SET FORTH A KEY BY WHICH PLATO'S dialogues may be interpreted. What I hope to show here is that the early or Socratic dialogues of Plato may be interpreted as not merely his tribute to the teaching of his beloved teacher (and thus as separate from his own doctrine developed in the other dialogues); but as expressing dramatically the first stages in the allegory of the divided line, that of the prisoners in the cave and those objects first illuminated by the sun and the beliefs thereby established. In other words the three famous allegories and analogies of the *Republic* open with a vision that is substantiated by the early dialogues. I should also say that it is my belief, although beyond my intentions in this paper, that a more intensive examination of the dialogues would indicate that as a body they express and fulfill the remaining parts of the allegories and analogies.

Plato tantalizes us by presenting a series of sequences of dialogues that appear as possible parts of a unified system of thought; nonetheless they contain enough stops and starts, enough themes tried on for size only to be rejected later, that unity disappears in diversity. (Ironically, this is one of the very themes, unity and diversity, which receives this sort of treatment.) In desperation the seeker of unity may force Plato's thought into a conceptual bed of Procrustes. Not that Plato suffers thereby, but rather does the interpretation of him. If that interpretation is used pedagogically the student may well be misled; and, as Socrates has indicated, the misleading of students is an evil not to be lightly taken. I hope my view does not end as Procrustean or vacuous; I trust no student will be misled by it.

In the pages that follow I shall review briefly and with some comments Plato's allegories noted before; I shall then give my characterization of the early dialogues, their personages to some extent, and the fittingness of my key to them. I shall then make some concluding remarks.

I

Plato states his three famous allegories of the *Republic* in Books VI and VII (508-518b). Socrates, having been asked to give an explanation of the good and its relation to knowledge as adequate as his recent attempt on the virtues of justice, temperance and the others, defers and offers instead to speak of the offspring of the good. It is stated somewhat as follows: When we consider the phenomenon of sight we recognize that that which has the power to see, the eye, and that which has the power to be seen, physical objects, are both powerless to bring about the 'perceiving-perceived' relation without the presence of light. Light in other words is neither that which sees nor that which is seen but that which permits the eye to see and the object to be seen. Socrates then points out that light is itself the 'subject' of the sun, its lord. The sun is certainly not the organ of sight although it is closely associated with the eye. Socrates does not discuss it here but he does indicate that the sun is no ordinary object of vision, if an object at all. Nonetheless, speaking metaphorically, the sun gives life to vision, sets it in motion, without itself being affected by the visual relationship. If there are things to be seen and there is a way of seeing them as they are, and if both of these depend upon light and the sun, then, for Socrates, it is meaningful to hold that the sun makes possible the reality of perception (and its objects, the eye and material things) and the truth or correctness of perception without itself being part of the ingredients of sight. To put it another way, the sun which is itself independent of the visual relation is nonetheless that which generates it and, more strongly, that which brings its parts into being; we see in Socrates' account a precursor to that kind of explanation which Aristotle gave of the gods when he spoke of them as unmoved movers.

Socrates holds that there is a similar relation in the intellectual world between that which has the power to know and that which may be known; a 'medium' is needed in order to bring this relationship to fruition. Just as we cannot see nor can things be seen without the sun so we cannot know nor can things (of the mind or better of the realm of forms or ideas) be known without the good. That which holds true of the sun vis-à-vis the eye and physical objects also is true of the good in relation to that which knows, the soul or mind, and the objects of knowledge, the forms or ideas. The good generates knowledge and may be said to be the author or creator of mind and its objects. It is also the case that just as the eye sees dimly and its objects are barely capable of being seen when light is low, so that only a hazy opinion may be formed about that which is perceived, so the mind is hazy in its judgements and barely understands those forms or ideas that are almost incapable of presenting themselves as understandable or knowable when the good is not known as that which empowers the mind and gives order, truth and being to the ideas. Just as in a hierarchy of things created and those entities that create, to wit, creators, the latter are held to be ontologically superior, so that we may say that the sun is lord of the eye as well as its objects (this for Socrates is true ontologically as well as epistemologically), so with regard to the good and mind and its objects we may say:

> This reality, then that gives their truth to objects of knowledge and the power of knowing to the knower, you must say is the

idea of Good, and you must conceive it as being the cause of knowledge, and of truth insofar as known. Yet fair as they both are, knowledge and truth, in supposing it to be something fairer still than these you will think rightly of it. (508e, 509a).

It can be seen in Socrates' account of the relation between the eye or the knower, their objects and that which generates the actual occurrence of opining and knowing, the sun or the good, that no one of the two entities related is sufficient to explicate opinion or knowledge. Thus, those who hold that opinion or knowledge rest ultimately upon one's point of view, that it is all in the eye of the beholder, fail to perceive that not only is it necessary that there be an object to be perceived, but that neither the eye which perceives nor the object to be perceived could enter into opinion or knowledge (the latter, of course, in terms of mind and forms) were there not a third ingredient to make the relation viable. The subjectivist, as we would denote him, blatantly ignores two features of opining or knowing without which there could be no point of view: something in the eye of the beholder, and stronger still both eye to behold and object to be beheld. The same kind of criticism applies to the 'objectivist' who holds that it is sufficient to account for the truth and knowledge (or opinion) of things by simply referring to the objects that exist in the universe independently of that which perceives or knows them or that which 'illuminates' them. It is obvious from Socrates' account that he does not liken the sun or its light to one more object in the universe of physical entities nor the good to one more form in the universe of forms. Both apparently give a structure and form to the collection of objects and ideas which results in their having the reality they have and the relations that they bear to one another. I suppose that it is something like the experience of grasping a philosopher's system so thoroughly that one sees not only his fundamental presuppositions and the propositions that he derives from them, but one has an insight into the manner in which he would consider problems, offer solutions and meet criticisms of his system. To take a possible but difficult example, it is as if one were confident of saying that one was in full understanding of the philosophy of Leibniz, saw his system as a 'whole' and was able to state and justify what Leibniz would say were he faced with such and such a problem. In this manner the truth of Leibniz's statements and the knowledge they intended would best be grasped when one saw them as integral parts of the system of Leibniz. This grasping of the system would amount to the form of the system, the good of it. So I think in the analogy of the sun with the good, Socrates holds that in order to grasp fully the objects seen and the eye that sees them, the forms known and the mind that knows them, one must grasp that which structures, orders and illuminates them; that which is not one of them but makes them possible.

A dramatic and important part of this and one that I shall return to is that in the dialogues themselves, especially the so-called Socratic ones, Socrates functions as the third ingredient present when discussion ensues. There are those who claim to know or opine about virtue(s) who have not examined (thrown light upon) their claims or that by which they establish them. The gadfly as midwife is neither that which knows ("I know that I do not know.") nor that which is known ("I do not know myself.") but nonetheless is that one who illuminates for others their quest. Socrates is the sun and the good who generates opinion or knowledge without being either the one who knows or who is known. He is the teacher as lamp. (It goes without saying that the lamp is the symbol of the teacher as well as of education.)

The analogy of the sun presents us with Plato's ontological vision of the entities necessary to the opining and knowing relationship as well as that entity which generates them and 'gives life' to their process. His second great analogy is that of the divided line by which he tries to express the qualities or characteristics present within the visible and intelligible worlds. (He asks us to keep in mind that there are two powers over these realms — the good and its offspring, the sun. [509d]) We are to imagine a line that is cut into two unequal parts, in the same propor-

Theodore Waldman

tion as the first division. The first division and its parts represent the visible world. The parts within each realm indicate the clearness with which the respective objects are perceived as well as presented. The emphasis, however, is upon the status of the objects as the appropriate epistemological designation of the kind or degree (it is not always clear which is appropriate) of opining or knowing that is related to each. In each division the lower is an image, copy or subordinate object or principle of those present respectively in the higher. Thus, in the visual realm we have shadows and reflections; reflections may be in water or from smooth, polished bodies. All these are images of the ordinarily perceived objects (animals, plants, physical entities, e.g., mountains, lakes, or plains, and those things that are made, i.e., artifacts). In Plato's scheme of things there is an order to the reality of objects that corresponds to the order in the knowing of objects. The copy of an object is less real than the object and the "knowing" (opining) of a copy less true than the knowing of that object to which the copy corresponds. In the visible world there is also a proportionate relationship between the copy and its original and the "knowing" of the copy and the knowing of the original which also implies that the same ratio pertains between the copy and the knowing of the copy and the original and the knowing of the original. Traditionally, the two different types of opining have been called "belief" and "opinion" and the divisions of their perceived correlatives, "images" and "objects." In the intelligible realm a similar division obtains, and there is a similar proportionate relationship between the sub-parts. Given the general rules of ratios the proportions noted first pertain not only within the divisions but between them since they were laid down similarly. Thus, the copy in the visible world is to its counterpart in the intelligible world ("hypotheses") as the original in the visible world is to its counterpart in the intelligible world ("Ideas" or "Forms"); similarly belief in the visible world is to its counterpart ("understanding" or "thinking") as opinion is to its counterpart ("reason" or "knowing"). In the intelligible realm we begin with the subject matter of the visible as that which presents the problems that require a "non-visible" or intelligible referent for their solution. The relations that are exhibited among physical objects are treated hypothetically in geometrical terms in order to reach a conclusion; both in teaching geometry and in working out the solution to the problems that are presented in the visible world either the visible objects or idealised images of them (to wit: geometrical figures) are used. Thus, not only the images but the originals of the visible world become the images of the intelligible world. In a very real sense the higher rests upon the lower and is constructed from it. This does seem to lead one to the conclusion that although the line is represented as divided, the division is not between kinds but a device for picturing a continuum. One passes from the world of shadows and physical objects to that of hypotheses and mathematical objects as part of a natural activity of perceiving and reflecting upon perceptions. Not that the natural activity proceeds without effort; as we shall see there is reluctance and resistance by the individual as he moves from one realm to another, even if those realms are part of a continuum. That is why Socrates likened the struggle to that of being born and why he who aided in that birth was a kind of midwife. I say this in spite of the view which holds that Plato argues for two worlds separate and distinct which bear only a distant image-like relationship to each other; a view that obviously lent itself to an interpretation compatible with the one that looked upon this life and this world as opposed to a spiritual one in which God is our home.

The upper sub-part of the intelligible realm Socrates held to be that of Ideas or Forms. In the 'hypotheses part' the activity of mind was directed toward the visible world and its objects using mathematics to solve problems peculiar to it. It was, in a way, what we would call "applied mathematics" or "engineering." In moving from hypotheses to those principles upon which they rest (perhaps, much like our study of the foundations of mathematics) the individual no longer uses hypotheses as if they were axiomatic and self-evident but as tentative and suggestive steps in an argument that has practical consequences. He seeks by use of his reason to structure the entire relationship so that the hypotheses now seen as Ideas or Forms in relation to one another are subsumed under some fundamental Forms. The subsumption of the Ideas apparently involves more than those we would ordinarily call "mathematical," that is, those of justice, beauty, love and truth, to name a few. As is well known, Socrates considers the kind of reasoning one uses in this search to be dialectical. Socrates concludes his analogy by noting that the soul has four powers of perceiving and knowing that correspond to the kinds of objects to be known; they are the aforementioned belief, opinion, understanding and knowing. (511e). It should be noted that these divisions of the soul or mind are different from and in a sense included in the more familiar three divisions of the soul — reason, spirited element and appetites. It is, by and large, in reason and the appetites that the four "faculties" of knowing are to be found, although the response of the spirited element to the world about it seems peculiarly suited to the virtue of courage and its "eros." It seems for Plato that the three divisions of the soul do have that power to perceive and the capacity to be affected along with the necessity to be "empowered" by a third ingredient that we noted in discussing the analogy of the sun. It should be pointed out that in this second analogy or allegory although he began by reminding us that the good and its offspring "hovered" above, the divisions of the line do not include the good as an element. He had said, of course, in the section quoted earlier that it was fairer still than truth and knowledge.

The last allegory is, perhaps, the best known and that to which most literary allusion has been made. Having presented us with a vision of the world of shadows and objects, of the sun and the good, of the eye and the mind, and of Ideas and Forms, and of the parts of the soul used for understanding the world of things and knowing the world of Ideas, he now turns to a poetic vision of the kind of life that we lead. It is a vision intimately connected with the views he had just given on knowledge and the good, but it also hearkens back to a discussion that had preceded the allegories. Earlier in Book VI (from 487b to 489d) Socrates had tried to answer Adeimantus' question as to the apparent rejection of philosophers and philosophy by the common people and to the spectacle of the followers of philosophy becoming strange monsters or rogues made useless to the world by the very pursuit in which they engage. For this allegory displays the condition of men in their everyday lives within which the philosophical natures find themselves, free themselves and ultimately return. It is Plato's allegory of the cave: (514-517d)

> Behold! human beings housed in an underground cave, which has a long entrance open towards the light and as wide as the interior of the cave; here they have been from their childhood, and have their legs and necks chained, so that they cannot move and can only see before them, being prevented by their chains from turning round their heads. Above and behind them a fire is blazing at a distance, and between the fire and the prisoners there is a raised way, like the screen which marionette players have in front of them, over which they show the puppets. (514a,b)

The bearers, behind the raised way, walk about, some talking, others silent, carrying many kinds of objects. All that the chained can see are the shadows of the objects, extended weirdly, dancing upon the wall. Not only do they see but shadows of the objects, but of themselves also. Since their "reality" is based upon what they see, they think that the shadows are real things and call them that. Truth for them then is nothing but the shadows of images. If one is freed and compelled to look toward the light,

> ...he will suffer pains; the glare will distress him, and he will be unable to see the realities of which in his former state he had seen the shadows;...
> ...if he is compelled to look straight at the light, will he not have a pain in his eyes which will make him turn away to take refuge in the objects of vision which he can see, and which he will conceive to be in reality clearer than the things which are now being shown to him?

Theodore Waldman

...And suppose once more, that he is reluctantly dragged up that steep and rugged ascent, and held fast until he is forced into the presence of the sun himself, is he not likely to be pained and irritated? When he approaches the light his eyes will be dazzled, and he will not be able to see anything at all of what are now called realities....

He will require to grow accustomed to the sight of the upper world. And first he will see the shadows best, next the reflections of men and other objects in the water, and then the objects themselves; and, when he turned to the heavenly bodies and the heaven itself, he would find it easier to gaze upon the light of the moon and the stars at night than to see the sun or the light of the sun by day? (515c-516b)

Socrates continues the allegory and indicates that he who is freed gazes finally upon the sun itself and finds it to be the cause of all. It would result in his recognition that those in the cave who honor those of their cohorts who are quick to note the passage of shadows, their order and sequence, are vying for and giving rewards in a world that has only the appearance of reality and truth. He who has seen the real and the true will not be eager for such honors nor will he envy those who have been granted them. He is happy to have left his former life, and those who yet live it elicit pity from him; nothing would induce him to return to it and he would suffer rather than do so. We may, however, imagine what it would be like for him to return to his old place in the cave after having 'seen the light.' (In point of fact, as we learn, Plato holds that he who has escaped from the cave and learned that the world of appearances is not the real one nor the statements about it the fundamentally true ones must be compelled to return to the cave to guide those who live only in shadows.) Returning from the light, he could not see in the darkness any more than he could see in the light when first he left. He would initially be at a greater disadvantage than when he had left the cave; for having seen the truth it would be more difficult to adjust once more to the darkness. Those around him, furthermore, would be little disposed to accept anything he had to say about their world, let alone another which they were told was the real and true one. They would instead think that he had ruined himself and if anyone tried to remove the chains of another so that he might ruin himself too, they would consider the liberator as a criminal and put him to death. Thus it is that philosophers, those who have pursued knowledge of the true and real, and their very pursuit, philosophy, have fallen into disrepute. The people, content with their shadows, would execute those who would chastise them and urge them to a new world and a new life. The allusions to Socrates' life and death seem apparent.

Socrates concludes this allegory by saying to Glaucon:

> ...the prison-house is the world of sight, the light of the fire is the power of the sun, and you will not misapprehend me if you interpret the journey upwards to be the ascent of the soul into the intellectual world according to my surmise, which, at your desire, I have expressed — whether rightly or wrongly God knows. But, whether true or false, my opinion is that in all the world of knowledge the Idea of good appears last of all, and is seen only with an effort; although when seen, it is inferred to be the universal author of all things beautiful and right, parent of light and of the lord of light in the visible world, and the immediate and supreme source of reason and truth in the intellectual; and that this is the power upon which he who would act rationally either in public or private life must have his eye fixed. (517b, c)

In this conclusion, Socrates seems to unite the allegories and analogies. The good and its offspring, the passage from the cave to the sun, the divisions of the line into opinion and its parts, and the intelligible world into understanding and reason or knowing are all seen in man's entrance into a blooming, buzzing confusion, his accomodation to it, his reflections upon that accomodation, his recognition that there is a world of intelligible objects and principles by which he comes to understand the visible world and his further reasoning upon the structure, form and origins of that intelligible world. For Socrates, a unifying principle ties together the noetic aspects of knowledge with the practical aspects of conduct and the spiritual values of beauty and love; it is that which he calls, "Idea of the good." It is within this attempt at unification that one may find the Socratic mission also. For philosophy is not merely an academic pursuit, albeit the Academy followed the death of Socrates. It is a way of analyzing one's self, one's friends and one's community in that conduct and those principles that characterize their respective activities. The allegories are an attempt at exhibiting the truth of this by example and narrative; they are not a proof, but a way of looking at those peculiar Socratic problems that later engaged Plato in the Academy and in his dialogues. Since the spur to the discussion in the *Republic* came from Thrasymachus' challenge to Socrates (343-344d) and Glaucon and Adeimantus adding to his argument (357-367e), Socrates has to justify how a man ought to live. That problem underlies the entire discussion and is not be be forgotten no matter what the divergence. How a man ought to live is central, also, to the drama of life. It is my contention, as I stated above, that the dialogues of Plato, and for the purposes of this essay, the early dialogues, are the dramatic enactment of the allegories. In participating in the dialogues one begins in the realm of opinion with beliefs and convictions about images and shadows, objects and artifacts, present in everyday life and proceeds along the path of the line, to the light of the sun, the offspring of the good, and from the cave, to the light, and back to the cave. The dialogues become, to use a melodramatic phrase, the living proof of the truths of the allegories. At this point I should like to give my characterization of the dialogues. I shall combine this with some evidence for my thesis and then briefly conclude this essay.

II

The dialogues of Plato are an amazing and exciting creation which unite philosophical insight and argument with dramatic form. Generally speaking, Socratic elenchus and Platonic dialectic are expressed through the conversation and disputation of the *dramatis personae;* for the dialogue is properly and beautifully chosen as the only written way to present the oral teaching of Socrates. Often the settings

Key to Plato's Early Dialogues

and actions of the dialogues exhibit the theses considered as much as does the give and take of the discussion. Plato recognizes that the dialogue form can make use of poetry and drama as well as argument and reason (not that these are exhaustive) to express philosophy much to the consternation and confusion of those critics and scholars who are well aware of his claims against the representative poet or imitative artist. As a counter to those critics one might mention in passing that in the magnificent myth of the journey of the soul in the *Phaedrus* (248d,e) we are told that by an ordinance of Necessity the soul first inhabits a human who shall grow either into a seeker of wisdom or beauty, a follower of the Muses or a lover. In its sixth "descent" the soul follows the life of a poet or some other imitative artist. Apparently Plato distinguished the follower of the Muses whose pursuit may include poetry or other artistic vocations from those poets who are imitative artists. He put the former, as noted, with philosophical natures, among others, whereas the latter were grouped as imitators. I believe in this distinction is to be found the difference between Plato the Poetical Philosopher and Plato the critic of imitative or representative poets.

It is his mastery of dramatic form that allows Plato to use the dialogue itself not only as the agora in which Socrates engages us in the pursuit of wisdom, but the stage upon which the life of Socrates in an odd and exciting way becomes the practical solution to many if not all of the philosophical problems presented. Richard Robinson in his *Plato's Earlier Dialectic*[1] correctly expounds the negative and destructive aspect of the Socratic elenchus but in his rather unimaginative portrayal of Socratic irony, he fails to see that at times Socrates himself (in his life) is the positive answer presented along with the negative turn of the early arguments. The dramatic form of the dialogues achieves this. In Alcibiades' magnificent portrayal in the *Symposium* (215a-222c) of Socrates the man, the soldier, the lover and

---

1. Richard Robinson, *Plato's Earlier Dialectic* (Oxford Clarendon Press, 2nd. edit. 1953), pp. 8ff.

dialectician, Plato combines the life and argument of Socrates so that he becomes the way, the solution to what might be called the "practical syllogism" developed in the dialogues. This, too, exemplifies the high drama of which I spoke. Paul Friedlander in his excellent introduction to Plato writes that Plato possessed what Socrates did not seem to need: the plastic eye of the Greeks.[2] He was able to see in Socrates' life and teaching the question and solution to the good life for all men, and to set it dramatically. He saw the one in the many, the form in the instances.

The allusions in the dialogues to the life of Socrates are many, too many to cite and already too often cited, but it would perhaps be of some value to recall at least one. (We recognize that the drama of the death of Socrates and Plato's ensuing despair is often presented by Socrates in the dialogues.) The *Euthyphro* is an excellent early dialogue concerned with a typically profound Socratic question, "What is Piety (or Holiness)?" One sees the negative aspects of the elenchus occur when Euthyphro, almost in despair says "Now, Socrates, I simply don't know how to tell you what I think. Somehow everything that we put forward keeps moving about us in a circle, and nothing will stay where we put it." (11b) Finally, Euthyphro, who claimed that he knew what holiness was, is either so confused or so disgusted or both regarding that so-called knowledge, that he begs off, leaves in a hurry, and Socrates remarks that he must face Meletus' indictment without benefit of Euthyphro's "wisdom." (15e, 16).

Dramatically the dialogue is magnificent in its ironical humor. Socrates, who is elderly, has been accused of impiety and of corrupting the youth of Athens through his teaching. In his way he has professed ignorance to the first charge in that he doesn't know what holiness is or for that matter, unholiness; and in effect pleaded not guilty regarding the second charge mentioned. Euthyphro, who is young, claims to know what holiness is (4e, 5a) and Socrates en-

---

2. Paul Friedlander, *Plato,* tr. from the German by Hans Meyerhoff (New York: Pantheon Books, 1958), p. 13.

joins him to teach him (the youth will be teaching the aged) so that he can answer correctly Meletus' charges and escape punishment. If Meletus does not accept his defense based upon this teaching, then it is Euthyphro who is guilty and should be indicted for corrupting the aged as well as for impiety. Thus Euthyphro would face charges that are a twist, as it were, upon those made against Socrates; these would also implicitly include the view that the teacher is responsible for the activity of his pupil in those actions relevant to the virtues taught by him. For Euthyphro as the teacher of Socrates would be responsible (apparently rather than Socrates or at least as much as him) for the inability of his elderly pupil to act virtuously. A common Socratic concern is with the responsibility of the teacher for the actions of his student. Socratic irony is at its best in this brilliant, dramatic reversal of the lives and opinions of the two men.

The dialogue in addition to its "negative" elenchus (as well as its dramatic merit) makes positive contributions toward the problem of defining any virtue as well as piety. I mention this to show that although an early dialogue may in general be destructive in its argument, it may yet contain elements that suggest the line that a solution might take. This may be but a suggestion for the reason that the tenor of the dialogue given its place in the scheme of things precludes a thorough examination of that line, yet permits a discussion to ensue which damages the opposite view. Thus Euthyphro (10d-11b) is led by Socrates to admit that what is holy is so because of some property or attribute essential to it and not because some (the gods) desire it or love it. This is a positive contribution to the argument even if Euthyphro (and perhaps Socrates) are unable to determine what that property is, and, even if that failure undoes their very attempt to settle the question and hastens Euthyphro's departure.[3]

In the *Euthyphro,* Plato, as noted earlier, has those who engage Socrates in disputation complain that the words they

---

3. Thus, as in the allegories, the "eye" (i.e., the desires of the individual to have, or perceive something external to it) is insufficient alone to account for knowledge of its object. It also apparently involves more than the object, but some relation between them.

use will not stand still. This is true ironically with those who most emphatically claim to have knowledge of that which is virtuous, whichever virtue happens to be the subject of the dialogue. Yet in the seventh letter Plato claims that the intelligent man whose reason has contemplated certain things will never put them into language because the words are unalterable, that is, the written word is fixed. Plato, of course, in his dialogues and letters (if not spurious) has presented his thought in a written form — that form which comes closest to the spoken in philosophical discussion and reflection. What an exciting turn of thought! The man who claims to know (e.g., Euthyphro) complains that words are not fixed; the man who knows points out that the written word is fixed and hence inadequate. One cannot say what one means; meaning is more than the use of words, whether one knows or knows not.

To return to my theme, I shall attempt to show that Plato expresses his vision of knowledge, opinion and reality in the dialogues themselves; that they exhibit both dramatically and in content or substance his theory of human nature. I do not mean this in the trivial sense that whatever view Plato had of knowledge, opinion, reality and human nature (or anything else for that matter), our knowledge of it can only be gained from reading and understanding his dialogues which contain his thought. Rather do I mean to say that the dialogues do not only present or perhaps describe his views but that they express them in their very form, order and dramatic development. In this sense it is similar to a play in which the author expresses, for example, temptation, greed and retribution by the action of the players, the words of the players, and the scene and spectacle of the drama. Plato is an artist and a philosopher (this may be redundant in his case); his philosophic truths are dramatically expressed. I shall not attempt to show nor at this time claim that all the dialogues can be so arranged as to prove my point. My claim is more modest: the spiritual and intellectual growth of the philosopher is paralleled by the procession of the dialogues. I do not claim that there is a one-to-one correspondence between the

Key to Plato's Early Dialogues

chronological order of the dialogues and the philosophical development of the dialogues; that there is more than an accidental correspondence is obvious. I also wish to point out that there are exceptions to my view in the dialogues themselves, but I do not think they are major. Lastly I cannot at this time claim to have made an exhaustive study of the dialogues nor to have a firmly set view of Plato's theory of knowledge and reality; but then, as Plato often puts it, let us try this view and see how it stands. (e.g. *Lysis* 218e, *Republic* 610b).

It is traditional to represent Socrates while accompanied by several of the youths of Athens, as engaged in discussion with his Athenian contemporaries over the moral issues of the day. The discussion often centers about the meaning or definition of a key moral term, e.g., "courage," "justice," or "holiness." The proponent of the definition is subjected to Socratic elenchus (cross-examination) and, as we saw in our brief résumé of part of the *Euthyphro,* he usually ends in confusion. Typically, none of the *dramatis personae* including Socrates appears to know more about the definition afterward than when he started; if they know anything it is that they know nothing, or, at least, do not know that which they professed to know when the dialogue began. Thus did Socrates pursue the truth of the Delphic priestess' oracular pronouncement that none in Athens were wiser than he, by showing that he knew he did not know whereas they did not. (Cf. *Apology* 21c, d).

In the three great allegories and analogies of the *Republic* (the Sun, the Divided Line and the Cave) Plato gives us an insight if not an argument into his vision of man's struggle from a creature of things seen (perceived) to things thought (conceived). The relation of the eye to the soul and of the objects seen by the eye to those recollected by the soul, of the sun and light to the Good and Forms is magnificently presented by him. This is reminiscent of the mythic explanation put forth in the *Timaeus* and Plato's injunction must be kept in mind that "He, however, who should attempt to verify all this by experiment would forget the difference of the human and divine nature. For God only has knowledge and also the power which are able to combine many things into one and again resolve the one into many. But no man either is or ever will be able to accomplish either the one or the other operation." (*Timaeus* 68d). The myth, allegory or analogy is our approach to the truth, a truth that we saw in the *VIIth Letter* was fundamentally inexpressible, for only the gods know and have the power to combine the many into the one and resolve the one into the many. Appearance and reality are unified in God alone.

In Plato's vision of opinion and knowledge one aspect is to perceive man as surrounded by the images of the sensible world; to put it another way, he is affected by the sensible world, the resultant being an image; and he responds to and even affects the images, perhaps the objects too. (cf. *Sophist* 239c-242B on *Eidolon* and 247e on Power as a mark or definition of being to account for "affect" and "be affected" or action and reaction). Until one responds to images or, better, reflects upon them I suppose it is not too harsh to say that one is not a human, a rational animal. One may have all sorts of valuable and useful responses based upon one's "contact" with and experience of the external world, but that is not knowledge, nor opinion, in a sense, but rather animal faith. It is human to reflect upon one's reflections, that is, to be aware of one's images. In the Cave allegory one begins with images or shadows on the wall, but one does not end there — at least not in the same way — for one has traveled to knowledge and the Good before one returns.

It is my claim that the so-called Socratic dialogues express Plato's belief (and presumably Socrates') that the Athenian man in the street who leads the unexamined life even if it be a life that is monetarily profitable or heroically adventuresome is a prisoner in the cave, is in the realm of images, shadows and reflections. The high point or culmination of this "set" of dialogues is the attainment or recognition of true opinion as expressed in the *Meno* (97a, ff). The Socratic dialogues, as I have mentioned, are commonly looked upon as inconclusive, as at times insincere in argument, as cursory, fleeting, as discussing concepts that will not be defined, that move around before one's eyes and are such that, to combine metaphors, one can neither fix upon them nor grasp them. The beautiful Charmides and the clever Critias are unable to settle upon the meaning of temperance, Lysis and Menexenus upon friendship, and Nicias, Laches and Socrates pursue vainly the concept of courage. In these dialogues the *dramatis personae* have exhibited, engaged in and performed the virtues discussed. In the world of human events, in the give and take of daily life, in the trials of the battlefield, they have been friends, lovers, courageous and self-controlled, harmonious, disciplined men. Yet upon reflection they are unable to state satisfactorily what it means to be a friend, a lover, to be courageous or temperate. They do not know themselves.

In most of these dialogues the action is either immediate (Lysimachus opens the *Laches* by presenting his problem to Nicias and Laches [178a-179e]' Meno [70a] asks Socrates whether virtue can be taught or not; Callicles invites Socrates to hear Gorgias [447a, b]; Socrates comes upon Hippothales who is in love with Lysis to whom they go to begin the discussion of friendship [*Lysis* 203 ff] and so, too in the *Euthyphro* and other early dialogues), or the dialogue is one that took place a short time, perhaps the day, before *(Charmides* 158a, *Protagoras* 310a-d, *Euthydemus* 27 ff, etc.). A problem, a situation, a visit, a chance meeting; the many yet ordinary ways in which conversation begins mark these dialogues. Yet the conversants in general open a discussion about that which is usual to them but which, as has been pointed out, they haven't thought through. To reflect upon what is usual to them has not been customary for them. The dialogues in their very immediate or near immediate setting express the separate, fragmentary and disorganized quality of the thought that has, or better has not, gone into a consideration of those activities. Or at least if they — the *dramatis personae* — have thought about their relations to each other, their ways of life, and so forth — that reflection has been a shadowy one; the reflection is of an image rather than a considered study. Both mirrors and souls reflect.

Socrates the midwife, ironic, mocking, teasing; professing

ignorance while revealing the ignorant, seeking but not giving when aid is sought by others moves as a kind of demon (*daimon*) through the lives of his fellow Athenians. It is he who exposes and makes plain the shadowy conjectures, the vague images of those who profess to know; it is he who shows them that their words will not stand still, that their ideas cannot be grasped, that their questions cannot be answered, that their answers are transparent.[4] Dramatically, noetically and genetically they express that part of the allegory of the cave in which the prisoners gaze upon images, believing them real without reflecting upon them or, perhaps barely freed, are confused and cannot relate image to object, half-blinded, swinging at shadows, stumbling about like punch-drunk, angry fighters. There are no conclusions to be found by prisoners in the cave. That is why there are no conclusions to be found in the Socratic dialogues, for Plato has dramatized and philosophized upon the first part of the allegory of the cave and the first division of the line of knowledge.

Keats concludes his *Ode to a Nightingale* by murmuring "Was it a vision, or a waking dream? Fled is that music: — do I wake or sleep?" And so those who are in the cave, and such is the quality of the Socratic dialogue. The dream-like aspect is seen in the likeness that Socrates finds in the Statues of Daedalus which run off as do the words in the discussion, in the inconclusiveness of these dialogues, in the will-o-the-wisp pursuit which shifts and changes before one's eyes, in the shadowy vague concepts that cannot be grasped, in the sense of unreality, of frustration and of anger that the most ordinary situation and conversation brings about. Through it all, again, floats the main reality — oddly enough — the daimonic figure, the Satyr, the gadfly of Athens stinging people to begin the pursuit, to free themselves from the chains that they seem to prefer and which appar-

---

4. As was noted earlier, he is the third ingredient, the sun and the good, the teacher as lamp whose light blinds, reveals, exposes and points the way to those in the realm of shadows and images. In argument with him one begins the ascent from below. The dialogues aim at this.

ently had tied down everything, including themselves. For if they would pursue that of which they had been ignorant, then must they ask, "Do I wake or sleep?" In *Republic* V (476b-d) Socrates states:

> Then here I draw the line, said I. On one side are the sight-fanciers and art-fanciers you spoke of, and practical men; on the other side again the subjects of our discussion, those who alone may rightly be named philosophers.
> What do you mean? he asked.
> The one class, I take it, said I, sound-fanciers and sight-fanciers, delight in beautiful voices and colours and shapes and all which craftsmen have made from such; but their mind is incapable of seeing and delighting in the beautiful itself.
> That is certainly so, he said.
> But the other class are able to approach the beautiful itself and to see it by itself; and would not these be few?
> Very few.
> Then if a man believes things to be beautiful, but does not believe in beauty by itself, and cannot follow when he is led towards the knowledge of it, what is his life? Is he awake, or is his life a dream? What do you think? Consider, what is dreaming but this, whether one be asleep or awake: thinking what is like something to be not the likeness but the thing itself?
> I at least would say, he replied, that such a one is dreaming.
> Take the opposite case. The man who believes in beauty itself, and can distinguish it from things which partake of it, who does not believe the things with beauty to be beauty or beauty to be those things: do you think that his life is a dream or is he awake?
> He is awake, said he, no doubt about that.
> Then could we not call this man's state of mind knowledge, as of one who knows, and the other's opinion, as of one who opines?

My claim, to repeat, is not that the Socratic dialogues are peculiarly Socratic in that they represent Plato's dramatic monument to his beloved teacher's life — albeit they are partly that — but that they present the beginning of his long dialectical and mystic-mythical argument for the examined life. (In this sense the totality of the dialogues is a monument to Socrates — not merely the Socratic ones.) The beginning, the realm of conjecture and belief, of images and objects, of false and right opinion, is a realm of irony, defeat and bewilderment; a shadowy, perplexing dream world in which one may ask in puzzlement or anger, "Do I wake or sleep?"

I would like to make a few remarks concerning my interpretation of the so-called Socratic dialogues. I have intentionally refrained from including the trial, incarceration and death of Socrates in my remarks of the first set. They have a peculiar status and although I think none does damage to my claims, I think it better not to include them.

I also see in the immediate or near-immediate character of the Socratic dialogues an attempt by Plato to present the beginnings of philosophical reflection as free from recollection or reminiscence as possible. No discussion and, perhaps, no learning, even of the instinctive or non-noetic variety, can occur without some kind of recollection or remembrance or some repetition of an impression in imagination, but Plato wishes to show us that in the realm of opinion men who may be very practical, very skilled and very successful are still philosophically barren when they speculate upon their activities.

As the dialogues I have recently mentioned progress, recollection becomes more and more important until in the *Meno* the high point of life inside the cave and within the division of opinion is attained. The introduction to the famous incident of the slave boy constructing a geometrical proof is through a chiding of Socrates by Meno over his wizardry, his witchcraft, his ability to drug his fellow discussant. Much in the manner of Euthyphro, Meno complains:

> You, seem to me to be a regular wizard, you dose me with drugs and bewitch me with charms and spells, and drown me in puzzledom. I'll tell you just what you are like, if you will forgive a little jest: Your looks and the rest of you are exactly like a flatfish and you sting like this stingray—only go near and touch one of those fish and you go numb,...my soul is numb and my mouth is numb, and what to answer you I do not know. Yet I have a thousand times made long speeches about virtue, before many a large audience...but now I have not a word to say...
> ...you are wise not to sail away or travel abroad, for if you did this as a foreigner in a foreign city, you would probably be run in for a wizard. (*Meno* 79e-80b).

Key to Plato's Early Dialogues

This passage not only brings out beautifully the dream-like quality that Socratic elenchus creates in those who begin to question their beliefs but it also dramatically introduces a biographical fact of Socrates' later life (as Plato often and imaginatively does) into the discussion. He did not have to leave Athens to be arrested as a wizard, and he refused to leave Athens to escape temporarily the consequences of his witchcraft.

The numb soul and mouth of Meno is reminiscent of those who in their dreams are struck dumb and motionless by the events around them. (Cf. Polemarchus, Socrates and Thrasymachus are struck dumb, *Republic* 333-337, wherein Socrates hints at the appropriate manner in which one may respond to that kind of situation). Of course, Meno's ability to speak upon virtue before large audiences takes us from the ordinary citizen of Athens who is the victim of Socratic cross-examination to the Sophistical teacher and orator who professes not only to know but to teach what virtue is. The *Euthydemus, Gorgias* and *Protagoras* are all preparations for the movement from conjecture to belief in that they introduce discussion by sophists concerning virtue or particular virtues. In these dialogues decisions are not reached nor doctrines agreed upon although important principles are stated as well as aspects of knowledge hinted at which properly belong in the waking world or the world outside the cave. Thus in the *Protagoras* we have the principle that no man does wrong knowingly (*Protagoras* 358a-360e), and a preliminary examination of pleasure as the good, while in the *Gorgias* occurs the question of the proper use of rhetoric and another examination of pleasure as the good (not necessarily a subsequent examination).

The Sophists, as the main target of Socratic argument, represent that way of life which Plato felt apparently was most like and yet most destructive to the philosophical quest. The Sophists proclaim, in Plato's view, that man is the measure of all things, that there is nothing eternal to be known or grasped, and that no principles guide our action which can be proclaimed both applicable to all men and universal or transcendent. It is in the world of conjecture and opinion in the way of the city, in the winning of friends and influencing of people, in the use of power for personal profit, honor and fame that philosophy is properly to be taught and used according to them. There, it follows, is to be found its subject matter. Plato holds that in the world of action, which is the realm of opinion, the highest kind of certainty we can have is true belief or opinion. This means that we have learned, through experience, to act correctly regarding that which we hope to achieve. Thus if someone has a right opinion about the road to Larissa (*Meno* 97A) then he can guide others correctly and his advice is no better nor no worse regarding that journey than that of him who knows the way. He does not, however, know the grounds or principles upon which his opinion is based. If he forgets the way, he is lost (presumably, if he had known the principles then he would not forget or, perhaps, could still work out the way — a dubious point at best); or if he were asked to map the way, in the sense that mapping might involve mathematical applications, he can not indicate those principles that would be used to convert his experience properly. The "end" of the quest for knowledge in the world of opinion is that condition which the senses can reach or attain for us; it is experience without principles, right opinion without knowledge. It is for that reason that Plato holds that those in the cave only think that they see truly in the world of shadows and physical objects; it is also why he likens them to blind men. The blind may learn the way along a path, but without sight cannot know it.

The *Meno,* as the *Gorgias,* are dialogues that bring the early or Socratic dialogues to the point in the line where opinion is 'fulfilled' and is shown to be inadequate. They also presage the next section in which knowing rather than opinion is examined. It is similarly the point at which the cave is left for the sun, and that wherein we pass from the offspring of the good to a glimpse of the parent. I would like to conclude this brief reference to the dramatic aspects of the dialogues which give credence to the use of the allegories as a key to them by remarking on some features of the *Meno.*

Socrates, after Meno's complaint about his wizardry and

stingray quality, suggests that he is as paralyzed as those whom he is said to paralyze. The scene is reminiscent of the one in the *Republic* alluded to earlier wherein he and Polemarchus were struck dumb with terror by the onslaught of Thrasymachus. Socrates had indicated then a way out of the terror and numbness: fix one's eye upon him who terrorizes one, and one can keep his wits about him. Apparently those whom Socrates stings are so concerned about being numbed that they forget the grounds for their arguments and complain about him instead. (This presumes that most of the arguments presented to Socrates have some grounds which might stand up were the proponent willing to examine them more fully.) Socrates also indicates to Meno that although paralyzed he does not intend to give up the quest for the knowledge of the meaning of virtue, thus asserting that the numbness will not halt his search. The various setbacks in the quest that the dialogues present are not sufficient to lead Socrates to abandon the movement from the cave or even within the cave.

Meno asks him how he will be able to look for that which he knows not; this, of course, brings up the 'old' sophistical puzzle about the impossibility of the quest for knowledge. Either one knows already and seeks not or knows not and cannot seek, not knowing for what to search. This, along with the numbness of Meno, presents the perplexity and the confusion in the world of flux and opinion, the world inside the cave, in spite of the fact that the prisoner has been freed from his chains. To seek knowledge among the many (things) is to search for the one (principle) within the many and to be able to recognize the many "contained" (implied) in the one. If we had only the perplexities of the senses, how would we know what to look for? If we knew what to look for would we have to look for it?

Socrates suggests that a possible solution to this would take us out of the realm of opinion, time and becoming and into that of thinking, eternity and being. One could understand the fundamental axioms of a geometry and not know the entire set of theorems that are implicit within them. One would not know and yet be able to search; of course, one would have to know (understand) something. Through Socrates' suggestion we are prepared for the next step in the journey, for the next truth in the allegory. We are ready to leave the first half of the divided line for the first section of the second half.

> They say that the soul of man is immortal. At one time it comes to an end — that which is called death — and at another is born again....
> ...since it is immortal and has been born many times, and has seen all things both here and in the other world, [it] has learned everything that is. So we need not be surprised if it can recall the knowledge of virtue or anything else which, as we say, it once possessed. All nature is akin, and the soul has learned everything, so that when a man has recalled a single piece of knowledge — *learned* it, in ordinary language — there is no reason why he should not find out all the rest. ... (81b, d)

By introducing the doctrine of recollection, Socrates indicates that mind is crucial to opinion as well as knowledge. To recollect is to recognize, through the activity of the mind, that in the blooming, buzzing confusion an event has been repeated. At least two important characteristics of opining and knowing are brought out in this doctrine. The world of phenomena must have that about it which is identifiable in terms of likeness or similarity so that not every, and possibly, no event is unique as if it bore no resemblance to any other event. If that were the case, knowledge and opinion would both be impossible, and nothing in nature would be akin. The recollection of likenesses also entails the recollection of differences.

The second important characteristic is that mind has the capacity to "hold" before itself an image of that which has occurred and is occurring as well as to imagine or conceive of that which will occur or might occur. Thus it has the power to recollect those events which have the power to affect it. This too is part of the view that all in nature is akin; both mind and the eye (opinion) are compatible with their respective objects. (Here nature too acts as a third ingredient which makes possible the relation between that which knows and that which is to be known). Without the ability to remember, neither perception nor cognition would result in knowledge. Recollection is strongly suggested in the analogy of the sun and the good as that which lights up the eye (mind) and its objects. Socrates, as noted, provides the light; the teacher as lamp through his midwifery, his questioning, sets recollection in motion. In the *Meno* the dramatic exchange between Socrates and the slave boy illustrates this and is the final preparation for the journey from the cave.

I hope that I have sufficiently suggested the fruitfulness of looking at the early dialogues as dramatically expressing the allegorical tales told in the *Republic*. That dialogue, of course, comes after the ones mentioned. (This, without arguing whether Books I, and possibly II, were written separably from the rest of the dialogue.) It contains a statement of the whole of Plato's program including where he had been, where he was, and where he had hoped to go. It provides us with keys to an understanding of the problems that he faced and the kind of solution that he envisaged. Whether or not he rested satified with any particular solution that he tried as he went along is not germane to my thesis; even if he abandoned the theory of forms as some have suggested, he did it along the way that he set out for himself. He yet hoped to account for knowledge and unite it with power so that wisdom might be had in the practical or virtuous activity of men.

Without going into the later dialogues and their relation to the allegories, which is beyond the scope of this introductory essay, one can at least indicate the manner in which they relate to them. The series including the *Parmenides*, *Theaetetus* and *Sophist* may be seen as representing the problems that face one when first leaving the cave and becoming accustomed to the sun; it also represents the movement from sun to good and the passage from the division of opinion to that of intelligible objects. The first part of the *Parmenides* (again, without considering whether or not it was written independently of the second part) presents the "blindness" that occurs when the forms are first encountered (the sun or good) as possible explanatory principles; the entire dialogue moves from a groping about and from rather impetuous suggestions to a more refined and presentable theory. Nonetheless it ends with some real difficulties of the theory yet unsolved. The *Theaetetus* as a dialogue in the realm of the upper division concerns its participants with such questions as "is perception knowledge?"; a question only admissible when one has left the realm of perception and can reflect upon it in the presence of principles that are not wholly reducible to opinion. The *Sophist* not only examines the character of the pretender to knowledge, but raises important questions as to the nature of power and being, as well as the relative merits of materialism and idealism. Here, too, Plato's allegories of the *Republic* form a useful key to the understanding of and the drama within the enacted dialogues. Without going into the *Philebus* (a search for principles that make possible "scientific" knowledge not always compatible with the theory of forms) or the *Timaeus,* I am nonetheless confident that they too lend themselves to my interpretation.[5] Finally, the *Symposium, Phaedrus* and *Cratylus* fit nicely into the movement from opinion to forms. All that I had hoped to argue for at this time was the usefulness of the allegories in seeing the early dialogues as a dramatic unfolding of them. In this brief essay I have not examined those in great detail but have only indicated the manner in which one might approach them. It is my hope to present this thesis in fuller form in the future.

In conclusion I wish to point out, also, that although my "ordering" of the dialogues rests not on stylometric tests but upon Plato's thought, it agrees with them, not surprisingly, to a great extent. Stylometric tests primarily aim at a chronological ordering of the dialogues as well as a settling of questions regarding the authenticity of the dialogues. My interests are rather along the lines of the development of Plato's thoughts as revealed within the dialogues themselves both in the form of outlines given by way of allegories and myths, and the substance of the drama presented.

In his dialogues, Plato discusses the education of a man of

---

5. The *Statesman* and *Laws* are concerned with the return to the cave as the philosopher attempts to apply principles to practical problems.

wisdom and of all men to some degree. Through his analogies, allegories and myths of the *Republic* as well as other dialogues, he pictures proper growth as from a realm of ignorance, of images, objects, of conjecturing, believing and opining to one of generalization, of unity and form, of justice, beauty, sameness and otherness, to a final beholding of the source and cause of all, the Good. The theme that I have hoped to develop and defend is that his dialogues, dramatically, logically, dialectically and mythically, present to us his vision of knowledge and power subsumed under the Good — the birth of wisdom which is the fulfillment of the pursuit of wisdom. I have limited myself to the earlier works but I have indicated my belief that the later works continue this development. Several of the well-known sayings of Socrates and Plato support this theme. Knowledge is a form of recollection or memory; no man does wrong knowingly; knowledge is virtue; love is crucial to knowledge; myth rather than dialectic expresses those truths which perhaps are better not expressed. They fit the theme because all of them are exhibited through the action of the dialogues, all of which are a kind of proof that thought is a form of action.

5

ON HOBBES' HUMANISM
Bertram Morris

HOBBES' POLITICAL PHILOSOPHY HAS BEEN MANGLED BY those commentators who have transformed his theory of politics into a formalistic ethics. Intent upon reading his philosophy in a quasi-Kantian style or even as a tract on theological Puritanism, they have obscured his rich and historically important insights by observing them through the mentality of a rigid moralist or that of a stern lawgiver. To be sure, Hobbes sometimes writes this way, but to read him in the larger context of his thought is to see him for the humanist that he was. Although his humanism has depths that cannot here be plumbed, yet we can extract something of its spirit by analyzing how he joins man's nature with the ways of peace.

In this analysis I hope to show how Hobbes' psychology and his reliance upon the arts of peace both gain in importance by the authentic interrelatedness they bear to each other. To carry out this analysis, I propose in this essay: (1) to distinguish between his naïve and his sophisticated versions of psychology, (2) to show how the latter entails man's social nature, and (3) to reveal the fulfillment of his institutionalism both as the result of man's nature and as the reality of the social contract.

On Hobbes' Humanism

I

Entranced by the new science, Hobbes regards man as a body capable of vital and voluntary motions. The latter he summarily calls desires and aversions, and quickly asserts their connection with what men think to be good and evil: "But whatsoever is the object of any man's appetite or desire, that is it, which he for his part calleth *good:* and the object of his hate and aversion, *evil* ..."[1] Hobbes adds that "These words ... are used with relation to the person that useth them." He then insists that to place good and evil in a position more secure than that afforded by the appetites and aversions, there must be a common rule of good and evil and that such a rule requires a commonwealth or an arbitrator created by the consent of men who otherwise disagree. Thus from the outset of his discussion of what moves men to act, he is torn by a simplistic theory of motivation towards the objects of satisfaction and a complex theory based upon rules and a prior agreement among men to be governed by rules.

As for the simplistic theory, men are readily equipped with desires and aversions of such a nature that they can easily determine what in the one case will satisfy the desires or what needs to be avoided in the other case. Even the simplistic theory, however, reveals that Hobbes is no naive hedonist; for the object of desire is always some thing, satisfying or menacing, not the pleasure or displeasure that accompanies it. He insists that vital motion or endeavor is that "which consisteth in appetite, or aversion, to or from the object moving." Pleasure and displeasure are not the end which is sought, but rather the "sense" of good or evil that *accompanies* the motion. As he specifically says: "And consequently all appetite, desire, and love, is accompanied with some delight more or less; and all hatred and aversion, with more or less displeasure and offence" (iii, p. 42). He is a utilitarian; not a hedonist.

Hobbes' utilitarian theory does provide for some complex-

---

1. *Leviathan,* iii, p. 41. (All subsequent references are to the *English Works,* Molesworth edition.)

ity inasmuch as one's desires do change and one does learn from experience. In this respect, he conceives of man as not different from the other animals. Having memory, man is also endowed with foresight. From much experience, he gains prudence, and is enabled to elude some objects of aversion. Ideally, the life that emerges from this psychology is the life of felicity, defined as *"continual success* in obtaining those things which a man from time to time desireth, that is to say continual prospering..." (iii, p. 51). In its utopian form, this is life in the Garden, where man lives according to his heart's desire and where every want readily finds its object. Hobbes in fact acknowledges the unreality of the Garden when he proceeds to contrast it with life in the Jungle, where man competes with man, faithlessly and abrasively. By the way he sets the problem, Hobbes has no alternative but to find a solution in something that falls between the Garden and the Jungle, which of course is in civil society. He needs therefore to develop a more realistic psychology, in order to mediate between the fictional states of perfect felicity on the one hand, and the war of all against all, on the other. Curiously enough, the simple psychology satisfies the demands of both fictional states, but not that of man in the civil state. An appeal to new principles becomes necessary.

Even in an early version of his philosophy, Hobbes was alert to the necessity of finding other than innate faculties by which men could become members of civil society. At the very outset of *De Cive,* he considers whether man is "born fit" for society. Observing that "we now see actually a constituted society among men," we need not fall into the absurdity of denying that men are fit for society. He therefore acknowledges that he "must plainly say, that it is true indeed, that to man by nature, or as man, that is, as soon as he is born, solitude is an enemy; for infants have need of others to help them live, and those of riper years to help them to live well."[2] If only it were allowed that ripeness begins

---

2. See this important footnote, ii, p. 2n. Indeed this is the fullest statement in which Hobbes, in referring to the "human nature" of "infants as well as those of riper years" explicitly avows that "man is made fit for society, not by nature, but by education."

with the beginning of life, Hobbes could not have better stated the question. For men truly to live well, they must, in his terms, create "civil societies [which] are not mere meetings, but bonds to the making whereof faith and compacts are necessary." If men can recognize this necessity, they can become apt for society. The question that faces Hobbes now becomes clearer: by what nature can men come to terms and live together peacefully?

The answer to the question is provided by reason, which suggests "articles of peace upon which men may be drawn to agreement" (iii, p. 116). To mediate between the felicitous life, that is, the continual success of the desires, and the life of peace and security presents a challenge to human motivation and accomplishment. Sometimes Hobbes avoids the challenge by merely postulating in men a desire for peace. This treatment is clearly cavalier. Aversions and desires have specific objects, but the desire for peace contains no such object. Peace may be a condition or mode of life, but has no such objects as those of desire, for example, the desire for a peach. Hence the postulating of a desire for peace is a restatement of the problem, not a solution of it. In his mature psychology, however, Hobbes shows that he does have a sense of what the solution requires.

He has told us that men, as well as animals, acquire prudence. Clearly, this is not enough for a person to maintain himself in civil society. He needs also a real sense of security, such as animals do not have, but such as men can have through bonds based upon faith and compacts. He sets a tone for the answer in his debate with Bishop Bramhall that it is worth quoting in full:

> The truth is, that man is a creature of greater power than other living creatures are, but his advantages do consist especially in two things; whereof one is the use of speech, by which men communicate one with another, and join their forces together, and by which also they register their thoughts that they perish not, but be reserved, and afterwards joined with other thoughts that they perish not, to produce general rules for the direction of their actions. There be beasts that see better, others that hear better, and others that exceed mankind in other senses. Man excelleth beasts only in making of rules to himself, that is to say, in remembering,

and in reasoning aright upon that which he remembereth. They which do so, deserve an honour above brute beasts. But they which mistaking the use of words, deceive themselves and others, introducing error, and seducing men from the truth, are so much less to be honoured than brute beasts, as error is more vile than ignorance. So that it is not merely the nature of man, that makes him worthier than other living creatures but the knowledge that he acquires by meditation, and by the right use of reason in making good rules of his future actions. The other advantage a man hath, is the use of his hands for the making of those things which are instrumental to his well-being. (v, pp. 186-7).

Unfortunately, Hobbes disparages the last suggestion, about the use of hands, which in other contexts, as we shall presently see, turns out to be of paramount importance. The other suggestions that speech and reason are crucial to man's living well, although already deeply entrenched in the philosophical tradition, are nevertheless highly significant in a way contemporary to Hobbes' own thought.

Memory leads on to imagination, and the latter to ratiocination, and finally to a kind of creative invention, the faculty of *sagacitas,* that Hobbes requires for the creation of that artificial person, the Leviathan. Thus prudence gives way to a life of the mind in which communication and rules occupy a central position. But most important would seem to be the interplay between ratiocination and "the faculty of invention." These two lead on to the most crucial factor: science, that is, the knowledge of consequences. The activity which is peculiar to men and which underlies science is that of seeking "all the possible effects that can by [imagination] be produced."[3]

---

3. iii, p. 13. See also pp. 14, 35. The question of science is complicated in that Hobbes relies so heavily upon names, and especially names of names, in order to formulate clearly the relation of cause and effect. Professor Herbert Schneider clarifies Hobbes' theory of science by suggesting that Hobbes connects *prudentia* or much experience with *sapientia* or much science. Thus, the formalistic aspects of science depend upon prior inductions. Finally, as Schneider points out, the case is made for establishing a kinship between Hobbes and Bacon closer than is customarily granted. See his review of Arrigo Pacchi, *Convenzione e Ipotesi Nella Filosofia Naturale di Thomas Hobbes* in *Journal of the History of Philosophy,* VI, 1, Jan. 1968, pp. 83-5.

By degrees we can come to see how Hobbes sets forth the conditions by which men are capable of leading a life which is qualitatively different from that of the beast. Finally, equipped with the requisite faculties, men are able to imagine a kind of existence that bears litte resemblance either to one in the Garden or in the Jungle. Two more steps are nevertheless required for reaching the good life: motivation and political means.

II

Commodious living is what man aims at in living well. It requires a disposition to peace, together with certain arrangements. In Hobbes' words: "The passions that incline men to peace, are fear of death; desire of such things as are necessary to commodious living; and a hope by their industry to obtain them. And reason suggesteth convenient articles of peace, upon which men may be drawn to agreement" (iii, p. 116). Through the combined effect of fear, desire, and hope to the end of peace, Hobbes can reasonably transform frustration into a powerful motive to achieve a life guided by reason and rule instead of fraud and force. The transformation is sponsored by reason, which happily turns up articles of peace, "otherwise called laws of nature." The function of reason now becomes clear: it is employed to place collective society before the individual, the commonwealth before the private wealth. Men can achieve this state, however, only when they are already social, or at least have guarantees that make anti-social conduct vulnerable to the heavy hand of law.

Now we begin to see why ethical formalism (and we may add, tyrannical autocracy) is a deficient way of coping with the problem Hobbes has set. The laws of nature are "precepts of reason," formal and ineffective until they are "interpreted" by a sovereign. They cannot even serve as rules of action for selecting a sovereign, for the laws of nature prescribe no methods to accomplish the purpose. Indeed, to prescribe them would require something like a "constitutional convention." That would of course require a prior agreement, not just as an intent or agreement to agree, but as a society or faction or clan which already has agreed precisely because it is already constituted as a working society. The problem of the members of such a society is to *re*constitute their society, that is, "to form a more perfect union." Or, more likely, the "constitutional convention" may turn out to be just a kind of "tacit acknowledgment" of the reality of a "commonwealth by acquisition," in which the members have become acculturated in a society and conform to the operative rules of it.

"Consent" surely does mean something in a civil society. It does not consist in the kind of formal contract that Hobbes sometimes suggests, but never quite takes seriously. Otherwise, he could not with such ease convert a *de facto* government into a *de jure* one. A mistake is committed when his ethical predilections are converted into his theory of the state. He does tell us that a "just man" is judged not by actions but by intention and conscience. Still, he never confuses this notion with that of a just act, which he defines as obedience to law.[4] If Hobbes can show that man as an agent can and does act justly, then he can dispense with the contract. He can do this if he can prepare his man in nature so to mature that he can live in civil society. Armed with speech and reason, memory, prudence, and creative imagination; knowing the frustration of acting alone and against others; and finally having a passion or informed feeling for peace, as well as the kind of knowledge it requires — so prepared, man is ready for civil society.

The laws of nature, with only one exception, which concerns drunkenness, are an imperative to seek peace. In

---

4. Hobbes often formally defines a just act as any which is not unjust, and the unjust as disobedience of law. He cannot and does not consistently hold to this position, because he acknowledges a condition in which justice and injustice have no place. Cf. iii, pp. 115, 257, 559; ii, p. 151.

substance, the imperative says, "Obey the law unless it is intolerable." Effective law, however, is positive law, not natural law; for there exists no civil state in nature, and as soon as man is in the civil state positive law supersedes natural law. Man is exempt from obeying the civil law only when it violates peace or when it exacts from him life or limb, or requires giving evidence against himself that would serve that end. The latter exemption, though not crystal clear, seems to be not unreasonably vague. The former is safeguarded by the fact that it occurs only when a whole structure of law collapses and, if not the war of all against all, at least civil warfare, is rampant. Except under these intolerable conditions, civil law both deserves respect and prevails.

III

Now we are in a position to see what a fully social person is. He is a moral being, not a beast. He acts, when obliged, according to rule, rather than from desire. The shape of his life is determined by the arts of peace, not by personal aggrandizement. Although inextricably intertwined, the factors are psychological, political, and institutional. The first requires no further comment, except for the explicit acknowledgment of the capability of man to be motivated *to act* upon rules, politically engendered. For this reason, Hobbes excludes "natural fools, children, and madmen" from obligation to obey the law, for they can neither enjoy "the title of just, or unjust" nor "authorize the actions of any sovereign" (iii, p. 257). The political and the institutional factors deserve consideration.

The political factor mediates between man as a self-defeating agent and man as a moral agent. In this is found the justification for political obligation. Justice and injustice are qualities of man in society, not in solitude. With the introduction of law a person can distinguish between what is his and what is another's. Otherwise, anyone has a right to anything. The implicit assumption is that man requires property, and that the only way of securing property (and also to make man secure) is to enact laws that can be enforced by a power stronger than any man or any faction of society. Thus *meum* and *teum* are the primary goods to be regulated by law. Granted that law enforcement is possible, should men consent, and, if so, why?

The ready answer is that of course they should, because it is law. This answer carries a long way. Law is a command of the sovereign. It is rational because it is a rule, known or knowable, and capable of being heeded. There can be no society without law and a sovereign is the only one capable of making law. It obliges therefore because it is law. According to this argument, Hobbes' view is the prototype of legal positivism, made more current by Austin and especially Kelsen. No doubt, law does have a quasi-independence, including a proper grounding of its own, together with agencies of interpretation and enforcement. Hobbes makes the very substance of it the basis of justice and thus does not confuse justice with matters irrelevant to it. But our question is less this than it is how it is indispensable for man as a moral agent.

The difficulty with natural law, as Hobbes repeatedly asserts, is that it does not provide unambiguous rules, and is therefore incapable of settling disputes; and, finally, since it provides at best a *disposition* to act, it contains insufficient sanctions to make civil society operative. Unable to be of practical use in the state of nature (Hobbes is reduced to some few observations of why a man should be bound to a band of brigands by the terms of his agreement for ransom), and unable to supply a framework for civil society, natural law can serve only as a weak theological sanction against the "iniquitous" laws that a sovereign may promulgate. Yet, however iniquitous the laws may be, they are nevertheless "just" laws, and, save for the exception noted above, a subject is obliged to obey the laws. This restriction surely creates a paradoxical situation. No one has the right to disobey an iniquitous law until such a number does that causes the breakdown of the legal system.

The paradox reveals that Hobbes needs an escape hatch so that men may disobey "just" laws that are nevertheless "iniquitous" to the point of tyrannizing them. At this point, one readily sees the limitations of the positivistic theory of the law, that is, that a legal system is dependent upon purpose or end, and not just upon a system defined in terms of due process or sheer machinery of the judicial process. Hobbes is in fact constrained to acknowledge the substantive character of law — a system that serves the needs of a society, not just as law and order, but as caring for interests intrinsic to the welfare of that society. Hence, at a crucial point, he observes that a sovereign needs to make "good laws." By such a law he "means not a just law: for no law can be unjust." He means a law that is *"needful,* for the *good of the people,* and withal *perspicuous"* (iii, p. 335. Emphasis in original.). Earlier Hobbes made it clear that the function of law in "limit[ing] the natural liberty of particular men" was to the end that men "might not hurt, but assist one another..." (iii, p. 254). The awkwardness of Hobbes' position is now that just laws do not, at least in extreme situations, suffice to create obligation. It takes just laws that are also *good* laws. Consequently, obligation cannot be defined solely in terms of justice, but must be defined in terms of "good justice," and then "right" cannot be dissociated from "good." So also, political obligation cannot be defined sheerly in terms of law: ultimately it requires an institutional base, which is the foundation of good, and in the absence of which political obligation is either absurd or a concealed form of tyranny.

IV

It remains to be shown that the institutional foundation of Hobbes' political philosophy is the arts of peace. When the practice of these arts has some coherence, the arts constitute the commodious life, or what may be called the culture of a society. Culture includes not only "labour bestowed on the earth" and "education of children" but also "worship" which is either of the people or of God.[5] The range of the peaceful arts is from those of public use to those which favor the understanding and celebration of life. Between the extremes are the productive and distributive factors, without which life would be impoverished and short.

Alert always to the need of the defense of the state, Hobbes is quick to insist upon the "Arts of public use, as fortification, making of engines, and other instruments of war" (iii, p. 75). His insistence upon using engines of war to protect the state is scarcely noteworthy. But it is noteworthy that in Bacon-like fashion he acknowledges the power of science that lies behind the instrumentalities by which a state can cope with the threats to it from without. Beyond this function, science serves the purpose of enhancing the other arts of peace by relating reason to human benefit.[6] Yet because science is inadequately developed, Hobbes concedes that the arts remain in a primitive state.

There is good reason to believe that Hobbes regarded the contract as that "meeting of minds" which men express in their common ventures, and which is absent in the state of nature. To fix this point as central to his political philosophy, we may well quote the classical passage in *Leviathan* in which he contrasts life in the civil state from that in the state of nature:

> Whatsoever therefore is consequent to a time of war, where every man is enemy to every man; the same is consequent to the time, wherein men live without other security, than what their own strength and their own invention shall furnish them withal.

---

5. iii, pp. 348-9. Intermediately, as civil worship is that which honors the ruler. See iii, pp. 647-8.
6. In his words: "... reason is the *pace;* increase of *science,* the way; and the benefit of mankind, the *end*" (iii, p. 36).

On Hobbes' Humanism

> In such a condition, there is no place for industry; because the fruit thereof is uncertain: and consequently no culture of the earth; no navigation, nor use of the commodities that may be imported by sea; no commodious building; no instruments of moving, and removing, such things as require much force; no knowledge of the face of the earth; no account of time; no arts; no letters; no society. ...[7]

Then comes the string of adjectives to describe how wretched life is in a world destitute of these arts.

Without these arts there is no need for a sovereign; for without property and exchange of goods there is little reason to control their actions by means of law. It appears axiomatic that society have a foundation such that "every man have a propriety in a portion of land, or in some few commodities, or a natural property in some useful art."[8] Since all manner of contracts between persons are necessary for arranging the use, exchange, selling, hiring, etc., of goods and services, some orderly and compelling rules need to be established and enforced. Otherwise, only the rule of the strongest could prevail. Observing that property and contract go to the heart of Hobbes' philosophy, Professor C. B. MacPherson argues that this philosophy is one of "possessive individualism." His work is instructive in that it reveals the way in which Hobbes' political theory is directed to the establishment of bourgeois capitalistic society. Although the end of peace and security need not have been spelled out in these terms, MacPherson amply documents the fact that Hobbes does so direct his theory.[9]

---

7. iii, 113. For somewhat parallel statements in the earlier versions, see ii, p. 177; iv, p. 72.
8. iii, 237. Hobbes adds parenthetically that "there is no art in the world, but is necessary either for the being or the well being almost of every particular man...."
9. See his *The Political Theory of Possessive Individualism* (Oxford: Clarendon Press, 1962). I have discussed this work, which is unique in acknowledging the institutional understructure of Hobbes' politics, under title of "Possessive Individualism and Political Realities," *Ethics,* LXXV, 3, Apr. 1965, pp. 207-214.

Whether or not Hobbes was an apologist for bourgeois capitalism, he certainly does insist upon the indispensability of the arts of peace, including their technological, as well as their proprietary, base. The question remains as to whether Hobbes had a sense of the innovative character of his politics and whether it would lead to the progress of human life. According to his initial assumption in *De Corpore,* progress is the keynote because the end or scope of philosophy is the benefit of man through knowledge, which is power. As a consequence, "lastly, the scope of all speculation is the performing of some action, or thing to be done" (i, p. 7). Thus, the "power after power" that men seek in the state of nature is dissipated, for power fulfilled is, except for God, a property only of civil society. Yet, Hobbes' practical proposals for achieving power fall short of the plenitude of his intent.

Absorbed as he was in the practical problems of government, he finally places his faith less in the growing knowledge traceable to science than he does in the supremacy of a ruler, who fashions society according to his own lights rather than according to the light of reason. Although Hobbes glimpsed the need for both political absolutism and for scientific enlightenment, he weighted the scales on the side of the former. Although Hobbes proposed machinery intended to perpetuate the political solution of the problem of peace, this solution did not exclude the benefits to be derived from science. His recommendations for peace contemplate that politics and science would re-enforce each other. Together, they would serve as the principle forces for liberating the human spirit.

What, finally, would be the other forces for liberating the human spirit? Hobbes rarely mentions the fine arts, and when he does, he speaks of them in terms of ornament and their accompaniments, delectation or delight. Yet, he did have a strong sense of the importance of *belles lettres* and of the consummatory worth they contribute to social life. These, taken together with his regard for moral philosophy, do provide clues to the liberating arts that, along with religion, make life more complete. Initially having acknowledged speech as a distinctive psychological factor belonging to man, Hobbes sees it evolve into moral philosophy, which he defines as "the science of what is good, and evil, in the conversation, and society of mankind." It becomes then "the science of virtue and vice," and their goodness comes "to be praised, as the means of peaceable, sociable, and comfortable living" (iii, pp. 146-7). Utility, justice, and knowledge thus meet in one.

By his humanism Hobbes repudiates the isolation of man from man. The territory in which the humanistic spirit grows is one which men enjoy in common. Having speech and reason, they transform prudence into sapience, acknowledge their common ties, and converse about their proper destiny. When the territory is too small, when knowledge is dissipated, or when speech becomes invective, the arts of peace are lost, and universal warfare begins.

University of Colorado
Boulder, Colorado

6

HUME AND JEFFERSON ON THE USES OF HISTORY

Craig Walton

IN 1775 DAVID HUME REJECTED BARON MURE OF CALDWELL'S request that he draft an appeal for greater discipline of the American colonies, countering that "I am an American in my principles, and wish we would let them alone to govern themselves as they think proper...."[1] Douglass Adair has shown that they thought it proper to make Hume's principles fundamental to the structure of the new constitution. Madison forged the tenth *Federalist* by close study of Hume's political essays. The theory of "interests" and the checking and balancing of "factions" through division of powers are Humean contributions to enlightenment "political science" vital to the American fathers.[2] Hume's works had begun to be available in the colonies at least as early as 1753 *(Political Discourses),*[3] the *History of England* as published,[4] *My Own*

---

1. David Hume, *Letters,* ed. Grieg (Oxford: Oxford University Press, 1932), Vol. II, p. 510, dated 27 October.
2. Douglass Adair, "That Politics May be Reduced to a Science: Hume, James Madison and the Tenth Federalist," in *Huntington Library Quarterly,* XX, (1956-57), pp. 343 ff. Hume first offers his theory of balance and checking of interests at *Treatise,* III/II/VII, 534-539 of Selby-Bigge.
3. E. B. Braly, *The Reputation of David Hume in America,* unpublished doctoral dissertation (Austin: University of Texas Press, 1955), p. 23.
4. *Ibid.,* pp. 13 ff.

Life in 1778, the *Treatise* at least by 1790,[5] and an American edition of the *Works* by 1817.[6] Most widely read and cited, of course, were the *Essays Moral and Political and Literary*, of which numerous editions and selections appeared both in book form and in gazettes.[7]

Thomas Jefferson bought Hume's *History* the first time in 1764; when his library burned in 1770, he replaced the Hume set.[8] In this period he lent Patrick Henry the two-volume Hume *Essays*,[9] and repurchased that set for his own library after each of the two fires. Yet by 1807, Jefferson's admiration for Hume changed to the most horrified disapproval, giving rise to one of the darkest and most puzzling efforts at thought control and censorship to be disclosed in the life of America's first renowned "champion of the free mind." While still in the White House, Jefferson began coaxing publishers to bring out John Baxter's *A New and Impartial History of England* (London, 1796) to replace Hume's, and at least until 1824 Jefferson sought to install this "editic expurgation"[10] as the official English history for use at the University of Virginia. Fortunately all of these efforts failed. But why were they prompted in the first place?

Apparently the cause of Jefferson's extensive efforts to stop the reading of Hume's *History* was his apprehension that the infant republic was in grave danger, part of which danger was conspiratorial "toryism." The future of the republic would hinge on popular belief in historical precedent for republicanism, and for popular sovereignty, such as was argued by the great Whig historians. Since returning from his ambassadorial duties in Paris in 1790, Jefferson increasingly encountered what he believed to be a new, "American toryism" which threatened to establish the same corruption

---

5. *Ibid.*, p. 22.
6. *Ibid.*, pp. 13 f.
7. *Ibid., passim.*
8. Marie Kimball, *Jefferson: The Road to Glory (1743-1776)*, (New York: Coward-McCann, Inc., 1943), pp. 167, 101.
9. Phillips Russell, *Jefferson: Champion of the Free Mind*, (New York: Dodd, Mead and Co., 1956), p. 16.
10. Letter of 25 October, 1825, to Geo. Washington Lewis; in *The Life and Selected Writings of Thomas Jefferson*, ed. Adrienne Koch and Wm. Peden (New York: Modern Library, 1944), p. 726.

and privilege his French patriot friends were just now defeating. By contrast, Baxter had been tried at Old Bailey in 1794, as a member of the London Corresponding Society, thereby acquiring excellent radical democrat credentials. After acquittal, Baxter took up his pen to establish a "true" historical case for liberty and Parliamentary reform. Jefferson had purchased Baxter's expurgation of Hume in 1805, and by 1807 he saw antidemocratic "factions" so virulent in New York and New England that he decided a cutting off of Hume's *History* would be one good halt to further decay of "republican principles" here at home:

> Baxter has performed a good operation on [Hume's *History*]. He has taken the text of H[ume] as his ground work, abridging it by the omission of some details of little interest, and wherever he has found him endeavoring to mislead, by either the suppression of a truth, or by giving it a false coloring, he has changed the text to what it should be, so that we may properly call it Hume's history republicanized...[if Mrs. Macauley's and a few other histories are read along with it,] a sufficient view will be presented of the free principles of the English Constitution.[11]

As controversy has increased in recent years concerning the intellectual origins of the American Revolution and subsequent years of the infant republic, Jefferson's attacks on Hume have received increasing attention.[12] Arthur Bestor

---

11. Letter of 11 June, 1807, to John Norvell, in *The Jefferson Cyclopaedia*, ed. Foley (New York and London: Funk and Wagnells, 1900), entry #3747, pg. 406.

12. Concerning intellectual origins of the American Enlightenment era, I have drawn considerably upon Herbert Schneider, *A History of American Philosophy,* Second edition (New York: Columbia University Press, 1963); Adrienne Koch, *Power, Morals, and the Founding Fathers* (Ithaca: Cornell University Press, 1961); Carolyn Robbins, *The Eighteenth Century Commonwealthman* (Cambridge, Harvard University Press, 1959); Douglass Adair, " 'Experience Must be Our Only Guide': History, Democratic Theory, and the United States Constitution," in Billington, R.A., (ed.), *The Reinterpretation of Early American History: Essays in Honor of John Edwin Pomfret* (San Marino: The Huntington Library, 1966), pp. 129-148; Bernard Bailyn, editor, *Pamphlets of the American Revolution,* Vol. I: 1750-1765 (Cambridge, Mass.: The Belknap Press of Harvard University Press, 1965), introduction (i.e., pp. viii-202); and R. M. MacIver, "The Philosophical Background of the Constitution," *J. Social Phil.* III (Oct.-July, 1937-38), pp. 201-209.

calls it a "painful episode," but is confident that Jefferson's general principles of tolerance prevailed.[13] Leonard Levy goes farther, finding material for an entire volume on Jefferson's "true believer" fanaticisms, most especially his notions of "verbal political crimes." But these are seen as moral "lapses" rather than acts indicative of a philosophical position.[14] Trevor Colbourn not only examines the attack on Hume, but studied the Baxter volume itself; yet his conclusion is that Jefferson the *philosophe* used history in proper "ideological" manner to promote a salutary and inspiring myth, without which America might have suffered the violence of the myth-less French radicals.[15] Meanwhile, the

---

13. Arthur Bestor, chapter on Jefferson in *Three Presidents and their Books* (Urbana: University of Illinois Press, 1955); quotation from p. 20. Bestor does not examine Baxter or Hume, nor does he discuss why Jefferson interpreted them as he did. He takes the "painful episode" as an exception to Jefferson's rule of toleration, rather than as exhibiting a view of the uses of history.

14. *Jefferson and Civil Liberties: The Darker Side* (Cambridge: Harvard University Press, 1963), *passim*. Levy discusses Jefferson's bill of attainder against Josiah Philips, his hope for the University of Virginia as a true republican "seminary" combating Harvard's American tories, his silence when others opposed the Alien and Sedition acts, and his view of political dissent or opposition as conspiratorial or unAmerican. Levy examines the campaign to publish Baxter, but does not examine Baxter or Hume.

15. *The Lamp of Experience: Whig History and the Intellectual Origins of the American Revolution*, (Chapel Hill: Univ. of North Carolina Press, 1965). Colbourn indicates sympathy for Jefferson's views that Hume had "royalist" sympathies and preferred established authority over liberty, and that history is a lamp of experience especially as it supports those myths which incite men toward bettering their condition. For example, at pp. 194-198, he argues that though the myth of Saxon liberty has been dispelled, Jefferson and his English radical democratic predecessors used the myth to substantiate their radicalism, such that less violence and more stability resulted from their efforts than was the case with French revolutionaries of the same period, who argued without such myths. Hence, Professor Colbourn suspects that our loss of myths may be a sad one. Jefferson and the English radicals before him had used history as a guide to a "perfectable future" by studying a "blemished past"; "it was Jefferson's ability to learn from and employ history for the present and future that contributed to his historical optimism" (p. 184). I am indebted to Professor Colbourn for his letters of encouragement over nine years, especially his help in finding a microfilm of Baxter. As he will doubtless recognize, what follows borrows from but differs somewhat from his valuable study.

controversy over Hume's *History* is also far from ended.[16] What makes the Jefferson attacks on Hume most interesting is that we are compelled to wonder whether, beneath a mound of ironies, there may lie buried some skeleton to account for how or why those ironies piled up here as they did: Did Hume the "philosophical historian" and foe of "metaphysics" violate his own philosophical logic and historical evidence in striking the balances offered in summary sections of his *History*? Did Jefferson the democrat despair of the people's ability to weather the onslaught of Hume's volumes? Was Baxter actually closer to Hume than to Jefferson? But most crucially, what are the deeper beliefs about human nature and the philosophic way of life from which the Hume and Jefferson positions emerge and collide? Recently Peter Gay has argued that, despite all differences, there is a "family" of traits characterizing one genus of Enlightenment man. He cites Hume as perhaps the single

---

16. Cf. E. C. Mossner, "Was Hume a Tory Historian?", *J. Hist. Ideas* II (1941), pp. 225-236; and "An Apology for David Hume, Historian", *PMLA*, v. 56 (1941), pp. 657-690; Marjorie Grene, "Hume: Sceptic and Tory", *J. Hist. Ideas*, 4 (1943), pp. 338-348; Geoffrey Marshall, "David Hume and Political Scepticism", *Philosophical Quarterly*, IV (1954), pp. 247-257; J.G.A. Pocock, *The Ancient Constitution and the Feudal Law* (Cambridge: Harvard Univ. Press, 1957); H.R. Trevor-Roper, "David Hume as Historian", *The Listener*, LXVI, Dec. 28, 1961, pp. 1103 ff.; F.A. Hayek, "The Legal and Political Philosophy of David Hume", *Il Politico*, XXVIII (1963), reprinted in V.C. Chappel, ed., *Hume: A Collection of Critical Essays* (Garden City: Doubleday Anchor Books, 1966), pp. 335-360; Laurence L. Bongie, *David Hume: Prophet of the Counter-Revolution* (Oxford: Clarendon Press, 1965); John Benj. Stewart, *The Moral and Political Philosophy of David Hume* (New York: Columbia Univ. Press, 1963), esp. chs. six and nine; Richard H. Popkin, "Scepticism in the Enlightenment," *Transactions of the First International Congress on the Enlightenment*, Vol. I (1963), pp. 1321-1345; Richard H. Popkin and David Fate Norton, *David Hume: Philosophical Historian* (Indianapolis and New York: Bobbs-Merrill Library of Liberal Arts, 1965) introductions, pp. ix-1, and also see their bibliography on the Hume-as-historian controversy, pp. liii-lv; Constant Noble Stockton III, "Hume-Historian of the English Constitution", *Eighteenth-Century Studies*, IV/no. 3 (Spring, 1971), pp. 277-293.

closest actual paradigm of those traits.[17] Yet something Hume took as central, his "mitigated scepticism,"[18] was not merely peripheral to, but alien and anathema to the *philosophes,* to many American intellectuals and most notably to Jefferson.[19] Consequently, study of Baxter's "editic expurgation" of Hume and of Jefferson's reasons for his campaign, followed by consideration of Hume's philosophical-historical conclusions in the *History,* may lead to some insight beyond the "painful episode" or "moral lapse" views of Jefferson's actions. If the incident reveals two conflicting notions of Enlightenment, warring on the common ground of the nature and use of history for purposes of life, then we must ask whether the conflict arose from deeply set and carefully developed positions. If so, suggestions of "lapses" or fits of pique will no longer serve as interpretations. In what follows I want to argue that Jefferson's attack on Hume, though partially due to personal and national stress and human fallibility, is also consistent with a particular notion of men, ideas, and their histories, and that Jefferson's position is one which Hume rejected. My theme might be caricatured as "history: *topoi* or *tropoi?"*

Little is known of John Baxter, except that after John Horne Tooke and Thomas Hardy (as leaders of the London Corresponding Society) were acquitted of high treason charges, Baxter as a lesser officer of the Society was also acquitted, desired to address the court and was denied that privi-

---

17. Peter Gay, *The Enlightenment: An Interpretation* [vol. I]: *The Rise of Modern Paganism* (New York: Alfred A. Knopf, 1966), "Overture", e.g., p. 13: and see ch. seven, sec. three: "David Hume: The Complete Modern Pagan", pp. 401-419, esp. 418 f.: "He was willing to live with uncertainty, with no supernatural justification, no complete explanations, no promise of permanent stability, with guides of merely probable validity; ..."

18. The phrase is from Hume's *An Inquiry Concerning Human Understanding,* sec. XII, pt. three; ed. Hendel (Indianapolis: Bobbs-Merrill Library of Liberal Arts, 1955), pp. 169 ff. Cf. *Treatise,* I/IV/ii, "Conclusion of this Book."

19. Cf. Bongie, *op. cit.;* Braly, *op. cit.,* and Popkin, "Scepticism in the Enlightenment", *loc. cit.,* for examples of attacks on Hume as "the Infidel", sceptic and so on.

lege.[20] His *History* appeared in London two years later.[21] It is largely a reprinting or paraphrasing of Hume's *History*, with a new preface. Hume's allegedly false statements and conclusions are cut out, and "truth" is supplied instead. To these he adds some chapters on the revolutions in France and Holland, plus Jefferson's Declaration of Independence as an appendix. Most histories, Baxter writes, are intended to deceive rather than inform; this is especially so with "party writers" (p.v). Though partisanship is presumably to be avoided, he also acknowledges the principle that "no individual or body of men, exercising power of the government, could become tyrants at once; the people can only be prevailed upon to part with their liberty by degrees, either by force, or on pretence of some necessity" (p.vi). Therefore a history of England would show when and how "liberties were invaded," and by examples of this sort discover how that evil is to be prevented. What follows, in the preface and throughout, might easily be predicted. Hume's considerations for Charles I are replaced with censure, his comments on popular excesses are replaced with praises, and in general Hume is rendered a democratic republican historian. Baxter caricatures, then disputes Hume concerning the present, as well: "Neither can we agree with those who say, the constitution, as it exists at present, is the height of human perfection, im-

---

20. T. B. Howell and Thos. J. Howell, *A Complete Collection of State Trials,....*(London: Printed by T. C. Hansard, Peterborough Court, Fleet Street, 1818), vol. XXIV, pp. 21-25, and vol. XXV, pp. 743-748.

21. *A New and Impartial History of England. From the Most Early Period of Genuine Evidence to the Present Important and Alarming Crisis; a Period Pregnant with the Fate of Empires, Kingdoms and States....* Including a History of the American War and Revolution, To which are added histories of the French Revolution, and the Revolution in Holland, etc... interspersed with Remarks, Observations and Reflections: By which former Errors are corrected, Absurdities pointed out, fabulous Narrations expurged, Party Prejudices removed, & what has hitherto appeared obscure and doubtful authenticated from the most respectable Evidences. By JOHN BAXTER. Member of the London Corresponding Society, and one of the twelve indicted & acquitted of High Treason at the Old Bailey, assisted by several gentlemen, Distinguished Friends to Liberty & a Parliamentary Reform....London: MDCCXCVI. Subsequent references are in the text parenthetically.

proved by time, and sanctioned by experience; for we have pointed out a time when it existed in much greater perfection, and had the universal suffrage of the people" (p.ix).[22]

In view of Professor Colbourn's comment that Jefferson's method is Baxter's,[23] a few examples of Baxter's method deserve notice. As to the purpose of his history, Baxter observed that although "standing armies, bastiles, and barracks" have walled the people off from each other and government chooses to prevent "public discussion, and dissolve popular societies," still a redress of grievances may be achieved by writing and reading history: "It is the duty of every true born Englishman, to read and imbibe the principles of his most worthy ancestors," and then propagate these principles by word of mouth (p.x). A history, then, should supply truth where government will not and open meetings cannot (because forbidden).

Concerning the popular element in ancient Saxon councils, Baxter tacitly admits Hume's point, though censoring it, but also finds it to be unimportant. True, the records are lost and we do not know the social or economic status of our ancestral popular councilors, but the lack of records is no bar to a conclusion, because people do not willingly give up a right they once had. The Normans must have destroyed the records. "We are therefore obliged to reason from analogy, and the imperfect records which remain. From these it appears, the *people* were *represented* in the Wittena-gemote, by persons chosen by themselves...." (p. 74). If history cannot complete the reformers' case, *a priori* argument as to human nature and political principles supplies the gaps. This "method" recurs in Baxter. On the Magna Charta, Baxter alludes to Hume's (censored) appendix two concerning its sections sixteen and seventeen (on representation), and tries to refute Hume in that, though Hume is correct that no reference is made there to a commons, still section seventeen names Earls, Barons and so on. "There is some ambiguity in

---

22. Cf. Hume's *History,* (Philadelphia: J. B. Lippincott Co., [no date]), II/514.
23. Colbourn, *op. cit.,* pp. 178-181.

the sixteenth article" (p. 134), but still "nothing is more incontestable that there was provision for [a commons'] attendance." On the controversy over Strafford's trial, Baxter sees Hume as wrongly lamenting the legal device used there since, even though there was no statute for crimes against the "rights of the people," there should be! Hence, punishment was justified (p. 425).

Either as a pang of conscience or as illustrative of his "method" in history, Baxter had noted that since the Magna Charta was based on a feudal order, it is not really a model for today (this from Hume). Its rules for securing liberty and happiness are so vague, he continued, that "it is not from them, but the common rights of mankind, and the customs of the Anglo-Saxons, that Englishmen must deduce their constitution and their liberties" (p. 134). Baxter does not indicate how we could discover those customs without evidence, though he may mean us to do it by "analogy."

But then, turning sharply away from the Saxon *vs.* Norman "origins" controversy, Baxter argues that in fact the present constitution owes its "radical *rottenness* and *mischievous effects*" to the "antient and glorious constitution" (p. 194), in that today's "trading interests" are deceived into believing they are represented, while "landed" interests prey upon them economically and by government control. To overcome this sort of present, and the past which produced it, a new theory of representation must be offered, "fair and equal," a universal suffrage but guided by "the most intelligent part of the people" in instructing elected representatives and "obliging" them to obey instructions or be recalled (p. 193). No historical precedent is claimed for radical democratic republicanism. But Baxter does note that Cromwell's commonwealth is not a counter-instance, for it was impure and, in fact, a military "tyrrany" [sic] (p. 485).

After discussing Henry VIII, Baxter adds to the Hume text his own argument for religious toleration, one which might well have struck Jefferson since it so resembles his own: "Good government has nothing to do with speculations in theology; it ought only to distinguish between the good and the bad citizen, by cherishing virtue and punishing vice, but

Hume and Jefferson on History

leave him to worship his Creator according to the dictates of his conscience, without prohibition or limitation" (p. 294).

Finally, after applauding the American Revolution and identifying George III as either weak or wicked, Baxter praises the Declaration of Independence as full of "great and useful principles of politics"; "it would be inexcusable to withhold it from public observation" (p. 789), so the text is then appended.

In 1810, Jefferson wrote to the publisher William Duane that "when young" he had read Hume's *History* with enthusiasm; only a long purge of "research and reflection" has relieved him of its "poison": "It is this book which has undermined free principles of the English government, has persuaded readers of all classes that there were usurpations on the legitimate and salutary rights of the crown, and has spread universal toryism over the land. And the book will still continue to be read here as well as there [in England] ...."[24] "This single book," he told John Adams, "has done more to sap the free principles of the English Constitution than the largest standing army...Hume has concentrated ...all the arbitrary proceedings of the English Kings, as true evidences of the Constitution, and glided over its Whig principles as the unfounded pretensions of factious demagogues."[25] In an 1824 entry to his *Commonplace Books,* Jefferson is still preoccupied with Hume and Baxter. He lists eight places in Hume's *History,* presumably the most offending passages: note AA to ch. 42; ch. 53; note GG to ch. 56; ch. 57, ch. 59 that revolutions rarely benefit the people; ch. 59 that popular sovereignty is of "specious" lineage; ch. 59 that obedience alone needs to be inculcated, and ch. 61 on Cromwell. Jefferson's comment to the list (or indictment?): "In a debate in the H[ouse] of Commons Mar. 23. 24 Sr. James McIntosh quotes Burke as having said in some speech, 'I believe we shall all come to think, at last, with Mr. Hume,

---

24. Letter to Wm. Duane, 12 August, 1810; in Koch and Peden, *op. cit.,* p. 606.
25. Letter to John Adams, 25 November, 1816; in Foley, *op. cit.,* #3749.

that an absolute monarchy is not so bad a thing as we supposed.' *The Globe.* Mar. 24. 1824."[26]

Jefferson's attacks are difficult to sort. At one point he seems to find toryism in Hume where Whig principles would be closer to truth. But then he favors Baxter who overthrows Whig *and* Tory appeals to precedent by arguing a natural and universal right of suffrage and representation. Again, Jefferson attacks Hume for doubting the Whig precedent, but endorses Baxter who opposes any past ("rotten") tie to the present and would reform whatever of the Whig precedent England did have (because illusory, a false representation). Jefferson apparently sees Hume in error as to the chances of popular excesses, yet himself deplored the "terror" in France. He scores Hume for the view that rights of rebellion need not be taught, though duties of obedience should, but he went far beyond Hume toward repression by acquiescing to the Alien and Sedition acts while Madison fought them.[27] Perhaps most ironic of all, he focuses on Hume's judicious verdict on Charles I as evidence of anti-republican sentiment, although that same verdict, *mutatis mutandis,* might be applied to Jefferson's own presidency with his use of embargo, censorship and strong state power to save the republic as he knew it and to combat political dissent as he saw it threatening.

Another ironic aspect of the attack on Hume reveals still another dimension to our story. In a letter to Peter Carr in 1787, Jefferson expresses two philosophic principles of considerable bearing. First, he argues (with Destutt de Tracy) that there is no philosophical science of ethics, for if God had so intended, most men would never acquire a "sense of right and wrong" at all; yet they do. That "sense," then, is a natural endowment, not a construction of reason, and is "as much a part of man's nature, as the sense of hearing.... It

---

26. *The Commonplace Book of Thomas Jefferson,* introd. by Gilbert Chinard (Baltimore: Johns Hopkins Press, 1926), entry #905, pp. 374-376.

27. Cf. Levy, *op. cit.,* pp. 50-55 on John Thomson of New York, James Madison and Tunis Wortman, all of whom argued that only deeds can count as treasonous, to Jefferson's position at the time; cf. also pp. 162 ff.

may be strengthened by exercise, as may any particular limb of the body."[28] Reason is able to guide it, but very little reason is needed — less than we need to have "common sense." In fact, a "plowman" would probably resolve a moral case more soundly then a "professor," as the latter's mind will be "led astray by artificial rules." But, second, Jefferson also argues in the same letter that Carr should "fix reason firmly in her seat" concerning religion in order to avoid "the fears and servile prejudices, under which weak minds are servilely crouched" (*ibid*). He does not explain why such prejudices cannot be combated by "moral sense" alone, or (alternatively) what is to happen to those with insufficient "artificial rules" here where "nature" has made no provisions. Rather, Jefferson goes on to fix a rule for judging what to believe about religions — and it is Hume's rule, almost *verbatim* from the essay "On Miracles"! "Examine upon what evidence [a writer's] pretensions are founded, and whether that evidence is so strong, as that its falsehood would be more improbable than a change in the laws of nature, in the case he relates... [finally,] Your own reason is the only oracle given you by heaven, and you are answerable, not for the rightness, but uprightness of the decision."[29] Apparently the dangers of religious "fears and prejudices" cannot be avoided unless reason is "firmly in her seat," but natural endowments and experience can avoid dangers of false moral beliefs. Many writers suggest Jefferson backed away from the "natural rights" doctrine after the Revolutionary War, but he seems to have retained (or acquired) the "moral sense" doctrine at least into the period of the attack on Hume. Jefferson's Humean rule of proportioning belief to evidence and always accepting the "lesser" miracle, is of especial interest to us here. For to Hume, this "general rule" or artifice of reason holds as much for the study of secular or moral history as it does for alleged or veridical religious histories. It is a rule for assessment of any testimony what-

---

28. Letter to Peter Carr, 10 August, 1787; in Koch and Peden, *op. cit.*, pp. 429-434.
29. *Ibid.*, pp. 432 f.; cf. Hume, *Inquiry, op. cit.*, sec. X, pp. 122-124.

ever, and is so treated in the *History of England*. But, for example, though Jefferson rejected Hume's conclusion that revolutions rarely benefit the people and normally simply change the identities of the rulers, neither Jefferson nor Baxter offers a preponderance of evidence for their optimism.

Further ironies deserve to be remarked. Either unknown, or unrecognized by Jefferson, Hume had taken a number of positions quite close to Jefferson's own. Though in the *History* he considered utopian writing the pursuit of a "chimera,"[30] Hume wrote such an utopian essay in which he opted for a republic formed by "hundreds" remarkably similar to Jefferson's republic by "wards."[31] As early as the *Treatise*, Hume argued the right of rebellion whenever government failed to preserve the public interest. And he made this *especially* applicable to countries with constitutional government, since there one would find less excuses for claims to obedience by virtue of possession or custom.[32] Again, Adrienne Koch noted that although Jefferson never developed a socialist theory of political economy, he did read the French socialist Mably and seemed sympathetic to an egalitarian approach to economic justice.[33] Yet as Marshall notes, Jeremy Bentham found Hume's treatment of justice in the *Treatise* to be perhaps the first time the case for a political economy of "the people" has been stated in terms of fundamental human needs and interests primitive to any subsequent governmental arrangement.[34] Again, as was true for Jefferson, Hume placed his hopes for improvement of

---

30. Hume, *History, op. cit.*, V/531-32, concerning Harrington and others who might write utopias: "The idea...of a perfect and immortal commonwealth, will always be found as chimerical as that of a perfect and immortal man."
31. "Idea of a Perfect Commonwealth", e.g., in *Political Essays,* ed. Hendel (New York: The Liberal Arts Press, 1953); compare Jefferson's "Wards" as described in Koch, *Philosophy of Thomas Jefferson,* (New York: Columbia Univ. Press, 1943) pp. 162-165.
32. *Treatise*, III/II/X, pp. 563-567.
33. Koch. *op. cit.*, p. 120, note 19.
34. Marshall, *op. cit.*, p. 250, citing Bentham, *Fragment on Government,* ch. 1, note to para. 36, that in Hume's treatment of justice, "the cause of the people [is] the cause of virtue." Cf. *Treatise*, III/II/secs. I-III.

the human condition not upon some form of government or system of institutions, but upon the condition of education, laws, arts and sciences and enlightened individual judgment (*The Federalist Papers,* no. 84, concludes with a long quote from Hume to this effect). Finally, on the matter of myth, in a letter to Turgot, Hume remarks that though evidence does not reinforce belief in ancient precedent for principles of popular sovereignty, it would be to the good if such were the case, because the "incitement" gained would strengthen the forces of liberty.[35] While we cannot conclude that Hume presented a full appreciation of the uses and abuses of myth as a social force, he did write an utopian plan in spite of its "chimerical" quality, and realized the value of the Whig "ancient origins" doctrine even though it, too, was a myth. He did not consider his own *History* to be myth in this sense, and apparently endeavored not to mix the two; but he gives myth some stature.[36]

If Jefferson's attack on Hume's *History* is not merely a "painful episode" or a moral "lapse," and if it cannot be understood as the straightforward collision of a democratic republican with an authoritarian monarchist, one further avenue remains to be explored. This is the examination of Jefferson's philosophical theories of human knowledge and of man's nature adapted from Destutt de Tracy, and as then contrasted with Hume's.[37] Jefferson labored long and hard to translate and publish works of de Tracy, corresponded with him and sang his praises to many correspondents. De Tracy's school of "Ideology" was founded in 1796 as *L'Institut National,* where philosophy was "the science of methods" (p. 72). De Tracy argues a biological foundation for all feel-

---

35. Letter to Turgot, 16 June, 1768; in *Letters,* ed. Grieg, *op. cit.,* vol. II, #417.

36. He considered "original contract" theories neither true nor false, but "philosophical fictions". Cf. *Treatise* III/II/II, and concerning Hume's wider notion of the place of "fictions" in philosophy, note Selby-Rigge's topical index, p. 662.

37. In this section, I rely on Adrienne Koch's *Philosophy of Thomas Jefferson, op. cit.* Further references to her discussion appear in the text parenthetically.

ings, and thence for all "ideas" as experiences of "resistance" from other things to our basic outgoing "faculty" of feeling. He also condemned Hume as too skeptical and Locke as too sensationalistic (pp. 65-79). His basic unit of judgment is a proposition, not a term or "idea," for knowledge begins with a "grouped judgmental action" rather than with isolated sense-data.[38] As thought and feeling are initially one whole and responsive experience, languages expressing experience suggest a range of thought and actions from least to most sophisticated. Jefferson's study of ancient Saxon dialects and of over thirty American Indian dialects is in accord with the scholarly interests of de Tracy's "ideological" program. In these and other empirical investigations, Jefferson shows a considerable skeptical reserve *as method,* just as did Dugald Steward and de Tracy. But also in their manner, he rejected Hume's "pyrrhonism"[39] because, as Dugald Stewart had put it, we need a scientific basis for action that is reasonable, not merely Hume's "custom" (p. 102). Adrienne Koch noted that Jefferson's references to resting on "the pillow of ignorance...[when faced with questions] which exceeded human knowledge at the time, may reveal a constitutional unwillingness to remain long in the sphere of skeptical doubt" (p. 102, nt. 31).

But reference to a "constitutional unwillingness" is, at least to readers of Hume, a begging of the question. For in the manner of Pyrrho, Montaigne, Pascal and Bayle before him, Hume admits it to be a constitutional (or "natural") propensity of all men to resolve doubts at the practical level and to "believe" when imperatives of survival or civility become pressing. It was not that Hume found his doubts "constitutionally" easy to manage, but that he saw the need for developing by philosophical art an ability to endure them long enough to discern how reason might (in Jefferson's phrase)

---

38. Koch notes that Wm. James found de Tracy's "ideology" as halfway between Lockean sensationalism and nineteenth-century "act philosophy" or voluntarism, at *Principles,* I/247.

39. Letter to John Adams, 15 August, 1820: in *Papers,* Memorial Edition, (Washington, D.C., 1905), XV, pp. 275-76; cited in Koch, *Ibid.,* p. 102.

be "fixed firmly in her seat," before beginning the rough ride of practical commitment to some course of action. That ability is a philosophical excellence, not a natural trait. Hume's question was never that of the (unmitigated) "rightness" or "wrongness" of the choice to be made, but rather (in Jefferson's phrase) "uprightness" that would separate the "mitigated" skeptic from the (affirming or denying) "dogmatist." Time after time, Hume's philosophical dialectic distinguished and evaluated positive and negative instances until as much illusion and self-deception could be closely examined as he had the talents and reach to accomodate. No judgment of beliefs could be made "safely," free from the tensions of paradox, ambiguity or partiality. But more than that, Hume often indicated that at the peak of suspension of judgment regarding a particular issue, the general field within which these tensions are generated *could* be recognized by philosophic man such that wherever his experience might move him when time for action arrived, it would be taken in a temperate and modulated manner. Moral excellence and philosophic excellence sustain each other. A separate study would be required to illustrate this view in the *Treatise, Inquiries, Dialogues* and *Essays*. But present purposes justify illustrations from his *History of England*.

Reflecting on the overthrow of James I, Hume observed that lovers of liberty acted as they did not because of harsh tyranny (for men had borne that before), but because the tyranny was founded on arbitrary and dangerous principles. Consequently "the wise and moderate" tried to see both sides. The people were divided, and civil war was coming. Both sides would be to blame. Faced with these realizations, "the good and virtuous would scarcely know what views to form; were it not that liberty, so necessary to the perfection of human society, would be sufficient to bias their affections towards the side of its defenders."[40] However, the revolution of 1688 decided "many important questions in favor of liberty;... it gave such an ascendant to popular principles,

---

40. *History, op. cit.,* IV/468 f.

as has put the nature of the English constitution beyond all controversy," such that if England's is not now the best system of *government,* it is "at least the most entire system of liberty that ever was known amongst mankind."[41] With this shift in the balance toward liberty and away from established government, however, new difficulties have arisen, chiefly the corruption among the Whigs and their party operatives, to the point where public offices and perquisites toward the arts are going to party hacks and mediocrity (a corruption reported to Jefferson by John Cartwright as a scandal to be avoided!). Hume now observes, "on forgetting that a regard to liberty, though a laudable passion, ought commonly to be subordinate to a reverence for established government,[42] the prevailing faction has celebrated only the partisans of the former, who pursued as their object the perfections of civil society, and has extolled them at the expense of their antagonist, who maintained those maxims that are essential to its very existence. But extremes of all kinds are to be avoided; and though no one will ever please either faction by moderate opinions, it is there we are most likely to meet with truth and certainty."[43] No matter which party governs, Hume's lifelong focus on the "balance" of the public interest, and hence the balance between government and the culture requires a fundamental civility to all vital claims. Those who claim priority for the "existence" of the government, its survival, will often oppose those emphasizing its "perfection"; but a wise governor will realize this tension to be vital, and will moderate his own partisanship toward the end of public well-being. He cannot avoid his own limits and inclinations, his own partisanship, but a "mitigated scepticism" would enable him so to moderate them as neither to

---

41. *Ibid.,* VI/363 ff.
42. The context here, and other passages such as I/171 and II/510 ff., indicate that Hume means a reverence for government within the laws. The Whigs were the "established government," but went outside or scoffed at the laws for the sake of patronage and spoils.
43. *History, op. cit.,* VI/365-66. The attack on Whig corruption is at VI/364; cf. also a letter to Mrs. Macauley, *New Letters,* ed. Klibansky and Mossner (Oxford: Oxford Univ. Press, 1954), #40, pg. 80, 29 March, 1764.

corrupt his own followers nor alienate his opposition. Either of these latter "extremities" weakens the "constitution." Real value differences are both predictable and salutory to the vitality of the people, their government and their culture. Stewart has argued that the *History* was intended to reduce Whig-Tory animus, by showing each side's anachronisms, and to show each that "because of the mixed, and therefore uncertain constitution, the other party had a part to play in contemporary politics, and that each should play its part with sedate restraint so as not to endanger that fabric of vulgar opinion of which the constitution was chiefly composed."[44] In the *History* as in other works, Hume's philosophical dialectic sometimes arrives at fundamental differences no longer beclouded with deception or fallacious argument. When he reaches those differences, he strives to moderate and civilize their inevitable interplay rather than to suppress one or more. It is his philosophical wisdom which led Whigs to see him as "Tory," and Tories as "Whig."

Hume concluded the final volume of this work by noting that history affords only slight positive assistance from the past, and teaches us to expect little latitude for human wisdom in the future: "A civilized nation... ought to be cautious in appealing to the practice of their ancestors, or regarding the maxims of uncultivated ages as certain rules for their present conduct. Any acquaintance with the ancient period of their government is chiefly *useful,* by instructing them to cherish their present constitution,... and it is also *curious,* by showing them the remote and commonly faint and disfigured originals of the most finished and most noble institutions, and by instructing them in the great mixture of accident, which commonly concurs with a small ingredient of wisdom and foresight, in erecting the complicated fabric of the most perfect government."[45]

---

44. Stewart, *op. cit.,* pp. 298 f. Cf. also Marshall, *op. cit.,* esp. pp. 252-257.

45. *History, op. cit.,* II/514. As Jefferson said, Hume wrote the History "backwards": Vols. V and VI published in 1754, then III and IV in 1759 and I and II in 1762. Thus, in point of time the conclusion to vol. II is Hume's summing-up.

Stewart had considered these sorts of observations to be "antihistorical" in Hume,[46] but it seems difficult so to separate the philosophical from the historical. For the greater part, Hume's "lessons" or *"obiter dicta"* seem to be consistent with his more philosophical writings.[47] David Norton has argued that Hume is as much an historical philosopher as he is philosophical historian.[48] But, Norton continues, is Hume not equally vulnerable in both areas, since his scepticism can only be "mitigated" by "proportioning" belief to evidence, whereas what shall count as evidence, and how it shall count, is determined by limited and fallible personal experience? Is Hume not up against a hopeless puzzle? Surely such was the judgment of Reid, Stewart and de Tracy, all Jefferson's mentors. They saw Hume's scepticism as "pyrrhonism" by which the "customs" one accepts are literally the prevailing political and moral arrangements of one's age, whether true or false, salutary or disastrous, and no scientific data could therefore resolve such philosophical conservatism. According to Sextus Empiricus, Pyrrho claimed we cannot know such ultimates. There is no "natural existence of anything good or bad or (in general) fit or unfit to be done," so that suspension of judgment alone is warranted and sane.[49] Jefferson takes Hume's use of "custom" to be Pyrrhonian, from which the case for Hume as apologist for the *status quo* seems to follow.

Yet whether or not Hume succeeded in revising Pyrrho and Sextus, such was his attempt; his notion of "custom" is not theirs. For in Hume, that word is a synonym for "the princi-

---

46. Stewart, *op. cit.*, p. 299.
47. Cf. Stockton, "Hume-Historian of the English Constitution," *op. cit.*, p. 293, where Hume is considered as dropping intuitive maxims here and there, such that his *History* takes on an *a priori* cast.
48. Popkin and Norton, *op. cit.*, introduction, pp. xxxii-l.
49. Sextus Empiricus, *Outlines of Pyrrhonism*, trans. Bury (London: Wm. Heinemann, Ltd., 1933), III/xxii, p. 483. Sextus finds the sceptic concluding that therefore, too, there is no place for ethics in philosophy since there is nothing it could study and no method it could use to teach if it did have a subject matter. Ironically, though the premises are the contrary of Jefferson's, the conclusion is the same, that philosophy does not study ethics.

ple of belief," whose natural operation can never be halted for long. But its operation can be studied by reflection and dialectical inquiry, until enough suspension can be achieved through *tropoi,* to offer some distance from which to begin taking perspective and doing the needed "proportioning." There is little reason can do; but that little makes the difference we are able to make; it is the difference between "dogmatism" and moderation. Hume's "experience" is not merely "personal," for the entire process of moral and intellectual development is interpersonal and cultural, top to bottom. Especially in the *History,* the experience on which he reflects and by which he reaches his "Lessons" or *obiter dicta* are, for better or worse, offered on a basis of common (informed and criticized) English experience. In his "anonymous" review of his own "still-born" *Treatise,* Hume wrote: "And as there is often a constant conjunction of the actions of the wise with their motives, so the inference from the one to the other is often as certain as any reasoning concerning bodies; and there is always an inference proportioned to the constancy of the conjunction. On this is founded our belief in witnesses, our credit in history, and indeed all kinds of moral evidence, and almost the whole conduct of life."[50]

Hume's notion of the status of evidence, "our credit" in history, of its uses as both *topoi* and *tropoi,* its lessons for "proportioning" of our lives as philosophic men, all require further study and criticism. But Jefferson and others sharing his notion of Enlightenment had made up their minds. As Lawrence Bongie tells it, the counter-revolution in France developed enthusiasm for some of Hume's doubts about popular excesses, and began to use those aspects of his *History* for rightist, (and others even for moderate left) purposes.[51] Concomitantly, "le Bon David" was abandoned by the *philosophes.* Such was the quickness of this shift, and such its severity, that by 1800 J. E. M. Portalis concluded that the Enlightenment of the *philosophes* had rejected medieval re-

---

50. "An Abstract of a Treatise on Human Nature", in *Inquiry, op. cit.,* p. 197.
51. *Op. cit.,* pp. 168 ff.

ligious superstitions only to replace them with modern political ones. Portalis specifically cited the two doctrines that any political act for "liberty" is good, and that history is to be made over into political propaganda.[52] Americans, and probably Jefferson, knew Baxter was reported to be a Jacobin, and that Hume was being used by the French right. And it is at just this time (1805) that Jefferson bought his copy of Baxter and began the attack on Hume's *History*. The doctrines of Reid, Stewart and de Tracy provided the "method" for overcoming Hume's alleged "pyrrhonism." Baxter provided the remedy for Hume's alleged "universal toryism;" the borrowing of Humean principles of 1787 is long forgotten. We might conjecture the same fate eventually befell Hume in Jefferson's mind, as Richard Popkin notices among the French *philosophes:* Hume's "... fundamental challenge to human intellectual security and peace of mind," was rejected. "What was to be done was to discover, within the limits Locke [and here, de Tracy] had prescribed, and with the method Newton used, what man could know about himself and nature, and to employ this knowledge to reform society, liberate man, and tame the future."[53] It is not that Jefferson's Enlightenment was naively optimistic; his great faith in the people had been shaken, though not broken, by their hearkening after "American tories". Nor was his ideology unchecked by any scholarly habits, for he continued careful research in areas of interest to him. But as Trevor Colbourn details, Jefferson held that in the writing and study of history for practical philosophical application one could be both scholarly *and* partisan.[54] Jefferson would utilize some histories for *topoi* they supply to current argument, and condemn other histories which counter or question the former. Though he boosted Baxter and attacked Hume in this way, he apparently did not realize either the folly of Baxter's man-

---

52. In *De l'usage et de l'abus de l'esprit philosophique durant le dix-huitième siècle* (Written 1798-1800, published 1820); cited in *ibid.*

53. Richard H. Popkin, "Scepticism in the Enlightenment", *op. cit.,* p. 1339.

54. Colbourn, *op. cit.,* pp. 179, 181, 184, 193-198.

ufacturing "evidence" by "analogy" when none other could be found, or Baxter's eventual decision that history is very slight use here anyway since the key issues are "natural" truths. To suggest that Jefferson's "method" here was Baxter's, is of little help when Baxter claims and then abandons two distinct positions in sequence, only to settle on a third lacking entirely in "method."[55]

The saga of Jefferson, Baxter and Hume is particularly poignant in view of the ironies that Baxter and Jefferson were championing radical democratic republican "eighteenth century commonwealthman's" views which Hume had shared before them. If we agreed with all three that no institutional reforms could supply hope where civic virtue in the people is absent, that foundations for liberty and law must be laid in accordance with man's nature if his artifice is to endure, and that even some role for myth may be necessary to vitalize civic reform; at least one question still remains: must the nonrational, the paradoxical and the accidental in man be explained away before civilization can be reconstructed, or can they be admitted and "mitigated"? Hume's *tropoi* in the *History* confront both irreducible value differences between men, and nonrational or paradoxical features in all of history.[56] Baxter and Jefferson seek to use history as the great empirical commonplace-book of a people, as would Hume, but without the paradox, accidents, real value differences, and nonrational elements he confronted and retained (at the expense of "system").[57] They could use

---

55. That is, (1) a nonpartisan history based on ancient evidence; then (2) a characterization of what "must have happened" by "analogy" with what Baxter would have done, to (3) urging what must be done, on humane and natural grounds, irrespective of the lack of precedent. Cf. Colbourn, *ibid.*, pp. 178, 181.

56. Cf. Richard H. Popkin, review of Geo. Boas's *Dominant Themes of Modern Philosophy*, in LVI, no. 2 (15 Jan., 1959), p. 67.

57. Jefferson's study of history did teach him that there are fundamental differences, but they are not equally human. Rather, for example, we find the "weakly" and corrupt vs. the healthy and virtuous (in a letter in 1823 to Lafayette); or (to Abigail Adams, 1804) that one natural sort fears the people as ignorant, another natural sort fears the powerful as selfish; and that

philosophy as "method"; they could not see it as the art of dialectical search for a human wisdom never secure. Finally, there seems some relationship, perhaps connection, between their notions of history and philosophy on the one hand, and their characterization of those they opposed as enemies of the party of mankind, and of some kinds of political thoughts as intolerable (irrespective of deeds). It seems especially important today to discover, if we can, whether the "lamp of experience" can guide us away from such civic vices as those, and whether our present wide varieties of parties and cultures can retain real differences yet be "mitigated" by artfully fashioning civil ways of coexistence.[58]

---

history is useful chiefly to control future social programs by inculcating proper beliefs (Koch, pp. 122-126).

58. I would like to thank Herbert W. Schneider, Jean Faurot, James T. King and Donald F. Koch for discussion, close criticism and helpful suggestions regarding an earlier version of this paper. At least they will barely recognize the present version, part of which was read Oct. 15, 1972 before the first annual meeting of the Southwest Society for Eighteenth Century Studies.

7

THE PHILOSOPHICAL BASES OF MODERN RACISM*

Richard H. Popkin

MODERN RACISM, DATING FROM THE 15TH CENTURY, HAS tried to develop justifications for the superiority of one group over another, and to base this superiority on biological, psychological and spiritual factors that may be permanent. Earlier racial views, such as those of the ancient Hebrews, the Christians and the Greeks, either proposed a way for overcoming alleged inferiority by conversion to the superior group, as the Jews and Christians did, or by allowing for a process of assimilation, as the Greeks did for those they called "barbarians" (namely, learning to speak, write, think and live Greek).

A new kind of racism began in Spain in the 15th century to deal with the large number of Jews who had been forcibly converted to Catholicism, and who were becoming the leaders of the Church. The Old Christians were separated from the New Christians, or *conversos* on biological grounds.

---

*I should like to thank Professors Harry M. Bracken and David F. Norton of McGill University and Professor James Groves of San Diego State University for their helpful suggestions regarding this paper. I should also like to thank the Guggenheim Foundation for their support while I was doing some of the research for this study. This study was presented at the conference on "Philosophy and Racism" at the Tuskegee Institute in April, 1973.

Richard H. Popkin

Anyone who had had a Jewish ancestor in the previous five generations was still a New Christian, and could not attend college, join most religious orders, hold government jobs and other restrictions. People had to produce certificates of "purity of blood" to prove they did not belong to the inferior group, the Jews. And the Inquisition was established in Spain and Portugal to police and control the situation, and to make sure those of Jewish ancestry were kept apart and out of the mainstream of society, regardless of what they believed, or what Church they belonged to.

This new form of racism differed from prior forms of discrimination against minority or conquered groups, in that it did not allow for leaving the group discriminated against by any legal process whatsoever. People could and did change their identities, go into hiding, or run away to another part of the world where the Inquisition did not function, all of this illegally. Theories justifying this kind of racism began to appear in Catholic Spain in the 15th century to deal with the Jewish converts, and then, after "the Discovery of America", were expanded to deal with Indians, and later the enslaved Africans.

The original theories ran counter to the dominant theme in Christianity that it was an essential Christian mission to convert everybody, and that once people were converted, they were equal members of the group. All sorts of famous Christian leaders including Popes and kings were converts from Judaism or paganism. But, starting in the 15th century, the Spanish authorities tried to separate the new converts from the old believers, and to make the former perpetual second-class citizens. They justified this on the grounds that biologically, and spiritually, Jews, (and later Mohammedans) had characteristics that could never be completely changed, and that these characteristics would lead to subversive or destructive behavior.

The basic cause of Iberian anti-Semitism may have been jealousy of the power, wealth and influence of those of Jewish ancestry in the society. When the Spaniards and Portuguese came to America, they confronted a new situation. The people whose land, assets and freedom they were taking over were outside of Europe and had no established role in European society. The elaborate racial theories and methods of enforcing them, already worked out in Iberia, were transferred abroad, but the theories had to grow to meet the new conditions. Things like certificates of whiteness were introduced, the American equivalent of certificates of purity of blood.

At first the Spaniards and Portuguese just took over whatever kingdoms they could, and looted them. Then, when they were challenged, racial theories were worked out to justify the conquest and rape of America, and later the enslavement of Africa. Among the first intellectual problems faced after Columbus arrived in the New World were (1) who were the inhabitants who had been discovered, and (2) were they really people? The previous Jewish problem came with a Biblical explanation of who the victims were, and Christian history had already given them the role of built-in villains, the killers of Christ and the eternal enemies of Christianity. But the Indians were an unknown quantity. Most of the theorizing about the origins of the Indians up to the 18th century went on within a framework presented in the Bible. The Indians must have come from some group traceable to migrations of Biblical people (as the Europeans had traced their own origins to various descendants of Noah and his family). So, theories were presented claiming the Indians were the Lost Tribes of Israel in a degenerate state, that they were of Phoenician or Arabic origins, that they were Asians, and even that they were Norwegians, descendants of members of Lief Erickson's expedition. The most dangerous theory, running counter to the claim that the Bible portrays the origin and history of all mankind, was that the Indians did not come from the Biblical world at all; that they were not descendants from Adam and Eve, but had a separate and independent origin; that they were pre-Adamites. This theory, which leads to the most virulent form of modern racism, will be treated at length shortly.

The original reports of the explorers and Conquistadores present two different theories on the second problem (whether the Indians were full and complete human beings).

Richard H. Popkin

One view was that the Indians were sub-human; the other that they were better than other humans in that they were noble savages. Those trying to establish the sub-humanity of the Indians adduced as evidence that the Indians were incapable of having abstract ideas, were incapable of running their own world, were incapable of becoming Christians, were incapable of morality (since they practiced sodomy and made human sacrifices), and therefore the Spaniards and Portuguese had to take over control of their lives, and had to supervise the entire world of the Indian. The Conquistadores did exactly that from the moment of their arrival. An opposition movement surfaced in 1512 when a preacher in Santo Domingo, Montezinos, denounced the mistreatment of the Indians, and insisted that they were human. His major convert to the cause, Bartholemé de Las Casas, who became the Bishop of Chiapas, was the great advocate of the humanity of the Indians, and debated the matter for almost half a century against Sepulveda and other Spanish theorists, insisting that, "...all people of the world are men...all have understanding and volition, all have five exterior senses and four interior senses, and are moved by the objects of these, all take satisfaction in goodness and feel pleasure with happy and delicious things, all regret and abhor evil.[1]"

Sepulveda, who had edited the best Renaissance edition of Aristotle's *Politics,* contended that the Indians were the people Aristotle described as being by nature slaves. And, if they were natural slaves, then, by God, they should be enslaved and put to work for the glory of Spain. Oviedo, another theoretician of the conquistadores, argued the Indians were lacking in rationality (a condition, according to Aristotle, for being human), morality, and were incapable because of this, of becoming believing or practising Christians. Therefore, they had to be dependent on Spanish domination for sufficient moral guidance to overcome their natural bestiali-

---

1. Cited in Lewis Hanke, *The Spanish Struggle for Justice in the Conquest of America,* (Philadelphia, 1949), p. 125. Hanke examines the debate over the status of the Indians in this work and in his *Aristotle and the American Indians* (Chicago, 1959).

ty. On the other hand, the first professor of philosophy in the New World, Alonzo de la Vera Cruz, argued in his first, and only course at the University of Mexico, that the Spaniards had no rights to the Indian domains, and therefore they should go back to Europe and leave the Indians alone. De la Vera Cruz was removed as professor and sent to lower Yucatan. Eventually he and Las Casas won the argument in theory, but lost it in fact. They got the Spanish government and the Pope to declare that the Indians were fully human, and were created in the image of God. Pope Paul III declared in 1537, "We...consider, however, that the Indians are truly men and that they are not only capable of understanding the Catholic faith, but, according to our information, they desire exceedingly to receive it."[2] Las Casas was convinced that the Indians were potentially better morally than the Europeans, since they had not become corrupt through all the baleful influences of the European Church and State. If properly instructed in Christianity they would become the ideal human beings that Christianity should produce — better Europeans than the Europeans.

Unfortunately, no matter how much good Christian humanistic argument Las Casas and his supporters could set forth, they could not stop the conquest and rape of America. In view of what was happening, racial theories were no longer idle speculations about the curious diversities of mankind, but were now crucial in justifying the mistreatment of the Indians, and the enslavement of Africans to replace the rapidly dying natives of America as the work force for the exploitation of the New World. The Spanish debate foreshadowed what was to come. The theories offered first by the Spaniards and Portuguese in the 16th century, mainly about Indians, and then the theories offered in the 17th and 18th centuries, mainly by the English, English Americans and the French about Africans, provide the basic structures

---

2. Cited in Hanke, *The Spanish Struggle for Justice*, p. 73. The Bull is dated June 9, 1537. There is a separate study of it by Hanke, "Pope Paul III and the American Indians," *Harvard Theological Review*, XXX (1937), pp. 65-102.

of racist thought for the next centuries. As I shall try to show, it is during the Enlightenment that what Hume called the application of the experimental method of reasoning to moral subjects, produced the basic justifications for modern racist theories with regard to people of color, as well as a secular basis for anti-Semitism.

The basic argument of the Spanish racist theorists was that the Indians were not fully human, as evidenced by their irrationality, their immorality and their inability to make prudential decisions. The evidence for all of this was alleged to be empirical descriptions of the state of affairs prevailing in America. The condition of the Indians and their behavior showed they needed the guidance and control of rational, moral men (i.e., European Christians), and hence were natural slaves. The humanistic opposition headed by Las Casas denied the facts adduced, and offered other ones seeking to establish the rationality and morality of the Indians, as well as the immorality of the Europeans. What might be lacking in their present performance could be overcome by training and education. Hence, for the humanists, the Indians had at least the potentiality to be fully human, though they might now be degenerate human beings.

The other side usually claimed that the sub-human condition of the Indians was either permanent or pretty much so. How could this be, if everyone, Indian, European, Asiatic, African, was part of the same Divine Creation of man? Except for a few hardy souls in the Renaissance, almost every thinker accepted the Biblical framework as the picture of where man came from (any other view would have been heretical). Hence most of the literature about the origins of the American Indians in the 16th and 17th centuries attempted to trace them back to a group whose connection with the Biblical world had supposedly already been established. Then the present state of the Indians and the present state of the Africans must be explained as the result of some sort of degenerative process, due either to climate and conditions of life, to isolation from the world of Christian "civilization," or to some Divine Action explained in the Bible.

The Biblical explanation that God in darkening the skin

Bases of Modern Racism

color of certain people was also cursing them and condemning them to an inferior human status, was, and still is, a popular explanation for the racist, desiring to explain first European, and then white superiority. The curse of Ham, the rejection of Ishmael, and the rejection of the Jews for refusing to recognize Jesus as the Messiah accounted for the desired colonial policy and the Inquisition attitude (and was adopted by many English and Anglo-American theorists). The Africans (i.e., Ethiopians) became black as a result of Divine Action, and were thereby made permanently inferior. The Jews were darkened by God's rejection of them, and developed a special obnoxious smell (and maybe tails and horns). All of this would remain true until the end of time.

The humanistic Christians, who denied much of the data employed by the racists, saw whatever degenerative effects there were as remediable, through Christianizing everybody and giving them the "benefits" of European education and culture.

— The modern philosophical defense of racism was to be worked out by those who either rejected, ignored, or revised the Biblical account, and tried to work out either a polygenetic account of human origins, with an associated claim that different origins implied different human natures; or a degenerative account in which being nonwhite or non-Christian was a biological or psycho-spiritual disease, making those so infected presently inferior.

— The theories of the nature of man that predominated in Western philosophy, especially from the Renaissance to the Enlightenment, should have had nothing to do with skin color or religion. The dominant theme, at least from Montaigne to Kant, is that man is seen, or defined, in terms of his psychological or psychic states. Montaigne painted himself (and presumably everyone else could do the same) in terms of his inner stream of consciousness, his thoughts and his emotions. Descartes defined himself as a thinking substance. And so on. Such theories imply that they should be neutral about the external features of people, their size, shape, color, or religious practices. Yet these theories quickly became transformed into justifications of the social superiority of white Christians over everybody else.

The transformations occur with the development of the degeneracy theory in terms of the emerging "science of man" in the Enlightenment, with detailed scientific explanations of how some human beings degenerated into their present miserable and awful state; they also occur with the development of the heretical pre-Adamite theory into forceful explanation of the fixed inferior status of non-Adamites (who were, of course, nonwhite).

The degeneracy theory started to come into its own in the views of John Locke, for whom everyone was *created* equal, and endowed with the natural rights of life, liberty and property. Locke tried to remain within orthodox Christianity, and apparently accepted the Biblical account of man's origins. However, the equality at creation and the endowment of natural rights no longer had to apply in 17th century America, because (a) the Indians and the Africans were not properly using their land, and (b) they had been captured in "just wars," and so could be enslaved. Locke, who was one of the architects of English colonial policy (and the drafter of the Constitution for the Carolinas), saw the Indians and Africans as failing to mix their labors with the land, and thus failing to create property as an extension of their persons. Hence they had no property as their natural right due to their own failings. They also had properly lost their liberty "by some Act that deserves Death" (presumably opposing the Europeans) and hence could be enslaved.[3] Their lands were wastelands. The Europeans were therefore justified in turning them into property, and enslaving the resistors.

Locke saw what was happening as due to the personal failures of the natives of Africa and America. Why they had failed needed more explanation. And the degeneracy theories worked out by Montesquieu, Buffon and Blumenbach would explain that the factors that led some peoples

---

3. Cf. John Locke, *Locke's Two Treatises of Government*, Lasslett ed., (Cambridge, 1966) *Second Treatise*, Sec. 23, p. 302. See also Harry M. Bracken, "Essence, Accident, and Race," *Hermathena* (forthcoming).

to change from white skinned to dark-skinned involved ways of life that were far inferior to those of Europeans.

During the 18th century there was a groundswell of interest and concern with why these people did not look and behave like Christian Europeans. There was a vast amount of literature on why blacks are black, why people speak primitive and inferior languages, and such matters. The application of the experimental method of reasoning to these problems brought forth two kinds of results, one a highly elaborated degeneracy theory, and the other a polygenetic explanation that claimed the differences between whites and nonwhites were fixed and permanent. Part of the battle between these basic accounts involved the question of whether there is a basic unity of mankind or a basic diversity.

Almost all of the degeneracy theorists took it for granted that the natural state of man is to be white and that Adam and Noah were white. (An exception to this theory was John Mitchell, M.D. who said, in 1745: " ... the white people who look on themselves as the primitive Race of Man, from a certain Superiority or Worth, either supposed or assumed, seem to have the least Pretensions to it of any, either from History or Philosophy; for they seem to have degenerated more from the primitive and original Complexion of Mankind, in *Noah*, and his Sons, than even the *Indians* and Negroes.")[4]

Montesquieu had given the most elaborate version of the ancient climate theory in his *Esprit des Loix* to account for the differences of human beings and their cultures. Linnaeus, the founder of modern biology, in his classification of mankind, though maintaining a unity of the human species, divided it as follows, as due to education and situation.

1. *Wild Man.* Four-footed, mute, hairy.
2. *American (i.e., Indian).* Copper-colored, choleric, erect. *Hair* black, straight, thick; *nostrils* wide; *face* harsh; *beard* scanty;

---

4. John Mitchell, "An Essay upon the Causes of the Different Colours of People in Different Climates," *Royal Society of London Philosophical Transactions,* XLIII (1744-45), p. 146.

obstinate, content, free. Paints himself with fine red lines. *Regulated* by customs.
3. *European.* Fair, sanguine, brawny. *Hair* yellow, brown, flowing; *eyes* blue; *gentle* acute, inventive. *Covered* with close vestments. *Governed* by laws.
4. *Asiatic,* Sooty, melancholy, rigid. *Hair* black; *eyes* dark; severe, haughty, covetous. *Covered* with loose garments. *Governed* by opinions.
5. *African;* Black, phlegmatic, relaxed. *Hair* black, frizzled; *skin* silky; *nose* flat; *lips* tumid; *crafty,* indolent, negligent. Anoints himself with grease. Governed by caprice.[5]

The classification obviously makes being white the best, and black the worst. Linnaeus suggested the differences were due to climate and social environment.

The pure climate theory was coming under scientific attack as an adequate explanation by the mid-18th century. Enough generations of Europeans had been living in Africa or Central and South America, and enough generations of Africans had been living in North America and Europe to indicate that no significant changes were occurring as the result of different climates. The greatest 18th century biologist, Count Buffon, tried to offer a more complete explanation in his *Histoire naturelle.* Buffon started from the premise that "White, then appears to be the primitive color of Nature" and that various people "have undergone various changes by the influence of climate, food, mode of living, epidemic diseases, and the mixture of dissimilar individuals".[6] These changes, resulting in black, tawny, yellowish, brown, and degenerate white (Laplanders and Eskimos) groups that are fairly permanent, have produced a pretty dismal picture of most of the human race. Buffon gave the following descriptions of some nonwhite groups; "they are gross, superstitious and stupid" (Eskimos); "they are gross, stupid and

---

5. Linnaeus, (Karl von Linne), *A General System of Nature through the Three Grand Kingdoms of Animals, Vegetables, and Minerals* (London, 1806), I, section "Mammalia. Order I. Primates."
6. Georges Louis Leclerc, Comte de Buffon, *Natural History, General and Particular,* trans. by William Smellie, 2nd ed. (London, 1785), III, *The Natural History of Man,* Sec. IX, "Of the Varieties of the Human Species," p. 207.

brutal" (Tatars); they "are effeminate, peaceable, indolent, superstitious, submissive, ceremonious and parasitical" (Chinese); "their indolence and stupidity make them insensible to every (useful) pleasure" (the Negroes of Sierra Leone); "though some were more savage, cruel and dastardly than others; yet they were equally stupid, ignorant and destitute of arts and industry" (the North American Indians). In contrast he claimed: "The most temperate climate lies between the 40th and 50th degree of latitude, and it produces the most handsome and beautiful men. It is from this climate that the ideas of the genuine colour of mankind, and of the various degrees of *beauty* ought to be derived.... The civilized situated under this zone, are Georgia, Circassia, the Ukraine, Turkey in Europe, Hungary, the south of Germany, Italy, Switzerland, France, and the northern part of Spain. The natives of those territories are the most handsome and most beautiful people in the world."[7]

Buffon's work, supposedly the result of the best empirical research of the time, accounted for human variety in racist terms. Whites were the best in terms of beauty, intelligence and civilization. Everyone else suffered from some degree of degeneracy. Now that the factors causing this were known, remedial action could be taken by moving everybody to the belt between Paris and the Caucasus Mountains, feeding them French food, and giving them a European education and way of life. Then, in several generations, everyone would be white and civilized.

Buffon provided the model for the degeneracy theories for the next century. His views were followed and improved upon by Lord Kames, Oliver Goldsmith, J. F. Blumenbach (the official founder of anthropology), and his successor, James Prichard. Some of the supporters of the degeneracy theory including Buffon, were against slavery, and some fought for the improvement of the conditions of nonwhites. Blumenbach and Prichard, while diagnosing the causes of present Negro and Indian inferiority in terms of physical

---

7. *Ibid.,* pp. 60, 65, 71, 146, 170, 181, 205-07.

and environmental factors, battled most forcefully against the more virulent racists who claimed the state of affairs could never be changed. Blumenbach called the Africans "his black brethren," and like the abbé Grégoire, kept producing evidence that nonwhites had the potentiality to achieve the same sort of civilization as whites; he pointed out cases where this had already happened — cases of black writers, scientists, and artists. Prichard (who gave the most idealized Europeanized pictures of nonwhites, looking like perfect Europeans, except dark-skinned) kept appealing to the fact that anyone could become a convert to Christianity, as missionaries were proving every day. Therefore, everybody had the potentiality to be as good as the best European.

Perhaps the leading antiracist of the late 18th century, the abbé Grégoire, was himself arguing from the degeneracy theory. Grégoire devoted his life to arguing for equality for Jews and Africans. His first work, on the Jewish question is entitled *Essay on the political, moral and physical Regeneration of the Jews*.[8] As the title suggests, Grégoire saw the Jews of his day as having degenerated from their former state and to be in need of regeneration. The degeneration in the Jewish case was due primarily to social factors, Christian anti-Semitism forcing the Jews to live unhealthful and indecent lives. Grégoire foresaw that by eliminating anti-Semitism, by giving the Jews citizenship, by changing the Jews' way of life, their basic spiritual goodness could emerge, and they would lead the world into the Messianic Age. The celebrated case of Moses Mendelssohn already proved that a Jew could be an important leader of the spiritual Enlightenment, if given the opportunity. What Grégoire envisioned, and was trying to bring about, was that the Jews could be emancipated by being made the best Europeans, the leaders of European culture, and of its religious spirit. Ultimately, he hoped this could lead them to become Christians, and the future leaders of the ultimate climax of human history, the Messianic Age.

---

8. Henri Grégoire, *Essai sur la Regeneration, morale et politique des juifs,* (Metz, 1789) (photoreproduced, Paris, 1968).

When he took on the black problem, as in *An Inquiry concerning the Intellectual and Moral Faculties and Literature of Negroes,* and in his role as Patriarch of Haiti, Grégoire started from the view of his time that Africans were at a low stage of culture and civilization.[9] Like his case in regard to the Jews, he insisted it wasn't their fault, but was due to oppression and lack of opportunity. Against the views of his contemporaries, he had to argue that the moral and intellectual qualities were there, but were being suppressed. That some Africans had already written books, were scientists, professors and artists, all in the European sense, showed the potentiality was there. Haiti was to prove it, under Grégoire's religious guidance. The Haitians, relieved of European oppression, uncorrupted by the worst aspects of Europe, its *ancien régime* and corrupt Church, would develop a republic that would be the beacon light unto the nations.

Grégoire's marvelous humanistic Messianism seems to be based in part on the degeneracy theory. He saw the oppressed, the Jews and the Africans, as functioning less well than they should or could, because of adverse environmental factors. The elimination of these through political and spiritual change would make the oppressed better Europeans than Europeans. Like Las Casas, whom he so admired, Grégoire saw the solution to racist oppression in making everybody an equal participant in European (and especially French) culture. This I submit, is a form of liberal racism, making the best of the European experience the model for everyone, and the eventual perfection of mankind consisting in everyone becoming creative Europeans.

The degeneracy theory had three reformist advocates — Grégoire, Blumenbach and Prichard — who wanted to improve the situation of those who had either been naturally or forcibly subjected to degeneration. On the other side, it had those who just wanted to portray or lament what had happened, and leave it at that. The author of the article "Ne-

---

9. Henri Grégoire, *De la Littérature des Negres,* Paris, 1808), translated by D. B. Warden as *An Enquiry concerning the Intellectual and Moral Faculties, and Literature of Negroes* (Brooklyn, 1810). Both works were photoreproduced in 1971.

gro" in the first American edition of the *Encyclopedia Brittanica* presented this view: "NEGRO, *Homo pelli nigra,* a name given to a variety of the human species, who are entirely black, and are found in the Torrid zone, especially in that part of Africa which lies within the tropics. In the complexion of negroes we meet with various shades; but they likewise differ far from other men in all the features of their face. Round cheeks, high cheek-bones, a forehead somewhat elevated, a short, broad, flat nose, thick lips, small ears, ugliness, and irregularity of shape, characterize their external appearance. The negro women have the loins greatly depressed, and very large buttocks, which give the back the shape of a saddle. Vices the most notorious seem to be the portion of this unhappy race: idleness, treachery, revenge, cruelty, impudence, stealing, lying, profanity, debauchery, nastiness and intemperance, are said to have extinguished the principles of natural law, and to have silenced the reproofs of conscience. They are strangers to every sentiment of compassion, and are an awful example of the corruption of man when left to himself."[10]

Presumably the African way of life had produced this degeneracy. And now one could recognize this sad state of affairs, but not do much about it.

The degeneracy theory at its best and worst still saw an original unity of human nature, and usually a pliability that allowed for improvement. Its most humanitarian advocates saw it as accounting for why at their stage in history, whites were superior and people of color inferior. The inferiority would be overcome either if the nonwhites became white, or if they acquired the culture and civilization of the whites. The white world was the ideal. (And it was Buffon and Blumenbach who created the term "Caucasian" for white primarily because their favorite people in terms of beauty, and their favorite skulls in terms of symmetry, came from Caucasian countries.)

In contrast to the degeneracy theory, a more hopeless kind

---

10. *Encyclopedia Brittanica,* 3rd edition (Philadelphia, 1798), XII, p. 794. The *Encyclopedia Brittanica* kept explaining why Negroes were mentally and morally inferior up to the 14th edition.

of racism emerged from the polygenetic theory. The first serious proposals of a polygenetic explanation of human origins already contain the germs of the racist views to be generated out of this theory. In the early 16th century Paracelsus contended that the inhabitants of the New World were not descended from the Biblical Adam, but had a different source, which had also produced nymphs, sirens, griffins and salamanders, all beings without souls. Paracelsus provided a possible justification for treating them as sub-human. Giordano Bruno, later in the 16th century, suggested that the Indians, the Ethiopians, the inhabitants of the caves of Neptune, the Pygmies, Giants, and others, "cannot be traced to the same descent [as the rest of the human world] nor are they sprung from the generative force of a single progenitor."[11] Again this would provide a basis for differentiating types of mankind.

The form of the polygenetic theory that was to provide the fundamental justification for the most thorough racism up to Darwin and the Civil War was the pre-Adamite theory, the view that there were men before Adam, who were the result of a separate (and unequal) creation. The classical formulation of this view was proposed by the heretical theologian, Isaac La Peyrère (1596-1676), in his work *Prae-Adamitae,* written in 1641 and published in 1655.[12] La Peyrère was primarily concerned with justifying his Messianic vision, that the Jewish Messiah would arrive soon and rule

---

11. Paracelsus discussed this in his *Astronomia magna,* and *Weiteres zum Astronomia magna*. Translations of the main texts are given in James Sydney Slotkin, *Readings in Early Anthropology* (Chicago, 1965), p. 42. Giordano Bruno's statement appears in his *Opera Latine Conscripta,* ed. F. Fiorentino et al. (Naples, 1879-91), I, part II, p. 282. On Renaissance polygenetic theories, see R. H. Popkin, "The Pre-Adamite Theory in the Renaissance," in Festschrift for Paul Oskar Kristeller, forthcoming.

12. Isaac la Peyrère, *Prae-Adamitae,* (Amsterdam 1655). The work appeared in several editions in Holland and Basel. An English translation, *Men before Adam* appeared in 1656, and a Dutch one in 1661. For details about La Peyrère's general theory, see R. H. Popkin, "The Marrano Theology of Isaac La Peyrère," *Studi filosophia,* forthcoming.

the world with the King of France. As central support of his thesis, La Peyrère argued that the Bible deals only with Jewish history, not world history. Prior to Adam, there were millions of people, pre-Adamites, who lived in a pretty awful state of nature. Then God created Adam and began Jewish history to save mankind. Jewish history developed through two stages, the Election of the Jews from Adam to Jesus, and the Rejection of the Jews from Jesus to the mid-17th century. Now the last stage will occur, the Recall of the Jews and after it the Messianic Age, in which everybody will be saved, pre-Adamites, Adamites, post-Adamites, regardless of what they believe or what they look like.

La Peyrère's evidence for his world-shaking view included much material from ancient pagan history which showed that various Near Eastern cultures had histories older than the Bible; that evidence from the Voyages of Exploration showed that Chinese and Mexican history was independent of, and older than, Biblical history; and that anthropological data about the Eskimos (about whom he had written a study), the Polynesians, and the Indians, and other critical information challenged the authenticity of the existing text of the Bible. La Peyrère was considered the greatest heretic of his day. His book was burned and banned everywhere. His views were condemned and he was forced to recant. His theory is only minimally racist in that he held that everyone would be saved, but that in this marvelous finale of human history, Jewish bodies would resurrect better than others. (He also held that the Jews would become less dark-skinned when they were recalled by God.)

La Peyrère's pre-Adamism accounts, as the author kept proclaiming, for the varieties of mankind, and for their different cultures and histories. In his view, all people except Jews are pre-Adamites. The explanatory power of the theory was lost on most of his contemporaries because of its heretical denial of the accepted Biblical account of man's origin. Although his work was constantly being refuted from 1655 onward, its polygenetic thesis kept being revived as the best explanation of the new findings in geology, biology, archeology, anthropology, and history that conflicted with the

Bible. The marvelous racist possibilities of the theory began to emerge during the Enlightenment among people who no longer took the Bible seriously, and these possibilities were developed into a powerful "scientific" defense of racism in 19th century America.[13]

One of Count Buffon's major and most lasting contributions was his definition of a biological species as any group of organisms that could crossbreed and produce fertile offspring. His interfertility criterion indicated that Africans, American Indians, Tatars, Mongols, Polynesians, Eskimos, Chinese, Europeans, Jews, Moslems, Hindus, and others were all members of the human species. The explorers, colonizers and slave traders had produced enough biological data in terms of illegitimate offspring to confirm Buffon's claim. However, this did not mean that there could not be basic and fixed differences among human beings that made some permanently superior and others permanently inferior.

— As long as the pre-Adamite theory was the scandal of European theology, few actually advocated it. David Hume apparently accepted a polygenetic view of man's origin, since in his *Natural History of Religion* he made no effort to trace a linear development of man from the ancient Jews to the modern world, and presented practically no historical connection between Judaism and Christianity (which he saw more as emerging from pagan polytheism.) In his *History of England,* he again did not follow the then usual attempt to derive British history from Biblical history, but began it with the indigenous pagan state of affairs at the time of Julius Caesar's invasion. In the essay "Of Miracles," Hume made clear that he thought the account of man's origins and of his development through Jewish history was extremely implausible, and that it would take a miracle to make a reasonable man believe in it.

Hume had claimed at the outset of his writings in the *Treatise of Human Nature* that "human nature" could best be

---

13. By the American school of ethnologists centering mainly around Dr. Samuel Morton and his followers. On the development of this school *see* William Stanton, *The Leopard's Spots* (Chicago, 1960).

studied by gleaning observations from human historical behavior, and generalizing from this according to the Newtonian method of experimental reasoning, that is, making inductions from observed cases. The results of this kind of research with regard to the race question appear in Hume's essay "Of National Character," written in answer to environmental and physical explanations of human differences. In a note added to the essay, Hume declared, "I am apt to suspect the negroes and in general all the other species of men (for there are four or five different kinds) to be naturally inferior to the whites. There never was a civilized nation of any other complexion than white, nor even any individual eminent either in action or speculation. No ingenious manufactures amongst them, no arts, no sciences. On the other hand, the most rude and barbarous of the whites, such as the ancient GERMANS, the present TARTARS, have still something eminent about them, in their valour, form of government, or some other particular. Such a uniform and constant difference could not happen in so many countries and ages, if nature had not made an original distinction betwixt these breeds of men. Not to mention our colonies, there are NEGROE slaves dispersed all over EUROPE, of which none ever discovered any symptoms of ingenuity, tho' low people, without education will start up amongst us, and distinguish themselves in every profession. In JAMAICA indeed they talk of one negroe as a man of parts and learning; but 'tis likely he is admired for very slender accomplishments like a parrot, who speaks a few words plainly."[14]

In this statement Hume, applying his method of historical experimental reasoning, appealed first to the alleged historical fact that there never has been a nonwhite civilization, while even the least cultured whites have been able to produce some kind of culture. Then the historical law governing the situation is offered, namely that "Such a uniform and constant difference could not happen in so many countries and ages, *if nature had not made an original distinction be-*

---

14. David Hume "Of National Characters" in *The Philosophical Works,* ed. by T. H. Green and T. H. Grose (London, 1882), III, p. 252n.

twixt these breeds of men" [my italics].[15] The countercase of the Negro in Jamaica is dismissed. Hume's own analysis in his discussion of general rules in the *Treatise* chapter on "Unphilosophical Probability" explained how prejudicial general rules like "all Irishmen are quarrelsome" could be believed in the face of counterevidence. And Hume seems to have been a perfect case of his own explanation of how prejudices can override evidence. (Hume referred to his learned friend, the Dutch economist, Isaac de Pinto, as a good man "tho a Jew.") With such views it is easy to understand why Hume was a good choice to run the English Colonial office in 1766.

Hume's view in the essay "Of National Characters" was quite influential. His relative, Lord Kames, put forth the view that the American Indians probably had a separate origin from the Europeans and this accounted for the superiority of the latter. The extreme racist, Edward Long, in his *History of Jamaica,* made Hume the source of the information that "the native Africans... are inferior to the rest of the species, and utterly incapable of all higher attainments of the human mind."[16] Long immediately attributed this state of affairs to the Africans having been separately created, or to their belonging to a separate (and lower) genus of the human species, a view also propounded by Charles White, in his *Regular Gradation of Man, and in Different Animals and Vegetables*....[17]

The explanation of the situation Hume described was soon

---

15. Cf. Hume, *A Treatise of Human Nature,* Book I, Part III, chap. xiii, Selby-Bigge ed. (Oxford, 1965), pp. 146-47. Hume's reference to De Pinto appears in an unpublished letter to Thomas Rouns, August 28, 1767. This, plus some other unpublished Hume letters concerning De Pinto will be published in a forthcoming contribution by me to the Festschrift for Ernest Campbell Mosner. Also see R. H. Popkin, "Hume and Isaac De Pinto," *Texas Studies in Literature and Language,* XII (1970), pp. 417-430; and "The Philosophical Basis of Eighteenth Century Racism," in *Racism in the Eighteenth Century* (Studies in Eighteenth Century Culture, Vol. 3), ed. Harold E. Pagliaro (Cleveland: The Press of Case Western Reserve University, 1974).

16. Edward Long, *The History of Jamaica* (London, 1774), II, Book III, chap. I, "Negroes," p. 376.

17. Charles White, *An Account of the Regular Gradation in Man, and in*

offered through a revival of Isaac La Peyrère's pre-Adamite theory. Various scientists and philosophers in England, France, Germany and America proposed the view in the early 19th century to account for new data, and to reconcile it with the Biblical account. The full development of the modern scientific version of the pre-Adamite theory came with the work of the American ethnologist, Dr. Samuel Morton of Philadelphia, and his disciples. Morton had patiently collected skulls, and measured their cranial capacity by filling them with pepper-seed, and then weighing the amount that could be fitted in each skull. His results first appeared in his masterpiece, *Crania Americana*....[18] This was followed by the work of his followers, Gliddon and Nott, and then the contribution of the great Swiss biologist, Louis Agassiz. The Mortonites set forth a powerful case for pre-Adamism, arguing (a) that skull measurements and paintings in Egyptian tombs showed that racial characteristics of various groups have been the same throughout recorded history, covering at least 3,000 years; (b) that the fixed racial characteristics included larger cranial capacity of whites, lower for Asiatics, still lower for Indians, and the lowest for Africans; (c) that the antiquity of these fixed differences could not fit in with Biblical chronology or with a theory of the monogenetic origin of mankind. Therefore, the best explanation of the data was the separate creation of different species of mankind, each with fixed characteristics including brain capacity.

While Morton and his followers were insisting that they were pure scientists, not moralists or theologians, the religious and racist implications were made clear in their presentations. Dr. Josiah Nott, in his two lectures at Louisiana

---

Different Animals and Vegetables; and from the Former to the Latter (London, 1799). On Long and White, see Winthrop D. Jordon, *White Over Black: American Attitudes Toward the Negro 1550-1812* (Chapel Hill: University of North Carolina Press, 1968), chap. XIII.

18. Samuel G. Morton, *Crania Americana; or, A Comparative View of the Skulls of Various Aboriginal Nations of North and South America: to which is Prefixed An Essay on the Varieties of the Human Species* (Philadelphia and London, 1839).

State University in 1848, on *The Biblical and Physical History of Man,* (which he called his "lectures on Niggerology"), claimed he was separating the actual history of mankind from the Biblical account by showing that the Bible dealt with the creation and development of the Adamites, the Caucasians, and not with the creation and development of the pre-Adamites, the rest of mankind.[19] Morton, Gliddon, Nott and Agassiz hammered at the supposed fixed differences between Adamites and pre-Adamites, insisting that these differences showed the perpetual inferiority of the pre-Adamites, and justified the continuous enslavement of the lowest of the pre-Adamites, the Africans. All this was always offered in the name of pure science.

Agassiz, who got into the argument late, started with a polygenetic theory about the origins of fish in the Atlantic and Pacific oceans. He came to America to get data, met Morton, and met his first Negro, a waiter in a restaurant in Philadelphia. He immediately wrote his mother in Switzerland of his horror, and his realization that blacks were a different species from whites. He then went to Harvard where he gave two lectures presenting the most complete version of the American pre-Adamite theory.[20] Agassiz insisted he believed in the unity of mankind in the sense that all people had moral and intellectual powers that made them human, all were in relation to the Deity, and all had the hope of eternal life. But this unity did not imply all people had the same origins. The scientific evidence showed that only a polygenetic explanation could account for the facts. The Bible did not dispute this, since it dealt only with Adamites (Jews and whites), and not Asiatics, Melanesians, Indians, Africans,

---

19. Josiah C. Nott, *Two Lectures on the Connection between the Biblical and Physical History of Man* (New York, 1849) (photoreproduced in 1969). On Nott's view, *see* Stanton, *op. cit.*

20. Agassiz's reaction to encountering a Negro is described in Stanton, *op. cit.,* pp. 102-04. His two lectures, Louis Agassiz, "The Geographical Distribution of Animals," and "The Diversity of Origin of the Human Races," appeared in the *Christian Examiner,* XLVIII (1850), pp. 181-204, and XLIX (1850), pp. 110-145. Cf. Edward Lurie, "Louis Agassiz and the Races of Man," *Isis,* XLV (1954), pp. 227-242.

and others. (Nott was so convinced of this that he wrote several papers contending the Hebrew term for black, or Ethiopian, "Kush", really meant "swarthy," and applied to Arabs, not Africans. The blacks just weren't in the Bible at all.)

Agassiz insisted he was only dealing with scientific matters — "Let the politicians, let those who feel themselves called upon to regulate human society, see what they can do with the results." By the end of the second lecture, Agassiz was pointing out the political racist results of his researches,

> ... it seems to us to be mock-philanthropy and mock-philosophy to assume that all races have the same abilities, enjoy the same powers, and show the same natural dispositions, and that in consequence of this equality are entitled to the same position in human society. History speaks here for itself.[21]

Then he suggested that since Africans had never developed regulated societies, had always been slaves, they should remain so, and that it was pointless to try to give Afro-Americans the educational or cultural benefits of European civilization.

American pre-Adamism was an extremely high-powered scientific theory geared to explaining the diversity of mankind on a polygenetic basis. Its adherents were happy that their theory, which they were convinced was vindicated by scientific research, was first stated by an heretical theologian, La Peyrère, who was martyred for speaking the truth. They wrote lots of essays on La Peyrère and made him the Galileo of anthropology. They were also delighted that their theory provided a "scientific" basis for racism and slavery. They offered it to leading Southern whites, Calhoun, Jefferson Davis, and others. When Morton died in 1851, the *Charleston Medical Journal* said

> ... we of the South should consider him as our benefactor, for aiding most materially in giving to the negro his true position as

---

21. Agassiz, "Diversity of Origin of the Human Races," p. 142.

an inferior race. We believe the time is not far distant, when it will be universally admitted that neither can "the leopard change his spots, nor the Ethiopian his skin".[22]

American pre-Adamism set forth a complete basis for justifying the permanent superiority of Caucasians over people of color, supposedly based on the best scientific evidence. Hegel had earlier elevated some of the central claims of this theory to the level of metaphysical truths in his *Philosophy of History*. He proclaimed that "In the Frigid and in the Torrid zone the locality of World-historical peoples cannot be found."[23] Then he tried to show by metaphysical geography that the Historical Spirit did not and could not operate among American Indians, Eskimos and Africans.

Scientific pre-Adamism fulfilled the intent of the original Spanish racist theories. It showed why whites were superior, and why the domination of the whites over the nonwhites was justified now and indefinitely into the future. It separated racial groups on a fixed and permanent basis. The theory left no hope of remedying or improving the condition of nonwhites (Nott worked very hard to establish that intermarriage wouldn't work by claiming the mixed breeds like mulattoes were biologically weaker than their parents. Morton insisted on constancy of type that would exhibit itself no matter how much racial mixing took place.)

The only price the racists had to pay for such a complete irremedial theory was to denigrate the Bible as the history of mankind. The Southerners by and large professed their racism consonant with their religion, and rejected Mortonism. Darwin's theory of evolution and Gobineau's theory of the inequality of races soon overwhelmed and supplanted Mortonism (though it survived for a while among the British anthropologists in the 1860's, and was revived by an American, Alexander Winchell in his *Pre-Adamites, or a Demonstration of the Existence of Men before Adam,* [1880], with

---

22. R. W. Gibbes, "Death of Samuel George Morton, M. D.," *Charleston Medical Journal*, VI (1851), p. 597.
23. Georg Wilhelm Friedrich Hegel, *The Philosophy of History* (London and New York, 1900), p. 80.

photographs of the pre-Adamites.) Nonetheless American pre-Adamism represented the paradigm case of a justification for permanent racial superiority of the Caucasians. And, unlike the degeneracy theories, it held up no hope for the gradual cure of nonwhite inferiority, since no process could turn pre-Adamites into Adamites. The rather benign theory of La Peyrère had become a sort of wonderful basis for modern biological racism.

An interesting twist on the situation was the use of the pre-Adamite theory[24] by Voltaire and Goethe to justify secular anti-Semitism, i.e., anti-Semitism not based on Christian theology. Voltaire was one of the first to assert that he believed the pre-Adamite theory. He believed it in La Peyrère's sense that only the Jews were Adamites, everybody else pre-Adamites, though the non-European ones were degenerate or inferior to the European ones. Voltaire saw the Adamites as a major menace to European civilization, since they kept infecting it with what he considered the horrible immorality of the Bible. Voltaire therefore insisted that Europe should separate itself from the Adamites, and seek its roots and heritage and ideals in the best of the pre-Adamite world — for him, the Hellenic world. Goethe's version was that the Jews were the descendants of Adam and Eve,

> But we, as well as Negroes and Laplanders, and slender men, who are handsomer than any of us, had certainly different ancestors; and this worthy company must confess that we at present differ in a variety of particulars from the genuine descendants of Adam, and that they, particularly where money is concerned, are superior to us all.[25]

Goethe's insistence that only Jews are Adamites was turned into a condemnation of them. It led German theorists to look for another source of mankind than the Biblical account. Their solution, the Aryan myth, denied the Jewish basis of

---

24. Voltaire's main discussions of this matter appear in his *Essai sur les moeurs,* the *Dictionnaire philosophique* articles on the Bible, and the appendices to the *Dictionnaire.*
25. Johann Wolfgang von Goethe, *Conversations of Goethe with Eckermann and Sort,* trans. by John Oxenford (London, 1882), 1828, p. 332.

Western civilization, indeed making the Jews the chronic enemies. Aryanism became a positive pre-Adamism that was finally used to justify German superiority over everybody.[26]

The two basic modern racial theories — degeneracy and pre-Adamism — were, of course, developed to justify what was happening in modern European history, the expansion of Europe and the exploitation of the Third World. As theories about why human beings differ, they could each be stated in nonevaluative terms. The first theory is a monogentic account of the human scene. If, as the late Louis Leakey and the French Nobel Laureate, Jacques Monod, claimed, the entire human race came from a single family originating in Central Africa, a family probably dark-skinned, then there must have been a series of mutational developments that has led to the present diverse state of affairs. But the developments should be describable without judging them either as forms of degeneracy or improvement.

Similarly a polygenetic theory, such as that of Carleton Coons, can explain human difference as resulting from different origins, without making any of the original or final results better or worse, superior or inferior. As Frederick Douglass pointed out in his answer to the Mortonites,

> I sincerely believe, that the weight of the argument is in favor of the unity of the origin of the human race, or species — that the arguments on the other side are partial, superficial, utterly subversive of the happiness of man, and insulting to the wisdom of God. Yet, what if we grant they are not so? What, if we grant that the case, on our part, is not made out? Does it follow, that the Negro should be held in contempt? Does it follow that to enslave and imbrute him is either just or wise? I think not. Human rights stand upon a common basis; and by all the reason that they are supported, maintained and defended, for one variety of the human family, they are supported, maintained and defended for *all* the human family; because all mankind have the same wants, arising out of a common nature. A diverse origin does not disprove a common nature, nor does it disprove a united destiny.[27]

---

26. On this *see* Leon Poliakov, *Le Mythe aryenne* (Paris, 1972).
27. Frederick Douglass, "The Claims of the Negro Ethnologically Considered," (1854), reprinted in Louis Ruchames, *Racial Thought in America* (New York, 1970), p. 490.

Richard H. Popkin

If we are to overcome our racist heritage, I think we have first to realize that the question of human origins implies nothing about the merits of present-day human beings. Secondly, I think we have to take seriously the view developed by Alexander Von Humboldt, first against the Mortonites and later against Gobineau. Von Humboldt, who had gathered much important information about human cultural differences during his travels in North and South America, Europe and Siberia, was at first impressed by Morton's work. When he saw the moral and social implications of it, he wrote at the end of *Kosmos*,

> Whilst we maintain the unity of the human species, we at the same time repel the depressing (désolante) assumption of superior and inferior races of men. There are nations more susceptible of cultivation, more highly civilized, more ennobled by mental cultivation than others — but none in themselves nobler than others. All are in like degree designed for freedom.[28]

Von Humboldt developed an almost complete cultural relativism, in which each culture was to be appreciated in its own terms, and none graded as more noble than another. One might have bigger buildings, more books, scientific academies, and such things, than another, but this only showed the differences between the cultures, not that one was nobler than another.

Morton and his followers were flabbergasted at this sign of mushy-headed liberalism on the part of Von Humboldt. Morton wrote:

> Humboldt's word désolante is true in sentiment and in morals ... it is wholly inapplicable to physical reality. Nothing so humbles, so crushes my spirit, as to look into a mad-house, and behold the drivelling brutal idiocy so conspicuous in such places; it conveys a terrific idea of the disparity of human intelligences. But there is the unyielding, insuperable reality. It is désolante indeed to think, to *know*, that many of these poor mortals were born, were created so! But it appears to me to make little difference in the *sentiment* of the question whether they came into the world without their wits, or whether they lost them after-

---

28. Alexander von Humboldt, *Cosmos: A Sketch of a Physical Description of the Universe* (London, 1888), I, p. 368.

wards. And so, I would add, it makes little difference whether the mental inferiority of the Negro, the Samoyede, or the Indian, is natural or acquired; for, if they ever possessed equal intelligence with the Caucasian, they have lost it; and if they never had it, they had nothing to lose. One party would arraign Providence for creating them originally different, another for placing them in circumstances by which they inevitably became so. Let us search out the truth, and reconcile it afterwards.[29]

The argument between the Mortonites and Von Humboldt bears much resemblance to that now going on between Jensen, Shockley, and Hernstein, and their opponents. Like Morton, the former are contending that they have measured something that establishes the mental inferiority of blacks. The opposition points out that the scientific evidence is not good, *and* that the moral consequences being draw constitute racism at its worst. If one took Von Humboldt's position seriously, then no matter what differences might be established between human groups in terms of physical, psychological or mental properties, each should still be evaluated in its own terms, and not graded as better or worse than another. All are human and entitled to express their humanity in their own terms, and none is nobler than another.

To conclude, this examination of the root theories of modern racism has, I believe, shown how two major kinds of theories developed to justify Christian European superiority over nonwhite and non-Christian groups. The application of the theories has caused an enormous toll in human suffering. The theories were designed to explain the diversities of mankind so that Caucasians must be the best. Part of the theories can be separated out as neutral scientific claims about human origins that can be evaluated on the basis of present and future scientific evidence. The rest, centering around the claims of Caucasian superiority, and justifying Western dominance of the Third World, have to be combated by a thorough-going cultural relativism and cultural plural-

---

29. Morton's letter to Gliddon, cited in Henry S. Patterson's "Life of Samuel G. Morton," in Josiah C. Nott and George R. Gliddon, *Types of Mankind* (Philadelphia, 1854), pp. li-lii.

ism. Until this is done, Western racism will continue to take its toll. As Grégoire pointed out, the soul has neither color nor sex, and those who believe in "the nobility of the skin will suffer the same fate as that of parchment"; namely, they will crumble.[30] When we can accept everybody both as created equal, still each an image of God, expressing his image in his own way, i.e., "doing his own thing," then the modern racist world will have ended. Then, perhaps, we can arrive at the goal set by Wilhelm von Humboldt:

> ... that of establishing our common humanity — of striving to remove the barriers that prejudice and limited views of every kind have erected amongst men, and to treat all mankind without reference to religion, nation, or colour, as one fraternity, one great community, fitted for the attainment of one great object, the unrestrained development of the psychical powers. This is the ultimate and highest aim of society.... Thus deeply rooted in the innermost nature of man, and even enjoined upon him by his highest tendencies — the recognition of the bond of humanity becomes one of the noblest leading principles in the history of mankind.[31]

---

30. Henri Grégoire, *De la Noblesse de la peau ou du préjuge des blancs contre la couleur des Africains et celle de leurs descendans noirs et sang-mêlés,* (Paris, 1826), p. 51. On this *see* Ruth Necheles, *The Abbe Grégoire 1787-1831, The Odyssey of an Egalitarian* (Westport, Connecticut, 1971), chap. 13.

31. Cited at the end of Alexander von Humboldt's *Cosmos,* I, p. 369 from Wilhelm von Humboldt's *Ueber die Kawi-Sprache,* Band III, p. 426.

Bases of Modern Racism

Appendix on Hume

THE MATERIAL ON PP. 142-144 ON HUME MAY SEEM SOMEWHAT inadequate to justify making Hume central in the development of polygenetic racism. In my brief comments, I tried to show (a) that Hume held, at least by implication, that mankind had no particular beginning, and that it did not develop from the Biblical world; (b) that he was attempting to find laws of human nature by making inductions from historical evidence; (c) that his law about the race question was based upon the application of his historical, experimental method of reasoning; (d) that his racial law influenced later racists, and formed a bridge to American pre-Adamism.

Since people may have doubts about some of these claims, I am here including additional evidence, plus some of the history of the impact of Hume's racial law on Kant and some American racists, as well as the attempts to disprove it by James Beattie, the abbé Grégoire and American abolitionists.

Hume's picture of the development of mankind is somewhat obscure, but certain general themes come out in his essays, which were the presentations of his major applications of the experimental method of reasoning to moral subjects. In the essay, "Of the Populousness of Antient Nations," Hume began by stating, "There is very little ground, either from reason or experience, to conclude the universe eternal or incorruptible." (Green and Grose III, p. 381). The world plus each individual form in it has "its infancy, youth, manhood, and old age; and 'tis probable, that in all these variations, man, equally with every animal and vegetable, will partake." (Green and Grose, III, *loc. cit.*) The general picture that emerges in several of the essays is that laws of human development involve a transformation from a state of barbarous human behavior to a more civilized state through the influence of various political, social and intellectual factors. The barbarous state of affairs existed all over the world, and Hume saw it as still existing in large parts of Asia,

Richard H. Popkin

throughout Africa, America and the polar regions. Nothing is said that indicates either that human development had a unitary place of origin, or a linear development. England was barbarous when Caesar invaded; the ancient middle East was barbarous in Moses' time; Africa was barbarous in 1750, and other regions at various times.

For Hume the study of history was the way (and the only way) to find information about what has gone on beyond our own experience in our own lives:

> And indeed, if we consider the shortness of human life, and our limited knowledge, even of what passes in our own time, we must be sensible that we should be forever children in understanding, were it not for this invention (history), which extends our experience to all past ages, and to the most distant nations; making them contribute as much to our improvement in wisdom, as if they had actually lain under our observation. A man acquainted with history may, in some respect, be said to have lived from the beginning of the world, and to have been making continual additions to his stock of knowledge in every century. *(Of the Study of History,* Green and Grose, *Essays,* Vol. II, p. 390)

Hume's method, as exhibited in several of his essays, was to survey the state of affairs in ancient times, on the basis of information given by various Greek and Roman historians, and to survey the modern scene on the basis of recent studies and accounts of what was apparent in various parts of the world. Then, he usually described a barbarous state of affairs, and showed how it had changed into the state of affairs in modern Europe, especially in England. Factors were then isolated that led to the transformation, demonstrated in his essays on "The Rise of the Arts and Sciences," and "The Natural History of Religion."

Hume was not seeking linear progression, but rather social, cultural and psychological factors that when active led men from barbarism to civilization, and when inactive or suppressed had reverse effects.

In his picture, Hume excluded Biblical history as relevant. His only explanation for so doing was offered at the end of the essay "Of Miracles" (which is thought to be one of his earliest writings, drafted probably in 1734). Considering the

Pentateuch "as the production of a mere human writer and historian," Hume then evaluated it as follows:

> Here then we are first to consider a book, presented to us by a barbarous and ignorant people, written in an age when they were still more barbarous, and in all probability long after the facts which it relates, corroborated by no concurring testimony, and resembling those fabulous accounts, which every nation gives of its origins. Upon reading this book, we find it full of prodigies and miracles. It gives an account of a state of the world and of human nature entirely different from the present: Of our own fall from that state: Of the age of man, extended to near a thousand years: Of the the destruction of the world by a deluge: Of the arbitrary choice of one people as the favorites of heaven; and that people the countrymen of the author: Of their deliverance from bondage by prodigies the most astonishing imaginable: I desire any one to lay his hand upon his heart, and after serious consideration declare, whether he thinks the falsehood of such a book, supported by such testimony, would be more extraordinary and miraculous than all the miracles it relates. (Green and Grose, IV, p. 108)

The fact that the *Pentateuch* is the work of a barbarous and ignorant people, that it has no supporting evidence, that it describes a world and human nature different from our own, that it looks like other fabulous stories of human origins and developments, makes it totally implausible to the reasonable man. Thus, it can be discounted as history (and could only be believed by a miracle occurring within the believer).

Having stated his conviction that the Biblical account has no status, Hume offered no other. He just began his consideration of the history of any society at the point where "credible" written records existed. So, the *History of England* starts with Caesar's invasion, since all information before then consists only of the memories and oral traditions of "barbarous nations."

> The only certain means by which nations can indulge their curiosity in researches concerning their remote origin, is to consider the language, manners, and customs of their ancestors, and to compare them with those of their neighboring nations. The fables, which are commonly employed to supply the place of true history, ought entirely to be disregarded; or if any exception be

admitted to this general rule, it can only be in favor of the ancient Grecian fictions, which are so celebrated and so agreeable, that they will ever be the objects of the attention of mankind. (*History of England,* Vol. I, pp. 1, 2)

The Biblical origin of mankind is removed. Other origins are just fables and fictions. So, no effort need be expended on the origin of mankind. Instead, human nature is to be studied where it is or was, in terms of how it developed from barbarism to civilization, without concern about the origin of the barbarous world.

This perspective, I submit, is an implicit polygenetic view. Hume rejected the major monogenetic view of his time, that of the Bible, and cut off inquiry into any alternative. His analyses are, by-and-large, comparative about already existing societies.

The essay "Of National Characters" is basically a discussion of whether cultural differences can be accounted for by moral or physical causes. Moral causes are defined as "all circumstances, which are fitted to work on the mind as motives or reasons, and which render a peculiar set of manners habitual to us;" (Green and Grose, Vol. III, p. 244), while physical causes are:

> Those qualities of the air and climate, which are supposed to work insensibly on the temper, by altering the tone and habit of the body, and giving a particular complexion, which, though reflection and reason may sometimes overcome it, will yet prevail among the generality of mankind, and have some influence on their manners. (Green and Grose, *loc. cit.*)

Hume then insisted that moral causes determine national character, using the effects of poverty, hard labor, and idleness as examples of moral causes making people useless, or ignorant. Surveying ancient and modern history, Hume found moral causes (which included government and religion), determining the national character, not the physical ones such as climate or air. England seemed best because its mixed government and the mixture of religions did not generate a fixed national character, but rather allowed each

Englishman "to display the manners peculiar to him," i.e., to express his individuality.

If physical causes were the determinate ones, as Hume claimed they were, on plants and irrational animals, then degrees of heat and cold should also have a great influence on people. Hume said:

> And indeed there is some reason to think that all the nations, which live beyond the polar circles or between the tropics, are inferior to the rest of the species, and are incapable of all the higher attainments of the human mind. (p. 252)

Lest this deny his thesis, Hume added,

> The poverty and misery of the northern inhabitants of the globe, and the indolence of the southern from their few necessities, may, perhaps, account for this remarkable difference, without our having recourse to *physical* causes. (p. 252)

Hume's contention that there never was a nonwhite civilized nation, or any eminent nonwhite figure in history, was added as a footnote to the above passage in the 1753-54 edition of his essays. Hume claimed that his racial law was based on a general historical survey both of what happened with barbarous whites (the ancient Germans, the present Tatars, and present uneducated Europeans) — among whom some civilized behavior emerged, or was lacking in Negroes in Europe or America when they never showed "any symptoms of ingenuity." Hume's historical induction, that there is and always has been such a uniform and constant difference between white and nonwhites in "so many countries and ages," led him to conclude that this must be due to a natural, original distinction between these breeds of men.

Hume's racial law seems to come down to the contention that moral causes tend to lead whites to develop from barbarism to civilization, but that nature has made it impossible for these causes to operate among nonwhites. The support for the law is similar to that which Hume offered for his other contentions about human developmental behavior. It fits into his general theme of the transformation of men from

Richard H. Popkin

barbarians to civilized Europeans, except that nonwhites cannot participate in this development, because nature has so ordained it. Thus, for Hume, the barbarous situation of nonwhites is irremediable.

Winthrop Jordan, who has probably studied the English and American racist literature more closely than anyone else, says that Hume put the case of black inferiority "more baldly than anyone" and outdid the ancient philosophers "by hitching superiority to complexion".[32] Hume's view became influential in the discussions of whether blacks were naturally inferior. Immanuel Kant simply took it over as establishing that "The Negroes of Africa have by nature no feeling that rises above the trifling." As evidence for this claim, Kant said,

> Mr. Hume challenges anyone to cite a simple example in which a Negro has shown talents, and asserts that among the hundreds of thousands of blacks who are transported elsewhere from their countries, although many of them have even been set free, still not a single one was ever found who presented anything great in art or science or any other praiseworthy quality, even though among the whites some continually rise aloft from the lowest rabble, and through superior gifts earn respect in the world. So fundamental is the difference between the two races of man, and it appears to be as great in regard to mental capacities as in color. [Kant then cited African religious practices as a case in point.][33]

Kant then went on to praise the American Indians: "Among all savages there is no nation that displays so sublime a mental character as those of North America." A couple of pages later, he quoted a report of what Father Labat had been told by a Negro about how wives should be treated. Kant then commented, "And it might be that there were something in this which perhaps deserved to be considered;

---

32. Winthrop Jordon, *White Over Black* (Chapel Hill: University of North Carolina, 1968), p. 253.
33. Immanuel Kant, *Observations on the Feeling of the Beautiful and Sublime,* trans. by John T. Goldthwait (Berkeley, 1965), pp. 110-111 (first published in 1764).

but in short, this fellow was quite black from head to foot, a clear proof that what he said was stupid." (p. 113)

The French edition of Hume's *Essays* (Amsterdam, 1764) reinforced Hume's view as being true about Negro inferiority. The translator added his own footnote to Hume's, saying,

> "J'ai eu occasion de faire une expérience qui confirme le sentiment de Mr. Hume. J'ai remarqué que les jeunes Negres qui ont le plus d'esprit & de vivacité, lorsqu'on les applique aux Arts, & aux Sciences, y font d'abord de rapides progres; mais passé un certain terme, leurs idées se brouillent, & l'on prendroit en vain toutes les peines imaginables pour les pousser plus loin. ...,"[34]

thus indicating education for blacks was a waste of time.

Hume's view became important in the arguments about slavery in England and America. The critic Hume despised most, James Beattie (1735-1803), wrote his answer to Hume, *Essay on the Origin and Immutability of Truth* in 1770. Hume dismissed him as "that bigotted silly Fellow, Beattie ..." (*Letters,* II, p. 301) and Kant held about the same opinion of him. In his chapter dealing with the causes of the degeneracy of moral science, after treating the value of the study of history and of classical authors, Beattie digressed to attack Aristotle's view that some men are by nature slaves. Beattie pointed out that, Aristotle notwithstanding, many Greeks became slaves and that "many nations whom he [Aristotle] would have consigned to everlasting stupidity, have shown themselves equal in genius to the most exalted of human kind ..." (1776 ed., p. 310). Beattie suggested Aristotle should have inferred "man's natural and universal right to liberty," rather than "to devise some excuse for servitude."

Then Beattie turned to Hume's racism, and quoted the footnote from "Of National Characters," as an argument of "the superiority of white men over black." Beattie com-

---

34. David Hume, *Essais moraux et politiques,* 2nd ed., (Amsterdam, 1764), "La Caractere des Nations", p. 434n.

mented "These assertions are strong; but I know not whether they have any thing else to recommend them ..." (p. 310). Then he went to work to show Hume's evidence proved nothing. Hume would have to show that if Africans and Americans were introduced to the arts and sciences, they would remain insusceptible of cultivating them. The British and French two thousand years ago were just as savage as Africans and Americans are today, but they overcame it, showing that the civilizing process takes time. "And one may as well say of an infant, that he can never become a man, as of a nation now barbarous, that it never can be civilized ..." (p. 311).

Next, Beattie pointed out that to reach Hume's inductive conclusion, one would have had to survey "all the negroes that now are, or ever were, on the face of the earth." Since Africans have not written histories, the explorers' reports would never amount to sufficient proof about all Negroes at all times.

Then, Beattie went on, Hume's law just wasn't true. The Peruvian and Mexican empires required "men eminent both for action and speculation." The Africans and American Indians do have "many ingenious manufactures and arts among them, which even Europeans would find it no easy matter to imitate." They don't have sciences, because they are illiterate. But the Indians have great orators, said to be greatly superior to Europeans.

Also, Beattie argued, slave conditions "are not favourable to genius of any kind," but nonetheless there are cases of slaves who have become excellent handicraftsmen and musicians. The slaves seem able to learn the virtues and vices of their masters. The slave who is illiterate, knows no European language, is completely oppressed and treated "as if he were of a species inferior to the human" can hardly be expected to distinguish himself among Europeans, and to be regarded as a genius. But to suppose him inferior therefore, "is just as rational, as to suppose any private European of an inferior species, because he has not raised himself to the condition of royalty ... ." (p. 312).

The Europeans, had they not been able to write and use

iron, would still be as barbarous as the Africans or the American Indians. But the inventors of these arts did not make the other Europeans a superior species.

Then Beattie launched into a bit of cultural relativism: "That every practice and sentiment is barbarous which is not according to the usages of modern Europe, seems to be a fundamental maxim with some of our philosophers ..." (p. 312). But if the Africans or Indians had a Voltaire or a Lucian, his "plain historical account" of European practices like duelling, gambling, adultery would "... exhibit specimens of brutish barbarity and sottish infatuation, such as might vie with any that ever appeared in Kamscahatka[sic], California, or the land of the Hottentots ... ." (pp. 312-313).

Finally, Beattie pointed out that those who held to the natural inferiority of Negroes denied the Biblical unity of mankind as all descendants of Eve, and all equal creations of God; while denying Scripture, the racists were vindicating slavery. Beattie closed his critique with a denunciation of slavery, and a plea for Britons to abolish it. Beattie's humanitarianism here, and in his later work, *The Theory of Language,* appears to have been based on the unity and basic similarity of all mankind as the result of their common origins in God's creation. In the latter work he stated:

> ...ever since the flood, men have had the same faculties, have been placed in the same or in like circumstances, have felt the same wants, have found comfort in the same gratifications, and acted from the influence of the same motives; it is reasonable to infer, that the *thoughts* of men must in all ages have been nearly the same ... . (p. 306).[35]

Hume refused to answer any of Beattie's long attack on him, and just added an "advertissement" to subsequent editions of his essays, disowning his *Treatise of Human Nature,* the main object of Beattie's criticisms, as "that juven-

---

35. Another Scottish common sense thinker, James Ramsay, wrote an even more extensive critique of Hume's racism in his *Essay on the Treatment and Conversion of African Slaves in the British Sugar Colonies* (Dublin, 1784), chap. 4.

ile work, which the author never acknowledged." The discussion of Hume's racism never was taken up. (There is a curious letter of Hume's to the Comtesse de Boufflers of December 2, 1766, where he looked into a case she had asked him about of an alleged African prince, who was said to have gone to England, and had had something to do with the Secretary of the Royal Society. Hume investigated and concluded that the person was not a prince, and never had had anything to do with the Secretary. This seems to be Hume's sole interest in any African who went to Europe.)

Hume's racial view was taken up in a very important racist work, Edward Long's *History of Jamaica,* 1774, which went to great length to establish that Negroes were an inferior species. Long cited all sorts of authorities and data, including Hume's claim. "Mr. Hume presumes, from his observations on the native Africans, to conclude, that these are inferior to the rest of the species, and utterly incapable of all the higher attainments of the human mind . . . ." (Book III, Chapter I, p. 376). Long then proceeded to reject Beattie's answer to Hume. "Mr. *Beattie,* upon the principle of philanthropy, combats this opinion; but he is unfortunate in producing no demonstration to prove, that it is either lightly taken up, or inconsistent with experience." Beattie, Long claimed, mixes up Negroes and Mexicans, and uses evidence of Mexican intelligence to say that it is probable that Africans have some. But two hundred years of commerce with Africa have not yet produced any civilized blacks. They are still "but little divested of their primitive brutality; we cannot pronounce them insusceptible of civilization, since even apes have been taught to eat, drink, repose, and dress like men."

Winthrop Jordan cites the use of Hume's view in the American debates about slavery in the 1770's in an anonymous work, *Personal Slavery Established, by the Suffrages of Custom and Right Reason. Being a Full Answer to the Gloomy and Visionary Reveries, of all the Fanatical and Enthusiastical Writers on that Subject,* (1773); and in Richard Nisbet, *Slavery Not Forbidden by Scripture* (1773) (Nisbet cited the whole footnote by Hume). An abolitionist, Charles Crawford, in his *Observations upon Slavery* (1784 and 1790), gave a defense of Negro mental capacities, and pointed out that James Beattie "had refuted David Hume's well-known diatribe against the Negro ..." (Jordan, p. 446).

The last indication I should like to offer of Hume's influence in the racist discussions of the time is that the abbé Grégoire, in *De la litterature des Negres* (1808), in his chapter on views about Negro inferiority, cited Hume first among those who stated this claim; and then went on to add Hume's French translator and others, including Thomas Jefferson. Jefferson had been much more tentative than Hume in his *Notes on the State of Virginia* (1784), merely saying "I advance it therefore as a suspicion only, that the blacks, whether originally a distinct race, or made distinct by time and circumstances, are inferior to the whites in the endowments both of body and mind." (Noah Webster, in opposing these views, had cited both Hume and Jefferson as raising the question of whether the blacks are a distinct and inferior race of beings [*Effects of Slavery,* 1793]).

Grégoire went on to claim that Beattie had refuted Jefferson (which I have not yet been able to confirm). Grégoire then offered a series of cases of blacks who had distinguished themselves in European arts and sciences (and tried to convince Jefferson of the force of this evidence in writing to him).

In the dedication of Grégoire's book "To all those men who have had the courage to plead the cause of the unhappy blacks and mulattoes ..." Beattie is listed as one of those who has fought for abolition and for the relief and freedom of slaves.

I hope this appendix shows that Hume's racist views are part of his implicit polygeneticism; that they are consonant with his analyses of human nature and how it develops from barbarism to civilization; that they were quite influential; and that they helped prepare the way for the "scientific" racism of the American anthropologists. Prior to the time of the school of Dr. Morton, Hume was taken to be one of, if not the chief, spokesman for the view that blacks were permanently inferior mentally to whites, and Beattie and Grégoire had to rebut his purported evidence. Beattie tried to

Richard H. Popkin

undermine it as poor induction and based on insufficient evidence; Grégoire tried to rebut it by producing cases of black writers, scientists and professors.

8

SCIENCE AND SOCIAL PROGRESS
Joseph L. Blau

THERE IS NO MORE APPROPRIATE WAY TO DO HONOR TO Herbert W. Schneider, teacher, colleague, and friend, than to present an investigation of the type he has done so well — a study of some aspect of the American past the results of which can be useful in their application to problems of the American present. Out of his background in the pragmatic tradition, Schneider knows and taught us, his students, that history is not merely to be learned *about*; it is to be learned *from*.

In our twentieth-century milieu, we have moved from an adulation of science and the scientist toward a more reserved and even suspicious attitude. At the very moment when the advance of biological science holds out the promise that men will soon be able to alter human heredity in the germ by genetic modifications, many of the most able of our youth are asking the cynical question: Who will determine what changes the scientists will make? A substantial segment of the most thoughtful people of our time foresee the possibility of a society controlled by scientific manipulation — and the scientists themselves controlled by military or political overlords. This is the context of current relevance in which I examine some earlier American theories of the relation of science to social progress.

Joseph L. Blau

I

If one holds to the theory that human nature is fixed and unchangeable, or alternatively that the nature of the human individual is completely determined by his heredity, it is most difficult to take the idea of revolution seriously. Theories of human nature of this sort suggest that the conclusion of the revolution, even if it were successful, would leave people in precisely the same life-patterns that they had manifested before the revolution. The tremendous expense of blood and time and resources that went into the making of the revolution would have been wasted if men were by nature or heredity unable to change their patterns of behavior. Perhaps one set of rulers would have been eliminated and replaced by another, but the character of society would not have changed. Every successful revolution would be merely a *coup d'état* or palace revolution. It would certainly not lead to the thorough social overhauling that its adherents had envisaged.

To induce people to expend their lives, if need be, in the cause of revolution, the possibilities of a successful outcome must be presented to them in terms of its making a real and lasting difference in the lives of men and women and children, especially their own children. Participants in a revolution must be able to believe sincerely that the new society that they hope to establish by their sacrifice will lead to a new humanity. To accept the idea of revolution, they must be persuaded of an environmentalist theory of the relations between society and human nature. To believe this, people do not have to reject all forms of determinism, but only the idea of determination by heredity. A very strict determinism is completely compatible with environmentalism. The more that developments in human nature are considered to be determined, even mechanically determined, by the social environment, the more vital seem the differences that revolution can make.

Revolutionary ardor must, then, be founded on the belief that human nature is malleable and that the primary influences in effecting changes in human nature are those of the environment. In modern times, at least, this belief has usually been accompanied by some form of egalitarianism. There must be no great stress placed upon hereditary differences; any such emphasis would tend to deny the possibility that change in the social environment could make basic and important changes in human beings. To many of the revolutionary generation and its immediate successors in the United States, the stress on hereditary differences was associated with the type of hereditary aristocracy that was maintained in England. One possible interpretation of the statement in the Declaration of Independence that "all men are created equal" is that there are no hereditary differences among men, but that each individual, when he is born, starts life with a clean slate. A position of this sort appears in the work of Thomas Paine and other extreme democrats.[1]

Thomas Jefferson had too much regard for the experience of the past ever to go this far in his belief in equality. On the contrary, as he wrote to John Adams in 1813, "Experience proves that the moral and physical qualities of men, whether good or evil, are transmissible in a certain degree from father to son."[2] He placed great emphasis on the limitations of hereditary transmission, however. He did not believe that the children of the "aristoi" would themselves necessarily belong to this group, nor that the children of the others would necessarily not be of the "aristoi" of their generation. He spoke, in the same letter to Adams, of "the accidental *aristoi* produced by the fortuitous concourse of breeders." Still his faith in the efficacy of education indicates the extent to which he accepted a theory of perfectibility and his recognition of the possibility of change within the limits imposed by heredity.

---

1. *See* in particular the argument in Paine's "Dissertation on First Principles of Government," *Works* (ed. Foner), II, 570ff.
2. To John Adams, Monticello, October 28, 1813 (Memorial Edition, XIII, 394).

I look to the diffusion of light and education as the resource most to be relied on for ameliorating the condition, promoting the virtue, and advancing the happiness of man. That every man shall be made virtuous, by any process whatever, is, indeed, no more to be expected, than that every tree shall be made to bear fruit, and every plant nourishment. The brier and bramble can never become the vine and olive; but their asperities may be softened by culture, and their properties improved to usefulness in the order and economy of the world. And I do hope that, in the present spirit of extending to the great mass of mankind the blessings of instruction, I see a prospect of great advancement in the happiness of the human race; and that this may proceed to an indefinite, although not to an infinite degree.[3]

As early as 1786, in a letter to George Wythe, Jefferson compared the new Virginia code of laws with those of France: "I think by far the most important bill in our whole code is that for the diffusion of knowledge among the people. No other sure foundation can be devised, for the preservation of freedom and happiness."[4] He regarded his part in the establishment of the University of Virginia as one of the three most important public services of his long career and left testamentary instruction that this achievement was to be listed on his tombstone along with his part in the writing of the Declaration of Independence and his composition of the Virginia Statute for Religious Liberty. For Jefferson, education was the crux of the environmental influence upon human nature.

John Adams, with his hearty enthusiasm for human differences, foresaw a different result of education. He suggested that those who were, by virtue of their inborn talents, better able to profit from education would become part of the "natural aristocracy" against which a democratic society had to provide checks.

---

3. To C. C. Blatchly, Monticello, October 21, 1822 (Memorial Edition, XV, 399-400).
4. To Mr. [George] Wythe, Paris, August 13, 1786 (Memorial Edition, V, 396).

> The increase and dissemination of knowledge, instead of rendering unnecessary the checks of emulation and the balances of rivalry in the orders of society and the constitution of government, augment the necessity of both. It becomes the more indispensable that every man should know his place and be made to keep it. Bad men increase in knowledge as fast as good men; and science, arts, taste, sense, and letters are employed for the purpose of injustice and tyranny as well as those of law and liberty, for corruption as well as virtue.[5]

As Adams wrote to John Taylor in 1814, "'Superior abilities' comprehend abilities acquired by education and study as well as genius and natural parts; and what a source of inequality and aristocracy is here!" In this respect, as in so many others, the acrid caution of Adams' opinions provided a much-needed corrective to the over-enthusiasm of Jefferson and, even more, of the Jeffersonians.

The views of Adams and Jefferson were formed primarily in the study of the literature of social theory. Their ideas were modifications, on the basis of experience, of the theories they had read. Both recognized the possibilities of alteration of human nature and the limits of that change. Adams, who was far closer than Jefferson to the traditionally pessimistic Christian theory of human nature, placed sharper limitations on the prospects of making a significant change by education than did Jefferson. Neither man was to any considerable degree familiar with biological science as it was presented in their age, although Jefferson was an amateur of zoology and of paleontology. Neither can be looked to for an exposition of the scientific status of environmental theory in the late eighteenth and early nineteenth century.

II

Benjamin Rush, however, was one of the most distinguished American natural scientists of the age and also a

---

5. From "Discourses on Davila," in Adrienne Koch and William Peden, *The Selected Writings of John and John Quincy Adams* (New York, 1946), p. 134.

man of political interests and concerns. In his writings both on medical and on general subjects, the importance of an environmentalist view to the Revolutionary generation is very clear. His social theories were dependent upon his larger scientific theory of the nature of life. Rush was a student of scientific method in medicine who attempted to find a way of harmonizing the claims of reason and experience. He rejected both of the extremes that were usually considered alternative in his time, the extreme of rationalism and the opposite extreme of empiricism, in favor of an attempt to combine the two.[6] In his chief scientific hypothesis, he combined the results of observation with the deductive and rational extension of these empirical findings into a statement that went far beyond both observation and reason. Rush's theory of life began with the observed phenomenon that every part of the human body is endowed either with the capacity to receive sensations, with "sensibility," or with the capacity to react to sensations by becoming active, which Rush called "excitability." The deductive extension of this observation was that the human body is so composed that the effects of the sensitivity of any part need not be the result of sensation at that part, but may be caused by sensation received at any part. That is to say, the human body is a unit; impressions made on any one part will stimulate either sensation or motion in every other part. From this rationally acceptable belief, Rush leaped to the conclusion that life itself is the effect of external stimuli acting upon the body:

> The action of the brain, the diastole and systole of the heart, the pulsation of the arteries, the contraction of the muscles, the peristaltic motion of the bowels, the absorbing power of the lymphatics, secretion, excretion, hearing, seeing, smelling, taste, and the sense of touch, nay more, thought itself, are all the effects of stimuli acting upon the organs of sense and motion.[7]

---

6. Cf. *The Selected Writings of Benjamin Rush*, ed. Dagobert D. Runes. New York, [c1947], "Observations and Reasoning in Medicine," pp. 245-53, and elsewhere.

7. *Ibid.*, pp. 135-37 (From "Lectures on Animal Life.")

Science and Social Progress

To have said this, to have made life and thought dependent upon external stimulation, is to have laid the groundwork for an environmentalist theory of human nature. If all is the effect of stimulation, then a change in the stimuli will inevitably be followed by a corresponding change in the effects. To produce the kind of human beings that we desire to produce, all that is necessary is to learn what kind of stimulation will have the effect we are looking for. A change in the stimuli involves a change in the environmental conditions under which the human being lives. Physical causes influence not only the physical situation of men but also their moral condition.[8] The American Revolution, by producing an alteration in the physical environment of men, would ultimately produce a change in their character. The belief that this is the case led Rush to strong sentiments in favor of republican government, an opposition to chattel slavery as well as to all other forms of human subordination, radical educational views, and a belief that all criminals are regenerable.[9]

Rush's discussions of education concerned more than the intellectual content of schooling. Following his own thesis, he asserted that the physical conditions that were maintained in the classroom — conditions of temperature and supply of air, the color of the walls, the physical activities that were permitted and encouraged — affect the intellectual results. "The influence of these physical causes will be powerful upon the intellects, as well as upon the principles and morals of young people."[10] The "mode of education proper in a republic" is one that brings physical stimuli to bear on the young in a way that will prepare them for the continuing physical stimuli of later life in a republic, and thus will change their characters in a desired direction.

So, too, with criminals. They are what they are because

---

8. *Ibid.*, "The Influence of Physical Causes upon the Moral Faculty," pp. 181-211.

9. Cf. the papers included by the editor in the section "On Good Government," *Ibid.*, pp. 3-84.

10. *Ibid.*, p. 92.

the environment in which they have grown up has directed them toward criminality. Criminality is the result of a bad physical environment. To regenerate criminals, all that is needed is a change to a different environment, marked by the presence of opportunities for religious observance, educational activities, and, especially, a change of occupation.[11] Rush believed that the best way of bringing a criminal back to society was to shift his occupation from the environment of the city to that of the farm. His agrarianism included the conviction that the agricultural life was conducive to moral health.[12]

Control of the environment would, of course, have to be scientific. Social science would mean the discovery of the precise physical causes necessary to the alteration of moral patterns in the desired degree. Because of the advances that had been made in the other sciences, and notably in the medical sciences, Rush was hopeful that the day for the development of moral science was at hand.

> Should the same industry and ingenuity, which have produced these triumphs of medicine over diseases and death, be applied to the moral science, it is highly probable, that most of these baneful vices, which deform the human breast, and convulse the nations of the earth, might be banished from the world. I am not so sanguine as to suppose, that it is possible for man to acquire so much perfection from science, religion, liberty and good government, as to cease to be mortal; but I am fully persuaded, that from the combined action of causes, which operate at once upon the reason, the moral faculty, the passions, the senses, the brain, the nerves, the blood and the heart, it is possible to produce such a change in his moral character, as shall raise him to a resemblance of angels — nay more, to the likeness of GOD himself.[13]

Thus early in the history of the United States was the connection between science and society discussed and made the basis for a theory of reform.

---

11. Cf. the writings of Rush on crime and punishment in the 1798 collection of *Essays, Literary, Moral, and Philosophical.*
12. *Selected Writings*, p. 290 and elsewhere.
13. *Ibid.*, p. 209.

Science and Social Progress

III

When Job Durfee, in 1843, elaborated his theory of technological determinism as a philosophy of history in support of the Whig program for internal improvements, he, too, was indicating a firm belief in the importance of physical causes in the supposedly "spiritual" matter of social life. He agreed with many other social theorists in asserting that governmental actions were responses to a higher law, but Durfee's higher law was not, like that of the other theorists, moral. [14] Although Durfee's conclusions were far different from those to which Rush had given expression, their similarity of approach was much more fundamental than their differences. Both Rush and Durfee argued that social developments were consequences of scientific advance.[15] To the extent that the scientist could be thought of as a pioneer, advancing beyond his contemporaries into uncharted realms, there might have been a combination of Durfee's views with an Emersonian individualism. Emerson's American scholar was, after all, a surrogate or representative selected to do the hard, pioneer thinking for the entire human race. But Emerson himself would have resisted any suggestion that his "scholar" was a scientist, because to him the work of the scientist was an earth-grubbing task that, although undoubtedly it produced useful results in practical matters, never led to any moral advance. There might, perhaps have been rather more attention paid to Durfee's theory among the small but very devoted group of Americans who followed the theories of the French pioneer of social science, Auguste Comte; but they were too busy with the attempt to gain an audience for the particu-

---

14. Job Durfee, "The Influence of Scientific Discovery and Invention on Social and Political Progress," reprinted in *American Philosophic Addresses, 1700-1900*, ed. Joseph L. Blau (New York, 1946), pp. 383-414; especially, pp. 383-84.

15. "If it be true that knowledge is power, then it would seem to follow that any change in the arts or sciences, favorable or unfavorable, must be followed by corresponding changes in society." *Ibid.*, p. 384.

Joseph L. Blau

lar gospel that they were bearing to spare attention to what others were saying. The result was that Durfee's important idea fell stillborn; more than twenty years were to pass before a similar view was able to gain a hearing.

The most general statement of Durfee's position that would be defensible for the American scene would run something like this: American social institutions are shaped by industrial and technological forces; within this framework the one sacred thing is the individual as *producer*. This statement retains the technological determinism of Durfee's thought, in combination with an individualism, though not the idealistic individualism of Emerson; it discards Durfee's emphasis on the development of the theoretical aspects of science. Perhaps a Martian examining the culture of the United States might have seen a view of this sort as inevitable in America even in the 1840s; but the view was not worked out until some thirty years later, as industrialization in the United States proceeded. One of the occasions for the acceleration of industrialization was the Civil War. The War brought about a direct need for increased production and the fact that the war effort itself cut down on the available manpower made it increasingly necessary that the additional production demanded of industry be the fruit of an efficient machine technology. There had, of course, been industry before the Civil War, but it was tolerated by many people rather than welcomed. In the 1840s, for example, the development of the early stages of the cloth-manufacturing industry in New England led to the employment of many young women in the mills. These young women were regarded as moral lepers; they had been, it was said, made unfit for marriage because they had worked in the factories. In the 1850s it was still possible to gain a sympathetic hearing for the view that Negro slavery was idyllic in its superiority to wage slavery in the factories. The growth both in extent and in respectability of the industries of the North during the Civil War period and the years that followed began the elevation of the industrialist to the pedestal that, for many Americans, he still occupies.

Science and Social Progress

IV

The dividing line coincides approximately with the publication of Charles Darwin's *Origin of Species* in 1859. Darwin's book was reviewed in America in 1860 and received a mixed reception. It was really not until after the Civil War, about 1870, that evolutionary discussion began to loom large on the American scene. Darwin was, by no means, the first to have maintained an evolutionary hypothesis; he was, however, the first to make a tenable suggestion of the method by which evolutionary changes came about. This method was that of "natural selection," which guaranteed the survival of those members of the group in whom there appeared variations favorable to survival. By and large, those better fitted to survive were those that survived; but their survival was not an isolated fact. By virtue of their survival, they were the more likely to be the parents of the next generation, transmitting their qualities to their offspring. Thus, each species went through a process of gradual improvement in its capacity to adapt to its environment. Darwin was, of course, speaking as a zoologist, not as a social thinker, and he himself gave no moral overtones to his discussion of natural selection. Survival of the fittest meant for him survival of the biologically superior, not of the morally best. In any case, his statement was descriptive, not normative. The fact of survival proved superior biological adaptation, but Darwin did not assert that those who were biologically superior — whatever that might mean apart from survival — *ought* to survive.

The first major application of Darwin's theory to social thought was made by Herbert Spencer, who had been working along the lines of a similar interpretation even before the publication of Darwin's study. Spencer's version of evolutionary theory emphasized the factor of struggle. Natural selection was the survival of those best fitted to struggle against a hostile environment; life was interpreted as a constant struggle for survival. The Yale sociologist, William Graham Sumner, adopted evolutionary theory in its Spencerian version. Sumner found in evolutionism an added dimension of the argument in support of a capitalistic organization of society. The new social theory envisioned the whole world under the rubric of struggle. Economic struggle took the special form of competition. The attempt to make a living under the artificial conditions of the market place was assimilated by Spencer and Sumner to the struggle to stay alive under the natural conditions of jungle existence. To the Tennysonian picture of "nature, red in tooth and claw," Spencer and those who followed him added a caricature of society, equally incarnadined. They interpreted any program for governmental control or for social welfare that in any way tampered with the "natural" process of economic struggle as a weakening of the human race in its struggle for biological survival. Thus a new rationale, grounded in evolutionism, bolstered the old "liberal" conception of a weak government, with limited police powers. Concurrently, a new version of the "self-reliant" individual was developed, the capitalist who was equipped to succeed without aid in the jungle of the market. The "rugged individualist" was born and became the culture hero of the Sumnerian mythos. Finally, the growing *de facto* respectability of the industrialists received a theoretical justification in the terms of this social — or, better, unsocial — interpretation of Darwinism.[16]

From the post-Revolutionary to the post-Civil War days, there were, thus, various theories of the relation of science to the social order. The later theories, those of Durfee and Sumner, inverted the earlier theories like those of Rush. For the purpose of science, as conceived by Rush, was to enable men to control the environment, to dominate the environment, for the good of society and of the individuals that made it up. For Durfee, and Sumner, and for the followers of Spencer, science served a different end; it described the environmental conditions that controlled and dominated men.

---

16. Much of the summary statement in the last part of this essay is based upon Richard Hofstadter, *Social Darwinism in American Thought, 1860-1915* (Philadelphia, 1944).

9

NATURALISM IN AMERICAN PHILOSOPHY
Paul Kurtz

I. Introduction

AT THIS LATE DATE, IT MIGHT BE CONSIDERED REDUNDANT to restate the naturalistic philosophy. For some critics naturalism, like an earlier moribund idealism, is rapidly becoming a remembrance of things past. Surely naturalism had been a considerable force in American philosophy, and its influence still continues in some circles, though admittedly much less than before. Lest analytic critics exult in naturalism's demise, let it be reminded that many histories of analytic philosophy are now being written, which may be a symptom of its own impending burial, and which only points out the fate that all philosophical movements seem to share: they are at the mercy of the winds of fashion. In any case, it is often easier after a movement has passed its prime to summarize it than during its heyday; thus it may be useful to view naturalism in America in historical sweep.

In a sense, naturalism was the heir, and perhaps the climax of what has been labeled, "The Golden Age of American Philosophy." Regretfully, even at this late date, all too little clarification has been offered of the definition of the term "naturalism." (The attempted definition in *The Encyclopedia of Philosophy* offered by an unsympathetic critic, Arthur Danto, is totally inadequate.) Perhaps the failure to find a precise definition of "naturalism" is the fate also suffered by most philosophical schools and tendencies, which are generally too broad to be given a specific platform, and which may count in one way or another many adherents and writers who are difficult to categorize. Most philosophers are notoriously individualistic and no sooner is a tradition announced than dissent arises and a new one is heralded in its place.

This is the case with naturalism, which has had a long career in the general history of philosophy. There are many varieties of "naturalism" and many meanings which have been attributed to the term. Broadly conceived, naturalism has two primary sources in philosophy: materialism in metaphysics and empiricism or experimentalism in epistemology. Thus the materialists, Democritus, Leucippus, Epicurus, Lucretius, Hobbes, D'Holbach, LaMettrie, and Marx provide historical antecedents to twentieth century naturalism. But naturalism also draws upon the empiricism of Ockham, Bacon, Locke, Hume, Mill, Russell, and Ayer. There are no doubt difficulties with this classification; for example, some materialists are rationalists and some empiricists are phenomenalists. Moreover, there are several distinguished philosophers who might not fit into the above tradition, yet have been labeled by recent naturalists as such. I am thinking here, for example, of Aristotle and Spinoza, of the Carvaka movement in Indian philosophy, and Lao Tzu in Chinese thought.

What is common in all of these philosophers is their commitment to science. Indeed, naturalism might be defined in its more general sense as *the philosophical generalization of the methods and conclusions of the sciences.* Insofar as America is pre-eminently a scientific-technological society and will most likely continue to be so, it may very well be that naturalism still provides the most appropriate philosophy for the future. But to say that naturalism is intimately related to science says both too much and not enough, for there are several other important characteristics which naturalism manifests.

Naturalism has been an especially prominent movement,

as I have said, in America in the twentieth century, though here again its delimitation is difficult. Undoubtedly its main sources are two strong philosophical tendencies at the beginning of this century: pragmatism and realism, and the subsequent importation of logical positivism in the thirties. Materialism, Marxism, and humanism in twentieth-century American thought also has been closely aligned with naturalism. Among the important American naturalists have been George Santayana, F. J. E. Woodbridge, Morris R. Cohen, W. P. Montague, Ralph B. Perry, Durant Drake, Roy W. Sellars, and C. I. Lewis. Undoubtedly the most important naturalistic philosopher in America is John Dewey, and there are a large number of writers influenced by him: Herbert W. Schneider, Ernest Nagel, Sidney Hook, John H. Randall, Jr., Abraham Edel, Morton G. White, Justus Buchler and Abraham Kaplan, among others.

Naturalism in America has had to contend since the Second World War with analytic philosophy, existentialism, and phenomenology, and there have been some attempts by naturalists to modify naturalism somewhat and to incorporate features of these alternative philosophies into its point of view. Although there is danger in blithely throwing all distinctions to the wind, features of existentialism, and phenomenology, and especially of analytic philosophy can be said to be naturalistic.

Naturalism thus cuts across many traditional philosophical demarcations, so much so that it perhaps would be wise to concentrate upon only one variety of naturalism — *pragmatic or experimental naturalism,* which those influenced by Dewey especially have advocated in the United States. At least these are the philosophers most likely to label themselves as "naturalistic." I will begin by stating what I take to be the dominant characteristics of naturalism — as will be seen the rationale for including so many diverse philosophical movements under the heading "naturalism" as I have done is that they have in some way shared many or most of these principles. But I then wish to concentrate upon what is clearly the central epistemological principle, naturalism's commitment to the methods of science, and to show how the naturalists have attempted to apply this principle to human behavior, morality, politics, art, and religion. Throughout, I shall be concerned solely with contemporary naturalism.

II. Does Naturalism Have a Metaphysics?

In interpreting the naturalists one must bear in mind the key point — that naturalism is committed to science in the broadest sense of that term. This is sometimes interpreted as the principle of continuity of inquiry. It means that all phenomena can in principle be described and explained in terms of natural causes and events, or at least there are no *a priori* reasons against their being so described and explained. Does this methodological principle entail a metaphysical view of the universe? Many naturalists have denied this, insisting that naturalism is a method, not a comprehensive account of the universe or of reality and that it is relatively neutral in its ontological commitment, thus allowing for a number of diverse metaphysical positions. Nevertheless, some naturalists have admitted that their methodology does presuppose or imply certain root categories, or a view of certain "generic traits" of nature and of human transactions. If scientific method is the fundamental principle of inquiry and if this involves a commitment to the explanation of things in terms of natural causes and processes, then everything that we can encounter, experience, or talk about must be considered to be "natural" and in some sense a part of "nature." Accordingly, any attempt to bifurcate nature into two realms, "appearance" versus "reality," the "phenomenal" versus the "supernatural," is for the naturalist based upon antecedent definitions which exclude as "non-natural" and prior to inquiry certain aspects of the experienced world.

Naturalism as so construed is dubious of transcendental metaphysical systems which claim that there is an "unknowable ground of being," a "divine essence," a "mystic presence," or a "theistic cause" over and beyond man's capacity to experience or understand. In modern and contemporary philosophy, a massive critique has been leveled by naturalists against the traditional transcendentalist views of the universe. This critique has been three-fold. It has maintained, first, that the traditional metaphysical views of the universe are based on prescientific or nonscientific grounds and that they come into conflict with rapidly developing scientific discoveries; second, that the claims for the existence of a theistic source or ground of being have not been conclusively "demonstrated" or verified and have failed to satisfy adequate methodological conditions; and third, and most devastatingly, that most of the terms, concepts, assertions, and propositions alleged about God are devoid of cognitive significance and incapable of confirmation or disconfirmation.

For the naturalists a key methodological criterion is that all assertions about the universe which are descriptive and informative in content and function must be confirmable directly or indirectly by the methods of science. Insofar as transcendental theories violate this principle, they are open to criticism.

Viewing the world as interpreted by the principles of science naturalists maintain that in some sense material processes and events or mass and energy are present in all things which we can describe or explain. In other words, material causes and events are basic to the universe, and all things which we can assert to exist, have in some sense material components or constituents. This suggests that the concepts and hypotheses of the natural sciences have a kind of priority in our accounts of the world and that to ignore the physical basis of things is to behave ostrich-like in the face of a whole range of tested hypotheses and observations in these sciences. However, while naturalism shares with materialism an appreciation for the physical-chemical basis of processes and events, it does not consider that an account of these processes and events simply in terms of their material or efficient causes is always sufficient. Naturalism is accordingly nonreductive, recognizing the manifold variety, diversity, and multiplying of things. Thus unlike traditional reductive materialism, which claims that nothing but material particles exist, or that only a reductive explanation suffices, present-day naturalism recognizes, indeed insists, that the plurality and richness of nature be admitted and that there are many kinds of events, properties, and qualities which we encounter in the world. In methodological terms, this means that sciences other than physics and chemistry (the biological and the behavioral sciences) are important in characterizing natural processes and events. It also suggests a contextualism; for if natural properties manifest diversity, then the characterization of things must take into account the various ways that things are observed to function in different contexts. Closely related to this view is the recognition that processes could only be understood in dynamic terms by reference to their historical origins, and an appreciation for the importance of evolutionary and developmental concepts. The universe appears to science not as a fixed scheme of eternal essences or of static structures, but one of dynamic processes and events in continuous change and flux.

The above is a brief account of the world as viewed by the naturalist. It is a naturalism which focuses on material events and processes, pluralism, contextualism, and historical evolution. But naturalism can also be interpreted in *methodological* terms as a philosophy which prescribes a set of regulative principles for dealing with the world. In this sense, naturalism attempts to be as neutral as possible in its metaphysics and is first and foremost a program of inquiry. Does this methodological program exclude *any* reference to the nature of man? Many naturalists would concede that their approach, at a minimum, *does* entail a "theory of human experience."

III. Theory of Human Experience

Naturalism's "theory of experience" is indeed central to its entire philosophical position. It is sometimes said that even though naturalism prescribes a methodology and has a theory of experience, it lacks an "epistemology." Even if an "epistemology" can be attributed to naturalism, it is unlike other epistemologies; for the "theory of experience" of naturalism is not subjectivistic; nor does it focus upon inner "mentalistic" processes; rather it deals with perception, cognition, and other psychological processes as forms of behavior. If all processes are to be explained in scientific terms, then this applies to man as well; for man does not have a privileged position in the executive order of events, but is part of "nature."

This twentieth-century naturalistic conception of human experience may be traced most directly to Darwinism and the radical reinterpretation of the human species that it entailed. Man was no longer a fallen creature from divine grace, but rather an animal like other animals; a product of evolution from simpler forms of life. Man's biological characteristics thus were not to be attributed to any special act of divine creation or teleological purpose, but rather a product of many factors: chance mutation, natural selection, differential reproduction, and transmission of genetic characteristics. Of causal significance in the evolution of the human species are the processes of its adjustment and accommodation to nature. All biological functions, such as respiration, digestion, and locomotion, have adaptive or survival value. But the same considerations apply to the so-called higher functions of perception, cognition, motivation, and valuation.

The most important consequence to the naturalistic philosophy of man and of the biologizing of human functions was the new interpretation of "consciousness" and other "mentalistic" properties of *homo sapiens*. William James in the article, "Does Consciousness Exist"[1] did not deny the existence of "consciousness," he simply asserted that it was a function, not a substance. But the significance of Darwinism can be nowhere more patently seen than in the writings of Dewey. If man is a product of natural evolution, like all other

---

1. From *The Journal of Philosophy, Psychology and Scientific Method,* Vol. I (1904).

animals, and if he can in principle be interpreted by a scientific methodology, then this will have far-reaching implications for many or most of the traditional problems of philosophy and epistemology, and especially to the conception of experience, knowledge, idea, concept, belief, meaning, and truth. In a famous article, "Charles Darwin and His Influence on Science," Dewey made clear the impact that Darwin had on pragmatic naturalism, when he said that the publication of *The Origin of Species* "precipitated a crisis" and "introduced a mode of thinking that in the end was bound to transform the logic of knowledge and hence the treatment of morals, politics, and religion."[2] For Dewey the destruction of dualisms between man and nature or mind and body is the inevitable result: all knowledge is to be considered as instrumental to the human being, a means by which he may resolve practical problems. C. I. Lewis in his work *An Analysis of Knowledge and Valuation* maintains a similar view when he states that "cognitively guided behavior is merely the farthest reach of adaptive response."[3]

Many naturalists thus have wished to avoid any commitment to a narrowly conceived epistemology; for much of traditional epistemological inquiry is based upon purely formalistic logical analysis independent of experimental inquiry. In spite of their disclaimers, however, the naturalists have presupposed a general theory of experience which, if not an epistemology in name, comes very close to it in function. Instead of a theory based on prescientific speculation, they have insisted along with most behaviorists that the starting point is always the behavioral action of the human organism, as viewed by the sciences. Thus man is properly conceived as an interacting field, not as split from his environing field. The term *transaction* best expresses the point. All human functions are organic functions related to a field which includes objects and goals. This is clearly the case for processes of digestion and respiration which could not proceed separ-

---

2. From *The Popular Science Monthly,* LXXV (July, 1909)
3. *An Analysis of Knowledge and Valuation,* La Salle, Ill., Open Court Publishing Co., 1946, p. 12.

ately from physical-chemical and biological causes, but it is also the case for sensation, thinking, and other so-called "psychic" functions, which historically were excluded from such treatment.

The point is that all "conscious" and intellectual processes are continuous with other biological processes and are to be considered as having natural causes and effects in the world. Conscious functions are not the inner spiritual or non-natural qualities of a human soul but merely instances of biological behavior. Perception and thinking are related to certain goals and purposes of the organism and stimuli in the environment. Thus for Lewis "the principle function of empirical knowledge is that of an instrument enabling transition ... from the actual present to a future which is desired."[4] Ideas are related to action and beliefs are implicit dispositional tendencies or plans of action, on the basis of which we are prepared to act. "Knowledge" for this view has a biological and psychological basis, but it also has, as G. H. Mead pointed out, a social fulfillment. For man not only has an enlarged cortex, which is an essential precondition for the emergence of intellectuality, but he is a social being interacting with others and communicating his wants, interests, and needs. It is only with the development of symbolic language in the communication process that advanced abstract conceptual thinking is made possible. And it is largely within the social process that such belief and knowledge develop.

IV. Language and "Meaning"

The study of language and of "meaning" is at the center of twentieth-century philosophy. Pragmatic naturalism like logical positivism and philosophical analysis has taken as fundamental the problem of the meaning of our concepts, terms, and symbols; though language is related to experience and behavior.

---

4. *Ibid.*, p. 4.

Paul Kurtz

Peirce's original formulation of pragmatism was as a criterion for the clarification of our ideas: "Consider what effects, that might conceivably have practical bearings, we conceive the object of our conceptions to have. Then, our conception of these effects is the whole of our conception of the object."[5] Peirce did not intend this criterion to be of universal applicability to all concepts. He limited it to abstract intellectual concepts, and he intended a rigorous experimental test. The meaning of abstract ideas can be clarified by reference to their consequences in practice. What does it mean to say that "salt is soluble," only that if salt were placed under certain test conditions, it would most likely dissolve. James later extended Peirce's original criterion, and especially the notion of "useful" consequences to include moral and aesthetic consequences, much to the objections of most other pragmatists. It is clear that the pragmatic criterion is too broad and imprecise to serve as a general theory of meaning and that the confusion of truth with utility was an unfortunate result. Language is far more subtle than the early pragmatic criterion allowed.

But Peirce had made a telling point, one that all subsequent pragmatic naturalists have accepted, and this I think remains in spite of limitations of the criterion itself; namely, that concepts, and the terms, and symbols which express them, are related to human *praxis* or conduct, and that they take on meaning and significance in relation to their effects upon such conduct. Language is not descriptive of the Logos, nor is to be construed simply as an abstraction from or reflection of "reality." It is adjectival and adverbial, an instrument of human desire and purpose, with functions and uses in human experience.

Language is biopsychological in function in that it serves as a sign in terms of which organisms may draw inferences. Ideas expressed in the form of beliefs are implicit dispositional tendencies and plans of action; they are vehicles by which man can interact within a natural and social environ-

---

5. From *Dictionary of Philosophy and Psychology,* ed. James Baldwin, New York, Macmillan, 1902, Vol. 2, p. 322.

ment. Language is thus a tool with jobs to perform. It is normative in that it presupposes grammatical and logical prescriptive rules, and it fulfills and satisfies our purposes and needs.

Language is social because it is used by a group of human beings in the process of communication. There is a trinitarian conception of language; for the linguistic situation includes interpreters, interpretees, and interpretants; that is, a linguistic context involves (1) individuals who use linguistic symbols or phrases, (2) symbols which function as dispositional proxies, and (3) ranges of reactions ("meanings") aroused in people who respond to the symbols. Pragmatic naturalism shares with analytic philosophy and Wittgenstein the view that (a) linguistic symbols, terms, and sentences have *many* uses and jobs to perform (the descriptive model is *not* the sole model), and that (b) their uses can only be discovered by reference to the concrete *contexts* in which they function.

Naturalism goes beyond analytic philosophy on one key point, and that is in the definition of the language context. For the naturalist, the analyst unduly tends to restrict the context of language to linguistic elements; whereas for him the context is eventually *behavioral,* for language is continuous with biosocial processes. Naturalism today is dubious of the formalist notion of "meaning," for this may suggest a kind of inverted Platonism. Language is best conceived in its broad sense as verbal or sign-behavior.

Although naturalism, like ordinary language philosophy, begins with common sense, it does not take ordinary language as beyond criticism or modification. Indeed, the pragmatic theory of language suggests that new uses for terms and concepts can be introduced into the language stock. If the scientific use of language is any guide, then we can stretch old terms, stipulate and introduce new terms, and reconstruct language, providing that we can justify our doing so as fruitful to the process of inquiry.

The analytic-synthetic distinction has raised a good deal of controversy in recent years. I do not know that there is any one naturalistic position here. Some naturalists (such as Lewis) have accepted the positivistic view that analytic statements, though necessarily true, are empty and tautological, saying nothing about the factual world, and that synthetic statements are descriptive and tested by empirical observation. Pragmatic analysts such as Willard V. O. Quine and M. G. White have considered the analytic-synthetic dualism as untenable, and have held that there are many border-line cases which are neither strictly analytic nor synthetic, but a combination of both. The criticism here especially applies to "analyticity" or "being synonymous with" in natural languages and the distinction between "essential" or "accidental predication." For all naturalists the analytic or synthetic distinction even if accepted, is based upon our purposes and determined by the conventional rules that we have adopted; it is not grounded on any alleged realistic foundation.

The naturalistic conception of logic is especially critical of formalism in logic. Logic is not construed in traditional Aristotelian or Thomistic terms as part of the nature of Being; nor in terms of the Hegelian view that the laws of thought are equivalent to the laws of Being. Many naturalists have sought to do logic without traditional ontology. Logic is conceived as a generalization from human inquiry, a statement of the most general propositions involved in effective thinking. The rules of logic — deductive, inductive, and the logic of practice — are *instruments,* tested by their demonstrated utility in investigation. Thus logic is not simply a formal discipline, but in its wider sense refers to the assumptions and methods employed in the search for reliable knowledge. Logical principles have the character of intellectual tools, even though they may in part be analytic and necessary; and these tools are the result of a slow process of evolution in which the habits of inference that are most adaptive remain as part of the stock of logical principles and distinctions.

V. Scientific Methodology

Naturalists who are willing to talk about "epistemology" generally take as their main concern methodology, i.e., the analysis of the criteria and standards for formulating beliefs and testing hypotheses. C. I. Lewis, for example, claims that his task in *An Analysis of Knowledge and Valuation* is not the "phenomenological construction of the real, but to discover by analysis the criteria of validity in knowledge."[6] An examination of the naturalistic position in methodology illustrates the importance of the methods of science, for as we have said pragmatic naturalism may be defined as a philosophy committed to the use of scientific methodology in the testing of knowledge. Thus Ernest Nagel defines the scope of his influential book, *The Structure of Science,* as "primarily an examination of logical patterns exhibited in the organization of scientific knowledge as well as of the logical methods whose use ... is the most enduring feature of modern science." The book accordingly ignores many of the issues of traditional epistemology, such as the epistemology of sense perception.[7]

Although the naturalists focus upon scientific methodology, their conception of science is much different from that which has usually been offered or defined in philosophy. This conception however, is continuous with the theory of experience and language discussed above. Science, for the naturalist, is primarily a way of behaving, a mode of acting or inquiring, and not a fixed body of knowledge. It is by viewing the process of scientific inquiry, and not simply the product, that we are best able to grasp its significance. The method of science is not something esoteric or mysterious; it is not a black art available only to a few specialists initiated into its cult. Rather scientific inquiry is continuous with the procedures and standards that we employ in ordinary life. Scientific thinking, though more sophisticated, is merely an extension of what the plain man uses in resolving everyday problems. According to Sidney Hook, there are effective working procedures on the level of practical life which everyone recognizes, and must recognize to some extent, if he is to live and function in the world, even at a minimal level.[8]

---

6. *Op. cit.,* p. 23.

7. Ernest Nagel, *The Structure of Science: Problems in the Logic of Scientific Explanation,* N. Y., Harcourt Brace & World, 1961, p. viii.

8. Sidney Hook, *The Quest for Being and other Studies in Naturalism and Humanism,* New York, St. Martin's Press, 1961, esp. Part 3.

Paul Kurtz

There are ways of using means to achieve our ends; there are canons of rationality, intelligibility, consistency, and practical tests of trial-and-error observation and experiment which are exhibited in behavior and involved in the arts and crafts. Scientific inquiry is nothing more than the refinement and elaboration of these commonly recognized procedures. It is acting responsibly and dispassionately, with care and caution in verifying judgments and testing beliefs. Scientific method is the method of ordinary intelligence at work in the most difficult and complex areas of inquiry.

The nature of the criteria and standards of scientific methodology has been vigorously debated in modern times, with the dispute between rationalists and empiricists commanding the center of interest. From the vantage point of the contemporary world, we now see that this dispute has in a sense been resolved and that the scientific method incorporates the contributions of both. If we ask, what are the criteria for adequacy of knowledge, we find, first, an empirical-experimental *criterion of verification:* if an hypothesis, proposition or belief is warranted, then it should be experimentally verified directly or indirectly by reference to a range of empirical observations. This point is fundamental to naturalism: that concepts without perceptual or observational rules of application to the concrete world are empty. Second, there is also a *consistency criterion:* if a hypothesis, proposition or belief is warranted, then it should be logically consistent with all other beliefs held; if not, either the belief in question or other beliefs with which it is inconsistent must be eventually replaced. This internal deductive test of noncontradiction applies to all propositions which are part of a system of propositions.

However, modern scientific methodology is more complex than this, and there are other characteristics which an objective methodology should satisfy. Thus we say with Peirce that human beliefs are to be considered as *fallible* in the sense that they are always corrigible and open to revision. In other words, beliefs are not certain or absolute, but only *probable,* since they are based upon a range of evidence. Moreover the grounds for the acceptance of scientific hypotheses must be *publicly repeatable* or *duplicable,* and based upon the tested judgments of a community of inquirers, who are committed to the canons of scientific objectivity. This fallibilism and probabilism of knowledge applies to the scientific method itself which is *self-corrective* in the sense that its rules, techniques, and procedures are open to possible revision and modification in the light of future practice and considerations of fruitfulness. One feature that the naturalistic theory of inquiry emphasizes and which has been previously overlooked is the view that hypotheses have an *instrumental* function, and are to be judged by their consequences.

Some have argued that this instrumental test of hypotheses refers to their ability to resolve existential problems of practice. Dewey's theory of inquiry holds that theories are related to practice and that all beliefs are a function of the situations in which they occur. A hypothesis is accepted if it helps to resolve an indeterminate or problematic situation, overcome the difficulty, and enable blocked action to continue.[9] It is generally argued that Dewey had overstated his case, for there are many contexts of inquiry in which no genuine practical problem is encountered as initiating inquiry. Instrumentalism thus must be extended to apply to problems which are primarily intellectual in character. Hypotheses in this sense are warranted in basic research as distinct from applied research if they overcome intellectual doubt in a community of inquirers.

For the naturalist it is the task of science to formulate hypotheses which function as instruments to fulfill our purposes and goals. The basic goal of science is the development of causal explanations and descriptions stated in hypothetical "if, then" form, on the basis of which a range of data can be ordered, accounted for, and predicted. Ernest Nagel, in *The Structure of Science,* has made explicit the role

---

9. Dewey defined "inquiry" as "the controlled or directed transformation of an indeterminate situation into one that is so determinate in its constituent distinctions and relations as to convert the elements of the original situation into a unified whole." (John Dewey, *Logic: The Theory of Inquiry,* N.Y., Henry Holt, 1938, p. 104-5.)

of explanation in science and the importance of the covering law or regularity model. According to Nagel:

> It is the desire for explanations which are at once systematic and controllable by factual evidence that generates science; and it is the organization and classification of knowledge on the basis of explanatory principles that is the distinctive goal of the sciences. More specifically, the sciences seek to discover and to formulate in general terms the conditions under which events of various sorts occur, the statements of such determining conditions being the explanations of the corresponding happenings.[10]

Naturalists have attempted to avoid the use of the term "truth," and prefer to talk instead of "warranted," "adequate" or "tested" hypotheses. For knowledge, and especially scientific knowledge, is not simply descriptive; it does not provide a simple one-to-one correspondence between a hypothesis or theory and the external world; rather hypotheses are functions of inquiry. Hypotheses are convenient if they fulfill their roles effectively within the process of inquiry. This methodological view of scientific inquiry does not deny or preclude realism. Indeed, although some pragmatists have refused to be drawn into the realist-phenomenalist controversy, it is clear that naturalists are in general sympathetic to realism (as Peirce noted) in the sense that there is a world independent of our wishes and fancies, and that the verification of our hypotheses only makes sense if we grant that they are related to an external world. Thus the context of inquiry and the transactions of human beings are not subjective but have an objective foundation in nature.

VI. Behaviorism and Neo-Behaviorism

Naturalism, as we have seen, is thoroughly committed to the extension of the scientific method to all areas of nature; but it is the application of this principle to the study of man

---

10. *Op. cit.,* p. 4.

himself which is at once the most distinctive and most influential characteristic of the naturalistic approach. And it is the principle that all events and processes, including human events and processes, can be explained by reference to natural causes and events that has contributed in no small way to the development in America of the behavioral sciences. Although not all naturalists accept all aspects of the behavioristic program, naturalism has been closely identified with its development, from James and Dewey to the present. Naturalism shares with other contemporary philosophical movements, logical positivism, philosophical analysis, and even with Marxism to some extent, the desire to create a behavioral science.

There are, however, various types of behaviorism; and, although naturalists would consider themselves sympathetic to some forms, they would not wish to be identified with all of them. In the early part of this century, Watson and Pavlov introduced mechanistic or reductive behaviorism within psychology. They attacked the reification of "mind" or "consciousness," wished to exclude subjective introspection as untenable, and to concentrate upon physicalist and mechanistic explanations. This view was later modified by functional behaviorism, as advanced by C. L. Hull, E. C. Tolman, and the pragmatists; the reductive model was held to be too narrow; and purposive or goal-directed explanations were to be admitted.

Since the Second World War a veritable explosion has occurred in the sciences which investigate man, and behaviorism is no longer restricted to psychology. Thus there are a great number of behavioral sciences which investigate man, from political science, sociology, anthropology, economics, education, and jurisprudence to cybernetics, information or communication theory, game and decision-making theory. I prefer to use the term "neo-behaviorism" here rather than behaviorism to characterize this new departure, and I think that most present-day naturalists are neo-behaviorists rather than simply behaviorists.

Most neo-behaviorists do not conceive of their inquiry as providing a general theory of man, aside perhaps from the minimal statements as discussed above under the naturalistic theory of experience: they are dubious of the postulation of any subjective "consciousness," "mind," or "self" separate and distinct from the body, and they wish to focus instead on the field of observable transactions. Unlike earlier behaviorists, they wish to avoid premature metaphysical speculation about the nature of man. Neo-behaviorism, they insist, should be interpreted primarily as introducing a set of regulative principles which recommend *how* we should go about studying human beings. The neo-behaviorists are interested in proposing prescriptive rules for investigating man, not in offering general accounts of his "essential traits," "nature" or "being." Thus neo-behaviorism is best construed as a strategy of research or a methodological program.

What does the neo-behavioral program involve? Unfortunately no precise platform has been worked out which would be acceptable to all of its proponents. What is clear is that neo-behaviorism cannot be identified simply with the Pavlovian-Watsonian program of physicalist reductionism; nor is neo-behaviorism today to be identified with any one school in psychology, such as the SR conditioned-response learning theory. The restricted definition of behaviorism which a B. F. Skinner in psychology might employ would hardly be acceptable to a neo-behaviorist in political science, sociology or economics. Virtually all neo-behaviorists, including even the most extreme physicalist behaviorists of earlier days, are now willing to deal with psychological areas which were formerly considered *verboten*, such as perception, thinking, and motivation, and they recognize the importance of introspective reports as psychological data to be explained. Some of the recent advocates of neo-behaviorism are also receptive to the use of functional, holistic, intentional, and motivational explanations. Many do not believe that a reduction of the many sciences of man to a single physical science is at this stage of research possible or even desirable. The term "coduction" best describes the existence within the social and behavioral sciences of many kinds of explanation drawn from many levels of inquiry.[11]

---

11. See: Paul Kurtz, *Decision and the Condition of Man*, Seattle, Univ. of Washington Press, 1965, Ch. 5 for a discussion of this principle.

Naturalism in American Philosophy

Some philosophical critics have interpreted behaviorism as "logical behaviorism," that is, as a theory of meaning in which every statement or definition of a psychological fact is equivalent to or must be translated into some statement of a physical fact. Others have interpreted behaviorism as an operationalist theory of definition whereby all definitions admitted into behavioral science must be framed in terms of a set of operations to be performed. But these interpretations of neo-behaviorism are also far too restrictive and would exclude a great number of inquirers who would wish to be considered as participating in the neo-behavioral program. It is clear that for the neo-behaviorist only a looser theory of meaning and definition is possible. He does not insist that all sentences in behavioral science be directly stated in physicalist or operational terms, but simply that they be related to other sentences which are, thus allowing for the admission of intervening variables and hypothetical constructs. Logical behaviorism and operationalism are wedded to early versions of logical positivism and pragmatism, both of which have been superseded.

We have said what the neo-behaviorist program is not, may we say more directly what it is? What is crucial to neo-behaviorism and naturalism is simply the insistence that all hypotheses introduced in science must be *experimentally confirmable* and these verifications must be *intersubjectively or publicly repeatable* by the community of inquirers.

While neo-behaviorists stress the role of experimental verification as essential to all scientific inquiry, this in no way precludes the use of mathematical models and theoretical systems, which all but the most extreme empiricists concede to be essential to any developed science. Many behavioral scientists today are reluctant to build high-level theoretical deductive systems, which they frequently consider to smack of premature philosophical speculation or intuitive guesswork. They prefer to concentrate upon the data and upon detailed experimental observation and statistical correlation. Most take as their immediate goal the development of hypotheses of the middle range, i.e., hypotheses amenable to some theoretical generality, yet closely related to concrete empirical contexts or particular facts. Yet behavioral science like natural and biological science has as its eventual goal the development of a set of mutually related hypotheses of wider deductive and theoretical significance. In the last analysis, however, neo-behaviorists insist that all statements that are considered warranted must be experimentally confirmed by reference to publicly observable changes.

Many philosophical critics have questioned the entire naturalistic-behavioristic program and have argued that a science of man is *in principle* not logically possible, and that intuitive *verstehen,* phenomenological description, or other methods must be employed. There are various forms to this critique. Thus one hears the following: that motives, intentions, and decisions are essential to characterize man, that teleological explanation and not causal explanation should be used, that historical method must be used, that man is "free," or that he possess a "mind" independent of causal explanation. I wish to respond briefly to each of these charges.

Neo-behaviorism surely would not wish to deny the first claim that motive explanations have an appropriate use in the social sciences and psychology. We could perhaps not very well understand many kinds of historical, political, and economic events unless we knew the plans and purposes of the human agents involved; nor could we operate fully in many psychological or psychiatric contexts without interpreting the motives and intentions of human beings (even though these motives may be "unconscious," as in psychoanalysis.) The question however is whether motives and intentions are capable of behavioristic treatment. The answer I think is in the affirmative. Motives and intentions can be interpreted as "intervening variables"; they can be put in operational and experimental form as "tendencies to act." Moreover, one can show that motive explanations are not logically different from causal explanations; for they involve dispositional statements. These are like hypothetical or conditional statements in that they satisfy the logical form of covering law explanations, i.e., given certain dispositions (motives) within the organism, then he will tend to behave in certain predictable ways. We must add however, that although motive explanations may have a use in the sciences of man, they are surely not the only kind of explanations that are employed.

Similarly, it is sometimes argued that in biological, psychological, and sociological contexts teleonomic,[12] functional, and holistic explanations are necessary; for they point to the purposive maintenance of the system as a whole. Clearly, teleonomic explanations which are purged of teleological overtones are used fruitfully in social and biological sciences along with others. But it can again be argued that these explanations indicate the conditions necessary for the maintenance of an organic system or social organization, and that in this sense they are an important aspect of causal explanation.

The claim of historicists that the sciences of man must be "historical" in a special way, for man has a past, not a nature, or the claim that human history is "unique" and incapable of generalization overlooks the argument that the historical method is an essential ingredient of the social sciences, and that historical inquiry is continuous with and dependent upon them. A great deal of discussion has been expended recently on the nature of history and whether it is a science. Naturalism and behaviorism share with positivism the covering law thesis (Popper-Hempel) that historical events in principle are explainable by reference to statements of general conditions or causal laws. Far from opposing the scientific treatment of man, historical inquiry is dependent upon the sciences for the derivation of many of its key causal generalizations and explanations.

There is another traditional objection to science based upon the argument from "freedom of the will," though recently this argument has been restated in different forms. There is, for example, the existentialist's view that man has no "nature" or "essence," only an "existence" as a subject. Man, it is said, is "free" to create his own nature; he is the sum and substance of his plans and projects. This view however, ne-

---

12. Teleological explanations without metaphysical overtones.

glects the large body of causal hypotheses that we have from the behavioral sciences, which enable us to explain much human behavior. Or there is the objection that man is a decision-maker, and that his choice can be "contra-causal", i.e., that an individual "could have acted otherwise" if he so wished. Few would deny that in many cases a man could have acted otherwise, *if* the circumstances and conditions under which he acted were somewhat different. It is difficult if not impossible to know, however, whether an individual could have acted otherwise, if all the conditions were *exactly* the same. The argument from contra-causality thus seems incapable of verification; it is nonfalsifiable and hence appears to be grounded in supposition. Another objection has been introduced to show the logical impossibility of a complete science — this is sometimes called the "self-fulfilling" and "suicidal prophecy" arguments. Science, it has been said, predicts that given the occurrence of a range of initial conditions, specific kinds of effects should follow. But in regard to human behavior, serious complications enter into our calculations, for our knowledge of a prediction, itself may influence the data. It may tend to either confirm what might have otherwise been false ("the self-fulfilling prophecy") or to disconfirm what might have otherwise been true ("the suicidal prophecy"). This kind of objection, I think, is the most serious that has been raised, but it can be answered perhaps in this way: for our initial theories to be adequate they must include as one of their conditions the role that knowledge of the causal hypotheses will itself play in future outcomes. Furthermore, prediction in science does not involve "prophecy" of the future, so much as it involves confirmation of an explanation.

All of these objections, however, are based upon a still more fundamental notion that is questionable, the notion that causal explanations involve hard determinism, compulsion or constraint between condition and effect. A science of human behavior does not entail strict determinism, only the principle of determinableness, i.e., that there are no *a priori* reasons for preventing us from inquiring into behavior, and of determining applicable causal explanations. Most naturalists and behaviorists today are weak determinists; they interpret "cause" not as a necessary constraining force, but rather as a statement of a hypothesis: given certain antecedent conditions, certain observed effects will most likely follow. Weak determinism need not deny the existence of decision-making in human life. It claims however that the fact that human beings make decisions that follow from their own motives, character, and personality does not in turn invalidate the possibility of causal explanation. On the contrary, one can argue that moral choice and responsibility, far from presupposing contra-causal freedom, would seem to require some regularity and order in human character and conduct, else punishment would be without foundation — one does not punish a man who acts without motive or cause. Punishing of offenders under this interpretation is still meaningful, for punishment operates as one of the regulative conditions of social behavior.

There is still another classic objection to the scientific treatment of man, which we have already touched upon, and that is the view that man possesses a "self," mind or "consciousness" entirely independent of his bodily processes or the context in which he interacts, and that this psychic entity is not amenable to objective treatment. The "mind-body dualism" or "ghost-in-the-machine doctrine" (as it has been called by Ryle[13]) has had, as we have seen, rough sledding in the behavioral sciences, for to postulate a separate "mind" for the behaviorist has little experimental warrant and is of little explanatory value in concrete contexts of inquiry. Moreover, the claim that the inner "subject" can only be known by a special "introspective, "intuitive," or "empathetic" *verstehen* raises the questions of what is meant by "knowledge," and how one can determine whether assertions about the "inner life" are adequate or inadequate. The behaviorist does not deny the existence of conscious awareness, or the life of feeling suffering, joy, desire or imagination; he merely asks that statements about phenomenological data be verified and tested by publicly observ-

---

13. Gilbert Ryle, *The Concept of Mind,* London, Hutchinson, 1949.

able correlations. Poetic insight may originate or suggest hypotheses, but it can never be held to confirm them.

Thus in answer to this range of objections, the naturalist does not maintain that a science of man is necessary or even that it is easy to achieve. There are profound experimental and practical difficulties in isolating and controlling the data under observation. The naturalist is simply denying that the alleged *a priori* arguments against a science of man have been conclusively demonstrated; for those who would seek to limit such a behavioral science generally do so from an untested theory of human nature that has been assumed beforehand. Nor can the naturalist *prove* the case for science. The question for him is still an open one. I reiterate that behaviorism should be construed primarily as a methodological program. Its basic justification as a program is that of convenience: given the great advances in the biological and natural sciences, there is some warrant to expect that application of similar rigorous methods of inquiry to the study of man will yield fruitful results. But to say this is not to argue in a vacuum, for the behavioral sciences have *already* achieved considerable success. Indeed, the growing body of behavioral research is both impressive and promising. There can be no more adequate justification for the behavioral sciences than its actual consequences. The test of the method is its pragmatic results: does it provide us with effective instruments which enable us to describe and explain how and why man behaves the way he does to test these explanations, and to apply this knowledge to human affairs? One has to beware of repeating the errors of the past: the history of philosophy is littered with dead metaphysical principles which have been adduced to demonstrate the alleged impossibility of the extension of the methods of the sciences to new areas of research.

VII. Naturalistic Ethics and Value

There is perhaps no area in which the naturalistic thesis has provoked more controversy than in the area of ethics and value. And this has involved a dispute not only with nonnaturalists but with other naturalists as well.

Naturalism in ethics and value has both a broad and a specialized interpretation. In its broad sense, all naturalists seem agreed that values are relative to human experience, and that any attempt to support or derive values from a transcendental source is mistaken. Nature is indifferent to man; she expresses no value preferences or moral purposes apart from the values and purposes of living organisms. Human values are in the last analysis *human*.

Pragmatic naturalists accept this basic humanistic thesis, but they go beyond it by also maintaining the more specialized thesis that value judgments are in principle at least amenable to objective empirical and scientific treatment. It is this latter claim that has engendered the widest dissent, particularly from positivistic and analytic philosophers. G.E. Moore charged that the naturalists committed the "naturalistic fallacy" when they attempted to provide an empirical definition for value terms; and this was later supported by the emotivist attack on objectivistic ethics.

What many often fail to see is that Moore's critique applies, if it applies at all, not only to naturalistic theories, but to all ethical theories, including metaphysical accounts of the "good." According to Moore, "good" was indefinable because it was a "simple nonnatural quality"; and any and all theories of the good failed. Accordingly, Moore's critique is not the naturalist's burden alone to bear, and it applies likewise to transcendental and nonnaturalistic theories. Similar considerations apply to the emotivist critique, which was offered by the positivists, who may otherwise be considered to be naturalists. The emotivists maintained that value judgments are expressive and imperative in function, and that any attempt to define value terms involves "persuasive definitions." But this critique, too, was intended to apply to any and all ethical definitions and theories, and not simply to naturalistic theories.

I think that a good case can be made for the view that the Moorean-emotivist critique of naturalism was an attack upon a straw man — possibly a crude kind of nineteenth-century scientism — but that it did not undermine the main thesis of pragmatic naturalism. I am here thinking of the kind of naturalistic position advanced by John Dewey, C. I. Lewis, Ralph B. Perry, Stephen Pepper, Abraham Edel, and others. In the first place, twentieth-century ethical naturalism, in America at least, has attempted to avoid many of the old issues by concentrating upon questions of value and valuation, rather than upon ethics or moral philosophy. "Value" has a wider denotation than "good" or "right"; and it refers to preferential behavior *in general.* Moral values are only one species of the broader class of values. In the second place, the basic problem of value theory for the naturalist is not that of definition. It is true that some naturalists, such as Perry, were concerned with providing scientific definitions of value (for example, that "value is the object of any interest"[14]); and no doubt the emotivists' charge of "persuasive definition" does apply in some sense. But the central issue for the naturalist has always concerned the question of the validation or verification of value judgments, valuations, and appraisals.

Lewis has stated clearly the key thesis: that valuations are "a form of empirical knowledge," and that they are in principle capable, to some extent at least, of empirical or factual verification.[15] The naturalist has simply maintained that valuation judgments concerning the preferences of human beings and their social norms grow out of concrete situations and are capable of modification by reference to the range of facts within such situations. For Dewey valuation judgments are hypotheses to be tested by reference to the conditions under which they arise, the means available, and the consequences of actions.

This naturalistic thesis in value is in many ways quite similar to the Aristotelian doctrine of the mean of the *Nichomachean Ethics:* what should be done is always a function

---

14. Ralph Barton Perry, *General Theory of Value,* New York, Longmans, Green, 1926.

15. C. I. Lewis, *An Analysis of Knowledge and Valuation, op. cit.,* Part III. Lewis, however, unlike other naturalists exempts ethical judgments of right and obligation from this classification.

of particular circumstances and is relative to the time, place, agent or agents involved. But the naturalist has attempted to go one step beyond Aristotle by claiming that there is a means-end continuum and that a deeper scientific knowledge of the conditions under which we act and of the alternative techniques available will enable us to evaluate plans and appraise ends.[16] Valuation judgments, including moral rules and principles, may be treated as hypotheses open to revision and modification in the light of new knowledge and altered circumstances. The naturalist is an objective relativist, in the sense that although he believes valuation judgments are relative to human experience, he does not think that this implies subjective caprice or the lack of all standards. Rather there are some canons of objectivity, he claims, that are available to the rational man. Linguistic-analytic philosophy has approached naturalism on this point, and there has been a "reunion" in philosophy.[17] Many ordinary language Oxford philosophers maintain that the emotive theory had misinterpreted what we do in every day life; there is a "logic of decision" which we can discover embedded in the stock of moral terms and judgments; there are standards and criteria of choice.

One point of confusion about naturalism on the part of its critics concerns the question as to whether valuation judgments can be resolved *simply* in factual terms alone, and whether these "facts" are neutral or "value free," i.e., whether normative judgments are deducible or derivable from nonnormative premises. Misconception about what the naturalistic thesis *is* on this key issue is so prevalent that perhaps no one should be blamed but the naturalists themselves for not clearly explicating their position. Yet a careful inspection of the writings of the naturalist will show, I think, that

---

16. See especially John Dewey, *Theory of Valuation,* International Encyclopedia of Unified Sciences, Vol. II, No. 4., Chicago, University of Chicago Press, 1939. See also Abraham Edel, *Ethical Judgment; the Use of Science in Ethics,* Glencoe, Ill., The Free Press, 1955; *Science and the Structure of Ethics,* Chicago, University of Chicago Press, 1961.

17. See Morton G. White, *Toward Reunion in Philosophy,* Cambridge, Harvard University Press, 1956.

naturalists have always *insisted* that part of what is given within the situation are the existing interests, prizings, likings, values and norms that men have, and that any normative judgment is always in terms of this "valuational base." Thus, valuation judgments are not antiseptic or devoid of values in content, but are intimately related to the *de facto* value experiences that human beings actually have. The very subject matter that our valuation judgments are about is the immediate experience of value, of enjoyment, liking, or need that people possess. But, say the naturalists, these value experiences are always open to modification in the light of a considered inquiry into the full factual situation, and they become *de jure* only after such inquiry. In any case, the primary need in ethics and value, according to the naturalists, is to develop "a science of valuation" in terms of which our judgments of value are facilitated and reconstructed.

One can argue on purely logical grounds about the adequacy or inadequacy of naturalistic methodology in valuation and social policy. But we should not overlook the remarkable and in many ways startling development that has occurred in the behavioral sciences in the past two decades, a development which can be traced in no small way to the influence of writers such as Dewey. I am thinking here of the new sciences or techniques of decision-making, operations research, game theory, etc., which have been attempting to develop scientific strategies of choice, and with considerable success, or of the policy sciences and applied sciences which provide important prescriptive rules for resolving problems of human conduct. To deny that there can be a "science of valuation," at least up to a point, is to overlook a whole body of tested valuation judgments which we already possess.

Most naturalists have also maintained that problems of value choice do not concern simply the isolated individual, but apply to social contexts and institutions. Thus pragmatic naturalists, perhaps more than most philosophers in the contemporary scene, have had a deep and abiding interest in social and political questions. Indeed, for the pragmatic naturalist, an essential function of the philosopher is his role in helping to resolve the problems of men in society. And here he has maintained that the same methodological approach that applies to valuation judgments in ethics also applies to the solution of social problems. John Dewey and Sidney Hook have written at length on the use of pragmatic or scientific intelligence and the need to develop an objective method for dealing with social issues. Under this interpretation, political and social policies and ideals should be treated as hypotheses and tested experimentally by their consequences in action. There are no absolute or universal ideological formulas which we can impose upon social life; rather our principles, rules, and laws grow out of, should be related to, and modified in the light of, the expressed needs and interests of human beings. Pragmatic naturalism as such has had a profound impact upon American life. For example, the movement known as progressive education in no small way can be traced to the writings of the pragmatic naturalists. Similarly, for the development of liberal democratic ideas in legal jurisprudence and political theory — liberalism under their influence has become not so much a fixed platform as a method of approach. But in being interested in the role of their theories in society pragmatic philosophers have only been acting upon their principle that theories must be related to their consequences in practice.

VIII. Aesthetic and Religious Experience

One complaint often heard against science and *a fortiori* scientific naturalism is that although naturalism claims to be concerned with experience as a basis for scientific knowledge, it fails to appreciate or do full justice to other dimensions of human experience, primarily aesthetic or religious experience. This charge had been hurled against historical materialism, which had been accused of ignoring and denigrating other qualities of human experiences; it has also been leveled against naturalism — but unjustly, I think. For naturalism, as distinct from reductive materialism, makes the special point that aesthetic, religious, and moral qualities can only be dismissed at a great price, and that any philosophy of experience, such as naturalism claims to be, must recognize the significance that these qualities play in human life. Far from excluding them from consideration, naturalism emphasizes and focuses on them: Santayana talks at great length about the "realm of spirit;"[18] and indeed, one of the most important collected volumes on naturalistic philosophy is entitled *Naturalism and the Human Spirit*,[19] so as to emphasize the fact that naturalism does not ignore the "human spirit." It is important to point out however that "human spirit" is herein being used metaphorically and that it does not represent any nonnatural or subjectivistic entity.

The naturalists do not deny that aesthetic and religious experiences are central to human life; in a sense they provide content to a rich and full life. The real issue for the naturalists however is how you interpret these experiences. Dewey constantly talks about the immediate experiences that we have, undergo, suffer, enjoy; but he denies that the term "knowledge" should be applied to this range of awareness in any special way. For it is one thing to have a raw, brute, and unrefined immediate experience, it is another thing to interpret, relate, organize, or deduce from this experience "concepts," to claim that they apply to the world, and to act upon them. Most naturalists have withheld the term "knowledge" from the immediately sensuous given and they have insisted that knowledge must be qualified so as to involve interpretation, reflection, manipulation, and prediction. "Knowledge by acquaintance" is often applied to that which is directly given, but unless the given is analyzed and related to previous experience, it hardly can be called "knowledge."

Aesthetic experience, for the naturalist, involves height-

---

18. George Santayana, *Realm of Being: The Realm of Spirit,* New York, Scribners, 1940.
19. Yervant H. Krikorian, ed., *Naturalism and the Human Spirit,* New York, Columbia University Press, 1944.

ened sensitivity, appreciation, and expression of feeling. It is not appropriate to say that such experiences are "true" in any but a metaphorical way unless we can restate and assert what it is that is contained in the aesthetic experience. Aesthetic symbols, a novel or a painting, for example, may denote and describe qualities of objects in the world, and this no doubt enhances their aesthetic effect. But a work of art is not true *per se,* and any claims that are made about the world on the basis of an aesthetic experience, however eloquent and moving that experience may be, must be submitted to independent tests of public confirmation. The primary function of art is to express and stimulate feeling and mood, not to communicate special or esoteric truths. Art may, as incidental to its aesthetic function, render and dramatize certain truths. But if we are to accept the "message" or "theme" of the work, then we must be able to state, define, and verify its claim. To allow the contrary is to open the flood gates to subjective feeling and romantic irrationalism and to overwhelm cognition as a basis for knowledge and belief.

Similarly, the naturalist does *not* deny the existence of reverence, awe, piety, or of mystical ecstasy, nor does he deny that the experiences can be prized or cherished by individuals who undergo them. The key epistemological issue, however, concerns what these experiences point to and what they assert, if anything, about the universe. It is one thing to *have* an experience, it is another to endow the universe with qualities in its name. And here we must proceed with care and caution, lest we read into nature any and all human experiences — love and hate, hope and fear, desire and aversion. The naturalist is unwilling to consider mystic claims as self-confirming unless they can be independently checked or publicly confirmed, no more than he would allow that the fact that people have dreams and hallucinations suffice that they are true. If a cognitive claim is to be drawn from such private experiences, then the naturalist insists that the same responsible criteria and canons of adequacy used in other areas must apply to it as well. Naturalists tend to be humanists in religion, for they believe that religious experiences are natural and that they can be explained by reference to natural processes and causes. A great deal of attention has been paid to religious language: naturalistic humanism would interpret its symbols and sentences primarily as moral and expressive in function. These do not designate or describe any alleged transcendental state of affairs, but rather recommend a way of life and an attitude of response. And they express our "ultimate concerns" and the basic ideals by which we live.

IX. Naturalism and First Principles

One last objection to naturalism must here be discussed, for it is the most frequent argument that is heard against it, and that is, that if scientific naturalism is not primarily a metaphysical theory of reality, but a methodological program of inquiry, then is not its basic epistemological criterion based upon a subjective value judgment? How can the naturalist justify, confirm, or vindicate his commitment to scientific method, other than by an act or leap of faith, and why is not the supernaturalist or transcendentalist entitled to his leap or act of faith in the same sense? If all first principles are matter of choice, why choose one rather than another?

This oft-heard criticism of scientific naturalism is most puzzling, and an analysis of it will reveal its speciousness. Are we to argue that *all* first principles are alike, since all are unarguable and indefinable? For example, are we willing to argue that the first principles of the Druid Cult or the Buddhist, the Fascist, the Communist, and poet, the charlatan, the scientist, and the theologian are all on the same level and one is as good as the next, but merely a question of taste or caprice? Surely not, responds the naturalist, for although first principles cannot be deductively demonstrated or inductively verified, without begging the question, this still does not mean that some principles are not more reasonable than others and that a range of evidence does not apply to some more than others. One test of a first principle is whether it carries with it a whole set of additional unsupported truth claims about the universe. The naturalist would be dubious of the transcendentalist's first principles precisely because they seem to presuppose further assumptions about the nature of the world, whereas the naturalist's commitment to scientific method does so only to a minimal degree. Another test of first principles is their consequences. Granted a rule of behavior, we may ask what follows. And here the pragmatist points to the profoundly dramatic results that have ensued upon the application of scientific method to the world and to human affairs. "Mysteries" concerning "depths unspoken" and problems which seemed beyond the ken of any human understanding *have been* resolved as science has proceeded step by step to push the frontiers of knowledge. But the claim here being adduced is not simply that scientific method is justified because it has provided us with powerful explanatory theories of wide generality and tested precision, but that scientific method also provides us with tools in terms of which we can modify and control nature. Indeed, no matter what our other first principles and values may be, we need to come to terms with the intractable world of events which resist our desires and fancies, our ideals and dreams; and we need adequate means to fulfill our ends. There is a world and there are the brute limitations of facticity, and only a methodological tool which is grounded in nature and tested by its effectiveness can enable us to cope with the encountered world.

Perhaps the strongest support of the use of scientific methods and of the standards of empirical verification and logical consistency in establishing our judgments and hypotheses is this: that science is continuous with ordinary life and that its methods are a product of historical evolution, the hard and difficult task by means of which civilized man has learned to turn nature to his purposes. Science is simply a more refined extension of the principles which we already employ in ordinary life and which the plain man uses to carry on the basic arts and crafts of social living. The first principles of naturalism are thus generic, as far as I can determine, to all humans and all cultures. For men are faced with common tasks and problems of living, functioning, and of responding to the challenges from the environment. Experience and intellect are the instruments of survival, and adjustment, and they are the common possession of mankind in general, transcending the limitations of custom and culture. Is it thus unreasonable to demand of naturalism that it justify the effective principles and criteria that we as human beings already use in ordinary affairs. Naturalism does not invent its principles out of thin air; it derives them from a reflection upon root human experiences and upon the assumptions and presuppositions that guide critical intelligence and action.

The real problem for the naturalist is not to justify the methods of critical intelligence in general — we could not live without them — so much as to justify their extension to other areas of experience, to human behavior, morality, politics, and religion. Naturalism does not wish to exclude human conduct, value, and social ideals from critical scientific treatment. Nor does it wish to exclude the "unknowable" by definition, as is sometimes claimed; it only asks that any claims about it be submitted to the same responsible critical standards that we use in ordinary life.

Naturalism considers all aspects of human experience to be a part of nature and hence available to scientific explanation and treatment. Yet, to borrow a phrase from Sartre, man expresses "bad faith" when he denies his natural roots, flees from the full use of his intelligence, or refuses to accept the responsibility for his own destiny. In the last analysis for the naturalist and humanist, it is man himself who is ultimately responsible for what he is; and it is the height of irresponsibility for him to renounce his capacity for critical intelligence and to look outside himself for blame or support. Naturalism's first principle is its commitment to and confidence in responsible and intelligent inquiry — whether in ordinary life, the arts and crafts, morals, religion, science, or philosophy. The application of this principle is a serious matter, and whether or not it is used fully may help to determine whether or not mankind will persist in a state of self-deception, or whether it will continue to develop and progress.

But is it "naive optimism" to place so much reliance upon the use of scientific intelligence by human beings? Surely there are some things which are within our power as human beings, but there are some things which are not. There are some problems that are difficult, if not impossible, to resolve, and even for those problems which have solutions, some solutions are only in terms of the lesser of many evils. The naturalist who is honest will recognize that there is no guarantee in life of complete success or of the avoidance of failure, but that both are part of the drama of human existence.

The naturalist is not unmindful of the tragic character of the human condition and the ever present possibilities of failure and betrayal, error and inadequacy; but at the same time he does not suppress the positive potentialities of human experience for achievement and adventure, discovery and fulfillment. He recognizes the limitations and frailties of men *and* the promises and capacities; and he has the "courage to be" in the face of the dual character of the human condition.

Philosophic naturalism today asserts that if mankind is to persist in the face of adversity and conflict, it must continue to express the best that is within it; and that its scientific reason (which many have thought most akin to the "divine"), if not perfect, at least is among the most effective instruments that it possesses. To renounce the use of this power or to deny its extension and applicability to other aspects of experience is for the naturalist morally irresponsible. And it is an irresponsibility that contemporary man can no longer afford to commit. For the complex problems and great crises of contemporary life are such that if man responds to them with anything less than the full use of his intelligence, then he is possibly betraying the last hope that he may have to continue to survive on this planet, at least in the form that he has heretofore known.

10

PHILOSOPHICAL PUNS
George L. Kline

I DEFINE 'PUN', WITH WEBSTER, AS "A PLAY ON WORDS OF THE same sound but different meaning, or on different meanings of the same word."[1] However, two qualifications are necessary: (1) Webster adds that puns are "always for the sake of ludicrous effect"[2]; I maintain that philosophical puns are typically serious in intent. (2) The difference of meaning is antecedent to the process of punning; in that process antecedently distinct meanings may be merged or joined. A philosophical pun is a philosophical play-on-words or, more precisely, a play on philosophical words. I shall exclude both nonphilosophical puns — whether or not per-

---

1. *Webster's Unabridged Dictionary*, second edition, 1947, p. 2011. Webster goes on to distinguish between punning and paronomasia, which "in rhetoric is a playing on words of similar but not the same sound, commonly for antithesis" (*loc. cit.*). Many philosophical puns could be regarded as cases of paronomasia. *See* especially secs. 2.1, 3.1, 6.112, 6.122, 6.132, 6.162, 6.212, 6.222, 6.232, and 6.312 below.
2. *Loc. cit.*

Philosophical Puns

petrated by philosophers — and philosophical near puns or nonpuns.[3]

A pun is *philosophical* if its operative terms are drawn from the philosophical lexicon, e.g., from such category pairs as 'one-many', 'universal-particular', 'abstract-concrete', 'continuous-discrete', 'being-becoming', 'subject-object', and 'necessity-possibility'. But not all philosophical puns are "categoreal." Plays on such word pairs as 'animate-inanimate', 'master-slave', 'force-justice', and 'know-will' may be considered philosophical so long as they make a broadly philosophical point.

Examples of philosophical near puns — they are "near puns" rather than puns *stricto sensu*[4] because the phonetic relation between their operative terms is slant-rhyme or echo rather than identity or near identity — are: (1) the Platonic claim that the soul is *ensema* in its *sōma* ('entombed' in its 'body') and that the *ouranos* is *horatos* (the 'physical universe' is 'visible [i.e., perceptible]'),[5] (2) the Hegelian assertion that *sittliche Gewissheit* ('moral certainty') is a higher dialectical phase which includes the parallel lower phase of *sinnliche Gewissheit* ('sense certain-

---

3. The play on 'nonphilosophical pun' and 'philosophical nonpun' is itself a prefix-switching, two-term permutational pun which combines my categories 4.1 and 6.11. I shall not attempt to decide whether it is a philosophical as well as a metaphilosophical pun. An example of a metaphilosophical pun which is *not* philosophical is Rabelais, name-dropping characterization of one who laughs through tears and weeps through laughter as a *Démocrite héraclitizant* ('Heraclitizing Democritus') and a *Héraclyte démocritizant* ('Democritizing Heraclitus'), i.e., a laughing philosopher weeping and a weeping philosopher laughing. (Cf. *Gargantua*, Bk. I, ch. 20.) In form this is a two-place permutational pun of the identifying noun-participle sort.

4. Examples (1) and (2) are not cases of paronomasia since they do not involve antithesis — rather, identification or parallelism — of the operative terms. Example (3) may be considered paronomastic.

5. *Republic* VI, 509D. Paul Shorey (in the Loeb Classical Library edition) renders the Greek pun by means of a near-philosophical English pun on the words 'skyball' and 'eyeball'.

ty'),[6] and (3) S. L. Frank's characterization of the absence of moral *samoopredeleniye* ('self-determination') as a *samopreodoleniye* ('self-overcoming').[7] The latter term is to be taken in a Stoic rather than a Nietzschean sense, i.e., as a "mastering" of the self by its appetites and impulses.

Dialectical thinkers such as Heraclitus, Plato, Hegel, and Marx are more given to philosophical punning, particularly of the permutational kind, than nondialectical thinkers. This is natural, since permutational and prefix-switching puns suggest the dialectical conversion of concepts into their (contrary or contradictory) opposites.

The seventeenth and eighteenth centuries are particularly rich in philosophical punning, e.g., in Pascal, Kant, and Gregory Skovoroda, thinkers widely different in other respects.

I distinguish six categories (and several subcategories) of philosophical puns according to the type of word-play and the number of terms involved. The arrangement of the categories is not strictly systematic, but it makes general sense in terms of three criteria: (a) *simplicity*: the progression is generally from the simpler to the more complex cases; (b) *frequency*: the progression is from the types of puns which, in Western philosophical writings, are rarest to the kinds which are most common; (c) *structural characteristics*: the first three categories (1. etymological puns, 2. ambiguity puns, 3. neologistic puns) comprise "semantic puns" — those that involve ambiguities or shifts of meaning. The last three (4. "switching" puns, 5. compositional puns, 6. permutational puns) comprise "syntactical puns," involving shifts in word order and parts of speech. The transition may be located between "prefix-switching" and "particle-switching" puns, both of which are included under category 4. The former are primarily semantic, the latter pri-

---

6. *Phänomenologie des Geistes* (ed. J. Hoffmeister), Leipzig, 1949, pp. 79-89, 318ff. Although Hegel does not use the expression *sittliche Gewissheit*, he uses the equivalent expression *Gewissheit des ... sittlichen Seins*.

7. *Realnost i chelovek*, Paris, 1956, p. 311.

marily syntactical. However, since most puns in the last three categories involve some shift of meaning, syntactical puns are also semantic, although semantic puns do not seem to be in any significant degree syntactical.

I. SEMANTIC PUNS

1. *Etymological Puns*

Curiously enough, the Greeks, who invented the philosophical pun — and perhaps the pun *tout court* — made relatively little serious use of etymological puns. However, the Pythagoreans were serious, I think, in linking *arithmos* ('number') to *rhythmos* ('rhythm'), even if their etymology was shaky (*rhythmos* is apparently derived from *rhein*, 'to flow', rather than from *arithmos*). They wished to stress the "rhythmic" or "harmonious" character of numbers and the "numerical" (or mathematical) character of rhythm and harmony. Of course, both numbers and rhythms or harmonies enjoy a privileged status within the Pythagorean cosmology.

Plato's *Cratylus* is full of etymologies, mostly quite fanciful, and often punning, but rarely serious. Three instances which Plato may have meant seriously are: (1) the derivation of *aēr* ('air') from *aei* ('always') and *rhei* ('flows').[8] But even if true, it is at most meteorologically, not philosophically, relevant that air is something which "always flows."

(2) The derivation of *anthrōpos* ('man') from *anathrei* ('he looks up at') and *opōpe* ('what he has seen').[9] But nowhere else does Plato characterize man as the creature who looks up (at the heavens). Quite the contrary. To behold reality, he reminds us, men should look not up, but *into* or *beyond* appearances.

(3) The derivation of *psychē* ('soul') from *physis* ('nature')

---

8. *Cratylus*, 410B.
9. *Ibid.*, 399C.

and *echei* ('has' or 'holds'), through the hypothetical intermediate form *physechē*.¹⁰ Aside from the problem of how the *phi* of *physis* becomes the *psi* of *psychē*, the etymology is singularly uniformative. For Plato everything "has a nature" — *sōma* ('body') no less than *psychē*.

Hegel, the most prolific of etymological punsters among philosophers, is also the most prolific of philosophical punsters generally. He describes *Wahrnehmung* ('perception', literally "taking-true") as a transition from the specious certainty of sensation to the (relative) truth of perception. Instead of merely sensing, Hegel says, I now "take the object truly" (... *nehme ich wahr*).¹¹

At an earlier point in the *Phenomenology* Hegel puns on the obvious and, in a broad sense, etymological, derivation of *gewesen* from *Wesen*. The *Wesen* ('being' or 'essence') of the sense-object *ist gewesen* ('has been'); its *Wesen* is its *Gewesensein* ("having-been-ness").¹²

One of Hegel's most convincing etymologies involves the derivation of *Gesetz* ('law') from what is *gesetzt* ('laid down' or 'established').¹³ But this derivation is perhaps too obvious to be philosophically enlightening.

His opposition of *Erinnerung* ('recollection'), with its etymological suggestion of "internalization," and *Entäusserung* ('externalization' or 'alienation'), is developed by Kierkegaard, who contrasts inward, "subjective" *Erindring* ('recollection'), characteristic of the ethical stage, with outward, merely "objective" *Hukommelse* ('memory'), characteristic of the aesthetic stage.¹⁴ Kierkegaard also follows Hegel in relating *Fortvivlelse* (=*Verzweiflung*, i.e., 'despair') to *Tvivl* (=*Zweifel*, i.e., 'doubt'). Doubt is cognitive and its overcoming leads to objective knowledge of the world; de-

---

10. *Ibid.*, 400B.
11. *Phänomenologie des Geistes*, pp. 89, 92f.
12. *Ibid.*, p. 85.
13. *Wissenschaft der Logik* (ed. G. Lasson), Hamburg, 1966, II, 124ff.
14. *Phänomenologie des Geistes*, pp. 563f. At p. 564 Hegel hyphenates the word *Er-Innerung*. For Kierkegaard, see *Samlede Vaerker,* Gyldendal, 1962, X, 212.

spair is passional and its overcoming leads to subjective choice of the self.[15]

The validity of the derivations in such etymological puns is of secondary importance. Etymological puns may be effective whether the derivations are demonstrably valid, demonstrably invalid, or indeterminate as to validity — so long as they are plausible and philosophically relevant.[16]

2. *Ambiguity Puns*

This is the category of philosophical plays-on-words that comes closest to puns in the ordinary sense of the term. Needless to say, this category has no monopoly on ambiguity; some degree of ambiguity is present in all types of semantic puns.

2.1. Ambiguity puns involving *heteronyms*, words spelled the same but pronounced (or stressed) differently and having correspondingly different meanings. The first and most famous is Heraclitus' *Onoma bios, ergon de thanatos* ('Its name is life [bow], but its work is death').[17] The heteronyms are *bíos* ('life') and *biós* ('bow').

This category can be stretched slightly to make it accommodate two cases of paronomasia, one Aristotelian, the other Nietzschean: (1) Aristotle insists that all *aitia* ('causes' or 'causal factors') must be *aidia* ('eternal' or 'timeless').[18] (2) Nietzsche scorns the *Kenner des Grossen ohne das Können des Grossen* ('connoisseurs of greatness who are unable to act greatly').[19] If the word *Kenner* is put in the

---

15. *Samlede Vaerker*, III, 197.
16. Between categories 1 and 2 — or possibly between 2 and 3 — an additional category of "polyglot puns" might be inserted. An example would be Nietzsche's invidious distinction between virtue in the "active, masculine" sense expressed by the Renaissance-Italian *virtù* and virtue in the "passive, feminine" sense expressed by the German *Tugend*.
17. Herman Diels, *Die Fragmente der Vorsokratiker* (ed. W. Kranz), 11th ed., Zürich, 1964, Fr. 48.
18. *Metaphysics*, 1026a 17-18. The paronomastic contrast is between the ordinary "temporalistic" conception of cause and Aristotle's "eternalistic" conception.
19. *Werke in drei Bänden*, 2nd ed., Gernsbach, 1960, I, 225.

infinitive form *(kennen)*, it becomes a near heteronym for *können*, and the paronomasia becomes a near pun: *Es ist möglich, das Grosse zu kennen ohne das Grosse zu können* ('It is possible to know greatness without being able to achieve greatness').

2.2 Ambiguity puns involving *homonyms*, words pronounced the same, whether or not spelled the same, and having different meanings. For example, Plato puns on the two senses of *eu prattein* ('to do well') — (1) to do what is right or good, and (2) to prosper, to "be well off."[20] Hegel puns on the adjective *mein* ('my') and the verb *meinen* ('to mean') to emphasize that at a certain stage in the dialectical phenomenology of human consciousness "meaning" is "*my* meaning," i.e., the meaning present to an individual consciousness.[21] He also relates the noun *Sein* ('being') with various forms of the adjective *sein* ('his') to make a parallel point.[22] Feuerbach contributes the notorious postulate of reductive physiologism: *Der Mensch ist was er isst* ('Man is what he eats').[23]

There is a similar ambiguity in the Russian words for 'world' and 'peace', originally spelled differently (міръ and миръ), but spelled exactly the same (мир) in the post-1917 orthography. Both Skovoroda and Vladimir Solovyov played on this homonymity to support the claim that the *universe* is, at least ideally, a *cosmos,* i.e., a totality characterized by harmony (peaceful relationships) among its parts or aspects.

Russian reproduces the ambiguity of the Greek *archē* and Latin *principium* in the word *nachalo*, which means both 'principle' and 'beginning'. Skovoroda plays on this ambiguity with the phrase *beznachalnoye nachalo* ('beginningless principle').[24] He means by it something like Aristotle's First or Unmoved Mover.

---

20. *Charmides*, 172A, 174B.
21. *Phänomenologie des Geistes*, pp. 83, 183.
22. *Ibid.*, p. 183.
23. *Sämtliche Werke*, Stuttgart/Bad Cannstatt, 1964, X, 22.
24. *Tvori v dvokh tomakh*, Kiev, 1961, I, 239.

Philosophical Puns

2.3 Ambiguity puns involving multiple meanings of a given term. (It might be objected that Plato's *eu prattein* belongs here. But *eu prattein* in the sense of 'to do right' is a term distinct from, though closely related to, *eu prattein* in the sense of 'to prosper'.) My examples are from Hegel: He uses [*geht*] *zugrunde* in the sense both of '[goes] to the ground, root (of a question)' and 'runs aground, is wrecked' — to support the claim that only by running into a deadend is thought, or consciousness, compelled to dig deeper and thus move from (subjective) certainty to (objective) truth.[25]

Hegel also plays on the three senses of the term *Erscheinung* in considering knowledge as *Erscheinung* (or *das erscheinende Wissen*).[26] Knowledge is (a) an event or occurrence, (b) something obvious or self-evident, and (c) something the obviousness of which is specious. The English terms 'apparent' and 'appearance' contain most if not all of these meanings. Finally, there is the famous term *Aufhebung*, with its three senses of 'canceling', 'preserving', and 'transcending' or 'raising to a higher [dialectical] level'.

2.4 *Pluralizing ambiguity puns*: the shift from grammatical singular to plural is accompanied by a shift from general to specific senses of the term, and, in at least some cases, an implied shift from *process* to *product*. Thus Kant's *Zeitbestimmung* ('temporal determination' or 'determin*ing*') as a general process or *determinatio* contrasts with specific *Zeitbestimmungen* (pl.), as products or *determinata*.[27] Similarly, with *Verbindung* ('connect*ing*') instantiated in *Verbindungen* ('connections'). Also, perhaps, *Anschauung* ('intuit*ing*' or 'perceiv*ing*') instantiated in specific *Anschauungen* ('intuitions' or 'perceptions'). When Kant contrasts the *Anschauung eines Mannigfaltigen* ('intuition of a manifold') with the *Mannigfaltige der Anschauungen* ('manifold of intuitions') he may intend an event-object or process-product distinction, i.e., a contrast between the 'in-

---

25. *Wissenschaft der Logik*, II, 52.
26. *Phänomenologie des Geistes*, pp. 66f.
27. *Kritik der reinen Vernunft*, A 177f.

tuit*ing* of a manifold' and the 'manifold*ing* ['rendering manifold'] of intuitions'.

A contemporary English example of a pluralizing two-term permutational pun: "intelligent artifacts" might be regarded as instantiations of "artificial intelligence."

"Word-stress-shifting puns" represent the extreme case of ambiguity puns. Michael Kosok has distinguished between 'negation of a *negation*', which is "positive," and '*negation* of a negation', which is "negative." Kojève, in his Hegel commentary, distinguishes between the self's directedness toward un autre Désir and un autre *Désir* ('another *Desire*' and 'an *other* Desire').[28]

3. *Neologistic Puns*

3.1 Coining of a word which matches or mirrors a given word (without such matching or mirroring there would be only a neologism, not a neologistic pun).

Nietzsche is one of the most prolific of neologistic punsters. He makes a neologistic contrast between *Fernstenliebe* ('love of the far-off', literally, 'of the farthest') and the standard German term *Nächstenliebe* ('brotherly love' or 'love of one's neighbor', literally 'of the next or nearest'). Of course, Nietzsche's contrast is not spatial but historical. What we should love is the "far-off" generations of the future, or rather the high culture that the few creative spirits of the distant future will have produced; we should cease to love our uncreative contemporaries. Nietzsche also coined the term *Zweisamkeit* ('twosomeness') to describe the mitigated *Einsamkeit* ('loneliness') of one who has found a single intellectual comrade. He applied the term to his own relationship to Spinoza.[29]

Whitehead has coined philosophical terms to complement or match traditional terms, e.g., 'prehension', related to 'apprehension' as 'perception' is related (in Leibniz) to 'ap-

---

28. *Introduction à la lecture de Hegel,* Paris, 1947, p. 169.
29. Letter to Franz Overbeck, July 30, 1881: *Werke in drei Bänden,* III, 1172.

perception'; and 'superject', related in a complicated way to both 'subject' and 'object'.

3.2 "Semantic neologism," i.e., giving a new meaning to an existing term, where such meaning matches or complements that of another existing term. Hegel uses the term *Gemeinschaft* ('community' in ordinary German) in contrast to *Eigenschaft* ('property', in both the philosophical and legal senses). The German adjectives *gemein* and *eigen* mean, respectively, (a) 'common' and (b) 'proper', 'peculiar', or 'one's own'. Hegel's point is that the sensed *EIGENschaft* turns out to be not proper or peculiar to the given perceptual object but common to many objects, thus a *GEMEINschaft*, i.e., a 'common element' or 'sense universal'.[30]

II. SYNTACTICAL PUNS

4. *Puns Involving Switches*

4.1 *Prefix-switching puns.* German appears to be richer in significant prefixes, and hence in possibilities for prefix-switching puns, than most other modern languages. In Hegel's account of the Enlightenment, *reine Einsicht* ('pure insight') is said to give way, or lead, to *unreine Absicht* ('impure intention'). There is a secondary play on two distinct senses of *rein*. In the first occurrence it means 'non-empirical' (Kant's usage); in the second its negation, *unrein*, means 'malicious' or 'nasty'. This shift from an epistemological to an ethical sense of *rein* would be sterile, however, without the meaning-shift from *EINsicht* to *ABsicht*.

Hegel puns on the words *INwendig* (literally, 'turning in') and *AUSwendig* ('turning out') to suggest that what is external is mechanical — on the model of the German idiom, *auswendig lernen* ('to learn by heart'). This is, of course, both a prefix-switching and an ambiguity pun.

Marx puns on *ENTäussert* ('externalized' and 'alienated') and *VERäusserlich* ('commercial') to support the claim that

---

30. *Phänomenologie des Geistes*, p. 93.

a commercial society produces alienated men and an externalized nature. Whitehead distinguishes between 'sense-*reception*' and 'sense-*perception*',[31] and Loewenberg differentiates, with respect to Hegel, between knowledge which is 'all-*in*clusive' and that which is 'all-*con*clusive'.[32]

4.2 *Particle-switching puns.* All of my examples involve a single particle, 'not' (or rather its equivalent in Latin or German), so perhaps this subcategory should be labeled "Negative-particle-switching puns."

Augustine contrasts the freedom of *posse non peccare* ('being able not to sin') with the greater freedom of *non posse peccare* ('not being able to sin').[33] Kant sets off his own view of the noumenon as *nicht Objekt unserer sinnlichen Anschauung* from the dogmatic rationalist view of the noumenon as *ein Objekt einer nichtsinnlichen Anschauung*.[34] The one is "*not* an object of our sense perception"; the other is "an object of our *non*-sensuous perception."

4.3 *Preposition-shifting puns.* This category is not strictly parallel to the previous two (4.1 and 4.2), because it involves not a switch but a shift of preposition. In each of the examples here given the shift is from the 'of' of possession (or its prepositional equivalent in French and nonprepositional equivalent in German) to some other preposition.

Marx asserts that the *gesellschaftliche Emanzipation des Juden* ('social emancipation *of* the Jew') is an *Emanzipation der Gesellschaft vom Judentum* ('emancipation of society *from* Jewishness').[35] Kojève says that, for Hegel, death is *une manifestation de la Négativité dans l'Homme*, or rather, *de l'Homme* ('a manifestation of the Negativity *in* Man' or rather '*of* Man').[36] Toynbee defines the term 'proletariat' as meaning 'any social element or group which in

---

31. *Process and Reality,* New York, 1929, p. 174.
32. *Hegel's* Phenomenology: *Dialogues on the Life of Mind,* LaSalle, Ill., 1965, pp. 359f.
33. *De Civitate Dei,* Bk. XXII, ch. 30.
34. *Kritik der reinen Vernunft,* B 307.
35. *Marx-Engels Gesamtausgabe,* Frankfurt, 1927, I, 1/1, p. 606. (Hereafter: MEGA.) (Italics modified.)
36. *Introduction à la lecture de Hegel,* p. 523. (Italics added.)

Philosophical Puns

some way is *in* but not *of* any given society at any given stage of such society's history'.[37]

5. *Synthetic or Compositional Puns*

My only example of a compositional philosophic pun is from Hegel. At the end of the master-slave dialectic the slave's *eigener Sinn* ('mind of his own') becomes *Eigensinn* ('stubbornness' or 'refractoriness').[38] This is probably both a compositional and an etymological pun, *Eigensinn* being historically derived from *eigen* and *Sinn*.[39]

6. *Permutational Puns*

This is the largest and probably the most important of all the categories of philosophical puns. It clearly has the greatest number of subcategories. Permutational puns normally function either to identify or correlate, or else to distinguish. The first type would be of the form, "x is characterized by Y and y by X," the second: "x is characterized by Y, but not y by X."

There is a difficulty of notation involved in any such formalization. *Principia Mathematica* notation, which I shall use for category 6.22 below, where

$$Y = \phi x \text{ and } x = \overline{\phi} y$$

is not appropriate where individual and predicate variables change places. I shall use lower-case 'x' and 'y' as individual variables (where the values of the variables are nouns) and upper-case 'X' and 'Y' as predicate variables (where the values of the variables are adjectives or participles).

It should be noted that syntactical shifts are more obvi-

---

37. *A Study of History,* Oxford, 1934, I, 41*n*3. (Italics added.)
38. *Phänomenologie des Geistes,* p. 150.
39. Compositional puns abound, for instance, in the works of Rabelais. But, while impressive, they are in no sense philosophical, e.g.:

> *Or donné par don*
> *Ordonne pardon.*
> ('Gold given as a gift
> Grants pardon'.)   (*Gargantua*, Bk. I, ch. 52.)

ous in the highly-inflected languages such as Greek, German, and Russian than they are in English.

6.1 *Two-term permutational puns* — where articles, conjunctions, prepositions, etc., are not counted in determining the number of terms.

6.11 *Noun-adjective pairs*

6.111 *Identifying or correlating cases*: Aristotle offers *orektikos nous* ('desiderative intellect') and *orexis dianoētikē* ('intellective desire') as alternative characterizations of deliberate choice.[40]

Hegel equates *verständige Vernunft* ('understanding reason') with *vernünftiger Verstand* ('rational understanding')[41] and correlates *die geistige Natur* ('spiritual nature') with *der natürliche Geist* ('natural spirit').[42] Marx says that men have a *geschichtliche Natur* ('historical nature') as well as a *natürliche Geschichte* ('natural history').[43]

According to Kojève, philosophy is a *dialectique pédagogique* ('pedagogical dialectic') or *pédagogie dialectique* ('dialectical pedagogy');[44] and man's historicity is expressed in *l'individualité libre* ('free individuality') or *la liberté individuelle* ('individual freedom').[45] Heidegger, of course, offers many two-term correlating noun-adjective puns on the model of *spontane Rezeptivität* ('spontaneous receptivity') and *rezeptive Spontaneität* ('receptive spontaneity').[46] But most of them strike me as more ingenious than philosophically illuminating.

Kojève provides an example of a two-term identifying noun-adjective permutational pun which also involves word-stress-shift: he correlates *le réel* passé ('the *past* real-[ity]') with *le Passé* réel ('the *real* Past').[47]

---

40. *Nicomachean Ethics,* 1139b 5-6.
41. *Wissenschaft der Logik,* I, 6.
42. Letter to Windischmann, May 27, 1810: *Briefe von und an Hegel* (ed. J. Hoffmeister), Hamburg, 1961, I, 314.
43. Marx and Engels *Die deutsche Ideologie,* (East) Berlin, 1953, p. 41.
44. *Introduction à la lecture de Hegel,* p. 281.
45. *Ibid.,* p. 521.
46. *Kant und das Problem der Metaphysik,* Frankfurt, 1951, p. 188.
47. *Introduction à la lecture de Hegel,* p. 368.

Philosophical Puns

6.112 *Distinguishing cases*:
Schiller points out that *eine leere Unendlichkeit* ('an empty infinity') is not the same as *eine unendliche Leere* ('an infinite emptiness').[48] Wittgenstein insists that a *zaghafte Behauptung* ('timid' or 'hesitant assertion') is not a *Behauptung der Zaghaftigkeit* ('assertion of hesitancy').[49] In his formulation the permutation is from an adjective-noun to a noun-noun pair. But the latter could be reformulated as an adjective-noun pair, viz., *behauptete Zaghaftigkeit* ('asserted hesitancy'), without loss of meaning, though perhaps with some loss of elegance.

Stanley Rosen juxtaposes the 'shaped process' of *logos* and the 'processive shaping' of *physis*.[50] Jan van der Meulen, in a participle-noun pair, contrasts *entäussernde Entfremdung* ('externalizing alienation') and *entfremdende Entäusserung* ('alienating externalization').[51]

6.12 *Noun-noun pairs*

It seems likely that at least some noun-adjective pairs can be reformulated as noun-noun pairs, thus exhibiting their categoreal character more clearly. An example would be the Heideggerian adjective-noun pair of Sec. 6.111 which could be reformulated as *Spontaneität der Rezeptivität* ('spontaneity of receptivity') and *Rezeptivität der Spontaneität* ('receptivity of spontaneity'). Such reformulations normally involve significant, but not drastic, shifts of meaning.

6.121 *Identifying or correlating cases.* Heraclitus' *ek pantōn hen kai ex henos panta* ('from all things one and from the one all things') is the first permutational pun on record in Western philosophy.[52] His famous *athanatoi thnētoi, thnētoi athanatoi* ('immortals are mortal[s], mortals immortal[s]') is a philosophical paradox, but not a pun in my sense.[53] Its formula would be: "not-x is X and x is not-X,"

---

48. *Werke,* Weimar, 1962, XX, 368.
49. *Philosophische Untersuchungen,* Oxford, 1953, p. 192.
50. *Nihilism: A Philosophical Essay,* New Haven, 1969, p. 147.
51. *Die gebrochene Mitte,* Hamburg, 1958, p. 198.
52. Diels-Kranz, *Die Fragmente der Vorsokratiker,* Fr. 10.
53. *Ibid.,* Fr. 62.

where it is not even clear whether the second of the two terms in each case is a noun or an adjective (hence whether, in my notation, the second '*x*' should be written in lower or upper case). The second part of this fragment, about "each living the other's death and dying the other's life" might be interpreted as a three-term verb-noun permutational pun of the identifying or correlating type.

Spinoza asserts that there is neither *Spes sine Metu* ('hope without fear') nor *Metus sine Spe* ('fear without hope'),[54] making a point pertinent for philosophical psychology.

Marx asserts the *misère* ('poverty') of a particular *philosophie*, namely, of the philosophy expounded in Proudhon's book *Philosophie de la misère*. Thus Marx is proclaiming the *misère de la philosophie de la misère*, in a "circular permutational pun" of a loosely correlating kind.

Earlier, Marx had said that the *Philosophisch-Werden der Welt* ('becoming philosophical [i.e., philosophical clarification] of the world') was at the same time a *Weltlich-Werden der Philosophie* ('becoming worldly [i.e., secularization and/or "practicalization"] of philosophy').[55]

According to Heidegger, the *Wesen der Wahrheit* ('essence of truth [as disclosure]') is the *Wahrheit des Wesens* ('disclosure [as truth] of essential being').[56]

6.122 *Distinguishing cases.* Hume denies — in effect — that the "succession of impressions" is or produces an "impression of succession."[57] Schelling sees a difficulty in conceiving *die Vorstellungen ... als sich richtend nach den Gegenständen* ('representations ... as conforming to objects') and the same time, *die Gegenstände als sich richtend nach den Vorstellungen* ('objects as conforming to representations').[58]

---

54. *Ethics,* Pt. III, def. 13, explanation.
55. MEGA I, 1/1, p. 64. Of course, *werden* ('to become') is a verb, but *das Werden* ('becoming') is a noun; hence *Philosophisch-Werden* is here treated as a noun.
56. *Vom Wesen der Wahrheit,* Frankfurt, 1949, p. 26.
57. *Treatise of Human Nature,* Bk. I, Pt. ii, Sec. 3. Hume's own wording is somewhat looser than this.
58. *Sämtliche Werke,* Stuttgart, 1858, Abt. I, Bd. 3, p. 348.

Philosophical Puns

For Marx the *Jenseits der Wahrheit* ('beyond of truth') is to be replaced by the *Wahrheit des Diesseits* (truth of the here-and-now', i.e., the 'non-beyond').⁵⁹ Here, of course, *Jenseits* (literally, the 'other-side') and *Diesseits* (the 'this-side') are contraries, which introduces a slight formal complication.

Whitehead says that "there is a becoming of continuity, but no continuity of becoming."⁶⁰ In my neo-Whiteheadian terms, this means that concreta ("ex-concrescences" or past actual entities) are individually divisible and form a continuous (past) series, whereas (present) concrescences are individually atomic and form a discrete series.⁶¹

Sartre insists that *l'être du phénomène* ('the being of the phenomenon or appearance') is not the same thing as *le phénomène d'être* ('the phenomenon, or appearance, of being').⁶² One would presume, however, that one of the aims of a "phenomenological ontology" would be to soften the distinction between the two.

Kolakowski contrasts the *reifikacja aktu* ('reification of the act') with the *aktualizacja rzeczy* ('actualization of the thing').⁶³

6.13 *Adjective-adjective pairs*

6.131 *An identifying or correlating case*: Hegel's celebrated epigram, *Was vernünftig ist, das ist wirklich* ('what is rational is actual') and *was wirklich ist, das ist vernünftig* ('what is actual is rational'),⁶⁴ could be considered an adjective-adjective pair. However, since the expressions *was vernünftig ist* and *was wirklich ist* function as grammatical subjects, the epigram could also be classified as a noun-adjective pair.

---

59. MEGA, I, 1/1, p. 608.
60. *Process and Reality,* p. 53.
61. See my "Form, Concrescence, and Concretum: A Neo-Whiteheadian Analysis," *Southern Journal of Philosophy,* Vol. 7 (1969-1970), pp. 351-360.
62. *L'Être et le néant,* Paris, 1943, pp. 14, 15.
63. *Kultura i fetysze,* Warsaw, 1967, p. 85.
64. *Grundlinien der Philosophie des Rechts,* "Vorrede," (ed. J. Hoffmeister), Hamburg, 1955, p. 14.

6.132 *A distinguishing case*: In poetry Aristotle prefers the *pithanon [kai] adynaton* ('probable [but] impossible') to the *apithanon kai dynaton* ('improbable but possible').[65]

6.14 *Adverb-adjective pairs*

I have found only one, distinguishing, case of this type: Kant's contrast between the man who is *bene moratus* (literally, 'well-moralled', i.e., one whose conduct is morally unexceptionable, whether or not he acts from motives of moral duty) and the man who is *moraliter bonus* ('morally good', i.e., who acts from motives of moral duty).[66]

6.15 *Verb-verb pairs*

Distinguishing case: Schopenhauer claims that, in terms of his own philosophy, the individual ERKENNT *was er will* ('*knows* what he wills'), whereas, on other philosophic views, the individual WILL ... *was er erkennt* ('*wills* what he knows').[67] This could be classified as a verb-noun pair, since the noun clauses *was er will* and *was er erkennt* function as direct objects.

6.16 *Noun-verb pairs*

6.161 *Identifying or correlating cases:* According to Feuerbach, who in this passage cites and paraphrases St. Augustine, *Gott ... vermenschlichte sich, um den Menschen zu vergöttern* ('God ... humanized himself in order to deify man').[68] Marx asserts that while *die Arbeit ... ist vergegenständlicht* ('work is objectified'), the *Gegenstand ist verarbeitet* ('the object is worked', i.e., 'elaborated, shaped').[69]

N. F. Fyodorov claims that primitive man *odukhotvoryal materiyu* ('spiritualized matter') and *materializiroval dukh*

---

65. *Poetics*, 1461b 11-12.
66. *Werke* (ed. E. Cassirer), Berlin, 1924, VI, 169. Only the Latin expressions contain adverbs in *both* formulations; the German counterparts are *ein Mensch von guten Sitten* ('a man with good morals') and *ein sittlich guter Mensch* ('a morally good man'). Only the second German formulation contains an adverb — *sittlich*.
67. *Sämtliche Werke*, Leipzig, 1891, II, 346. This example also involves word-stress shift.
68. *Sämtliche Werke*, VI, 62.
69. Marx and Engels, *Werke*, (East) Berlin, 1962, XXIII, 195.

Philosophical Puns

('materialized spirit').[70] Wilfrid Sellars has equated "particularized qualities" with "qualitative [i.e., qualitied] particulars."[71]

6.162 *Distinguishing cases*: Epictetus says that in the opinion of the unenlightened, *ouk epitrepomen paideuesthai, ei mē tois eleutherois* ('only free men may be educated', i.e., only the well-born need or deserve an education), but that in fact *ouk epitrepomen eleutherois einai ei mē tois pepaideumenois* ('only educated men may be free', i.e., only men trained in Stoic self-control can escape the bondage of the passions).[72] Pascal remarks drily that, *ne pouvant fortifier la justice* ('not being able to enforce [or strengthen] justice') men have *justifié la force* ('justified force').[73] Karl Popper proposes that we "moralize politics" and not "politicize morals,"[74] i.e., that we subordinate political policies and actions to moral principles rather than subordinating moral choice and action to political principles.

6.2 *Three-term permutational puns*

6.21 *Cases with two repeated terms and one unrepeated term*

6.211 *Identifying or correlating cases*:

Skovoroda calls *veshchestvo* ('matter') both *krasnaya gryaz* ('painted mud') and *gryaznaya kraska* ('muddy paint').[75] For Hegel *nous* or intellect is *bewusstlos-wirkende Vernünftigkeit* ('unconsciously-effective rationality') as well as *bewusstlos-vernünftige Wirksamkeit* ('unconsciously-rational effectiveness').[76] The hyphenated expressions are regarded as single words.

---

70. *Filosofiya obshchevo dela,* Verny [Alma Ata], 1906, I, 28. Earlier, Feuerbach had asserted that love *idealisiert die Materie* ('idealizes matter') and *materialisiert den Geist* ('materializes spirit') (*Sämtliche Werke,* VI, 59). Clearly, his use of the terms 'matter' and 'spirit' is rather different from Fyodorov's use of these terms.

71. In a paper read at a meeting of the Metaphysical Society of America at Vanderbilt University, March 14, 1969.

72. *Discourses,* Bk. II, ch. 1.

73. *Pensées et opuscules* (ed. L. Brunschvicg), Paris, n.d., No. 299, p. 470.

74. *The Open Society and Its Enemies,* New York, 1963, I, 113.

75. *Tvori v dvokh tomakh,* I, 245.

76. *Werke* (ed. H. Glockner), Stuttgart, 1928, XI, 389.

For Hegel, on Hyppolite's interpretation, *la vérité devient subjective* ('truth becomes subjective') at the same time that *la subjectivité acquiert une vérité* ('subjectivity acquires a truth [of its own]').[77]

6.212 Distinguishing cases

For Kierkegaard *Tvivl er Tankens Fortvivlelse* ('doubt is the despair of thought') and *Fortvivlelse er Personlighedens Tvivl* ('despair is the doubt of personality').[78] Here *Tanken* ('thought') would appear to mean 'man as thinker' and *Personlighed* ('personality' or 'person') — 'man as existing individual'. This pun involves prefix-switching, with one "null" prefix between *-Tvivl* and *For-tvivlelse*. (Cf. German *Zweifel* and *Verzweiflung*. Etymologically, in both languages, *despair* is an intensified *doubt*.)

Sir James Baillie has said that "wonder is reverent ignorance" while "superstition is ignorant reverence."[79] Here 'wonder' and 'superstition' are species of a genus, something like 'naïve feelings of awe'.

According to Whitehead, "physical time" expresses "some features of the growth, but *not* the growth of the features."[80]

6.22 Cases with two repeated terms, the third term appearing once in positive and once in negative form:

$$x \text{ is } \phi y \text{ and } Y \text{ is } \bar{\phi} x$$

6.221 Identifying or correlating cases

For Aristotle the *doulos* ('slave') is an *empsychon organon* ('living or animate tool'), while the *organon* ('tool') is an *apsychos doulos* ('lifeless or inanimate slave').[81] This pun includes a kind of prefix-switching in the adjectives *EMpsychon* and *Apsychos*.

According to Pascal, *la nature* is *une première coutume* ('nature' is 'a first habit') while *la coutume* is *une seconde*

---

77. *Genèse et structure de la Phénoménologie de l'Esprit de Hegel*, Paris, 1946, p. 216.
78. *Samlede Vaerker*, III, 197.
79. *Reflections on Life and Religion*, London, 1952, p. 17.
80. *Process and Reality*, p. 434.
81. *Nicomachean Ethics*, 1161b 4-5.

Philosophical Puns

nature ('habit' is 'a second [i.e., non-first] nature').[82] Marx says that the *Kapitalist* is a *rationeller Schatzbildner* ('rational miser'), while the *Schatzbildner* is a *verrückter Kapitalist* ('insane [i.e., irrational] capitalist').[83]

Marx also calls *der Christ* ('the Christian') a *theoretisierender Jude* ('theorizing Jew'), and *der Jude* a *praktischer Christ* ('practical [i.e., not merely theorizing] Christian').[84]

6.222 Distinguishing cases

Whitehead contrasts the "collective kinds of the entities" with the "individual entities of the kinds."[85] If the term 'collective' is taken to mean 'non-individual' and the term 'individual' to mean 'non-collective', this could be formalized as:

$$\phi y \text{ of } x \text{ in contrast to } \overline{\phi} \ x \text{ of } y$$

6.23 Cases where all three terms are repeated
6.231 Identifying or correlating cases

Aristotle claims that, just as there is no *hyperbolēs kai elleipseōs mesotēs* ('mean of [either] an excess or a deficiency'), so there cannot be any *mesotētos hyperbolē kai elleipsis* ('excess and deficiency of a mean').[86]

For Hegel, *das Absolute [ist] allein wahr* ('the Absolute alone [is] true') and *das Wahre [ist] allein absolut* ('the True alone [is] absolute').[87] Here the adverb *allein* is taken as one of the operative terms.

According to José Ferrater Mora, *hay preguntas insolubles que no son filosóficas y las hay filosóficas que no son insolubles* ('there are insoluble problems which are not philosophical, and there are philosophical [problems] which are not insoluble').[88]

---

82. *Pensées*, No. 93, p. 373.
83. *Das Kapital*, Hamburg, 1909, I, 116.
84. MEGA, I, 1/1, p. 605.
85. *Process and Reality*, p. 44.
86. *Nicomachean Ethics*, 1107a 25-27.
87. *Phänomenologie des Geistes*, p. 65.
88. *El Ser y el sentido*, Madrid, 1967, p. 97.

6.232 *Distinguishing cases*

As Pascal sees it: *ne pouvant faire qu'il soit force d'obéir à la justice, on a fait qu'il soit juste d'obéir à la force* ('Not having been able to force men to submit to justice, they have declared it just to submit to force').[89]

Jacobi, discussing Spinoza, asserts that *das Denken ist nicht die Quelle der Substanz; sondern die Substanz ist die Quelle des Denkens* ('Thought is not the source of substance, but rather substance is the source of thought').[90]

William Hamilton insists that the contemporary "experience of the absence of God" is entirely different from the classical mystics' "absence of the experience of God."[91]

6.3 *Four-term permutational puns*

6.31 Cases where the two non-repeated terms designate species of a given genus.

6.311 *Identifying or correlating cases*

According to Marx, *wie die Philosophie im Proletariat ihre materiellen, so findet das Proletariat in der Philosophie seine geistigen Waffen* .... ('Just as philosophy finds in the proletariat its *material* [weapons], so the proletariat finds in philosophy its *spiritual* weapons ...').[92] This means something like: (Left-Hegelian) philosophy is used by the proletariat to realize its practical aims, and the proletariat is used by (Left-Hegelian) philosophers to realize their theoretical aims. There is a further equivocation on 'philosophy' and 'philosophers'; but it is possible to interpret *proletariat* (i.e., proletarians) and *philosophy* (i.e., philosophers) as species of the genus *social groups*.

6.312 *Distinguishing cases*

Kant claimed that for realists knowledge must conform to its object, whereas for transcendental idealists the object must conform to (the structure of) knowledge.[93] Here I take

---

89. *Pensées*, No. 299, p. 470.
90. *Werke*, Leipzig, 1819, Bd. 4, Abt. 1, p. 67.
91. Thomas J. Altizer and William Hamilton, *Radical Theology and the Death of God*, Indianapolis, 1966, p. 28.
92. MEGA, I, 1/1, p. 620.
93. Cf. Schelling's reformulation of this Kantian point in Sec. 6.122, above.

realist and *transcendental idealist* to be species of the genus *epistemologist*.

Whitehead writes: "For Kant the world emerges from the subject; for the philosophy of organism, the subject emerges from the world."[94] Here 'Kant' means 'Kantian philosophy' and 'philosophy of organism' means 'Whiteheadian philosophy'. These two are thus species of the genus *philosophy*.

6.32 *Cases where the two non-repeated terms are, in a broad sense, correlative, but are not species of a genus.* This may be formalized as:

All x that is not-y is P; all y that is not-x is R.

'P' and 'R' are the correlative terms. No term is repeated in its positive form, but 'x' and 'y' appear in negative form ('not-x', 'lacking x', 'without x', etc.)

According to a celebrated Kantian formula, *Gedanken ohne Inhalt sind leer, Anschauungen ohne Begriffe sind blind.*[95] Here *blind* means 'lacking form' and *leer* means 'lacking content'. *Gedanken* is synonymous with *Begriffe*. Since 'form' and 'content' are correlative terms, their negatives are also correlative terms. Kant is thus saying that *Begriffe ohne Anschauungen* are *inhaltlos* and that *Anschauungen ohne Begriffe* are *formlos*, i.e., "concepts without sense-perceptions are empty of content; sense-perceptions without concepts [i.e., unconceptualized] are formless."

In a metaphilosophical pun Cieszkowski maintained (in 1838) that, in the history of philosophy, just as Aristotle was the *Ende des Anfangs* ('end of the beginning') so Hegel was the *Anfang des Endes* ('beginning of the end').[96] Here 'beginning' and 'end', like 'form' and 'content' in Kant, are correlative terms — more specifically, contraries.

Philosophical puns often function mnemonically or peda-

---

94. *Process and Reality,* pp. 135f.
95. *Kritik der reinen Vernunft,* A 51.
96. *Prolegomena zur Historiosophie* (1838), 2nd ed., Posen [Poznan], 1908, p. 99.

gogically; they may occasionally function heuristically. But I would deny — although I cannot argue the point here — that such puns are merely aids to memory, communication, or invention. The most successful of them also play a substantive or systematic role in the formulation of philosophical positions.[97] Perhaps philosophical puns can be reformulated in nonpunning terms as poems can be paraphrased in nonpoetic language. But, in both cases, something essential is lost.

---

97. The question of the "validity" of punning arguments, and of the "invalidity" of punning paralogisms, invites exploration on another occasion.

11

KANT'S ETHICS AS A PART OF METAPHYSICS: A POSSIBLE NEWTONIAN SUGGESTION?

with Some Comments on Kant's
"Dreams of a Seer"

Giorgio Tonelli

I

ONE OF THE MOST REMARKABLE TRAITS OF KANT'S SYSTEM of philosophy is the fact that Ethics is classified as a part of Metaphysics, as it appears in the titles of two of Kant's major works: The *Foundation of the Metaphysics of Morals* and *Metaphysics of Morals*. It is just too bad that no commentator, as far as I know, ever stressed the importance of this fact, and of the underlying problems; the fact was taken for granted, the problem ignored.* It is high time to call some attention to it.

Actually, this is one of the most dramatic changes Kant in-

---

*I wish to express my gratitude to Prof. Anthony Preus for reading this manuscript and making some useful suggestions.

troduced into the structure of philosophy as a whole; before him, a subordination of Ethics to Metaphysics was, as far as I know, totally unheard of. Metaphysics had been subordinated to Ethics by Spinoza, probably under the influence of the later developments of Stoicism, but the opposite had never been attempted.

This of course does not mean that before Kant Ethics never had been *founded* on Metaphysics; on the contrary, this foundation of Ethics is certainly one of the most generally accepted positions. Nevertheless, Ethics had been considered all the same as an independent science, and not as a part of Metaphysics.

On the other hand, if Kant considers Ethics as a part of Metaphysics, this does not mean that in his thought the dependency of Ethics on Metaphysics is increased; on the contrary, Ethics becomes systematically totally independent of Metaphysics *stricto sensu;* but, as we shall see, it becomes a part of Metaphysics because it is transformed into a *foundation* of it, and this is quite new.

The expression "Metaphysics of Morals" *(Metaphysik der Sitten)* appears, as far as I know, for the first time in Kant's letter to Herder of May 9, 1768, where Kant states that he is working on a Metaphysics of Morals which should be completed within that year. But, in a letter to Lambert of December 31, 1765, Kant had already announced a work on the "Metaphysical Foundations of Practical Philosophy." The expression "Metaphysics of Morals" is repeated in Kant's letter to Lambert of September 2, 1770,[1] where our author states that he is busy right then writing a treatise (which never was published) on that subject, without adding any further comments.

In the *Logik Blomberg* (1771) and in the *Logic Philippi*

---

1. I. Kant, *Gesammelte Schriften,* Akademie-Ausgabe (Berlin und Leipzig), X^2, pp. 74, 56 and 97. Professor Norbert Hinske called my attention to the letter of 1768, and to another letter from Hamann to Herder of February 16, 1767, where Hamann states: "Kant arbeitet an einer Metaphysik der Moral" (J. G. Hamann, *Briefwechsel,* Wiesbaden 1956, Vol. II, p. 390); in another letter to Herder of August 28, 1768, Hamann writes: "Kantens Metaphysik der Moral hält mich in Erwartung" *(ibid.,* p. 421).

Kant's Ethics

(1772), moral philosophy is not subordinated to the general heading of metaphysics.² In the *Metaphysik L₁* (1775-1780), Metaphysics and Moral philosophy are said to be the two *pure* philosophical sciences,³ and in the *Lectures on Ethics* of 1780-1781, philosophy is divided into theoretical and practical philosophy,⁴ but a Metaphysics of Morals is not mentioned. In his lectures Kant frequently takes a more conservative stand than in his private correspondence, in his personal notes or in his published works.

In a letter to Herz, written towards the end of 1773, Kant announces a detailed plan for his own work: he intends to write a treatise on "transcendental philosophy," which would be a *Critique of Pure Reason;* afterwards, he intends to publish a *Metaphysics,* which would be divided into a *Metaphysics of Nature* and a *Metaphysics of Morals.* The last one would appear first.⁵

Towards the end of the decade, in his lectures on *Philosophical Encyclopaedia* (1777-1780),⁶ Kant expounds his new notion of ethics even in class. Practical philosophy should be divided, in his saying, into: (1) *transcendental practical philosophy,* dealing with the use of freedom *in general;* (2) *practical rational philosophy* viz. *Metaphysics of Morals,* dealing with the *good* use of freedom; (3) *practical anthropology.*⁷ We need not consider (3) here, because this section clearly does not belong to *pure* philosophy.⁸ As for (1), it is easy to identify it with that section or aspect of a *Critique of Pure Reason* which deals with the transcendental founda-

---

2. *Op. cit.*, XXIV, 1, 1 pp. 31, 314.
3. *Op. cit.*, XXVIII, 5, 1, p. 173.
4. I. Kant, *Eine Vorlesung Kants über Ethik,* hrsg. v. P. Menzer (Berlin, 1924), p. 1.
5. Kant, *Ges. Schr.,* X, p. 145.
6. For the correct datation, see my review of its edition, *Filosofia,* XIII (1962), pp. 511-514.
7. I. Kant, *Vorlesungen über Enzyklopädie und Logik,* Bd. I, *Vorlesungen über Philosophische Enzyklopädie* (Berlin, 1961), p. 38. (This edition of Kant's lectures, although published by the Berlin Academy, is not a part of the *Gesammelte Schriften.* This edition was discontinued after Vol. 1.) Nevertheless, on p. 67, *Moral* and *Metaphysik* seem to be distinguished.
8. *See ibid.,* p. 68.

tions of morality.⁹ Therefore (2) corresponds to the *Metaphysics of Morals* properly.

It is well known that in the section on *Architectonic* of the *Critique of Pure Reason* metaphysics is divided into *Metaphysics of Nature* and *Metaphysics of Morals*. But Kant felt the need of adding a few words of explanation for a denomination so unusual:

> The term 'metaphysics,' in its *strict* sense, is commonly reserved for the metaphysics of speculative reason. But as pure moral philosophy really forms part of this special branch of human and philosophical knowledge derived from pure reason, we shall retain for it the title 'metaphysics'.¹⁰

Still, in the *Prolegomena* (1783), Metaphysics and Morals are mentioned separately.¹¹ But in a Reflection dated by Adickes in 1783-84, Metaphysics is divided again into Metaphysics of Nature and of Morals.¹² In the *Metaphysik Volckmann* (1784-85), Kant expands on this distinction.¹³

In 1785, the publication of the *Foundation of the Metaphysics of Morals* lends a final official character to this denomination, referring to a science belonging to *pure* philosophy in as far as this is limited to particular objects of the understanding.¹⁴ The need for a special *Critique of Pure Practical Reason* is also acknowledged.¹⁵

---

9. It is well known that Kant realized the need to write a *Critique of Practical Reason* only after 1781. The *Critique of Pure Reason* was supposed, at least until 1785, to take care of the transcendental foundation of both the Metaphysics of Nature and the Metaphysics of Morals.

10. B. 870. I quote the *Critique of Pure Reason* using the pagination of the second edition (B). Where the second edition (1787) does not conform to the first, that will be pointed out. For translation into English, I follow N. Kemp Smith.

11. Kant, *Ges. Schr.*, IV, p. 363 (§60).

12. *Op. cit.*, XVIII, pp. 284-85 (Refl. #5644).

13. *Op. cit.*, XXVIII, 5, 1, p. 364. On p. 362 a justification of sorts is given for the presence of metaphysics in ethics; but it cannot serve our purpose because, according to this justification, metaphysics is present in *all* rational sciences, including mathematics (p. 363).

14. *Op. cit.*, IV, p. 388. Kant adds: "Auf solche Weise entspringt die Idee einer zweifachen Metaphysik, einer *Metaphysik der Natur* und einer *Metaphysik der Sitten*" (*ibid.*). But what precedes hardly can be considered a clear explanation of this conclusion.

15. *Loc. cit.*, p. 391.

Kant's Ethics

The question, in fact, is settled from now on. In the later years, only after 1790, Morals is distinguished from Metaphysics in the division of the parts of a certain conception of philosophy in general, called "cosmopolitan," which conception seems to have been unknown before, and which seems not to replace, but to flank, the older conception and division.[16] In fact, the established denomination reappears in the *Metaphysics of Morals* published in 1797.

II

Kant, of course, gives some reasons for classifying Ethics as a part of Metaphysics. For instance, in 1781, he states that:

> All pure *a priori* knowledge, owing to the special faculty of knowledge in which alone it can originate, has in itself a peculiar unity; and metaphysics is the philosophy which has as its task the statement of that knowledge in this systematic unity.[17]

Still, one may wonder why the best way for stressing the unity of pure *a priori* knowledge should be to bring it all under the heading of metaphysics, instead of using, e.g., the denomination of "pure philosophy," as Kant does on other occasions. But in 1787, in the Preface to the second edition of the *Critique of Pure Reason,* Kant offers a perhaps better justification:

---

16. The first appearance of this doctrine which can be dated with certitude is that in the *Metaphysik L₂* of 1790-91 (*op. cit.,* XXVIII, 5, 2, 1, pp. 532-33). The same notion of "cosmopolitan" philosophy reappears in the *Wiener Logik* of 1794-96 (*op. cit.,* XXIV, I, 2, pp. 798-99), but there is no division. This leads me to think that the section of the *Logik Jäsche* expounding the same doctrine, and giving the same division *(op. cit.,* IX, pp. 24-25), derives from the *Kollegheft* of 1790 which, along with another from 1782, was used by Jäsche to compile his text.

17. B 873. This inclusion of moral philosophy in pure philosophy had already been introduced in the *Dissertatio* of 1770, as a reaction to the sentimental morality of Shaftesbury and others. *See:* J. Schmucker, *Die Ursprünge der Ethik Kants* (Meisenheim am Glan 1961), p. 268-269.

Giorgio Tonelli

> ... when all progress in the field of the supersensible has thus been denied to speculative reason, it is still open to us to enquire whether, in the practical knowledge of reason, data may not be found sufficient to determine reason's transcendent concept of the unconditioned, and so to enable us, in accordance with the wish of metaphysics, and by means of knowledge *a priori,* though only from a practical point of view, to pass beyond the limits of all possible experience.[18]

In fact, pure *speculative* philosophy is barely negative in the area of the knowledge of reason: the traditional basic problems of metaphysics remain unanswered in this field; but the "wish of metaphysics" is fulfilled, in as far as this is possible, by pure *practical* philosophy. Thus ethics is, in a certain way, systematically incorporated into metaphysics in order to provide metaphysics with a tenable "Unconditioned" which cannot be established otherwise.

Other reasons as good as this one could possibly be found in order to explain the doctrine under consideration: a doctrine both original and eventful, which is obviously of central importance in Kant's system. But the justification given *post factum* for a certain doctrine frequently does not correspond to the historical origin of the doctrine in question, which sometimes was first suggested by considerations of a different order, perhaps less original and more casual. This was probably the case with Kant's unification of metaphysics and ethics, which may have been originated in a parallelism proposed as early as 1766, between physical and moral laws. If this is true, from this initial parallelism to the final systematic unification, Kant certainly had a very long way to go. I intend to explore in the following the modest beginnings, not the glorious developments of this approach.

III

In his book, *The Dreams of a Seer Compared with the Dreams of Metaphysics* of 1776, Kant presented in a merely

---

18. B xxi. *See* also B xxv.

hypothetical way a rather inspiring doctrine: if it is true that lifeless matter constitutes a system ruled by mechanical laws, immaterial beings could also be considered to constitute a system of their own, ruled by "pneumatic" laws. This "spiritual" or "immaterial world" could be "a whole subsisting by itself," in as far as spirits could act upon each other directly, without the mediation of matter (i.e., of their bodies), the more as some of them are not connected at all with a body (are not souls).

The two worlds, the material and the immaterial, would be linked with each other through the organic bodies belonging to some of the spirits. In fact, organic life itself could be considered at all its levels as originated by the connection of an immaterial substance with matter. This would be difficult to deny at least in as far as motile organisms (animals) are concerned, because the capability to initiate a movement (activity) presupposes a free will, and therefore the presence of a spirit.[19]

> In as far as all principles of life in the whole of nature are interconnected in this way, as many corporeal substances in a community with each other, but also as partially linked with matter, one comes to think of a great whole of the immaterial world, of an immense, but unknown chain of beings and of active natures, which alone vivify the dead stuff of material world.[20]

According to this hypothesis, the situation of man would be the following:

> Thus, the human soul should be considered already during the present life as connected with two worlds at the same time; of them, the soul would sense clearly the material one only, in as far as the soul is connected into a personal unity with a body; but, as a member of the spiritual world, the soul would receive and impart the pure influences of the immaterial natures, so that, as soon as that connection ceases, the standing community with spiritual natures alone is left, and should become manifest to the soul's consciousness in a clear intuition.[21]

---

19. Kant, *Ges. Schr.*, II, pp. 329-32. On the connection between life and free will (Willkür), see also p. 327, n.
20. *Loc. cit.*, p. 330.
21. *Loc. cit.*, p. 332.

Giorgio Tonelli

As we have seen, a mutual communication between the human soul and the other spirits would already take place during lifetime, although the soul could not communicate material representations to spirits, and could not grow *clearly conscious* of the concepts pure spirits have, at least in the *proper form (eigentliche Beschaffenheit)* of these concepts, or as intuitive representations of immaterial things.[22]

Kant is very prudent in presenting these views: he knows that it is fashionable to deride them as "dusty obsolete fancies," and he confirms in principle his allegiance to the mechanistic approach in science: in fact, if he is persuaded that Stahl's vitalism is closer to the truth than the mechanical explanations of life, he is also persuaded that it will at most be possible to establish the presence of this influence of immaterial nature on matter, but not to explain how it works, or to set its boundaries.[23]

Anyhow he remarks that, if these considerations are very far from being evident, still they seem to bring about some "not unpleasant" conjectures.[24]

IV

In fact Kant develops on these presuppositions a further hypothesis. The "secret power" of moral motivation in man, as a "rule of universal will," could be an effect of this spiritual community.

> If we want to call *moral feeling* this compulsion of our will we feel in ourselves to agree with the general will, we are speaking of it merely as a phenomenon of what actually happens in ourselves, without deciding about its causes. So *Newton* called *Gravitation* the ascertained law of the effort of all material things to move towards each other, as he did not want his mathematical demonstrations to get involved in an irksome participation in the philosophical quarrels about the cause of it. But he

---

22. *Loc. cit.*, p. 333.
23. *Loc. cit.*, p. 331.
24. *Loc. cit.*, pp. 333-34.

Kant's Ethics

did not hesitate to consider this Gravitation as the true effect of a universal activity of material things on each other, and he called it *Attraction*. Should it not be equally possible to consider the phenomenon of the moral tendencies in the thinking natures, in as far as these refer to each other, as the consequence of a true active power through which spiritual natures influence each other, in such a way, that the moral feeling would be *to feel this dependence* of private will from general will, and a consequence of that natural and general reciprocal action, whereby the immaterial world reaches its moral unity, constituting one system of spiritual perfection according to the laws of this peculiar connection?[25]

So, the basic analogy acquires a *second dimension*. At first, we saw the "spiritual world" used as a principle founding the phenomenon of organic life; now, it is used as a principle founding the phenomenon of moral feeling, formulated as "general will," probably on Rousseau's suggestion.[26] In the first case, the laws of the spiritual world explicitly interfere with the mechanical laws of matter; in the second, they implicitly interfere with the laws of psychological determinism. Moreover, the second dimension of the analogy points at a particular aspect of the material world: the law of gravitation, as an established element of it that had not found an explanation.

I do not want to insist on this last point because, although Kant had tried, more than twenty years before (1745-46), to "explain" metaphysically gravitation in a way which certainly could not be called mechanical in an impulsionistic sense, he had given up this pretension very soon: in his *Monadologia physica* of 1756, he had tried to construct a system of natural philosophy *presupposing* (not explaining) attraction and repulsion as basic forces, without attempting to reduce them to impulsionistic agents;[27] it seems that Kant

---

25. *Loc. cit.*, p. 335. I translated "einfliessen" as "to influence," which is one of the eighteenth-century meanings of this verb (*see* J. Chr. Adelung, *Grammatisch-kritisches Wörterbuch der Hochdeutschen Mundart*, Leipzig, 1793, s.v.), in the sense of "the influence of one substance on another."

26. See J. Schmucker, *Die Ursprünge der Ethik Kants* (Meisenheim am Glan, 1961), pp. 156 f.

27. See G. Tonelli, *Elementi metodologici e metafisici in Kant dal 1745 al 1768* (Torino, 1959), Vol. I, Cap. I and IV, A.

in 1766 had given up that doctrine too, and had resorted to a prudent agnosticism; however, he was for a long time firmly to believe that all physical phenomena unrelated to life could be (although they may not yet actually have been) explained mechanically. Only very late, at the time of his last attempt towards establishing an all-comprehensive theory of the physical world in the *Opus postumum,* was Kant to give up this basic conviction, and to try to set up a finalistic foundation of physics.

But, in order to understand Kant's different positions in their precise relationship, it is important to realize in general that a "mechanical" explanation, for Kant, did not necessarily mean an "impulsionistic" explanation; it only meant a process taking place (1) by *efficient,* and not by final causes, and (2) in a strictly *deterministic* way. The notion of "mechanicism," in fact, had undergone in general some basic changes after Newtonian attractionism had been generally accepted.

Referring for a moment to the *first* dimension of the analogy, I only want to recall the fact that this hypothesis of a spiritual world as the source of life was bound to have a lasting influence on the shaping of Kant's philosophy; as I pointed out on another occasion, this theory would very soon be identified by our author with the ancient doctrine of the Soul of the World, and as such it would play an important role in the foundation of the notions not only of life and of freedom, but also of "genial" works of art and of a "system" of philosophy. The interconnection of these notions had probably been suggested to Kant by Swedenborg.[28]

Now, focusing on the *second* dimension of the analogy, what I intend to explore is the origin of the parallelism between the moral law and the physical law of attraction, a parallelism unaccounted for by any precedent in Swedenborg (who anyhow always refused to accept attractionism). As he did on many other occasions, Kant creatively combined suggestions of disparate origins.

---

28. *See* G. Tonelli, " *'Divinae Particula Aurae';* Genial Ideas, Organism, and Freedom: A Note on Kant's Reflection N. 938," *Journal of the History of Philosophy,* VII (1969); *id.,* "Kant's Early Theory of Genius (1770-1779)", *ibid.,* IV (1966).

Kant's Ethics

V

A parallelism between moral inclinations and the motion of bodies had already been established by Malebranche,[29] and certainly not for the first time: it is, among other things, an old Stoic doctrine. But this doctrine had been largely developed only among the British Newtonians, as Professor Macklem pointed out.[30] As early as 1688 John Norris had asserted a "Moral Gravity," as a "radical *Complacency* and Connaturality of the Soul towards Good," which he explained as "nothing else but that first Alteration or Impression which is made upon her by the streaming Influences of the Great and Supreme Magnet, *God* ...," in the same way as the earth attracts the bodies. Norris knew Malebranche's main work very well; but the terms he uses rather suggest that he had combined Newtonianism with some doctrines transmitted by Cabbalists and Hermetic philosophers, establishing a series of analogies between "sympathies" and "antipathies" or "sexual unions" at the metaphysical, physical, biological and psychological levels.[31] By 1740, not less than seven other authors expressed the same views: among them there are prominent philosophers such as Bentley and Turnbull. We may add that Hume had mentioned a kind of attraction in the "mental world" which "will be found to have as extraordinary effects as in the natural ... Its effects are everywhere conspicuous; but as to its causes, they are mostly unknown ..."[32] Hume did not refer this attraction to ethics; and, unlike most of the speculative Newtonians I mentioned, he did not take attraction as a basic force for

---

29. N. Malebranche, *Oeuvres complètes* (Paris, 1958 ff.), II, pp. 9-10 *(Recherche* IV, I, i): "Or il me semble que les inclinations des esprits sont au monde spirituel, ce que le mouvement est au monde matériel."

30. M. Macklem, *The Anatomy of the World: Relations between Natural and Moral Law from Donne to Pope* (Minneapolis, 1958), esp. pp. 100-02.

31. L. Thorndike, *A History of Magic and Experimental Science* (New York, 1958), vols. VII-VIII. *See* Vol. VIII, General Index, "Sympathy." H. Sérouya, *La Cabbale* (Paris, 1947), pp. 264 ff. On English mysticism, *see* S. Hutin, *Les disciples anglais de Jacob Boehme* (Paris, 1960).

32. D. Hume, *A Treatise of Human Nature* [1739-40] (Oxford, 1888), pp. 12-13 (Bk. I, Pt. I, Sect. IV).

granted, and expressed his agnosticism concerning its cause.

Now, it is of course possible that Kant may have originally elaborated the doctrine in question independently of any British suggestion, and this could appear the more likely, as none of the English works mentioned by Professor Macklem were translated into French or into German, nor was Hume's *Treatise* for a long time to be translated, and it is still dubious whether Kant could read any English. Only, Professor Macklem did not mention two other authors, whose influence may actually have reached Kant.

The first is Andrew Michael Ramsay, a Scotsman who spent most of his life in France, and who published in French, in 1727, a famous and extremely successful novel, *Les voyages de Cyrus*. There he expounded a version of Newton's attractionism, metaphysically founded on an "invisible" or "aetherial matter" pervading the material universe, and being, as it were, God's body, while God's soul acts on the mind of man, filling it with love. Love and hatred, in fact, are the opposed principles originating all the phenomena of the universe.[33] Ramsay was obviously combining Newtonianism with cabbalistic and hermetic ideas, largely diffused in that time in Freemasonry: our author greatly contributed to introducing this sect into France.[34] This particular doctrine, however, does not seem to have been successful in France, where Newtonianism was accepted very late, and never developed into a speculative philosophy. Only Montesquieu, in a posthumous note, expressed a somehow related idea,[35] and Voltaire hinted at the parallelism in 1766.[36]

---

33. A. M. Ramsay, *Les Voyages de Cyrus* (Paris, 1730), Vol. I, pp. 110-11; enlarged in the London, 1730 edition (in French), pp. 65-67.

34. See R. Mercier, *La réhabilitation de la nature humaine, 1700-1750* (Villemoble [Seine], 1960), pp. 278-79.

35. Mercier, *op. cit.*, pp. 83-84. In *De l'esprit des lois*, L. I., Ch. 1, Montesquieu establishes a parallel between the laws of the "monde intelligent" and those of the "monde physique."

36. Voltaire, *Le philosophe ignorant* (1766), XXXVI: "La loi de gravitation qui agit sur un astre agit sur tous les astres, sur toute la matière: ainsi la loi fondamentale de la morale agit également sur toutes les nations bien connues." F. Hemsterhuis, in his *Lettre sur les désirs* of 1770, estab-

Kant's Ethics

The second, philosophically more significant personality, is George Cheyne, the major figure among speculative Newtonians. The first edition (1705) of his most important work did not contain anything on the subject, but later he wrote:

> ... we have in the *material World Gravitation,* which wonderfully analogises to the *Faculty* or *Desire* in the *spiritual World,* and this to that; both being the *active, cardinal,* and *energetick Principles* of either *Systems* respectively. Next we have a *Mass* of extended sensible Matter, if collectively considered, or a *System* of *material Bodies,* diversely figured and situated in regard to one another, if separately considered: And in both these Views, they admirably represent the Subject or Object of the *Desire,* which is analogized by *Attraction* or *Gravitation* ...[37]

> There must of Necessity be some *Principle* of *Action* in intelligent Beings, *analogous* to that of *Attraction* in the material *System;* and that is, the *Principle of Reunion* with the supreme Infinite, by him originally impressed on their *supreme Spirits* ...[38]

This attraction lies at the foundation of moral "natural Conscience," and is contrasted by "contrary Attractions," corresponding to "Sensuality."[39]

Cheyne's work was not translated into German, but J. P. Eberhard (1729-1779), one of the most reputed German physicists of that time, gave in 1752 an account of this doctrine in one of his works.[40] Kant knew Eberhard's writings

---

lishes a parallel between moral law and the physical law of inertia, which he opposes to attraction (*Oeuvres philosophiques,* Leuwarde, 1846, T. I., pp. 57-58). Moral law is founded on religion, and its aim is the greatest good of the individual; it is opposed to, and balanced by, the "vertu civile," the aim of which is the greatest good of society. The "Vertu civile" is analogous to attraction (*op. cit.,* pp. 63 f.).

37. G. Cheine, *Philosophical Principles of Religion* (London, 1734), Pt. II, pp. 77-78. I have not been able to see the *second* edition, published in 1715. In any case, the story of this work is not very clear. The 1734 edition is sometimes considered the third, sometimes the fourth.

38. *Op. cit.,* II, p. 84.

39. *Op. cit.,* II, p. 87.

40. J. P. Eberhard, *Betrachtungen über einige Materien aus der Naturlehre* (Halle, 1752).

quite well: in 1756, 1757, and 1758, he used Eberhard's main treatise, first published in 1753,[41] as a textbook for his lectures on physics,[42] so that we can assume that he knew the other work as well.

Eberhard is one of the first German physicists who accepted Newton's theory of attraction; he declared its nature incomprehensible, and, still preserving the traditional notion of mechanicism, declared that attraction did *not* act mechanically.[43] Kant's choice of Eberhard's handbook as a textbook is easy to understand: this handbook was the first which systematically expounded in German physics on an attractionist basis.

Eberhard's account of Cheyne's analogy between moral impulse and attraction is rather accurate,[44] although he does not show much sympathy for this doctrine which could, in his opinion, lead to mysticism.[45] But on the other hand, he also indulged in rather daring speculations about spirits, who are supposed to act upon each other at a distance and directly, i.e., without the mediation of matter; this action, which he declares to be analogous to attraction, should explain among other things the apparitions of ghosts, and premonitions.[46]

---

41. *Erste Gründe der Naturlehre* (Halle, 1753).
42. Kant, *Ges. Schr.*, I, p. 502; II, pp. 10, 25. As of 1778, Kant still considered J. P. Eberhard "a very good teacher" of physics: *loc. cit.*, Vol. X, 2nd ed., p. 228.
43. Eberhard, *Betrachtungen,* p. 46. For the diffusion of Newtonianism in Germany, see Tonelli, *Elementi,* pp. 67-68.
44. Eberhard, *op. cit.,* pp. 56-57: "Solte nicht auch etwas ähnliches [*to attraction*] in der Geisterwelt stat finden? *Cheine,* ein Englischer Medicus und Weltweiser, nimmt eine dergleichen Kraft bei denen Geistern an, welche algemein sein soll, und aus welcher sich hernach viele moralische Handlungen eben so gut herleiten und erklären lassen, als die Würkungen der Körper, aus der anziehenden Kraft. Er nimmt es als einen algemeinen Grund an, dass jeder Geist sich mit seinem Ursprung wieder zu vereinigen suche ... Diese Kraft, würde freilich, wenn sie würklich vorhanden wäre, eine grosse Aehnlichkeit mit der anziehenden Kraft der Materie haben. Denn so, wie sich durch diese die Körper einander nähern; so werden sich auch die Geister durch jene einander zu nähern bemühen."
45. *Op. cit.,* p. 58.
46. *Op. cit.,* pp. 62 f.

As the notion of the immediate interaction of the spirits is, as we know, another component of Kant's hypothesis, this is one more reason to believe that Kant was actually influenced by Eberhard's work; especially as Eberhard's and Kant's quite peculiar explanations of the apparitions of ghosts are almost identical.[47]

The notion of a spiritual world consisting in a "pneumatic" connection among the spirits, and co-existing with the material world, was also present in Baumgarten,[48] Meier,[49] and Gunner.[50] Only, in the first place, Baumgarten was a panpsychist, and Meier did not reject panpsychism as an hypothesis, while Kant's hypothesis clearly rules out panpsychism by introducing a clear-cut distinction between spirit and matter; secondly, Baumgarten and Meier considered the spiritual world as a connection among intelligent spirits only, while Kant seemed to hypothesize a universal connection of all kinds of spirits, including the souls of the lowest living

---

47. Kant, *Ges. Schr.*, II, p. 340; Eberhard, *op. cit.*, pp. 71 f.
48. A. G. Baumgarten, *Metaphysica* (Halae Magd., 1739), §403: *"Nexus spirituum alicuius mundi inter se est pneumaticus (Verbindung der Geister)*. Iam in omni et hoc mundo, cui spiritus insunt, singulis singuli connectuntur. Ergo in hoc et omni mundo, cui spiritus insunt, est nexus pneumaticus universalis (mundus pneumaticus, intellectualis, moralis, regnum gratiae)." A spirit is a monad "intellectu praedita" (§402).
49. G. F. Meier, *Metaphysik* (Halle, 1755-59), §375: "... Da es nun in unserer Welt Geister giebt, so ist in dieser Welt ein allgemeiner Zusammenhang aller endlichen Geister, die in derselben entweder auf einmal, oder nach und nach, würklich sind. Diesen Zusammenhang nennt man, *die Geisterwelt* ... Diese Geisterwelt wird auch *die verständige und moralische Welt* genannt, weil nur denen Geistern Verstand und Moralität zukommt." Meier takes care to distinguish, within his panpsychism, the "spirits" from both the "sleeping" and the "merely sensibly thinking" substances. But one should not forget that Meier's panpsychism was merely hypothetical: see *op. cit.*, §367-370.
50. J. E. Gunner, *Institutiones metaphysicae* (Hafniae et Lipsiae, 1757), §326: *"Nexus alicujus spiritus dicitur pneumaticus*. Ergo nexus inter plures spiritus, qua tales, itemque inter operationes alicujus spiritus, qua tales, nexus pneumaticus dici meretur." §327: *"Mundus pneumaticus* est unio omnium spirituum finitorum, ut actualium cogitatorum. Ergo tam mundus materialis & mechanicus quam pneumaticus sunt partes mundi proprie dicti."

beings; thirdly, for Baumgarten and Meier all finite spirits have a body,[51] while for Kant superior spirits have not; fourthly, Baumgarten and Meier were universal harmonists,[52] while Kant always had been a partisan of the *influxus physicus,* inclusive of the relation between soul and body.

The fact that Baumgarten and Meier were universal harmonists increases the significance of their doctrine of the spiritual world, as a particular connection within the general connection of monads of all kinds; and this was in accordance with some doctrines of Leibniz' *Monadology,*[53] which Hansch had already pointed out.[54] In this spiritual community or "City of God" all the spirits are connected with God;[55] as for the question of the connection of the spirits with each other, Baumgarten and Meier do not establish whether this action is immediate (direct), or whether the spirits only can act on each other through their bodies; in fact, Baumgarten does not discuss the problem, and Meier does not reach any decision on the subject, stating that he does not know whether substances can act directly on each other at a dis-

---

51. Baumgarten, *op. cit.,* §797; Meier, *op. cit.,* §791.
52. I.e., they explained the interaction of *all* substances on the basis of Leibniz' pre-established harmony (see G. Fabian, *Beitrag zur Geschichte des Leib-Seele Problems,* Langensalza, 1925, pp. 79, 84-85), while Wolff, who assumed that there was a basic distinction between spiritual and material substances (having shaped his system of philosophy on Leibniz' *Système nouveau de la Nature* — the *Monadology* was published as late as 1720), restricted the pre-established harmony to the connection between the soul and the body. Material substances, according to Wolff, interacted through a real influence (Fabian, *op. cit.,* p. 40). It must be noted that Meier, though inclined towards universal harmonism, prudently stressed his basic agnosticism: *Metaphysik,* §731-759.
53. G. W. Leibniz, *Opera philosophica,* ed. J. E. Erdmann (Berlin, 1840), p. 712: there is a difference between ordinary souls and finite spirits *(Monadology,* §83), because the latter "sont capables d'entrer dans une manière de société avec Dieu" (§84), together composing a "city of God" (§85). "Cette cité de Dieu, cette monarchie véritablement universelle est un monde moral dans le monde naturel" (§86).
54. M. G. Hansch, *G. G. Leibnitii principia philosophiae* (Francofurti et Lipsiae, 1728), prop. LXXXVIII, theor. LXXVIII, LXXXIII.
55. Meier, *op. cit.,* §§1063-1064.

tance.[56] This suggestion that a direct action among spirits would have been a kind of action at a distance may have been one more reason prompting Kant to establish the analogy between pneumatic nexus and attraction.

Of course, there were other thinkers supporting the doctrine of the existence of a spiritual world, but their speculations were so wild, and the result of these speculations so remote from Kant's hypothesis, that they cannot be considered in any definite way as precedents of Kant's doctrines. For instance, among the Wolffians, Canz had maintained that there is a spiritual world where all spirits live (i.e., the souls of the dead, and superior spirits — the souls of living human beings and of animals belong to the material world); they all have a body, whereby they communicate with each other, and therefore their world, the City of God, has a material component of its own and a precise location in the universe.[57] Reusch expounded the same doctrine,[58] and Darjes, one of the major eclectics of the time, shared some of

---

56. Meier, *op. cit.*, §375: the spirits, at least in the majority of cases, are spatially *distant* from each other — they do not *touch* each other. Is an *immediate* action possible between things which do not touch each other? Meier declares that he does not know the answer (§220). (It should not be supposed that Meier could have assumed an *harmonic* action among spirits *at a distance* from each other; in his view, all actions, mediate and immediate, are brought about through the pre-established harmony, and the issue he does not decide is precisely that of the possibility of *immediate* harmonic action *at a distance*.) Of course, for Meier, space is a *phaenomenon bene fundatum,* and "contiguity" is defined as immediate action; thus, in principle, immediate action between non-contiguous substances is a *contradictio in adjecto*. But Meier proposes another definition of non-contiguity (§220): "wenn man durch Dinge, die von einander entfernt sind, solche Dinge verstehet, zwischen welche etwas anders gestelt werden kan, ob gleich ofte zwischen sie würklich nichts gestelt ist: so ist es nicht klar genug, ob es möglich oder unmöglich sey, dass ein Ding in ein anderes unmittelbar würke, welches von ihm entfernt ist." What is not clear to me, is *this* definition of non-contiguity.

57. I. G. Canz, *Iurisprudentia theologiae seu de civitate Dei, ex mente Leibnitii Monadologiae* (Tubingae, 1731¹, 1737²), Sect. II, Cap. 3, §30 f.; Sect. III, Cap. 1, §46; Sect. IV, Cap. 5, §60 f.

58. J. P. Reusch, *Systema metaphysicum* (Jenae, 1753; 1st ed. 1734), §1122 f., 1125 f., 1131 f.

these views.⁵⁹ Swedenborg, of course, fully accepted and greatly expanded the tenets of this school of thought (which obviously derived from an ancient tradition very diffused among mystics of all kinds, and widely received by divines in general), indulging in the description of the beauties of the material world of the spirits.⁶⁰

Canz and Reusch belonged to a widely speculative wing of the Wolffian school, a wing which was tolerated but certainly not encouraged by Wolff himself, who was a much more sober thinker. Canz in particular indulged in this kind of

---

59. J. G. Darjes, *Elementa metaphysices* (Jenae, 1743-44), I, p. 14; II, pp. 110, 152, 265, 295-96, 298.

60. E. Swedenborg, *Arcana Coelestia* (Londini, 1749-1753), N. 969; *id., De ultimo judicio, et de Babylonia destructa* (Londini, 1758), N. 27; *id., Sapientia angelica de divino amore et de divina sapientia* (Amstelodami, 1763), N. 83, 321, 322. Later, Kant attributed to Swedenborg the doctrine that there is a spiritual world as a community of the spirits, comprehensive of both the souls of living men and of other finite spirits; so that the soul of a virtuous living man is in connection with all other good souls however distant, although he is not aware of it; and viceversa for the souls of the wicked which are in connection with the other evil spirits: Kant, *Ges. Schr.*, XXVII, p. 298-299 *(Metaphysik L_1, 1778-1780)*. See also p. 768-769 *(Metaphysik K_2, 1791-1794)*. Now, I could not find in Swedenborg's *Arcana Coelestia* or in his other works precisely these doctrines, but as the bulk of his writing is enormous, I may have overlooked the pertinent passages. Otherwise, it is quite possible that Kant's memory deformed Swedenborg's doctrines (as there is no evidence that he had re-read Swedenborg after 1766, or at the very latest, after the middle of the seventies: see my article "Divinae Particula Aurae", *Journal of the History of Philosophy,* VII, 1969), and that this deformation vaguely followed the line of thoughts developed by Kant himself in the *Dreams.* However, even if these doctrines actually derive from Swedenborg, they basically differ from Kant's theory of morality as a kind of attraction, or as a natural law of the community of the spirits, disregarding the virtue or wickedness of the individuals. In fact Swedenborg thought that the mind of man is influenced by God for the good (*Arcana,* N. 6240), both immediately, so that he should live from the good which is from the Lord (general influx), and mediately through the spirits (particular influx) (ibid., N. 657, 6472 and 9683; *De commercio animae et corporis,* Londini 1769, N. 7); the properly moral influence is the particular which is mediated by some angels and spirits who are connected with each individual man; otherwise, man would be entirely egoistic *(Arcana,* N. 5850, 6323). Each man is influenced by two angels and by two spirits from hell *(Arcana,* N. 5470*)*.

distraction,[61] as later some other Wolffians would do, especially Schubert.[62]

---

61. See I. G. Canz, *Überzeugender Beweiss aus der Vernunft. Antreffend die Unsterblichkeit sowohl der Menschen Seelen insgemein, als besonders der Kinder-Seelen* (Tübingen, 1741).

62. J. E. Schubert, *Vernünftige und schriftmässige Gedancken vom ewigen Leben und dem Zustand der Seelen nach dem Tod* (Jena, 1742); *id., vom jüngsten Gericht* (Jena, 1742); *id., vom Ende der Welt* (Jena, 1742); *id., von den letzen Zeiten* (Jena, 1744); *id., Trauerrede von der Seelenwanderung nach dem Tode* (Jena, 1746); *id., von dem Seelenschlaf* (Jena, 1746); *id., von der Bekanntschaft der Seelen nach dem Tode* (Jena, 1746); *id., von dem Zeitvertreib der Seelen nach dem Tode* (Jena, 1746); *id., von der Erscheinung der Seelen nach dem Tode* (Jena, 1746); *Vernunftige Gedancken von der Ewigkeit der Höllenstrafen* (Jena, 1748); *Vernünftige und schriftmässige Gedancken von den Engeln* (Jena, 1748). See also G. Büchner, *Von den zweimal Verstorbenen* ... (Jena, 1756); C. F. Goede, *Demonstrationes philosophicae de existentia corporum angelicorum* (Halae Magd., 1744); J. D. Müller, *Die vertheidigte Gewissheit der Unsterblichkeit der Seele aus der Vernunft* (Frankfurth am Main, 1747); *Possibilitas et certitudo resurrectionis mortuorum ex principiis rationis excitatae* (Marburgi, 1752) (with a Preface by I. G. Canz); *Neue Bestätigung der vernünftigen Beweise für die Gewissheit der Unsterblichkeit der Seele* ... (Marburg, 1752); J. J. Plitt, *Dass in dieser als der besten Welt eine Auferstehung der Toden zukünftig sey, wird aus der Vernunft erwiesen* (Marburg, 1748); *Vernunft- und schriftmässige Gedanken über diejenige Menschen, welche bald nach ihrem Tode wieder aufgeweckt* ... (Marburg, 1752); J. F. Scholze, *Beweis dass eine Seelen-wanderung bei denen Tieren gebe* (Helmstädt, 1753); H. V. Stange, *Schrift- und vernunftmassige Gedanken von dem Zustand der Seele nach dem Tode* ... (Nordhausen, 1751); W. G. Vangerow, *Dissertatio historico-philosophica* μετεμψύχωσις *Veterum sistens* (Halae, 1765); G. Wernsdorf, *Disputatio do metempsychosi Veterum non figurata sed proprie intelligenda* (Vitembergae, 1741). Meier showed a certain restraint in this field; as we have seen, he presents doctrines of this order only in a hypothetical fashion. The same is true for the metempsychosis *(see* Meier, *op. cit.,* §450). But many of his speculations are rather wild *(see* §775 f., §789 f.) in spite of the prudence he occasionally recommends *(see also* §472). After the middle of the century, with the advent of Neologist theology, this kind of speculation became, at least for a while, unfashionable, and survived only in some mystical trends. In any case, the importance of Crusius' school, which is related to neither the Wolffians nor Swedenborg, but which developed highly fantastic speculative doctrines, should not be underrated. See G. Tonelli, *Einleitung* to Chr. A. Crusius, *Die philosophischen Hauptwerke* (Hildesheim, 1969), p. XLI f., XLIX f. A not disreputable independent thinker who advanced doctrines about the future state of the soul, ghosts, etc. was C. von Creuz in his *Versuch über die Seele* (Frankfurth und Leipzig, 1754).

Giorgio Tonelli

In fact, Leibniz himself had advocated metempsychosis at a certain time;[63] and all those thinkers who held that all spirits must have a body, as many Wolffians did (as we saw), were bound to admit a form of metempsychosis. The same doctrine circulated in Germany in Spinozistic, Stoic and Cabbalistic circles,[64] so that it is not astonishing to find it supported by independent thinkers such as the French-Swiss Crousaz,[65] Edelmann, Curtius, Mylius, Lessing, Sulzer, and the French-Swiss Bonnet.[66]

However, Kant was by no means alone in asserting that spirits above the level of human souls have no bodies: Crusius, for example, maintained the same point of view.[67] This could be a further Crusian element in Kant; and this is of some interest, because this element appeared at a time when Kant was definitely polemical against metaphysics in general, inclusive of Crusius'. But Crusius' influence would act on Kant for several more years in different ways.

The fact that Kant attributed in general "pneumatic" laws to the spirits, versus the mechanical laws of matter, was in itself quite atypical: the idea was of course very old, and many thinkers in Kant's immediate environment had accepted it explicitly, some of them using the expression

---

63. *See* N. Lossky, "Leibniz' Lehre von der Reinkarnation als Metamorphose," *Archiv für Geschichte der Philosophie,* XL (1931).
64. *See* L. Bäck, *Spinozas erste Einwirkungen auf Deutschland* (Berlin, 1895), pp. 64 f.
65. J. E. De La Harpe, *Jean-Pierre de Crousaz (Genève-Lille, 1955),* p. 235.
66. *See* H. Kofink, *Lessings Anschauungen über die Unsterblichkeit und Seelenwanderung* (Strassburg, 1912), p. 20 (Lessing expounded his views on metempsychosis for the first time in 1754, in his Preface to Mylius' *Works),* p. 178 (J. Chr. Edelmann), p. 181 (Bonnet, Sulzer); also, W. Arnsperger, *Lessings Seelenwanderungsgedanke,* Diss. (Heidelberg, 1893), pp. 18-19 (M. C. Curtius, Chr. Mylius). *See,* in particular, Chr. Mylius, *Vermischte Schriften, gesammelt von G. E. Lessing* (Berlin, 1754), pp. 139 f. For later developments of this doctrine, *see* R. Unger, "Zur Geschichte des Palingenesiegedankens im XVIII. Jhdt.," *Deutsche Vierteljahrsschrift für Literaturwissenschaft und Geistesgeschichte,* II (1924).
67. Chr. A. Crusius, *Entwurf der nothwendigen Vernunft-Wahrheiten* (Leipzig, 1753²), §485 (the passage in question is added in the second edition). *See also* §434.

"pneumatic laws."[68] But this expression covered a wide range of disparate specific conceptions: we have seen those which were closer to Kant's.

VI

The *Dreams of a Seer* were written by Kant on the occasion of some indirect contacts between him and Swedenborg;[69] in fact, Swedenborg's theosophy had become better known in Germany in 1765 through Ötinger's propaganda;[70] Ötinger himself, a mystic of pietist extraction, indulged in rather wild speculations.[71]

We should not think that Kant's sobering reaction to this trend was anything particularly original: a sound distrust for theosophic distractions had already been propagated by Thomasius as early as 1688,[72] and was most naturally in con-

---

68. *See*, for instance, Baumgarten, *op. cit.*, §403; Reusch, *op. cit.*, §630; J. J. Koethen, *Principia metaphysicae wolfianae* (Coloniae Allobr., 1737), p. 19; Gunner, *op. cit.*, §326. These were all Wolffians. *See also;* J. G. Darjes, *Introductio in artem inveniendi* (Jenae, 1731), Praec., §179; Crusius, *op. cit.*, §365.
69. *See* E. Benz, *Swedenborg in Deutschland* (Frankfurt-M., 1947), pp. 241-271; C. O. Sigsted, *The Swedenborg Epic* (New York, 1952), pp. 335 f. (ch. XXVI: "Reactions in Germany").
70. Fr. Chr. Ötinger, *Swedenborg und anderer irdische und himmlische Philosophie* [1765], in *Sämmtliche Schriften* (Reutlingen, 1855), II Abt., II B.
71. Fr. Chr. Ötinger, *Theologia ex idea vitae deducta* (Frankfurt und Leipzig, 1765).
72. Chr. Thomasius, *Introductio ad philosophiam aulicam* (Lipsiae, 1688), p. 141, where this kind of speculation is attacked for the same reason that Kant later used: "*Substantiam spiritualem ratio nostra nescit,* quia ipsius modus essendi non incurrit in sensus. Et miserandum profecto est, quod tot homines ratione pollentes se excrucient, et unus alteri conceptum rei, quem non habent, verbis obscuris & ignorantiam parum palliantibus communicet." He adds that these problems should be left to the meditation of divines, based on revelation. Thomasius pokes fun at this kind of distraction: "Et considera modo, quo excreverint ineptiae Pneumaticorum, dum multi conati fuerint explicare *Loquelam Angelorum.* Cur non etiam eorum *matrimonia, Respublicas, contractus, cibus & potum?*"

Giorgio Tonelli

formity with the spirit of the "Aufklärung" from the fifties on (with the partial exception of Lessing and of some of his friends); Semler, Nicolai and others, are excellent examples of this school of though pervading Neologist theology.[73] Swedenborg in particular had been attacked by Ernesti in 1750 and in 1763,[74] and in 1766 the Württemberg government had prohibited Otinger's book on Swedenborg.[75] In fact, it is only *after* 1776 that the Swedish seer began in general acquiring a significant number of adepts.[76] Thus, in his *Dreams of a Seer*, Kant had set upon a fashionable controversial theme. Mystical pneumatic distractions, very diffused in the XVIIth Century, had been pursued in Germany in the XVIIIth Century by theologians such as Bengel and Ötinger, and survived the "Aufklärung's" attacks in the works of Ötinger himself, and of Crusius, who was elaborating his own theology, and organizing his vast theological school after the middle of the Century.[77]

Kant chose this occasion in order to participate in the Neologists' attacks against these trends, but his approach to the subject cannot be explained in these simple terms. In fact on the one hand he did more than attack a mystical

---

73. K. Aner, *Die Theologie der Lessingzeit* (Halle, 1929¹; Hildesheim, 1964²), pp. 234 f., 270 f.; F. W. Kantzenbach, *Protestantisches Christentum im Zeitalter der Aufklärung* (Gütersloh, 1965) p. 132.

74. Sigsted, *op. cit.*, pp. 301, 310. Swedenborg's mystical works had been attacked in Holland (1763-64), France (1764), Britain (1764), and Sweden (1763): *see ibid.*, pp. 310-11.

75. *Ibid.*, p. 337.

76. *Ibid.*, pp. 326 f.

77. Different kinds of mysticism would quickly gain momentum, since Hamann's reputation was established and Lavater, Obereit, and, in particular, Herder became productive and popular. Mystical trends would become extremely fashionable in the late eighties. *See*, for instance, H. Schneider, *Quest for Mysteries: The Masonic Background for Literature in Eighteenth-Century Germany* (Ithaca, N.Y., 1947). It should be noted that Crusius' wild speculations were confined to his works on *revealed* theology, while his *philosophy* was very sober, relative to contemporary standards. The same is true for Ötinger. Kant always referred to Crusius' *philosophical* works; he ignored, or rather, preferred to ignore, the latter's theological distractions.

trend: he compared the "dreams of a Seer" with the "dreams of metaphysics," putting on the same level doctrines usually discussed by "sober" metaphysicians (such as the spirituality and the immortality of the soul), and the wildest speculations about spirits. In so doing, he attacked the basic trends of that traditional German metaphysics which was dominant until the middle of the century, and he did it in a spirit which was certainly more extreme than that of the "popular philosophy" developing in that time. But he probably intended to reach a further aim as well: attacking the "dreams of a Seer" meant *a fortiori* to expose the same "dreams" which were offered by the speculative wing of the Wolffian school as the product of *rational* philosophical inquiry; from this point of view, this book is a further episode in the anti-Wolffian campaign Kant had carried on from the very beginning of his philosophical career.[78]

On the other hand, Kant's book reveals a general pattern of basic importance, a pattern that the commentators have hitherto failed to recognize. In fact, our author constructs his doctrines on *two different levels:* on the *first,* he stresses the limits of reason with a vigor very unusual in the Germany of that time,[79] denying to rational inquiry the access to areas traditionally open to it; on the *second,* he elaborates in a merely hypothetical way some doctrines that the majority of the traditional "sober" metaphysicians would have considered as trespassing on the boundaries of human reason.

Now, the basic justifications for the hypothesis in question are the difficulties raised by two related problems, that of organic life, and that of the moral law (of freedom): both of them imply a break from natural *mechanism,* and therefore cannot be approached by a valid philosophical method leading to rational knowledge, because rational knowledge of natural beings can be gained only in accordance with the mechanical way of explanation which proceeds by establishing regularities in the phenomena, and discovering their

---

78. *See* Tonelli, *Elementi, passim.*
79. *See* G. Tonelli, "The *Weakness* of Reason in the Age of Enlightenment," *Diderot Studies,* XIV (1971).

laws through the application of mathematics.[80] Moreover, it is clear that morality, as a psychological event, cannot be studied in a mathematical way, as physical phenomena are, thus, it is a "phenomenon" *sui generis:* so, its affirmed presence points for its justification towards another posterior development: morality will not be founded in the future on the presence of a dubious psychological phenomenon, the "moral feeling," but it will receive a "transcendental" foundation of its own as a *fact* of pure practical reason, founding that phenomenon, and not being founded by it.

When Kant, after having humorously discredited his own hypothesis of the spiritual world from the point of view of what he considers as strictly rational knowledge,[81] tries to draw a balanced conclusion, he refers again to the problem of life, and states that, from a purely rational point of view, the question, in his opinion, is completely settled, but in a merely negative way: that is, that we are completely certain that we will *never* be able to gain any positive knowledge of the nature of spirits because they lie beyond the world of sense.[82] But he adds a very significant remark: . . . "that even the possibility of this kind of negation is based neither on experience, nor in inference, but on a fiction where reason, deprived of all aids, takes refuge.[83]"

In other words, this "fiction" *(Erdichtung),* this hypothesis, is *necessary* to reason in order to make the *negative rational knowledge* in question acceptable, i.e., in order to show that these things known are *possible,* which means that their presuppositions, viz., consequences, can be thought in a noncontradictory, although merely hypothetical, way.

But there is more: in the final Conclusion of the book, Kant reconsiders this problem from the moral angle, and establishes one of the basic tenets of his "critical" ethics: being virtuous just in view of a future life does *not* mean to be virtuous. Our ignorance about the spiritual world belongs to our

---

80. Kant, *Ges. Schr.,* II, p. 371.
81. *Op. cit.,* pp. 342-48.
82. *Op. cit.,* pp. 351-52.
83. *Op. cit.,* p. 352.

nature, because it is the very foundation of the possibility of morality. Moral prescriptions are present in the heart of man *immediately,* they are not accepted as the most convenient consequences of some ascertained speculative truths.[84]

> Therefore, it seems to be more adapted to human nature and to the purity of customs: to found the expectation of a future world on the feelings of a goodnatured soul, rather than to found, on the contrary, its moral behavior on the hope of a future world. And such is the moral belief too ..., which is the only thing adapted to man in every condition, because it brings him without distractions to his true aim.[85]

Thus, morality is present as an immediate feeling in our hearts, but morality implies, in order to be possible, the hypothesis of a future life (which, from the rational point of view, is a pure fiction); and so we must *believe* in this hypothesis.

If, in the case of organic life, the necessity of admitting merely *negative* concepts implies the acceptance of the *possibility* of a certain hypothesis, in the case of morality, with its *positive* prescriptions, we must *believe* in the possible hypothesis morality implies.

It seems to be rather clear that Kant has established a position which is very near to the general structure of the *Critique of Pure Reason:* our metaphysical *knowledge* is restricted within the very narrow boundaries of possible experience; but the "fact" of morality lies at the foundation of the *belief* in some ideas we can (and we must) *think,* although we cannot *know* their objects: God, freedom, immortality.

And, if we think of one of the basic structures of the *Critique of Judgment,* we will realize that some elements, including freedom and the idea of organic life, compel us to admit a *transcendental* principle, which is *necessary* but *subjective,* and which belongs to the *reflective,* not to the *determining* faculty of judgment. In the more exoteric terminology of

---

84. *Op. cit.,* p. 372.
85. *Op. cit.,* p. 373.

1766, and according to the corresponding earlier frame of reference, this principle would be an hypothesis which is not founded *positively* in knowledge, but which we must admit as a *presupposition* to other knowledge.

So, it seems that in the *Dreams of a Seer* Kant established some basic traits of the master plan of his future system.

It is evident that the objects of *belief* in the *Critique of Pure Reason* are just traditional objects of "sober" metaphysics, and have nothing to do with the fabulous hypothesis advanced in the *Dreams;* but what counts is, in my opinion, the general similarity in structure, in spite of the dissimilarity of its application. On the other hand, I have shown elsewhere[86] that the fabulous hypothesis in question played an important role as a background frame of reference and as a directing principle in the further evolution of Kant's system.

VII

Another conclusion we can draw is that in the *Dreams of a Seer* ethics is already incorporated *de facto* into metaphysics, as it lies at the foundation of the belief in immortality, a basic metaphysical tenet.

Now, in the same work, Kant has established the parallelism we saw between moral law and gravitation. The "spiritual" is a counterpart of the material world: it has its own sphere, and its own law, but it is closely related to the material world; they are both of them parts or aspects of Nature. Thus, the moral law is a law of nature,[87] and ethics studies a part of nature—the spiritual part of it: it is a metaphysics of the spirits.

This conclusion is conditioned by two premises. (1) That

---

86. *See* Tonelli, "Kant's Early Theory of Genius," and " '*Divinae Particula Aurae*' ... ."

87. This was meant, of course, in a completely different sense from that in which moral law is considered as *natural law,* in so far as it derives from the nature of man (is founded on his right reason, etc.).

Kant's Ethics

the spirits, inclusive of the souls, constitute a world of their own. But this must be a world parallel to the material one, and interacting with it through the connection between the souls and their bodies, therefore a world belonging to "nature" in the strictest sense, and not a fabulous "paradise" or "hell" confined in some remote regions, half way between nature and miracle. (2) That, within this world, the spirits interact *directly* on each other, so that their world is actually ruled by the moral law, as the material world is ruled by attraction. If the interaction of the spirits in general is mediated by their bodies (as it happens for Kant for human beings, although, in his hypothesis, he does not rule out the possibility that the souls may interact not only through their bodies, but also directly), then the law of the spirits, the moral law, is just a rule affecting the individuals, insufficient to account for a general order: it is still an ethics which cannot grow into a metaphysics.

Now, it is clear that this doctrine definitely points at an incorporation of ethics into metaphysics; but one could raise the question, whether the final doctrine of the *Dreams,* the moral foundation of the belief in immortality, would not be sufficient to account for this incorporation.

But a moral proof of the immortality of the soul was nothing new; and, what is more important, many philosophers had offered moral proofs of God's existence,[88] but none of them had come to the conclusion that Ethics should be considered for that reason as a part of Metaphysics. So that it seems to me very likely that Kant needed a stronger motivation in order to take this step — and that this motivation was provided by the parallelism we studied.

A reasonable objection could be that the subordination of Ethics to Metaphysics appears in the documents we have only a few years *after* 1766, and that therefore one should prove that the doctrine of parallelism was not abandoned soon after 1766, before assuming that it played an important

---

88. *See* J. N. Frobesius, *Brevis ac dilucida scriptorum atque argumentorum quibus nominis divini existentia comprobatur recensio* (Helmstadii 1746), pp. CIV f.

role in that subordination. Now, the parallelism reappears on two occasions in the 1st *Convolut* of Kant's *Opus postumum*,[89] i.e., in the middle nineties. It is true that about thirty years had elapsed, and that the general trend of the *Opus postumum* may have *revived* mystical doctrines of the early period which had been suppressed in the following years. But the soul-of-the-world theory, still present in the seventies,[90] testifies that a version of the "spiritual world" doctrine had survived the time of the *Dreams;* so that we are entitled to assume that its moral implications had not been abandoned either, and still actively shaped some aspects of Kant's system.

The doctrine of parallelism is indeed a strong motivation: *moral* law, present in everybody's conscience, is considered as a symptom of the existence of an entire sector of the natural order, that of the superior spirits, whose existence otherwise can be supposed only on the foundation either of far-fetched metaphysical arguments, or of dubious and irregular phenomena (the apparition of ghosts). It must also be noticed that organic *life* can be considered at best as a symptom of the existence of the souls of living beings, not of superior, incorporeal spirits.

So, the moral law discloses, although only hypothetically, an entire, remote sector of nature; it does not require us to believe in its existence, but the hypothesis it allows us to establish has a metaphysical redundance far exceeding the more important, but much more sober and meager ideas of God and immortality, which are objects of belief.

I must stress that the role I attributed to this doctrine as a motivation for Kant's development towards a metaphysical ethics is founded much more on the assumption of an action of psychological rather than of strictly speculative factors on his development; but history of philosophy has to take into account many irrational or semi-irrational elements of explanation.

---

89. Kant, *Ges. Schr.,* XX, pp. 35, 51-52.
90. *See* Tonelli, " '*Divinae Particula Aurae*' ... ."

12

PROMISE AND PERIL IN PRAGMATIC HISTORICAL THOUGHT:
A Contemporary Dialogue
Whitaker T. Deininger

Setting

A COMFORTABLE ROOM IN A RATHER UTILITARIAN FACULTY club at an urban campus where three professorial colleagues sit discussing some relationships between pragmatism and aspects of thought about history. Naturally, they are also sipping occasionally from coffee cups. Nearby each person, in easy reach, sit stacks of relevant books, both paperback and hardcover, awaiting uses in later classroom scenes.

Characters

Professor Present A. Focus — an historian seated next to copies of H. Zinn's *The Politics of History* (Beacon Press, 1970); H. Lynd's *Knowledge for What?* (Princeton, 1946); M.

Whitaker T. Deininger

Curti, Ed., *American Scholarship in the Twentieth Century* (Harvard, 1953); John Higham, Ed., *The Reconstruction of American History* (Hutchinson, 1962) and a neat stack of cards containing research notes pertinent (and some impertinent, no doubt) to writings by John Dewey, J. H. Randall, Jr., Charles A. Beard and other scholars.

Dean Value Humanist — a person learned in literature and philosophy, who has "gone administrative," whose available books include K. R. Popper's *The Poverty of Historicism* (Routledge, 1957); I. Berlin's *The Hedgehog and the Fox* (Weidenfeld Goldbacks, 1967); H. Fain's *Between Philosophy and History* (Princeton, 1970); plus books by Herbert Marcuse, E. Auerbach and Morris Cohen (including notes on the latter's essay, "Some Difficulties in John Dewey's Anthropocentric Humanism," retained from long-vanished graduate-school days).

Dr. Clio Muse — a soft-spoken woman scholar, an historian widely read in other fields, seated near copies of G. M. Trevelyan's *Autobiography and Other Essays* (Longmans Green, 1949); H. Butterfield's *The Whig Interpretation of History* (Scribner's, 1951) and a well-used paperback volume from Lord Macaulay's multi-volumed *The History of England*.

Each of the participants in the relaxed dialogue also owns, as a part of a personal library, marked-up copies of Herbert W. Schneider's *The Puritan Mind* (Michigan Paperback, 1958) and *A History of American Philosophy* (Columbia, 1946). (*Both* are known as worthwhile works. *Author.*)

Prof. Present Focus. How the times are a-changing! I'm reading Samuel B. Gould's suggestive *Today's Academic Condition* (McGraw-Hill, 1970) along with a number of studies of counter-cultural communities and educational reforms. A revival of pragmatism seems in the offing. Shades of John Dewey and the "old" New Historians like Robinson and Beard! I'll drink to the quest for contemporary relevance and renewal of pragmatic historiography.

Promise, Peril in Pragmatic Thought

Dr. Clio Muse. You pragmatists never learn from history how ephemeral are all the "pragmatic" revivals. The stress on contemporaneity, activism, confrontation and immediacy should also be resisted by historians. Scholars still worry about pragmatists' enthusiasm for the immediacies of their version of something known as The Present.

Prof. Present Focus. I sense I'm walking on eggs again. Perhaps you can state some of the so-called scholars' worries?

Dr. Clio Muse. Delighted to oblige! The leading worries about professions of the value of pragmatic historiography are moral and ontological. Disinterested historical study may be subverted to raw political activism, inside as well as outside our libraries and classrooms. Pragmatic historiography may "go" gung-ho ideological, so to speak. Such activism can weaken younger historians' allegiance to truth, to what the evidence suggests. Knowledge of the past as it was will get pushed aside for evaluative proposals about the future of society. And genuine scholars, whatever their social views, know that truth counts for more than self-interest in genuine scholarship and historical research.

Dean Value Humanist. Maybe it's easier to talk about historical truth than to arrive at it, no matter what our philosophical orientations. Didn't Charles Beard once claim, perhaps a bit jokingly, that history is like a cat being dragged to places it doesn't want to go?

Dr. Clio Muse. A bit cynical, that remark of Beard's! Historians and philosophers may have differing interests in life, but about truth they should tend toward seriousness. They should listen to one another.

Dean Value Humanist. My impression is that hardworking historians prefer to avoid extended discussions with epistemologically oriented philosophers. Oh, I realize that historians occasionally write books on historiography and, sometimes at luncheon, make methodological and logical remarks about their enterprise. But often they act as if they're in pain when they take part in such talk, while the philosophers are obviously happy. On the whole, historians shy away from intellectual discussion with philosophers.

Whitaker T. Deininger

Dr. Clio Muse. Didn't Ludwig Wittgenstein somewhere claim that philosophers are word-secreting animals? Probably philosophers simply enjoy talk more than historians. The latter tend to want to talk only about the immediate research they're at work on. Like lawyers, historians perhaps constitute something like a guild in a self-conscious way while philosophers are never quite sure about their subject matter or their professional relationships with other philosophers.

Dean Value Humanist. Perhaps so. In any case, the fact that historians don't discuss methodological and logical matters openly and easily across departmental lines needn't imply they're uninterested in these concerns. Many academic persons who teach also tend to shy away from general public discussions of teaching methods and aims. Nonetheless they do care about teaching. But they don't openly display this concern. That sort of thing simply isn't done in some academic quarters, you know.

Prof. Present Focus. Nonetheless historians can't hide their methodological and valuational tracks completely. In their historical works they often open up small windows on their own personal views. True, they seldom spell out the logical implications of these knothole views, so to speak — nor do they pause to engage in detailed philosophical analysis. These often significant and suggestive capsule-like assertions, pronouncements or recommendations are the kinds about which philosophers would want to talk if they could get the historians to linger long enough for varied and civilized conversation.

Dr. Clio Muse. Does a person converse or argue with a philosopher?

Prof. Present Focus. Why, a few of my philosophical colleagues are civilized persons quite capable of conversation as well as argumentation. And they are capable of analyzing the implications of some of the shorthand views of men, events and institutions which creep into historical works.

Dean Value Humanist. That's so. These "whispered" asides in historical works can surely intrigue any thoughtful reader. Only yesterday while looking through Herbert

Schneider's famous *The Puritan Mind* I came upon one of these highly concentrated yet undeveloped suggestions for a philosophical canvas.

Dr. Clio Muse. No secrets allowed here, you know. Tell us it.

Dean Value Humanist. Better than that, I'll read it to you. I brought the book along for use in my afternoon class. Here's the passage:

> The perspectives of history are ever-shifting, for human experience, being itself continually subject to change, affords no fixed point of reference for the mind. Not only does each generation find itself compelled to interpret a more or less alien past by the categories of the present, but even this specious present is itself unintelligible unless it be illuminated by the past. Neither the mental world nor the physical has a center and a circumference.[1]

Dr. Clio Muse. Schneider is a lively intellect and a solid historian. But I'm not sure I understand fully what he means to claim by that rather vague, even puzzling assertion.

Dean Value Humanist. Perhaps another brief "aside" selected from the same work will prove a help. "Past and present are in themselves alike mysterious, but they mysteriously illuminate one another; and though things are never intelligible in themselves, they nevertheless make each other intelligible."[2] Does that passage clear up Schneider's meaning?

Dr. Clio Muse. Not for me. That's quite an emphasis on mystery for a scholar who became known as a leading American philosophical naturalist. Of course, as you know, Herbert Schneider lived among all those brilliant Columbia University pragmatists and naturalists. He is both an historian of ideas and a philosopher. I'm not completely sure the philosophical environment was always best for his outstanding qualities as intellectual historian, though he survived and

---

1. Herbert W. Schneider, "Prologue," *The Puritan Mind* (Ann Arbor Paperback: University of Michigan Press, 1958), p. 3.
2. *Ibid.*

wrote some fine things. At least he didn't "see" historians of ideas as activists and prophets, as do some of our contemporary younger pragmatic colleagues. In his excellent *A History of American Philosophy* (Columbia, 1946) he admitted that historians must end their historical works where their own reflections begin.[3] I like that.

Prof. Present Focus. You *would* like that! Your garden-variety humanistic conception of historical inquiry and writing, seen as a narrative account of what has happened, strikes me as irresponsibly simplistic in our highly sophisticated age. Knowing what has happened in the past isn't the clear-cut kind of enterprise you literary historians would like to believe. You object to a pragmatic interest in present problems and to historians' self-conscious concern for social relevancy, yet just such concern can enrich historical subject-matter and broaden our notion of what is most worth looking into.

Dr. Clio Muse. Bosh! Humbug! Rhetorical nonsense! You can't pragmatically ignore a noble Englishman like G. M. Trevelyan if you want to retain the historical sense of truth and disinterestedness. Some of you pragmatically inclined historical theorists become too confused, too easily, to suit my methodological and logical fancy. If by pragmatic historiography you mean to refer to an enlargement of our *human* vision about men and events and a rich inclusive notion of subject matter, then I've no serious objection. Such inclusiveness needn't be a matter of party or class, you know. No "standard measure" exists by which to choose our historians by philosophical labels. After all Marxists, neo-Marxists, Thomists, Existentialists and other philosophically oriented persons can become sound historians in spite of their philosophical standards. Getting an A-grade in Introduction to Philosophy won't in itself qualify a person for historical work. Historiography without metaphysics, that's my motto!

---

3. Herbert W. Schneider, "Preface and Acknowledgements," *A History of American Philosophy* (New York: Columbia University Press, 1946), p. vii.

Dean Value Humanist. You're both getting too excited. After all, there is no one model for educating would-be historians, whether literary or pragmatic. The care and feeding of existing and promising historians no doubt needs a varied and rich recipe book. Most historians like to "read around" quite a bit, much as experienced travelers enjoy looking about. Descartes wasn't too far wrong when he insisted that history is like travel in its influence on an educated person. Knowing how things are and how they operate needn't involve a person in advanced "theory" — a bias of a scientific and overly intellectualized age. *Seeing how things are* counts for as much as mastering philosophical views and theoretical models of knowing. Many kinds, shapes and sizes of historian exist. Perhaps we should keep this fact in mind during our discussion?

Dr. Clio Muse. I'll go along on that. But can we get Professor Focus here to do so? He strikes me as one who confuses a strategy for enriching men's conception of worthwhile subject matters (which is essentially a matter of educational strategy) with more strictly methodological matters (which can assume technical dimensions). We don't produce fine practising historians just by setting up broad educational aims, since these aims may be poorly realized through shoddy teaching or learning.

Prof. Present Focus. You seem unable to grasp my main point. Traditionalist views of historiography and historical research were much narrower at one time than Clio pretends. Pragmatism loosened these traditionalist rigidities, just as the empirically-minded William James insisted it would. Self-conscious preoccupation with the ways in which race, class, sexual, nationalist, religious and psychological factors may influence both the choice of historical topics and how they are investigated and interpreted has in fact helped to produce better historians as well as historians who *collectively* study a wider range of topics. Today's historians are professionally freer to include formerly ignored topics in the province of legitimate scholarly work.

Dr. Clio Muse. I admit there's *something* to what you say. But how much? Historians' interests have been broadened, especially with regard to selection of appropriate topics for research. True. But probably there's much more general "opinion-izing" of a weak sociological and quasi-sociological kind, which at the periphery of scholarly work can threaten to engulf genuine investigations by authenticated methods under the bilge water of various self-righteous ideological dogmatisms. Relevant *interests* cannot in themselves become the basis on which to determine whether written histories based on them are sound or not. And the great historians, seldom read widely today, knew much about society and politics and human psychology long before specialized departments in the social sciences taught the myth that such knowledge began in the last century.

Dean Value Humanist. Apparently you tend to agree with Professor A. O. Lovejoy's claim that the only way in which historiography concerns the present has to do with historians' interests and not their procedures nor their conclusions?[4]

Dr. Clio Muse. Indeed I do. Interests are only the very beginning — though admittedly more important than some traditionalists had once cared to grant. And as R. G. Collingwood pointed out,[5] such interests may concern a whole past century rather than contemporary matters. The execution of interests in light of available evidence is what determines the scholarly worth of written results.

Professor Present Focus. Pragmatists' historiographical emphasis on the present-sideness of valuable historical inquiry often got caricatured rather than analyzed, leading to much misunderstanding.[6] Perhaps I can state my under-

4. Arthur O. Lovejoy, "Present Standpoints and Past History," *Journal of Philosophy,* 36 (1939), p. 482; and his "Historiography and Evaluation: A Disclaimer," *Journal of the History of Ideas,* 10, No. 1 (1949), p. 142.

5. Nonetheless, Collingwood looked most favorably on aspects of the pragmatic stress on the contemporaneity of historical work in relation to the historian's *thinking* about the available evidence: *The Idea of History* (Oxford: Clarendon Press, 1946), pp. 282-302.

6. In his *Nature and Historical Experience* (New York: Columbia University Press, 1958), p. 51, in *footnote* 7, John H. Randall, Jr., points to what he considers an example of a "confused" argument, namely, Chester A. Destler's "Some Observations on Contemporary Historical Theory," originally printed in *The American Historical Review,* 55 (1950), pp. 503-529.

standing of the legitimate ways in which historiography concerns our present?

Dean Value Humanist. That might clear the intellectual fog a bit. What *are* the legitimate ways in which historians are concerned about the present rather than the past?

Professor Present Focus. Let me give you a nutshell version of my special lecture on this topic. Pardon the brevity and the schematic format! I'd say that pragmatic historiography stresses an *evaluative,* an *epistemological* and an *ontological* sense of the present-sidedness of historical inquiry. By the ontological emphasis, I mean the conviction that history-as-events involves a plurality of actual as well as possible happenings, such that some of the possible events are more probable than others, given what we know about what has already happened. This need not mean inevitability. The epistemological emphasis involves the generalized claim that historians employ canons of evidence and principles of procedure which are contemporary ones. By the elusive and controversial evaluative stress, I mean to refer to the strong claim that historians *ought* positively to write histories about what they take to be the most pressing problems in their own age. And this means their attempts to appear absolutely disinterested will often be weakened when we observe the kinds of subject matters they choose to write about and the types of interpretive criteria they employ.

Dr. Clio Muse. The philosophical distinctions are already beginning to make my head spin. Can you say something about each, in order?

Professor Present Focus. Let's take the evaluative sense first, since it may be the most controversial. Every historian ought to be concerned with how the present came to be what it is, in so far as he gives some attention to general historical tendencies, whatever his own specialty. An imaginative concern with what most matters in the present enriches rather than diminishes historical research. In this way the historian can put questions to the past in light of values of the present, though the "answers" from the past may differ from those we might prefer in our own day and age. A moral concern for present perplexities and difficulties also makes a scholar more sensitive to the possible "binds" faced in past ages.

Dr. Clio Muse. As with most pragmatists, what you say strikes me as too strongly oriented on present values and problems. It is quite possible for an historian to have the most minimal connection with his own age and yet to write excellent histories about past events. The historian may even write from a minority viewpoint. The values reflected may be those of sects, parties, or ideals which are declining or suffering severe reversals in his own day. Aren't you concerned that great concern about contemporary values will emphasize only histories of success rather than sympathetic insight into *all* aspects of historical existence, including defeat and desperate loneliness? Won't your present-mindedness inevitably produce an educational orthodoxy about values, though you do not intend this to occur?

Dean Value Humanist. Everyone who knows anything knows there's something to this worry. There's a significant difference between academic orthodoxy (even if it's an official liberalism) and genuine scholarship.

Prof. Present Focus. You don't avoid orthodoxies by holding no views at all. I'm not sure what you mean by "official liberalism" either, though it is being bandied about by cautious conservatives and does carry an ominous ring!

Dean Value Humanist. So be it, then. You choose to pretend not to know what most scholars worry about, especially those who study the workings of academic and other orthodoxies. I'm not interested in the hard-core right-wing politicians' and public's anti-intellectualistic criticism of academic life. But their bad motives needn't blind any of us to the recent emergence of academic liberal "lines" concerning what is proper to say and do about educational and political theory and practice. Traditionalist academic values are on the defensive against upstart confrontationists inside and outside the ivy-covered fortresses. The nonteaching power of deans of men and women and public relations cares little, too, about traditional classroom values. Pragmatic historiographical views play into their hands. Every innovation is viewed as superior to solid work already being done.

And pragmatic concern for the present produces a restless impatience with cautious treatment of evidence, logical analysis and awareness of alternative viewpoints. Pragmatism always means emphasis on activism rather than on thoughtful deliberation.

Prof. Present Focus. Shame! Your caricature of pragmatic historiography overlooks the pragmatic insistence on prudent use of human intelligence in judging the relevance of evidence and alternatives. *Of course* any general view of education or history will be subject to varying applications and interpretations because of its very generality. No pragmatist who is also an historian plans to give up the required professional training that is essential. Nor is pragmatism a subjectivist doctrine. A sound philosopher-historian, J. H. Randall, Jr., has pointed out how any history must relate to some set of particulars which form the "objective" evidence for the writing of that history.[7] *Which* histories happen to get written in a specific era or civilization becomes itself a fruitful subject matter for historical investigation. And concentration by contemporary historians on the deepest problems of a society or an era, across the whole range of human activities and thought, cannot help but liberate historical scholarship from innocent-looking but restricting academic formats. Ideological conformity can occur in any academic camp, including that of traditionalists!

Dr. Clio Muse. Aren't we spinning mental wheels just to cover standard arguments? The journal-articles on these matters during the past thirty or more years indicate no obvious orthodoxy as having won the day. These articles often concentrated on specialized topics — like that of the philosophers who worry about the logic of historical explanation[8] or on liberal efforts to encourage reconsideration of

---

7. J. H. Randall, *op. cit.,* pp. 51-54.

8. A fine representative collection of such thinkers can be found in Patrick Gardiner, Ed., *Theories of History* (Glencoe, Ill.: The Free Press, 1959); and a fine current bibliography in Haskell Fain, *Between Philosophy and History* (Princeton, N. J.: Princeton University Press, 1970), pp. 319-326.

our existing views of the past,[9] either for educational reasons related to the classroom or in order to make sense of recent social-political movements.

Prof. Present Focus. Sometimes I think that critics of pragmatic historiography like to believe pragmatists want only to write general textbooks. After all, the older "new" historians, like James Robinson and Charles Beard, emphasized the need to produce histories for the generally educated masses. They did not mean to confine written histories to the General Education curriculum or the general lecture circuit!

Dr. Clio Muse. But may not pragmatists overlook the extent to which many fine historians had classical and literary training? Men like Thomas Babington Macaulay, Henry Adams and Edward Gibbon sought primarily to give us detailed, complicated descriptions of real men and events. They sought to study sources and to visit original sites. They aimed at thorough treatment of past events on the basis of evidence.

Dean Value Humanist. Let me interrupt here. Remember that Macaulay was a Whig whose synoptic "portraits" of famous personages reflected whiggish prejudices and the unquestioned conviction that 19th-century Victorian industrialism marked a highwater mark in civilization. Isn't that rather pragmatic?

Prof. Present Focus. Thanks for the attempt at assistance. But let's not discuss Lord Macaulay's Whiggism here. Clio won't admit, in any event, that great historians had pragmatic interests, even unconscious ones. And about Macaulay I'd be among the first to admit he did write a full-scale institutional and political history of England, containing brilliant economic insights as well as masterful descriptions of city life and battles. We'd better not go too far afield, though, if we want to complete our discussion.

Dean Value Humanist. Is it time to say something about the other two meanings of pragmatic historiography — the ontological and the epistemological?

---

9. See John Higham, Ed., *The Reconstruction of American History* (New York: Harper, 1962) which will serve as one example.

Promise, Peril in Pragmatic Thought

Prof. Present Focus. The ontological version simply insists there is no monistic or common historical subject matter "out there" waiting for historians to discover and to write it down. That is all. History-as-process is plural rather than unitarian, in other words. The historical quest after one underlying pattern, which would "see" all historical events as related to one another, turns out philosophically as a pursuit of something which doesn't exist.

Dean Value Humanist. You seem to mean by pragmatic ontology nothing more than pluralism, pure and simple. Your position doesn't deny existence of structures but only of a single structure. But is it a bit idealistic in its emphasis on how our perspectives help to determine which historical structures shall be said to have existed?

Prof. Present Focus. Not in the least. Idealist theories of historical inquiry tended to imply that the historian's perspective lent meaning to processes or helped to create them. Pragmatism merely asserts there are as many genuine histories, objectively speaking, as there are perspectives which open up evidence into their past emergences. Pragmatism tends toward philosophical realism, in fact. It wants to assert that perspectives which matter historically help to bring into being knowledge of what happened. But the perspectives are significant, for without them no historical inquiry would be possible. Any question about which perspectives among competing ones is the most important, itself perhaps a pragmatic one, must be settled on evaluative grounds.

Dr. Clio Muse. I fail to discern any great peril in the ontological implications of pragmatic historiography as you've stated them. Indeed I find much merit and even promise in them.

Historical pluralism — the view that numerous historical strands exist, sometimes in a parallel fashion and at other times interwoven in causal ways — strikes me as a view which few persons would deny. Is it in any significantly essential sense "pragmatic"? Of course, it is possible that stress on pluralism can weaken some persons' intellectual determination to seek for those empirical, basic underlying themes in history beyond the surging immediacies of contemporary happenings. But this may be more a matter of individual historians' character and talent. On the other hand, monistic and monarchical views of history ("History" with the large "H"!) emphasizing single preordained aims in historical process often blind historians to the rich varieties in tendencies, past and present. Even Hegel admitted that philosophical History is *a priori,* requiring a notion of History-as-unity which empirical historians need to bring to their studies of history since they won't find it empirically among the evidences. Of course, we know how Marxists claim to find an empirical unity in economic events; while liberals following J. S. Mill "see" the basic pattern in struggles between authority and individuals. Still, pluralism is more or less philosophically neutral so far as I can discern!

Dean Value Humanist. I'm also a bit unsure of the pragmatic aspects of this stress on plural actual "histories" as process-in-the-making. Surely there are also cultural unities in terms of which music, painting, religion and the like may contextually be interrelated, if only we knew how to get at them? And some events are historically *normative* — wars, revolutions, scientific "breakthroughs," say — counting for more than other events occurring in the same era. Such events are culturally fruitful. They are more inclusive of wide-ranging sub-events and are causally influential over wide areas and times.

Prof. Present Focus. If so, they exist as limited unities — national or economic. Their day will also come, as suggested by a hymn — "Our little systems have their day, they have their day and pass away." No single version of unity is ultimate. Pragmatic historiography is insistently empirical and pluralistic on this point.

Dr. Clio Muse. Perhaps too much so. However the details change, there may be ground-swell problems and concerns in every age with which the learned must deal. And there are predictable qualities of men. Like statesmen, great historians even perceive those ground-swell events and direct attention to them. This has been true from Thucydides to Marx to Beard! Not all possibilities are historical, as Sidney Hook has maintained in his stimulating little study,

The Hero in History: "The trend toward collectivism and the intervention of the state into economy are 'unavoidable.' To hark back to the era of free enterprise is just another futile call, of the same kind but not of the same desperate degree as the call to return to an agrarian economy."[10]

Dean Value Humanist. I agree there are more or less universal human sympathies, plights, predicaments. These permit us to identify with aspects of the situations of persons long dead and gone, simply as human beings, in more than narrowly pragmatic ways. I suspect that pragmatists understate the tragic aspects in human existence — the boredom, defeat and frustration; the senseless repetitions; the perpetual rediscovery of iron-like limits; the irony; the obduracy of difficult problems and of human stubbornness. Pride, anger, shame and other emotions do not alter fundamentally from age to age. Nor do our tendencies, at times, to overstep boundaries in dangerous ways.

Prof. Present Focus. And what of *living* pragmatists — do they not bleed, suffer, sometimes experience defeat in given circumstances? Pragmatists can be as aware of human limitations as others.

Dean Value Humanist. But will they in light of their educational concern with the present and with *their* problems and *their* perspectives?

Prof. Present Focus. John Dewey knew that pragmatism is no protection against possible failure. He thought that if intelligent choice failed, then we'd be forced to face the consequences. In his famous *Experience and Nature* he replied to some critics by writing:

> When theories of values do not afford intellectual assistance in framing ideas and beliefs about values that are adequate to direct action, the gap must be filled by other means. If intelligent method is lacking prejudice, the pressure of immediate circumstances, self-interest and class-interest, traditional customs, institutions of *accidental* historic origin are *not* lacking, and they tend to take the place of intelligence.[11]

---

10. (New York: The Humanities Press, 1943), p. 264.
11. (Chicago: Open Court, 1926), p. 265.

Whitaker T. Deininger

Dean Value Humanist. The question is whether, for a pragmatist like Dewey, any traditions will be left after a large-scale secular dismemberment of past values in light of what he termed "intelligence." But we'll put aside that disturbing issue for another time. Now I'd like to hear about the epistemological aspects of the present, as pragmatic thinkers see them.

Prof. Present Focus. Pragmatists make some simple epistemological points about the present. Most importantly, the conception of evidence used by historians is always a contemporary one. So, too, the notion of explanatory models able to aid historians in their historical interpretations of complicated phenomena. And a scientific, even sceptical era has made some old-fashioned models no longer useful. They are no longer believable. And finally, the historian in the present understands how past events have worked out as they did by virtue of living in that present. For this reason new histories need to be written every decade or so. The reason is that we see how the implications of value-ridden events get spelled out in factual terms. To say that histories are about the present means only to insist their truth rests on canons of evidence, inquiry and interpretation alive in the present.

Dr. Clio Muse. The point about evidence, though trite, is unassailable. But didn't logical-minded philosophers point out it meant, on the basis that the truth of a statement is in its verification, that historical statements are really about the *future* — since all our present statements will be subject to continual reverification?

Prof. Present Focus. Yes, but in doing so they missed the important pragmatic point. This is that *when* a historical (or other) statement is verified in some future, it will exist in what is then a living present for the person conducting the verificational techniques. Neither they nor we can escape this involvement in a conceptual, methodological and verificationist present. Pragmatists insist that we be aware of this epistemological limit.

Dean Value Humanist. Isn't this sort of talk about a "conceptual present" either a trivial truth or a tricky philosophical issue? Bodies of evidence in the present may point to established happenings of the past in fairly unequivocal ways. And they may be found to agree with evidence in previous eras. The validity of evidence historiographically useful is its purported relevance to past events. The claim about the *indirect* reference of historical statements (like *all* statements) to future verificatory experiences, though logically sound, strikes me as logic-chopping of the worst sort. It implies we never know anything for certain! Many a realist philosopher has challenged that rather absurd notion.

Prof. Present Focus. As we learn more about our world and the methods of the sciences, as well as about human motivation, we do alter our canons of evidence. And our conceptions of past events — how they came about, why, and under whose jurisdiction — change along with our general world views. Pragmatists want to make us aware that no evidence is self-interpreting.

Dean Value Humanist. Nonetheless, however new our notions of evidence in what you call "a conceptual present," our aim is to find out what others in earlier times, places and circumstances thought, felt and did in light of how they understood their problems *then*. It is only in one type of present-oriented historical inquiry that our interest is in the consequences of historical events for our times.

Dr. Clio Muse. I think so. Many pragmatists tend to confuse a type of historical inquiry with the whole of it. This is a serious error. Still, the point they do make is worthwhile. The present-sidedness of historical inquiry can be made more manifest, as an aspect of historiographical reflection, if we study the history of how historians tended to "see" important events, especially large-scale ones like the Renaissance or Romanticism or Medievalism. As the consequences of these large-scale events unfold into later eras, or get worked out by living persons, historians do sometimes come to interpret them afresh. This causal historical view, seeing events as often incomplete and ongoing, loosens the view of history as locked exclusively into hard-and-fast, finalized past happenings. A concern to know more about how historians have interpreted events is surely a justifiable aspect of a pragmatic emphasis in historiography. Perhaps it is the most significant one.

Dean Value Humanist. I'll accept your evaluation with a proviso. The proviso is that the fact World War I, say, has ongoing social-economic-political consequences for contemporary events must not blind us, or historians, to its own distinctive historical character from 1914-1918. We need both kinds of historical awareness.

Prof. Present Focus. Right on. I'm happy for this little island of agreement among us. But this increasing awareness helps to direct historians to the constant reinterpretation of existing historiographical views and to the reconsideration of histories already written. These great written histories need not be ignored nor dismissed. But history-as-written begins to look more like what goes on in lawcourts, in England and this country, than like what goes on in scientific laboratories. Our little stacks of research notes must often be submitted, as it were, to new "juries" for interpretation and judgment. Disagreements on historiographical matters, among historians, is something like disagreement among "strict constructionists" and "sociological jurists" concerning interpretation of the Constitution. Neither emphasis will disappear; but their fruitful competition will keep each new generation on its historiographical toes!

Dr. Clio Muse. Again we must remind ourselves that while many things change, so, too, some do not! Our contemporary stress on change, novelty, innovation should not blind us to our ideological bent toward these values. Perhaps we are evading serious moral readings of historical events. Each new generation of historians may think itself possessed of special divinizing and prophetic social powers. Temptations to such self-applied dogmatisms about method and purpose can appear in subtle forms. No one generation of scholarly historians can claim the right to make a final verdict on the value of the histories its historians write. Why give in to our rage for contemporaneousness? Why not keep our ears tuned, also, to historical warnings from past thinkers, in different climes, who knew much about human motivation and self-deception?

Promise, Peril in Pragmatic Thought

Dean Value Humanist. I suppose this suspicion of the pragmatic present-centeredness can never wholly be assuaged. Some pragmatists tend always to adopt a priest-prophet-professor combined role, acting as if they know *the* real problems of our present and *the* required techniques for dealing with them. Pragmatism harbors something of a sectarian bias. And elements of pragmatic historiographical views strike me, ultimately, as trivial — especially their value-oriented claims! Consider this model:

> If H (an historian) had not been interested in Y (a specific historical subject matter) *and adequately judged Y's value to his present* (pragmatic "justification" of the present), then Z (a researched and complete historical account) would not now exist.

How would this model fundamentally be altered if the italicized phrase "... and adequately judged Y's value to his present" — the justificatory phrase — were dropped? Not at all. That justificatory phrase adds nothing to what is contained in the historian's interest in the specific subject matter in the first place. Too much of the pragmatic historiographical position has been concerned, from the beginnings of pragmatic thought, with such "empty" justifications.

Dr. Clio Muse. It seems that we are returning to former arguments again! Perhaps our dialogue should come to an end. Hopefully we're more aware of what pragmatic historical thinkers want to emphasize. Yet we've been able to state our own doubts and convictions.

Prof. Present Focus. I see that much of the criticism of pragmatic historiography involves a fear of excessive stress on the present. I'll try to keep it in mind. But I'd be untrue to my deepest convictions if I failed to propose a toast to thinkers who do try to make historical knowledge relevant to our present concerns. Men like Charles Beard and ...

Dr. Clio Muse. Herbert W. Schneider, philosopher and historian, and ...

Dean Value Humanist. We'll all drink to such men. But now ... it's off to the classroom once again!

13

INSTITUTIONS AND THE ALIENATED MAN
Darnell Rucker

IN A WORLD THAT SEEMS TO BE LOSING ITS BEARINGS BEcause its members already have lost theirs, philosophy is helping little, if at all. Continental philosophers, at least in the popularly received versions of their views, have exacerbated the rampant egoism and individualism that are the dominant symptoms of the modern malaise. When Camus gives up all hope of understanding the world, saying "you give me the choice between a description that is sure but that teaches me nothing and hypotheses that claim to teach me but that are not sure,"[1] he expresses the widely held notion of our more intellectual young that the individual somehow must be *one* with his world — absorbed into it — or remain alienated from it forever. "If I were a tree among trees, a cat among animals, this life would have a meaning, or rather this problem [the absurd] would not arise, for I should belong to this world. I should *be* this world to which I am now opposed by my whole consciousness and my whole insistence upon familiarity."[2] But sad to say for Camus, one-

---

1. Albert Camus, *The Myth of Sisyphus* (New York: Vintage Books, 1955), p. 15.
2. *Ibid.*, p. 38.

Institutions and The Alienated Man

ness with the world *would* reduce men to trees among trees or cats among animals; it would mean the end to consciousness, knowledge, action, values. A stone is completely at home in the world. A self-conscious being can never be completely at home — even when he is not conscious of not being at home. Men *are* part of the world, but as knowing beings they must distinguish themselves from that world.

Our problem is that we seem to have arrived at a stage of history in which that self-distinction has become an extreme self-centeredness — a hyper-self-consciousness accompanied by an alarming loss of the sense that we are also and essentially social beings, nurtured, formed, channeled by the social relations within which we come to be and continue to exist.

Even the British language analysts do not succeed in making clear to their followers that what they are analyzing is an *institution,* a socially organized body of tools of communication. The fact seems evident enough, but the reality and the significance of the fact escape us in our private, myopic concerns. The American pragmatists — Peirce and Dewey in particular — insisted upon the social nature of man.[3] Peirce seems fated to a rather narrow logical interpretation, however, and Dewey continues to be treated as an educator, on the one hand, or as an intellectual fossil, on the other. To be sure, there are sources of help in understanding the social turmoil of our time in these and other philosophers, but the most illuminating message is too easily lost in the dust of side battles.

There is one American philosopher whose message about man's ineradicable dependence upon institutions cannot be missed — *if* he is read at all, that is. Unfortunately, Elijah

---

3. Dewey, for instance, offers trenchant criticism of modern individualism in a number of works, notably *Individualism Old and New* (New York: Minton, Balch and Co., 1930) and *The Public and its Problems* (New York: Henry Holt and Co., 1927). In fact, he shows some of the same awareness of and attitude toward the effects of business that Jordan has. But Dewey does not center his thought in the institutional problem as obviously or as dramatically as Jordan does.

Jordan is hardly known beyond a handful of scholars—most of them former students of Jordan at Butler University. Jordan's style is too old-fashioned, his approach too much his own for him to attract much interest amidst the fads and fancies of academic philosophy. He reflects the idealism he was exposed to briefly at Cornell in 1907-08, the social psychology of E. A. Ross from his year at Wisconsin, and the pragmatism of Mead, Moore, and Tufts from his two years at Chicago. But he made what he found his own, and no convenient label identified his ideas.

Jordan also was handicapped for popularity by the fact that he was not a man to suffer fools gladly and that he found a plethora of fools, to his mind, against whom he spoke out regularly and openly. Even some of his most ardent followers deplored the publication of *Business be Damned,*[4] a strident, vitriolic attack on our whole business system. But Jordan wrote that book before 1931 and he still believed in it when it finally was published in 1952. He never concealed the depth of his feeling about and his concern for those matters he considered important, and his prose could be purple indeed:

> At its best, at its nearest approach to beauty, life remains sordid, vulgar, brutal, and obscene. For the benefit of those optimists who in the fatuous shallowness of their muddled vacuity remonstrate, I point to the fact — the reality of the world wallowing in the mire of its own filth and prolonging for the moment its futile existence in fevered draughts of its own dripping blood. This the eternal truth of the Christ: the blood is shed.[5]

And this near the end of a highly technical work on aesthetics.

Behind what appears to be unphilosophic bombast—or at the least an unscholarly directness — lies a tough mind intent upon *seeing* the world directly and restoring to it the objectivity it has lost. Jordan's theory of institutions does

---

4. (New York: Henry Schuman, 1952).
5. Elijah Jordan, *The Aesthetic Object* (Bloomington, Indiana: The Principia Press, 1937), p. 246.

help make sense of the lost individual, swallowed by giant corporations he does not comprehend. His ideas are of vital importance as counterbalance to our ego-oriented world.

I

In *The Aesthetic Object,* Jordan distinguishes three moments or aspects of knowledge: the intellective or discursive, the contemplative, and the speculative.[6] Only the speculative yields real objects, in Jordan's sense, and is knowledge proper. The intellective and contemplative forms are stages on the way to knowledge, stages necessary to the understanding of the end result. One of the two preliminary forms of knowledge may well be the best we can attain under certain circumstances with regard to some matters, but in such cases it remains important to be aware that our knowledge is a preliminary, not a realized, form.

Jordan distinguishes the three moments on the bases of their purposes or basic urges and of their objects. The intellective urge is directed toward the discrimination of presentations into relational schemes or networks. Intellection is the structure-seeking endeavor basic to mathematics and science, as well as to art. It abstracts from all content of presentations in order to achieve precision and clarity in the expression of bare relations or form. The resulting object is an abstract relational object — the mathematician's point or the physicist's atom. Jordan calls it the existential object, identifiable only as the terminus of relations connecting it with other such objects. The object lacks quality altogether, and because of this abstractness, it can be moved from one relational context to another without serious distortion, as is exemplified pre-eminently in mathematics. The intellective object — as bare form —

---

6. *Ibid.,* Chapter II.

also is the ground of the aesthetic object (pure shape), the truth object (logical structure), and the practical object (routine habit).

An object, however, must have qualitative content to be real; it must have value, and quantity as such has no value. As Jordan says, the abstract object is useful for devising techniques for action as set patterns and for formulating abstract ideas or goals for action where rigid patterns are relevant. The meaning of the existential object lies only in anticipation of the realization of the abstract form as a real object with emotional content. Considered as purely intellectual, intellective knowledge cannot encompass action; it is restricted to mechanical repetition of endless process.

On the other hand, Jordan conceives of contemplative intellect as directed toward synthesis or comprehension of presentations into wholes of individuality. The mind comprehends the abstract forms of thought in a unity with the substance of sense perception. The result is an individual object in which the creative act of mind is identified with the substance of the external world. The cognitive act is embedded in feeling, and feeling is made permanent or objective in the value object produced. Science, according to Jordan, has no real objects; it has only skeletal forms which never acquire sensuous meaning. The contemplative act of thought constitutes the moral, religious, and aesthetic objects that then constitute the substance of the real world. In Jordan's words, "The object of the discursive reason is existence; of the contemplative reason, value; the object of the speculative reason in logic is the real. The three objects are cumulative in the direction indicated."[7]

Speculative reason yields the real object, for Jordan, embodying both the form and the substance derived from the first two stages of thought. Existence and value are united in what he calls the logical object. Logic, in this sense, is that which gives the underlying conditions which make the object possible as the object it is. The object is grasped in its relation to its metaphysical ground in reality. Logic is the

---

7. *Ibid.*, p. 35.

Institutions and The Alienated Man

whole system of relations which constitutes experience, including thought, sensation, emotion, and feeling, and to which any object must be referred for its meaning. The logical object is the object thus located and valued within the whole of experience.

It seems obvious that action is not based upon full speculative knowledge, as Jordan describes that knowledge. The object of an act cannot be known in advance in any such complete sense. There is always an element of surprise, an element of risk in action. But Jordan maintains that we can have speculative knowledge *of* action (as contrasted with knowledge *in* an act), and *The Good Life*[8] is a search for just that logical meaning of action. He approaches that meaning through an analysis of the act into the three traditional categories, Person, Act, and World.

Intellective or discursive thought enables us to grasp those processes or forms that are the foundation for person, act, and world; and in Jordan's treatment intellection has special reference to the concept of person in its initial development in incomplete, isolated, hence abstract, form. Contemplation presents us with the feeling content of each of the three categories, and it holds a special relationship to the category of act as acts are analyzed in terms of the subjective virtues or the qualities that are good in the person. Speculation makes possible the realization of person, act, and world as full objects of knowledge, but that full realization can be attained only in the context of the world as objective eventuation of the act and as fulfillment of the person.

The analysis of the person proceeds from the biological capacities (process) through the psychological capacities (content) to the social capacities and the person as moral agent. The subjective virtues, in a similar progression, are sympathy, generosity, and friendship, culminating in integrity. The world is made manifest in discussions of progressively more inclusive institutions: the family, industry, education, religion, art, and politics. It is in the ways indicated that each stage of thought plays its part in cognition of

---

8. Elijah Jordan, *The Good Life* (Chicago: University of Chicago Press, 1949), pp. 6, 25, 128.

action. But the important consideration here is that intellection cannot by itself produce a moral theory at all. There can be no biological ethics, much less a physical one. Those positivists were correct who judged that their approach ruled out ethics altogether. Contemplation can eventuate in an ethical content, but it cannot reach knowledge. Only speculation can do that, and speculation has as its object something more than the subjective agent and act as viewed by most modern thought.

The starting point for Jordan's discussion in *The Good Life* of the psychological capacities of the agent is perception, by means of which we are given objects as qualitative. Memory stabilizes these objects by making possible a past linked with a present, and imagination gives them a future (in the form of plans or ideals) by moving from the object as quality or variety to the object as value. Imagination serves as the connection between thought and action in its capacity as what Jordan calls "the cognitive phase of will or the volitional phase of thought."[9]

The difficulty for contemplative intellect, however, is the fact that it is impossible to know what the end of an act means before the act is completed, while knowledge of the end is the sole basis we have for guiding action. We act in reference to ends as *forms,* but the meaning of the ends will be changed by the actual feeling-value they acquire when they are actualized. Intellect cannot anticipate the feeling-content of the object. But that feeling Jordan calls religious intuition — prophetic feeling impregnated with a cognitive element — can anticipate the meaning of an end to some extent. It is religious intuition that keeps the act from being a matter of pure chance. This intuition cannot be rendered an object of knowledge, however; we cannot establish a logical basis for the intuition itself.[10]

Yet even at this stage, reason has a logical function with respect to action — that of demonstrating the continuity of nature and culture.[11] By "nature" Jordan means the world,

---

9. *Ibid.,* p. 113.
10. *Ibid.,* pp. 317-318.
11. *Ibid.,* pp. 4-5, 129, 257.

including man, prior to any effects of man's activity; by "culture" he means the world as shaped by man or as embodying the thought and action of man. The act and the end of the act have their value in relation to the unity of nature and culture, and thus the judgment of an action must rest upon a demonstration of its conformity to this unity.

However, Jordan sees two problems connected with any such judgment. First, the unity of nature and culture can be formulated only as a result of an examination of the past, that is, of situations and actions resembling the situation we recognize now and the act as we hold it in idea.[12] Consequently our formulation is only probable with reference to the future. Second, even after the act, the meaning of its end can never be stated fully. Insofar as it is an end, it has its meaning in its reference to the past and the future — for all time. It is never, as an end, completely realized as a "thing;" it always has unknown implications for future action. It is in light of these two problems that action is always risk.

The risk must be calculable, in order that we can have action and not just random movement, and such calculation depends upon there being some stability in the environment of action, some elements in the circumstances surrounding a proposed act remaining unchanged. Insofar as that environment is composed of other *agents,* it certainly will change before the act is complete. We cannot look to individuals to supply the stability action requires. In the face of this situation, Jordan turns to the relatively fixed structure of institutions within which our act and the actions of others take place.

It is here that the distinctive character of Jordan's thought emerges. He says that men act, in any real sense of "act," only institutionally, that is, through some kind of corporate structure. He states this view most dramatically when he says that "thinking is the only act of which the individual is capable that does not also complicate his activity with that

---

12. *Ibid.,* pp. 40-41.

of other individuals. Objectively, thinking is the only act within which the individual can complete an object."[13] Thought can come only from an individual, but the individual *acts* through and in institutions. Institutions provide the necessary instruments for action and, at the same time, limit the scope and point the direction of action. Therefore, ethics must center in the attempt to understand institutions and the kinds of action possible within them.

The end of an act cannot be known in advance except abstractly. But the major conditioning and limiting circumstances can be known. Consequently, the end can be characterized within a set of limits, and the issue of the act can be anticipated to a degree. Coupled with religious intuition of the meaning of the end, this knowledge of corporate structure yields the best guide for action possible under human circumstances. Chance and change still operate to make any act an adventure, but such knowledge as can be had serves to keep the act from being blind wandering. We can have speculative knowledge of institutions; we can discover the logical grounds for judging institutions in terms of their operations and ends as related to the structure of the world.

II

Mind, for Jordan, may be described as an order of objects.[14] One meaning of "object" in this context is purpose, as when we talk of having an object in view. Mind then can be dealt with as a system of purposes, ordered by thought and action. The ordering activity of mind can be distinguished from the objects ordered, but Jordan insists that we can *talk* about mind only as involving those objects. Mind manifests itself only in and through objects. In another

---

13. *Ibid.*, p. 81.
14. *Ibid.*, pp. 308-310. See also his *Forms of Individuality*, (Bloomington, Indiana: The Principia Press, 1927), pp. 169-170, and *The Life of Mind* (Indianapolis, Indiana: Charles W. Laut and Co., 1925), pp. 317-318.

sense, "object" means merely that which is distinct from or outside the activity of mind. Yet, for Jordan, the object in this sense is a stage of purpose. The thing is viewed as outside under some elementary kind of order dependent upon our practical purposes.[15]

As individual, these objects can be realized only partially, in Jordan's view; we cannot give them permanence or stability. But purposes in their full sense are not individual; they are shared, and as shared they can be made objective. Their objectivity consists in their being related consistently to other purposes and thus fitted into the matrix of human activities. As objective, purposes are embodied in external objects, and these embodied purposes, in turn, are what Jordan calls institutions. Institutions are composed of physical things which contain subjective elements in their constitutions. Subjective elements thereby become accessible in a form in which intelligence can deal with them.

From the most basic point of view, an institution is an ordering of property objects as means to some particular kind of end.[16] In this sense, an education system is a set of buildings containing desks, chairs, blackboards, maps, and other equipment, together with a number of teachers, administrators, and service personnel. These objects are related by virtue of their common end — however vaguely conceived that end may be. An institution is the established way of thinking and acting people have for dealing with certain ends. An education system is a relatively stable way of thinking and acting in the province of developing the intelligence of the young. (These same kinds of remarks can be applied to such an institution as language. Jordan calls words objects, and language a collection of words and rules for their use organized for the purpose of communication.[17])

Institutions are the outgrowths of the objective conditions of the world. They contain purposes of men and those pur-

---

15. *The Good Life,* pp. 223-227.
16. *Ibid.,* pp. 5-6, 37, 110.
17. Elijah Jordan, *Essays in Criticism* (Chicago: University of Chicago Press, 1952), p. 16.

poses make up a part of the conditions giving rise to institutions. But by and large, institutions or corporations are not the *products* of conscious purpose of individual men.

> The corporation is the natural embodiment of a social purpose, when a social purpose is regarded as the objective logical medium in which individual purposes are realized. It is the more or less consciously formulated institution, and has come to take the place of the older institutions which were established reflexly and unconsciously under the influence of imitation and custom. It is not created by anything outside itself, it is the product of its own dynamic life, of its own order effective as will; it is a fact-synthesis principled by its own law, and in this sense it has no origin. To speak of its originating out of some specifiable thing or act or even out of a complex of tendencies is absurd. It grows up within the system of reality as a form which represents both the permanence of realized or objectified purpose and the creativeness of purposive process, and the distinction between created and creator is within it, hence, neither of the terms of the distinction can be asserted of it. It neither creates itself or is created by anything; it grows.[18]

However, the growth of institutions, for the most part, reflects the effects of changing conditions on old forms. This means that institutions generally reflect the purposes of men in some anachronistic fashion. They are outgrowths of previous circumstances, altered in some way by the intervening changes in conditions. At a given time, objective conditions call for a particular kind of corporate structure in any realm of action. The pressing question of the present is whether those conditions are to any extent under the control of men. And Jordan is clear in his answer: no, they are not under our control.

> In matters of destiny it is not man's prerogative to choose either ends or means. Destiny has ordained civilization, and history dictates its methods. The type of method changes as the course of civilization elevates man above or drops him below his previous states.[19]

---

18. *Forms of Individuality*, p. 433.
19. *Business be Damned*, p. 236. See also *The Good Life*, pp. 228-229.

Institutions and The Alienated Man

This does not make man a mere pawn on history's chessboard, however. History does not determine what *happens* or what *is;* it only determines the circumstances within which whatever happens does occur and to this extent must shape the occurrence. The methods of civilization do not assert themselves. Men have to discover them and implement them.

> It is the province of man's reason and his choice to modify the method for the attainment of the good which history puts into his hands, and to adapt it to the accident and circumstance that make up the environment in which he, at each moment, must act.[20]

Again, man's first duty is to know, to know what is called for by the situation in which he finds himself. Yet his job is not that of devising new institutions to cope with changing facts. Mind does not create institutions any more than institutions create minds. Jordan views both minds and institutions as aspects of the factual situation considered from the standpoint of its logical ground. "Mind is the natural order of fact; institution is minded order."[21] Mind does the ordering of fact, and it can be recognized as mind only as the order is made real in institutions. Stated in terms of mind and matter, mind is determinative of culture within the limits set by the material circumstances. Mind and culture are the same order looked at in the one instance as a dynamic force, in the other as a pattern of action. Matter constitutes the conditions of order, and mind is the ordering.

The ordering, of course, may not conform to the facts. Mind may be a muddle and institutions abortive. One reason may be that men do not change their methods consonant with historical changes, or they may completely misinterpret historical changes. In either case, the attempted ordering of objects is at variance with what the situation requires. Jordan views most institutions as anachronistic in one or the

---

20. *Business be Damned,* p. 236.
21. *Forms of Individuality,* p. 178.

other of these ways.[22] Men's purposes are thereby thwarted; their actions become futile or worse. Men so order the means for action that unwittingly they channel their activities away from the ends for which the ordering came about. Thus institutions become perverted, and minds in their disarray cannot understand what is going wrong.

If, on the other hand, institutions were in harmony with the historical situation, mind would be at the same time a proper ordering of that situation. And the institutions would make available to men the appropriate means for the attainment of their ends. These ends would be right in that they would be objectified in institutions that reflect and collectively constitute reality. (An end is right in its harmonious relations with other ends and with the whole of nature and culture.)

Because of the intimate relation Jordan sees between any institution and the whole of reality, he argues that we cannot deal with the problems of *an* institution in isolation. An institution may have the correct form for current achievement of the purpose it embodies, yet the influences of other institutions less well constructed may prevent the proper functioning of that institution and in time may pervert the well-adapted structure itself. For instance, Jordan says that it is *possible* that art in some of its forms still can attain aesthetic ends in a relatively satisfactory manner. And since the aesthetic act is the only act that approaches perfection (in the perfect objectification of the act itself[23]), we still can have a model for the form of action. This model is threatened, is hindered, is more and more often debased, however, by other institutions which are not in harmony with reality or with each other.[24] To the extent that the cultural system is not made up of parts that are harmonious and integrated with each other, men are not agents but tools of their own institutions. Thus the artist is corrupted by commercialism and cynicism and exhibitionism, and he does not achieve his

---

22. *Ibid.*, pp. 437-440.
23. *The Good Life*, pp. 324-325.
24. *Business be Damned*, pp. 162-163.

own artistic ends but the ends of a confused and confusing culture. The human body becomes the obscene source of ephemeral titillations and the mind is depicted as a private insane asylum.

Institutions not only interfere in and deflect the operations of other institutions, they directly oppose other institutions both in purpose and method. Jordan maintains that the whole must be relatively well adjusted or none of the parts can long continue to function as it should. Moreover, even given a comparatively harmonious situation, the cultural structure must be such as to provide for continuous adjustment of the whole as conditions alter.[25] Primitive societies may for some time remain functional by means of the crude adjustments that take place in the gradual alteration of customs and habits in response to slowly changing environments. And in more complex cultures, certain self-adjusting mechanisms may operate within very narrow limits. Diet habits of custom-bound people may gradually conform to changes in the rainfall or in the animal population of the region. Adam Smith's market does indeed effect a sort of balance between the prices of goods and their scarcity or abundance. It makes some allowance for the differing amounts of hardship and creativity that different products entail, but as Smith says, that adjustment is made "not by any accurate measure, but by the higgling and bargaining of the market, according to that sort of rough equality which, though not exact, is sufficient for carrying on the business of common life."[26] A traditional condition stated for the market to work even thus roughly is "other things being equal;" and, of course, other things never are equal. A free market requires delicate adjustments of a great many elements in order to work limpingly, much less robustly.

One of the primary concerns Jordan has tried to make

---

25. *Forms of Individuality,* p. 308.
26. Adam Smith, *The Wealth of Nations* in *Adam Smith's Moral and Political Philosophy,* ed. by Herbert W. Schneider (New York: Hafner Publishing Co., 1948), p. 347.

clear is that civilized societies cannot hope for gradual habitual accommodations or built-in mechanisms of control to take care of the need for maintenance of the wholeness and health of the culture. There is for civilized men no alternative to thinking. The bare passage of time, the calculations of computers, or the psychological conditioning of our responses will not save men from the wild careening of institutional change. Mind, Jordan insists, must become aware of the nature of changes and the actual functioning of institutions and so make possible the re-ordering of the world of cultural objects to accord with the cultural and natural possibilities.

It is important to note that Jordan holds that there is no basis in the nature of things for the conflicts of ends we see all around us.[27] The recognition that, under our conceptions of the nature of property, we inevitably seem to encroach upon the property rights of others, even in the absence of any malice or lack of concern, points to the inaptness of those conceptions in a world where property *is* public and general in its fundamental functions, *not* private and particular. In Jordan's words,

> ... rights to use are not necessarily exclusive, and where uses "conflict" it is not a question necessarily of the principle that the stronger will prevail, but that supposedly conflicting uses *are* often naturally, and can quite generally be made in practice confluent to a common end where both may be enjoyed to the full.[28]

If we posit conflict as essential, conflict will appear in our social arrangements, without doubt.

A social theory based on a final acceptance of what actually exists at any moment, or even over the course of time, usually will amount to no more than an attempted rationalization of an essentially irrational state of affairs, as Jordan sees it. A theory must look to the relation between

---

27. *Business be Damned,* pp. 110-111; *Forms of Individuality,* p. 338; *The Life of Mind,* pp. 251-252.
28. *Forms of Individuality,* p. 334.

culture and nature for its ground, if it is to deserve the name social or practical. Culture, as the totality of men's efforts to bring nature into the arena of men's purposes, is the all-inclusive institution, on this view.[29] It is the whole of man's embodied or instituted purpose. But men, as individuals, cannot comprehend this super-institution in its wholeness, even though it is, at least in part, their creature. That is, men cannot take in the cultural whole as what Jordan calls value-substance. We do not have culture as a logical *object*. We can, however, arrive at a logical *concept* of culture, and it is as a logical concept that culture is of primary importance. For Jordan, an analysis of the structure of an act implies the logical structure of culture. An act or an object of any sort can be given meaning only within a larger structure. Behind the act must be the institution, and behind the institution must be the cultural whole. The necessity for a successive ordering of objects in order to explain the significance of *this* object leads us from the particular to the whole.

The logical concept of culture contains the ground for action. Institutions, as objectified modes of action, are significant in relation to this concept, and individual acts take on meaning by being judged in light of the concept. The logical function of the concept of culture is analogous to that Jordan describes of a table we know is in the next room. He says, "The table as it stands in the next room as the dependable basis and center for other objects [books, chairs, etc.] is a simple instance of a logical object, and by this we mean that *when* we think of the table *as* the center of a group of experiences, it will help us to organize our thought to the form and degree where it has meaning."[30] Even though we do not have culture as a value-object in the sense that we do have the table as such, the concept of culture plays an organizing role just as the concept of the table does. And what we lose by not having a comprehension of culture is more than compensated by the gain in richness, breadth, and profundity of the concept in its logical use:

---

29. *The Good Life,* pp. 254-255.
30. *The Life of Mind,* p. 216.

Darnell Rucker

> When we speak therefore of action with reference to ends, we mean that the act finds its meaning ultimately in this system of culture. Also when we refer to the right and the good as standards of judgments about acts, we mean to refer to the cultural system in some of its generalized aspects; and we indicate, by using the terms "right" and "good," a place or locus in that system to be occupied by a typical object or a set of qualitative conditions to which the object must conform.[31]

Institutions are objectified purposes, modes of action, ways of thinking that have come into being because of cultural circumstances. If the materials at hand are adapted to the purpose called forth by the cultural reality, then the institution gives expression to a genuine need and provides means—organized and accessible—for its satisfaction. Such apt adjustment of means to an end for Jordan means that the instituted purpose fits into the total scheme of purposes which makes up the cultural world. But where an end is out of harmony with reality or where unsuitable materials are used or the materials are improperly organized to direct action for that particular end, the institution becomes a crippling one—crippling to the individual who holds that end in view and crippling to society by the disruptive effect of its lack of harmony with the objective situation. A weak institution of this sort may well be destroyed either by its own inner conflicts or by its conflicts with other institutions. (Third Party movements in American politics would seem to illustrate this kind of weakness.) On the other hand, an ill-adapted institution that attaches itself to a firm base of traditional, entrenched forms which, perhaps, once were suited to their ends can assert itself for a considerable period of time to the detriment of other social structures that are better adapted to the facts of the world. (The tenacity of some big-city political machines is a case in point.)

Jordan asks that we judge our institutions by two intimately related criteria. We should judge them first by the way in which they interact with other institutions to form a whole of human purpose. That purpose would be the provision of conditions for satisfactory modes of action such that sub-

---

31. *The Good Life,* p. 110.

sistence, reproduction, education, science, art, philosophy, and any other human ends would play their appropriate roles in the lives of individual men. That means that we also should judge an institution by its effectiveness in making its means readily available for the attainment of its particular purpose. Of course, neither criterion will be met satisfactorily in the absence of the other. In the case of the institution of art mentioned above, Jordan could claim that the institution was meeting the demands of aesthetic purpose to some extent precisely because it, unlike some other institutions, was capable of an integration into the cultural potential of the time. American painting, poetry, and fiction earlier in this century, had a kind of strength that grew out of American culture and enabled them to make concretely available a feeling-sense of what was good and what was bad in that culture. But Jordan points out that isolated institutions cannot long survive intact against the opposition they encounter on all sides from corporate structures that have broken loose all ties with reality. Just so, those most promising literary and artistic trends in the United States have been thwarted and seduced all unawares by the dominant commercialism of the time. Television, for instance, captive from its inception to advertising, has infected the theater and motion pictures (both already ill) with its virus. The novel and painting have become emotional exhibitionism, and even the dance becomes more and more a freak show. Those artists who somehow manage to maintain an integrity of vision are hard put to gain any foothold in the world with what they produce. What it finally comes down to is that the parts that compose culture can be understood and evaluated only as they are viewed in relation to the whole they constitute. A relatively adequate institution in a disorganized world is in much the same predicament as the good man in a very bad society.

Jordan tells us that our culture is gravely ill. He says this in words ranging from statements of desperate urgency to those bordering on utter hopelessness. What has gone so badly awry in our culture? And what, if anything, can be

Darnell Rucker

done about it? His principal answer as to what is wrong is that men do not apply their *intellects* to their institutional problems.[32] He does *not* mean that individual men, by taking thought, can reform their institutions. But by thinking, men can devise plans, point to areas of breakdown, clarify goals, and exhibit the possibilities of existing resources. When men attempt to act directly to change the world, they produce what Jordan calls techniques, fixed tools and means that then stand between the purposes men have and any actualization of those purposes. The efficiency expert and the designer of mass-production machines, for example, devise a world of actions that are partial, isolated, and inherently unsatisfactory. In Jordan's words, a part has its sole significance in the extent to which it reflects the whole to which it belongs. The more we try to make the part an end, the less it can have any genuine purpose at all. If the man whose activities have been efficiently mechanized retains a sense of purpose, that purpose becomes merely "intellectual," disembodied, airy, wistfully or desperately unattainable.

The role of the individual's intelligence is that of play (as opposed to work and reproduction).[33] Play is the free activity of intellect in ordering man's relations to the world apart from any purpose other than the order or design itself. Work has as its end the production of the material conditions necessary for the biological, psychological, and aesthetic health of men. Reproduction aims at the range of activities essential for the production of a continuing line of adequate individuals through the family, the school, the church, the community, and the like. Play has no end beyond the activity of inventing systems adapting the materials of nature and culture to each other and both to human actions. Only in play is intellect focused on wholeness and adequacy, rather than diverted toward partial concerns and immediate, therefore distorted, problems. In this sense, Jordan says that "play is the essentially institution-building activity of

---

32. *Business be Damned,* p. xiii. See Dewey, *The Public and Its Problems,* p. 147.
33. *The Good Life,* pp. 86-94.

man."[34] Institutions cannot concoct their own schemes; they must rely upon individual thought to create and revise the plans required to maintain institutions as competent instruments of purpose and to prevent their degenerating into blind, aimless monsters.

The act of intellect in ordering the relations between nature and culture gives form to the materials of the world, since any act of mind remains inchoate so far as it fails of embodiment in some way. Therefore, the free activity of intelligence, apart from any deliberate intent, creates institutions as the embodiments of ideas and, when adequately thought-out, as the effective instruments of human purposes. In much the same sense that the worst way to try to be happy is to make happiness itself a direct end of action, the worst way to try to control the instruments of action is to aim directly at altering those instruments. Hence the failure of intellect lies in the utilitarian and pragmatic activity of intellect — precisely those activities modern man so prides himself upon, the intelligence of the engineer, the medical researcher, the agronomist, the model-builder and the language analyst. The urge toward immediate results imposed upon us by our biological natures overrides any recognition of the need for detachment suggested by intellect, and intellect remains subordinate to our bodily impulses even in our most sophisticated uses of intellect. But men are what they are *because* their bodily impulses do not have sufficient built-in direction and control to provide for the organism's survival. Intellect is requisite for the necessary guidance of impulse, and the role of intellect in the human constitution introduces demands that, even though they rest upon a biological foundation, transcend the biological and make any merely biologically controlled pattern of action impossibly inadequate. To play its ultimate necessary role, intellect has to stand above the materials it orders and to recognize that in the ordering of those materials it is itself constituted as intellect and that the ordering, in turn, constitutes the world of culture within which intellect must subsist and act.

---

34. *Ibid.*, p. 93.

Darnell Rucker

III

Why, however, do we seem in so much worse a plight than men in the past? Surely, men in other times and places were not superior in intellect to contemporary men. Other civilizations have flourished and died or been transformed. The dislocations of modern civilization hardly can be unique. Why, then, this sense of urgency and of despair on the part of those who appear most aware of and most sensitive to the situation we find ourselves in? Why such violent and widespread reactions on the part of the young, who hold whatever hope there is for a future?

What Jordan sees is the impending collapse of culture, not because our world is made up of strange new elements, but because the elements are dominated by the institution of business — a new *domination* in the world and one that has taken its definitive form in the United States and is spreading throughout the world.

Common characterizations of the cultures of ancient Greece, Rome, and the Middle Ages serve to illustrate the way in which a particular institution sets the tone for a whole culture and affects the range of possibilities the culture affords.

The ancient Greeks certainly had bad institutions by any standards, such as slavery, the subjection of women, and homosexuality. Yet they attained forms of activity such that some few individuals could achieve real greatness and more could find real satisfactions. The dominant institutions in Greek life were aesthetic, not commercial, and therefore those crudenesses and evils that existed in the social orders they had were tempered by the grace and beauty embodied in those orders. Religions that could have been raw superstitions and fears were transformed by art into imaginative, though impractical, structures of thought. Sexual practices that in themselves were bestial became at times sublimated into charming, though sterile, acts of love.

The Romans were saved from being nothing more than barbarians by their pervasive concern with law and the legal orders they devised to make it effective. Brutal conquest was tempered by the conquerors themselves, by their instituting and maintaining Roman law as the defining mark of the conquest.

Medieval life, dismal and slavish as much of it undoubtedly was, carried a religious vision into every corner of life and gave a glow and a significance to things otherwise unbearable. The depravity of a pope did not erase the courage of a martyr or the grandeur of a cathedral.

What does our over-arching institution do to alleviate the weaknesses and breakdowns of *our* culture? Jordan's reply is that it does nothing for us by way of either construction or salvage. It acts like a cancer and infects every other cell of the social organism in turn, one way or another. "Culture and civilization are breaking down because of the lapse of intelligence; and the lapse is due to the transformation of the man into the businessman."[35] Where art, law, and religion tend to expand awareness and concern, business tends to narrow them; and in Jordan's terms business produces only techniques and mechanical processes at the expense of the creative thought culture requires.

Business, for Jordan, is a perversion of necessary economic forces; and in an economic era, business is the motive that perverts all our institutions. Business is not the same thing as industry.[36] It is not concerned with either production or distribution of goods; it is concerned only with control of the process of exchange, exercised through the market and its price system. Buying and selling should serve as a means whereby the producer and the user can exchange goods without losing valuable time from their productive endeavors. Jordan is objecting that the servant has become master.[37] The producer and the consumer are manipulated by the businessman for the sake of abstract control of the exchange process itself. The businessman has no idea of or interest in the purposes of the parties to the exchange;

---

35. *Business be Damned*, p. xiii.
36. *Ibid.*, pp. 32-35, 38-42.
37. *Ibid.*, p. 16.

he is interested simply in maintaining control of the market for the power that control represents.

The market is the practical embodiment of business; economics is its theoretical embodiment.[38] To Jordan, economics is the attempt by intellective mind to account for value (which is the province of contemplative mind) and for action (which speculative mind alone can deal with adequately). Intellective mind cannot comprehend culture as the embodiment of human purposes; consequently it must ignore purposes altogether and introduce purposeless natural urges as man's only motivation. It cannot understand (much less account for) the continuity of nature and culture, so it reduces man's activities as nearly as possible to the level of nature:

> It [business organization] shows on the one hand the elevating of the blind energies of nature to a sort of semi-awareness, and a reduction of the conscious visions of cultural persons to a point where they coalesce with this low awareness, the combination forming the conscious but conscienceless energies of the business organization.[39]

The market is characterized for Jordan in three ways.[40] First, the elements of the market are discrete individuals and property objects which these individuals appropriate. The value of the objects themselves is lost sight of in the operation of the market; and the abstract values in terms of which the exchange system operates are based on the actual or potential exclusion of interested individuals from property objects. Thus property, under this conception, does not constitute the embodiment of the relations among men; instead it constitutes the separation and distinction of men into isolated groupings of "things," each grouping regarding all other groupings as potential threats to its possessions and as potential sources of additions to its possessions. And even within a grouping, the individuals regard each other with suspicion wherever their individual posses-

---

38. *The Good Life,* p. 295.
39. *Business be Damned,* p. 19.
40. *Ibid.,* pp. 9-14.

sions are involved. The market approaches an economic war of all against all.

Second, the motivation of the market is the motive to control — not control of objects for use, but control of the whole exchange process and hence of the parties to that process. For Jordan, the value placed on property objects from the standpoint of control is almost altogether negative: the more inaccessible the object is made to potential users the more valuable it becomes. This negative valuation has nothing to do with anything inherent in the object or connected with its possible use. The objective of the man in the market is not the object in any sense at all but the manipulation of the exchange situation to create an advantage to himself in regard to these exclusion possibilities. Exclusion value, even once attained, is not translatable into goods values, except as we regard other goods also as exclusion values. In this view, market value has meaning only as power — economic power over the market and over other men.

Third, the operations of the market necessarily take place through the price system. Money is the abstract, artificial measure of market value, and money value need have no relation to the goods involved, as goods. Money is merely the means by which the manipulators keep score in their power game. As the control motive becomes more pervasive, price is related less to supply and demand, too. Whatever is advantageous for the manipulators to supply is what can be bought; and demand is conjured up by clever use of the rawest natural urges, which are cut off from any genuinely cultural objects for human satisfactions.

The serious threat to civilization that the market mentality poses is made clear when we look more closely at Jordan's conception of culture. As has already been said, there must be a continuity of nature and culture, but the crucial consideration lies in the fact that culture reshapes, re-forms the raw matter of nature to human specifications— the specifications of an intelligent being capable of moral, aesthetic, and intellectual activities.[41] Whatever there is of goodness,

---

41. *The Good Life,* pp. 254-256.

beauty, and truth in the world man creates by his corporate activity. Of course, corporate activity can and often does create evil, ugliness, and falsehood, as well. Men cannot create values as individual agents, and neither can they *find* values ready-made in nature. *All* values, positive and negative, are corporate human products.

Life, the blind biological drive, is, from the standpoint of human purposes, in essence failure and frustration. By this, Jordan does not mean that there is failure and frustration because we have not yet reached success in harmonizing culture and nature, value and existence. Success is impossible and failure is the very nature of life. There is an unbridgeable gap between value and existence. Only intellect can close this gap. Speculative knowledge alone can unify value and existence, but only at the cost of the realization that this unity cannot be realized completely. Jordan, like Camus, sees man's nature as consisting in his demand for what nature cannot supply. But whereas Camus tries to live with the absurd by an act of the individual will creating a harmony out of nothing, Jordan holds that only in corporate activity can man bring nature, even though it retains its ultimate bruteness and recalcitrance, into objective relation with value as embodied in culture.

Truth, then, from Jordan's perspective lies in recognition of the essential negativity, the futility, the failure that is life. Beauty is attainable by the artist at the cost of life itself, by producing a dead perfection. Good can lie only in negating in action the negation that is life, in turning away from what is to what should be:

> Life is sweet then for the hog, the fox, and the practical man. But for the man whose knowledge of the conditions and limitations of life is even moderately clear, who knows conditions as they are and as determined by existence, life is a troubled dream. It is for this reason that philosophers and saints and the aesthetically competent persist in living in conditions not as they are but as they ought to be; conditions as they are or would be in a world under moral principles and as such directed by aesthetic design; the *meaning* of the New Jerusalem *is* its eternal Beauty. Incidentally, this breach between existence and value is cosmic, and the consequent limitation it imposes on life is the ground of

rational, that is, moral, action, and action is thus, when rational, principled by the motive to reform. "Practical" action has therefore no moral status.[42]

"Practical" action here means action premised on an acceptance of what happens to exist: the hardheaded businessman's "facing the realities of the world." For Jordan, the good, the moral, lies in an entirely different realm from that of the actualities of the world. And here lies that basic distinction he makes between nature and culture. Nature is the brute world in all its aimless cruelty, tawdriness, and obscenity — much the same vision of nature Schopenhauer had in his darker moments. Culture, on the other hand, is nature adorned with man-made covering. "Culture itself is carrion vestured in cloth of gold."[43] It is not nature altered from its bruteness; it is that bruteness made bearable by hiding its true nature from sight. The good man never forgets what life actually is, but he also never ceases trying to make it appear to be something else or acting as though it were something else.

The values brought into being by the creation of culture are genuine values. Truth, goodness, and beauty are true goods, real satisfactions as anyone knows who has experienced them. Jordan simply insists that we lose sight of the underlying crudity and chaos of nature at our peril. The shocking phenomenon of Nazi brutality emerging in the most highly cultured nation in the western world serves very well as an example for the point he wants to make. The marriage ceremony, domestic customs, parental love, and marital devotion can cover over and tame the blind lust that marks the naked reproductive urge; yet that lust is never eliminated (as any Freudian will testify) and in fact cannot be eliminated, any more than can any other of the natural bases of human life, without destroying the race. Consequently, the avarice and rapaciousness that culture tempers remain beneath the veneer and can burst forth in terrify-

---

42. *The Aesthetic Object,* pp. 223-224.
43. *Ibid.,* p. 246.

ing fashion unless the cultural substance that coats them is kept in repair.

In Jordan's classification of man's biological capacities, work and reproduction are the functions that have contact with the existent world of nature. They represent man's necessary recognition of his natural existence. But it is man's capacity to play that makes culture possible. It is his ability to rise above physical necessity in his purposeless activity in the realm of ideas that enables man both to exist as distinctively human and to bear such an existence in the face of the natural world.

It was mentioned earlier that Jordan calls play the essentially institution-building activity. And he adds what in the context in which it appears is a cryptic statement: "The adequate theory of play is thus the aesthetic theory of comedy."[44] The statement becomes less cryptic when we see what he means by "comedy."[45] Whereas, as he says, tragedy represents life as it is — a faithful objectification in art of the cold truth of life, comedy represents both the truth of life in all its negativity and the ideal of life as it might be. It is thus that all the institutions that comprise culture are what Jordan calls creatures of the comic purpose. Institutions are created systems embodying a more perfect relation between existence and value than can be realized in life. It is solely in and through man's institutions that any purpose or positive element can be brought into being. Therefore the objects of knowledge *are* these institutions. Speculative knowledge is the grasp of the unity of existence and value, and that unity exists only in the comic creations of man. Men have succeeded in their corporate endeavors in objectifying, making concrete what can never be in the natural world.

Whatever the historic origin of human beings, what has emerged from nature is an animal that cannot rest satisfied with its animal nature or with its animal world. The human being demands a moral world, an artificial world he must create in order that he may act, that he may feel, that he may

---

44. *The Good Life,* p. 93.
45. *The Aesthetic Object,* pp. 254-262.

be fully human. Consequently the man who wants to live with the raw facts of nature and to destroy the artificial facts of culture as being pipe dreams is a fool, in this view. He is proposing to destroy the very fabric of human existence. The man who views as guides to action the formal structures intellective mind creates is bound to produce a gross negativism of all human values out of his positivism, however well intentioned. Mind which never gets beyond its intellective stage is self-destructive. And while contemplative intuition can produce an ideal vision, so long as it remains in the contemplative phase, it yields sterile, hopeless yearning. Speculative mind alone can give us human life. Speculative mind combines intellect's contact with nature and contemplation's soaring above nature, and it creates a synthesis of the two in its cultural object. "And what we call culture was called into existence for just this purpose, to hang a wreath of posies upon the misfits within the tragedy which is life."[46]

The business system, because it is based upon division and conflict and can operate only at the level of intellection, is a perversion of what an institution should be. It is a denial of the possibility of that on which culture rests; it is an acceptance and a reinforcement of life in the raw that only can submerge us in confusion or numb us into insensibility. To Jordan, any appeal to the bare facts of nature, to our animal instincts, is not only foolish for men but basically immoral. The world within which action is intelligible is the result of turning away from bare facts while retaining the awareness that the facts are still there.

Camus' demand of his absurd man that he never lose sight of the cosmic gap between man's rational claims and the world's irrational indifference to those claims already had been demanded by Jordan of *his* moral man. But with the important difference that Jordan recognized that the world man can make is made institutionally, not individually. Camus' absurd hero defying the world in his lone attempt to create an order in his own life, to shoulder the entire enormous burden of responsibility for his actions, is doomed to

---

46. *Ibid.,* p. 260.

the very despair Camus so desperately tries to escape. Jordan's moral hero knows that he acts only through institutions and that intelligence is the sole source of better-ordered institutions. The moral man is not alone. He may be lonely in his morality but he is aware that his being is inextricably involved with other men in the organizations that make up his world. It is precisely *that* awareness Jordan sees absent in the businessman, and a culture shaped by the business mind is a culture devoid of that awareness.

Technology is applied piecemeal to the half-formulated problems modern men encounter. Technology is intellective mind concocting with a minuscule clarity and a social blindness mechanical devices that seem doomed inevitably to create more difficulties than they solve. In just as piecemeal a fashion, the specialist in culture bemoans the loss of first one value and then another as they are destroyed by technological advance. Contemplative mind is cut off from its intellective base and reacts to the destruction by a rejection of technology in the manner of the Luddites. This isolated contemplation has the virtue of a sense of the value content of culture, but it has little sense of the precarious but precious interrelatedness of the whole of culture and nature. As a result, the romantic culture advocate is rather an easy target for the tough-minded structuralist. The mechanistic theories and schemes of the intellective mind can be spectacularly successful in limited situations and in the short-run. The contemplative man appears mush-minded in his protests at the longer-range effects because there always are new marvels of technique being produced so as to prevent most men from seeing the real significance of those effects and to prevent their seeing what is the source of our accumulating troubles.

The unavoidable implication of Jordan's analysis of action is that man's sole hope is intelligence in its full sweep—speculative mind with its logical grasp of reality synthesizing the form and the content provided by intellection and contemplation. Jordan's moral law is a corollary of his analysis of action:

Institutions and The Alienated Man

> The good life posits a person or actor endowed by nature and by culture with all the capacities that are possible to him, with these capacities developed to their fullest possible degree; the person living in a world so organized and ordered as to guarantee to the person full and free access to all the means and instruments necessary to the adequate and appropriate expression of his capacities and to the realization of his acts in satisfying objects.[47]

When he says that the moral law is a faithful formulation of the essential relations of human life as it is actually lived, he means life complete with its wreath of posies. When he says that the moral law is true of the total fact of active life and needs no other recommendation to enforce its claim upon the intelligence, he means that speculative mind recognizes its object for what it is.

IV.

Jordan's solution to the problem of the breakdown of culture is the reordering by speculative mind of our culture so as to remove business from its central position and, probably, to eliminate business altogether. To eliminate business, for Jordan, means the end to any sort of market for distributing goods and the end to the use of money as a measure of goods.[48] Exchange will be of concrete objects, not of abstract symbols of any *quantity* of value. The businessman will be replaced by the Merchant.

> Then the Man and the Merchant, the Professor or Knower of Exchange, shall unite in the moral Person. His function will be to see that mankind are supplied with all the materials necessary to the completest action and the fullest use. He will supervise the creative process by which the raw materials are placed in the hand of the acting person.[49]

---

47. *The Good Life,* p. 59.
48. *Business be Damned,* pp. 9-10, 263-267.
49. *Ibid.,* p. 266.

Darnell Rucker

He views business as entrenched in culture through the market and the market as dependent upon money and the price system. Therefore money must go so the market can go. But it does not seem to be necessary to accept this demand for the abolition of money in order to find Jordan's theory of action a valuable aid in our attempts to understand our world. He may be right with regard to money and the market, but then again money and the market may be techniques capable of use for human purposes should speculative mind ever assert itself effectively. They are techniques men might find necessary in some form in any conceivable alteration of culture as it now exists. True, we cannot foresee the forms speculative mind might bring into being, but lack of foresight applies equally to the possible utility of old forms as it does to the nature of new ones.

The conception of speculative mind, instituted in the world, by indirection shaping that world to the moral form Jordan finds required by action smacks of a kind of idealism that is largely alien to the predominant shape of American thought. Pragmatism is conceived in terms of a directness of action that for Jordan keeps us vacillating between technology and dreams, with no hope of connecting the two. The fact remains that the confusions of the modern mind do reflect the confusions built into our institutions. And it does seem a hopeless task to try to assign any cause-effect connection between the two. Mind and its world are mutually determinative. As individuals, we flounder in frustration and despair in our feeble, ineffectual efforts to protest what we *feel* is wrong in our world. If we only could *think* (in Jordan's sense of that word) what is wrong, even as individuals we could live our lives in a humane awareness of why we fail. And who is to say that thought — speculative thought — would not *be* a reordering of the objective world — the very sort of reordering the absurd man so vainly tries to invest his private life with by an act of sheer private will? Once begun, that reordering *might* be infectious. The whole world does vibrate even now when a change occurs in any part of it.

Most men long ago have given up the hope that God will

save us from our follies and usher us at last into eternal bliss, whether in heaven or on earth. And many men are beginning to give up the hope that science and engineering will save us with a constant stream of gadgets of increasing complexity and increasing potential for misuse. We are busy in the field of education, only as one example among many, devoting time, energy, and physical resources to the development and promotion of contraptions and programs we are told will solve our educational problems if only we place our faith and our money in them. The path behind us is littered with the wreckage of machines and lives abandoned on the way by education; yet we are lured on along the selfsame path by the promise that, while the old schemes were stupid, the new marvels will prove to be the philosopher's stone.

Jordan is right, of course, as others have been before him: there is no philosopher's stone. There are no possible natural or mechanical solutions to the problems that beset man because he is man. Nature does not equip us as natural organisms for bare *survival;* we are compelled to act and acting so changes the world that no habitual or otherwise fixed patterns of action can sustain us. Acting and thinking are not individual manifestations. There must first be social organization to make action and thought possible. The individual acts only in and through instituted channels of action. He thinks only as the peculiar creation of those institutions. We have evolved from instinctual social groupings through semiconscious formations to the point that the structure of culture so overlays nature that deliberate organizations are the only possible means for supporting human life. We do not now *know* that such intelligent control of the world is necessary. We can *say* that it is so but our continued thought and action belie our words. Elijah Jordan, even in his rage, is trying to bring us closer to that knowledge. It would seem clear at this juncture that we have little to lose by at least lending his voice an attentive ear. If we heed him at all, we will have to look hard at a number of our really basic shortcomings as men.

A central shortcoming Jordan brings into bold relief is the

failure of our thought patterns to make significant contact with the external, concrete world. The result of this failure is that the objective structure of society goes its own way without the benefit of intellect, carrying men along with it, while the men being carried cannot comprehend what is happening. We patch the structure here and we patch it there, crying out for a change in men's hearts. But though our hearts bleed, our bodies continue to reinforce the machinery that dehumanizes us. Our President exhorts us to virtue while our social organizations promote antisocial vices of every description.

The relations among men exist as property objects, not as feelings and thoughts. Feelings and thoughts are made solid in property objects and, as solidified, relate men to each other and to their world; but the relations are made real in the object, not in the subject. Concrete property relations are accessible, whereas bare feelings and thoughts are not. Feeling is the stuff of all value and thought is the only source of social control, but both are effective only as they are embodied in the value-objects of culture.

Men exist as active beings in an institutional framework, and the kinds of action open to them depend upon the nature of that framework. The significant actions in our world are institutional actions, which our traditional individualistic categories do not enable us to understand. Only as we see how the structured means to various ends embodied in institutions direct the actions of men can we understand the relations between individual efforts and social results.

If we ever come to see the meaning of a corporate world that seems to spawn bewildered individuals, we will need to look critically at some of Jordan's excesses in language and in idea, especially his bitterness toward economics and business. But until that time, the truth of his basic vision of modern society stands as a badly needed antidote to the easy sorts of art and science and religion and philosophy that seem to gain most currency—easy in that they celebrate failure or promise miracles. Whatever else Jordan does, he does not celebrate failure or promise miracles. There is no substitute for hardheaded thought, and Jordan certainly provides us with a rare example of it.

14

THE EXPERIENCE OF VALUE
Ralph Ross

OUR LANGUAGE IS INESCAPABLY GENERAL. IN ORDINARY DIScourse it readily conveys ideas, although somewhat loosely, but it resists the statement of particulars. Of course, we can always point to a particular, but unless we also say something about it, it is hard to know which particular we mean in the complex that confronts us. And what we say is rather vague; if it were accurate we wouldn't need to point. Unlike discourse, the arts deal with particulars, not making statements about them in any usual sense, but presenting new particulars so arranged that statement is implicit in them.

To talk discursively about particulars one may have to use terms and make distinctions that help call attention to aspects of experience otherwise neglected. Because I want to talk about values, to begin with, as experienced particulars, I shall speak of qualities *in* experience and qualities *of* experience, and distinguish each from the other.

Values are found in experience and clarified in reflection. Sometimes clarification brings change and a new value is substituted for an old one, or the original value becomes less or more valuable. We start, logically, by finding qualities in things and events which are instances of "primary" qualities like figure, solidity, motion, and rest, or of "secondary" qualities like color, sound, odor, and taste, and are simple value-qualities, a term I will explain below. For this argument it is irrelevant to deny Locke's distinction between primary and secondary qualities on the ground that they are equally dependent on sense or mind, or to defend the distinction. It is relevant to point out that Locke's words for qualities are all general and that one experiences particulars.* A color, as we all know, must be some color and not another. Let us suppose the color is blue. That is general still, for there are many shades and intensities of blue, but even if we name the shades and intensities we are naming types. When blue is experienced, it is *this* blue, an instance if you like of a type of blue, though perhaps a little different from all other instances of the same type, as when we say "I never saw a blue like that before."

I find a value when I note that a particular experienced figure is balanced, a color vibrant, a sound rich and deep, an odor pungent, a taste sweet. A simple value is, initially, a quality *in* experience, not a quality *of* other qualities. Language misleads us here, unless we are very careful. When we say an odor is pungent we do not mean there is an odor, or quality, which has an additional quality, that *of* pungency; we mean we smell a pungent odor, thus characterizing the odor. Indeed, to say that what we smell is pungent (a value), is better than saying it is an odor, which is empty and redundant. The vibrant blue is not both blue and vibrant, but is one kind of blue, not another, and its value consists in what it is. Although it is one *kind* of blue (which is also a general description, for that is the way our language makes us talk) it is *this* perceived blue, which may be somewhat different from all other vibrant blues. And it is *this* "vibrancy-in-the-blue" that is its value, or, to put it better and less

---

* A particular is sometimes thought of as a single thing, and a quality is then a distinguishable perceived element in it, like the red of a rose. But sometimes a particular and a quality are thought of as identical. I use the words in both ways, relying on the context to clarify each use.

colloquially, it is this particular vibrant blue; there is a vibrant blue, after all, not a vibrancy in the blue.

But a value is not always simple, in the sense that it does not arise from other qualities; it is often a quality or character that does arise from other qualities, or from things and events. The magnificence of a mountain, the beauty of a face, the deadliness of a shark cannot be so distinguished from other qualities of the mountain, face, and shark, that they are perceived independently of them. This is quite clear and can be stated in a variety of ways, almost equally apt. Yet we can again be deceived by any statement of the relation between the simple qualities in these things and the emergent quality, for we may assume that the simple qualities must be thoroughly apprehended if a new quality is to emerge. And it is more likely that the configuration and the emergent quality are perceived first, or at the same time, and more vividly than the simple qualities.

Nor is a value of the kind I am calling emergent the result of a process of evaluation in which the object perceived is analyzed into its elements and relations, *standards* of value applied to those, and a *judgment* of value elicited. A turn in the road reveals a mountain rising magnificently from the valley below. We do not first identify the rock as sedimentary or igneous, measure the angle of thrust from the valley and then, by applying appropriate criteria of beauty, decide the mountain is magnificent. The very idea is ludicrous; it is as if I know I am running only if I can describe my activity in detail, learn a good definition of running, and then find that the definition fits the activity described. We see a magnificent mountain. Afterwards, if we like, we may ask why we think it magnificent or, for that matter, why we think it a mountain.

Magnificence in this instance is a quality *of* (not *in*, for quality is here a character and arises from the whole) the configuration of qualities that make up a mountain, yet the mountain's magnificence is perceived as much as its colors are perceived. Very often the magnificence is perceived before the colors are, as a face's beauty is seen before the shape of the ears is.*

* For a fuller discussion of this matter, see Ralph Ross, "Art as Knowledge," *The Sewanee Review,* Autumn, 1961.

Ralph Ross

On the standard subjective account, we first see, and then respond to, the mountain, judging or feeling it magnificent. But what are we judging? To what are we responding? The mountain? A configuration of qualities? And why is our response a feeling of magnificence? There must be something about the configuration that evokes that response, something that other configurations do not have, unless we find them, too, magnificent. What is that something? Can we put a name to it? Perhaps the best possible name is "magnificent"; what other name can one use? The mountain's magnificence is an emergent quality, a quality of the total configuration, or at least of what we perceive of it, what we experience in the viewing. "Emergent" should not be thought of as something after the fact; it is the logical result of what the simple qualities make up, the configuration itself, which is usually what, psychologically, we perceive first.

The configuration is magnificent, and we feel what we see. We feel a vibrant blue, too, as we see it, and feel as we taste a peppery sauce. Our feeling is perhaps less total, less moving, in our perception of simple qualities, than in our perception of emergent qualities. But that is because the fully aesthetic perception and response are not of and to simple qualities, which are elements of beauty, but to the way in which they are composed, by nature or art. In this respect, the aesthetic is what evokes total response. But the response is not separate from the experience, any more than the response to peppery sauce is. The response is the full experience.

I do not want to talk the issue to death, but another element might increase clarity. It may seem that certain chemical combinations exist objectively in the sauce, and are discovered by the practice of chemistry. When the sauce enters the mouth, it mingles with the saliva and stimulates a response of the taste buds which we call peppery. Thus we have objective existence, subjective response, and intellectual evaluation (we call the sauce peppery because we relate its taste to other tastes, many of which are blander). First, the taste, even if it is thought of as a response to a stimulus, is at least as real as chemical elements are. Second, introducing those elements and giving them a status of their

The Experience of Value

own, moves us away from experience to its natural conditions. We don't experience the conditions; they are conclusions of scientific inquiry which have a probabilistic claim to truth. They are not qualities of experience, value-qualities or any other kind, because we don't perceive them or experience them at all; we are said to respond to them, which is a different thing entirely.

In this context of stimulus and response, intellectual evaluation of qualities becomes a tertiary quality. The very idea of tertiary qualities assumes that primary and secondary qualities are approximately what Locke said they were, and contain no values. As primary qualities are essentially qualities of phenomena and secondary qualities dependent on the senses, so tertiary qualities are value-qualities dependent on the mind. Secondary or sense-qualities are projected on phenomena by the senses and tertiary qualities are read back into phenomena by the mind.

This account of tertiary qualities is false to experience in implicitly denying perceived value qualities. It is only by discrimination in attention, and then in analysis, in reflection on experience, that we can distinguish tertiary from other qualities. We perceive all qualities at once, a sturdy red square, for example, and only afterwards, intellectually, distill the values. The sturdy red square becomes, in thought, a square (primary), red (secondary), and sturdy (tertiary). The virtue of our distillation depends on its intellectual uses. One use, of great importance, is the need in scientific observation to eliminate portions of ordinary experience because they are irrelevant to science or even hamper it.

An explanation of tertiary qualities that still has great currency was well stated by Santayana in a discussion of beauty before the turn of this century. We respond to what we perceive in an evaluative and emotional fashion, the perception and response being distinct, and project that response onto the object perceived. Thus the aesthetic pleasure a perception gives us is objectified by being projected onto the percept, which is then called beautiful, beauty being pleasure objectified. Unfortunately for this explanation we can go back to secondary and even primary qualities and offer the same explanation on the same principle: the sweet taste of sugar is a response of the taste buds which is then objectified by being projected onto the sugar; red is a discharge in the brain projected through the optic nerves to the surface of an object; solidity is the objectified experience of resistance. If an explanation can hold of all qualities, then it has no special virtue in the case of tertiary qualities.

It is much more useful, and much closer to what underlies our talk about it, to treat scientific statements, at least physical and physiological statements about perception, as statements of conditions under which each perception occurs. Then physical statements about light reflected from a surface and reaching the eye in a particular wave frequency, and physiological statements about the stimulation of the rods and cones of the eye by that frequency and the optical phenomena resulting, are statements of the conditions under which a particular color is seen. They are not statements about the color itself and surely not statements about the values of the color. Those value statements are, at their best, made implicitly in art, if we can use the word "statements" metaphorically in a realm in which there are no literal statements.

My concern at this point, however, is with experience. And I am saying that there are not two stages in it to be distinguished, a physical substratum, which is the natural conditions of experience, and experience itself, because the conditions are not in experience at all, but are a presumed basis for experience, a basis moreover discovered by intellectual methods themselves based on experience, in that observation is the ultimate ground of science. And there are probably not two further stages to be distinguished within experience, one perception and the other response, unless we want to use such a distinction as the beginning of further, postexperiential analysis. On our standard account of experience, as I have said, perception is itself a response to stimulation by what is not itself perceived, light waves and sound waves, for example, and that would be followed by a second response, which includes feeling, and that in turn by a third stage, which involves evaluation. It is too much like De Morgan's fleas.

What seems more likely to me, truer to life, is that perception and response are one in experience, when experience is not partial or fragmented, and that values, too, are contained in the experience. The peppery sauce in the mouth is an experience that is peppery, liquid, and good, bad, or neutral. One quality in the experience may predominate. If the sauce is very peppery, we may be overwhelmed by that and only later remember liquidity, and perhaps aversion. Yet they were all together in the experience. When experience is more complex, as in the case of the magnificent mountain, we will be told by many that not only is magnificence separate from the perception of the mountain, but that the proof it is separate is that people raised in different cultures have quite different aesthetic standards, and so evaluate the mountain differently. That claim of proof needs clarification. The standards must be internalized and condition response or we would all see a magnificent mountain or a non-magnificent one. And we don't all see the same thing, i.e., have the same experience. If the standards are internalized, we must add that they are internalized somewhat differently in people within the same culture, for we do not find uniformity in what they say of a mountain, a painting, or a piano sonata, for example. Yet we should expect to find a greater difference from culture to culture than within any one culture.

Does the same thing hold true of simpler experiences? In the case of the peppery sauce it does, for what tastes very hot and unpleasant to midwestern Americans tastes lightly spiced and delicious to people from Thailand, India, and Mexico. The "response" to the sauce and the taste of the sauce are one thing, and the full experience to a midwestern American may include being bathed in sweat. Can we separate desire and aversion from the experience itself? I don't think so, because just as some people taste a hot sauce and some a mild one (although the dish is the same), depending on the cuisine to which they are accustomed and on individual differences, they also taste a delicious sauce or an unpleasant one. Those who taste the former want it; those who taste the latter, avoid it. And I think a vibrant blue and shimmering orange are in the same case logically as a peppery sauce. Thus the internalization of the characteristics of a culture alter experience itself, not only judgments about experience. It is hard to believe that people who think perception, response, and evaluation are all separate within experience have contemplated such matters as the joyful slaughter of others so common in history, or the gleeful flaying of others alive, in contrast to the horror, repugnance, and actual illness that would be the overwhelming element to so many in experiencing such sights, if indeed they could bring themselves to look.

The internalization of cultural standards and of familial standards, and the special sensory and emotional makeup of each person (based on genetics, a personal environment, or whatever) are what makes each of us the kind of experiencer he is. This is the other side of the natural conditions under which we experience one thing rather than another. Thus the social sciences, psychology, and physiology are used to explain us, and the natural sciences are used to explain what it is we experience. Between them they do provide an account of why experience is what it is. Yet in the course of all this explanation we can too easily reduce experience to the content of these sciences, while all that has been stated in them relative to experience is what we think are the conditions under which experience takes place. Even language and analysis may deceive us, for magnificence and beauty are general terms (or universals, if one likes), as are pepperiness and vibrance. Qualities of experience may be generalized into these indispensable abstractions, or may be called instances of them, although as particulars they vary and each abstraction refers in extension to a range of particulars which includes dubious and borderline cases.

When we find value in particular *experiences* of magnificence or beauty we generalize easily to the value of "magnificence" or "beauty." A shorthand statement of our values is made in general terms, as so many other shorthand statements are, for such is our language. We say we value beauty, song, health, or contemplation and imply we value certain qualities in experience.

As values become even more complex and our treatment of them more purely verbal, we have difficulty in finding in-

The Experience of Value

stances of them. Honor, virtue, and justice are hard to define in intension or extension. But that does not mean there are no qualities in experience that give rise to complex values. There are two difficulties in knowing what honor, virtue, and justice are. First, such values are not qualities in other particular qualities nor are they configurations, or qualities of other qualities. Rather they are qualities of situations, conduct, or human dispositions, and are experienced not as instances of pungency or magnificence are experienced but as instances of stealing or cheating are experienced. Second, complex values are handed on from generation to generation by language. The original experiences which were regarded as instances of justice, honor, and virtue are not transmittable, but words are, and words often gain in approval what they lose in content. That the renewed search for their content is based properly on an attempt to identify relevant qualities in human conduct and situations is witnessed by the early dialogues of Plato, where values are defined or definitions rejected because of the qualities in experience which are instances of them.

The example of Plato assumes we know that an action, event, disposition, or situation is valuable, and so to be approved, or its opposite, and so to be condemned, even when we cannot generalize what we approve or disapprove. Thus we may think justice consists in always keeping promises, and then imagine a special situation in which a man keeps his promise, and discover we disapprove of his conduct. We have learned from this that our generalization was wrong, not that our response to the conduct was wrong, and we have learned also that we derive our values from experience. The situation is the same with all definition of things in extension, things we actually experience. Such definition is not just conventional or arbitrary; it must account for qualities in experience or it will not do. I may be able to recognize a dog whenever I see one, yet be unable to define "dog." When I attempt definition, that must be based on the animals I recognize as dogs.

For Plato all this could be explained by precognition. We know from birth what justice is and what dog is, but we may need help in giving tongue to what we know. For us, culture and habituation are more likely explanations. We may know a great deal about dogs, their temperaments, habits, and responses, while some biologist who knows far less about these things may be better at defining "dog." In the matter of justice, it is likely that people in different cultures find different situations just or unjust, and that there is variation within each culture. And just as it is with aesthetic standards, ethical standards are internalized, although with both the aesthetic and the ethical it is harder to define the standards than to *find* them realized in particulars. Again, experience is the basis of thought; and again, the values we may or may not be able to articulate are found in experience.

Because we internalize ethical standards, we experience ethical qualities. Although it is common to say we approve or disapprove someone's conduct on a particular occasion, it does not follow that our experience of that conduct is one thing and our approval or disapproval another. We experience, I think, approved, disapproved, and ethically neutral conduct, and there is great variation in the extent and intensity of approval and disapproval. When we respond to an action with embarrassment or shame, annoyance or repugnance, anger or rage, our feeling is not merely evoked by our perception of the act, but is part of it. The full experience, as with the aesthetic, includes what we call perception and what we call response. This becomes more obvious when we realize the extent to which what we call response alters what we call perception, and the extent to which it affects attention. The odor of food cooking will be attended to differently by a hungry man and a man who has just eaten too much. And the experience of the odor (which is neither more nor less than the odor) is quite different. In the same way a sadist's sexual arousal colors his perception of a flogging and a nonsadist surely perceives the flogging very differently.

Ordinarily we minimize the experiencer when we discuss experience, treating him first, implicitly, as a bundle of senses and nerve-endings, and then as a set of emotions and a

The Experience of Value

mind. Perhaps we take our cue from the ideal scientific observer, who has been trained to perceive in a special way. But whatever the reason for our descriptions of experience, we usually forget how much the experiencer counts, and the importance to his experience of what he knows, remembers, and imagines. We may hear someone "make a statement," as it is ordinarily put, yet actually hear him tell a lie. And that aspect of the experience may so predominate that we have difficulty remembering what he said. The ethical quality of the experience only exists for an experiencer with particular knowledge, or he would not know he heard a lie, and for an experiencer who had internalized an attitude toward lies, or he would not have an experience which lying dominated. The elements of experience we call perception and response interact, and interact as they do because of the character of the experiencer. In consequence, I think it fair to say that in witnessing what we call the same event, experiences themselves differ, not just subsequent responses and judgments. In a scene described by William James, cannibals chased a group of visitors, shouting, "Meat, meat, meat." That is scarcely the way noncannibals perceive visitors.

When reflection clarifies values and relates them to other values and to consequences, we may hold the values more or less firmly than before, alter them, or give them up. This is true in both ethics and aesthetics, but is perhaps more evident in the experience of art, for we all as we mature and grow old have quite different experiences of the same work, at first perhaps finding Swinburne enchanting and Wordsworth dull, later experiencing Swinburne as puerile and embarrassing and Wordsworth as noble and stirring. We have all had the experience of liking a poem, a painting, or a musical composition at one age and later finding it banal, sentimental, or foolish. And we have had the reverse experience of disliking art at one age that we like immensely at another. The explanation often given is that we have changed psychically and so respond differently to an unchanged or identical experience. The first part of that explanation is correct: we change psychically; but the second part is incorrect: the experience is not identical at both ages.

We learn to perceive meanings and relations in the poem, the painting, and the musical composition differently, and we learn to perceive things and qualities in them that we did not perceive before, or perceived dimly. This is not a matter of changing post-experiential judgment of an identical experience but, as all introspection reveals, a change in the experience itself. I think our experience of ethical values, indeed of all values, changes in the same way.

When young, we may experience the assumed heartiness of the salesman as friendly, courteous, and heart-warming, and we may walk away in a glow of pleasure. In a few more years, we may experience the same sort of behavior as false, meretricious, and essentially dishonest, and walk away irritated or unhappy. In this example, we have not lessened the value we place on "friendliness" and "courtesy," but we have changed in the kind of experience we have of supposed instances of those general terms. In a different type of example, we may, over the years, change our estimate of the constant disputation of young (and some older) thinkers, which we once thought vital intellectual concern, but which we now characterize, with Socrates, as like puppy dogs biting and tearing everything they see. We may have found that the disputatious generate much heat and little light, and that they would rather score debaters' points than discover truth. Quiet contemplation now seems a value and disputation does not.

Here we have reflected on past and present experiences, thought about their consequences, and come to a new conclusion about values. Surely both the reflection and the nature of our experiences were part of a single process of change, in which perhaps one once reveled in disputation, finding it a needed stimulant to thought, while solitary contemplation was lonesome and was not self-generating. Later, one experienced excessive disputation as an irritant and felt that thought was distracted by its noise and passion; therefore he much preferred intellectual conversation, but above all experienced contemplation as joyous and anguished creativeness, deeply satisfying and complete.

The greater the attention to value-qualities in experience,

The Experience of Value

the better we perceive them. Attention is a function of interest and concern, although it often seems forced on us, rather than chosen by us, especially when the value-quality is dramatic, unexpected, or urgent. When attention is directed to one element in an experience, other elements are relatively neglected, to the point where they are not consciously perceived. The experiencer may be the most important factor in attention, although the experience is sometimes so structured that a high point of value grips almost all who have the experience. Dramatic art offers many examples. Thus the idea that some qualities of experience are just perceived more universally than others may be too simple and too mechanistic.

One reason, originally, for the distinction between primary and secondary qualities was the supposed greater universality of primary qualities. It seemed reasonable to attribute the more universal qualities to phenomena themselves and the less universal to human responses to phenomena, which should be more relative to the senses and minds of perceivers. When it became apparent to those who accepted Berkeley's analysis, that primary qualities were as sense-dependent and mind-dependent as secondary qualities, and that figure was no freer of human perception than odor, little more was said about a greater or lesser universality of qualities. Yet figure and motion still seem to many people more universal than taste and odor.

Now do we, as a matter of fact, agree more readily that a thing is square than we do that it is sweet? I think not. Indeed, the opposite is the case if we mean exactly square, and do not measure. As for primary qualities like motion and rest, the phenomenon of autokinesis shows us that we all see stationary objects, under certain conditions, as though they were moving. Is there less agreement about what is perceived when the percept is heavily value-laden? Perhaps that is the case, and that may be one reason to minimize values in scientific observation. But agreement is not, I think, a matter of primary and secondary qualities. Primary qualities are not really perceived as having few elements of value. There is a sturdiness in a square that comes out in the word "foursquare." We never see motion; we see moving things;

and the flight of a gull is memorably graceful. Some things, as we all know, are wonderful to touch, to hold, to handle, to press against; other things are repulsive. How bland is the word "solidity," which embraces all these "tactile sensations," and how false is the notion of "tactile sensations," when the term is used to suggest feelings in the epidermis alone. Finally, the shape of an object, especially when it is a total configuration, may dominate a powerful aesthetic experience.

Agreement and disagreement about what we experience may be in the end a matter of human biology, cultural diversity, and psychological difference, rather than a matter of types of experience. We probably vary as much or as little in calm and relatively emotionless experience as we do in vivid and stirring experiences. Commotion and confusion may mix us up so that we give rather incoherent accounts of what happened; but relatively emotionless experience may insufficiently fix attention, and we may not be aware of much in an event we experience dimly. Perhaps extremes of confusion and inattention bring the greatest disagreement; that sounds, at least, like a testable hypothesis.

Yet one extreme, that cannot properly be called confusion, probably leads to almost incredible attention to a single element in experience, and a vast disregard of the rest. That occurs, I think, when an experience is dominated by one aspect of it, the ultimate example being pain, which blots out almost everything else when it is severe. Pain not only exists on a continuum from the annoying to the unbearable; it is also many kinds, from the observation of another's embarrassment to one's own physical agony. I don't think that pain is logically different in kind from any other dominant element in experience, and that is why I called it an example of such elements. Pain is not a special kind of experience, entirely a response to particular stimuli, but not in itself a perception. Experience, I have been suggesting, is a perception-response, involving the whole person, except when it is fragmented. And pain, too, is perception, not only response, an experience of the whole person, even when it has a location, like an ankle.

The tactile perception of a lighted match is one kind of

pain. The visual perception of a blinding light is another kind of pain. The auditory perception of a loved one's scream is still another. This may sound stranger when put another way, although it says the same thing: one kind of pain is the tactile perception of a lighted match; another kind of pain is the visual perception of a blinding light; and so on. We don't experience pain; we experience pains, and they are of many kinds. And we perceive these different pains, which are qualities in or of things and events. An immediate rebuttal seems supplied by the obvious, that pain is in us, not in the objects we experience. Yet consider the pain I have called a tactile perception of a lighted match. It is quite true that one can look very carefully at a lighted match and see no pain in it; indeed it is absurd to think one might. But if that is the heart of the rebuttal, it is useless, for it is a confusion of categories. I may feel, taste, and try to hear a sapphire, and conclude that careful examination reveals no blue in it. But that is because I haven't looked. Equally, visual (or auditory, or olfactory) examination of a lighted match reveals no pain in it, because I haven't touched it.

If, finally, it is objected that the physical injury inflicted by the lighted match is what hurts, and is all that hurts, it may be that we are slipping into a use of words that seems ordinary and normal but that, like so much ordinary and normal language, is the result of one way of seeing the world and talking about it, a way that gets fixed and continues to reinforce a set of ideas. One of those ideas is that the perceiver is not changed by perceiving; yet that depends on what is perceived. The act of perception is not necessarily an act that leaves the perceiver unchanged. Many people have learned this in making and experiencing art. But it is also true of much experience outside of art. I don't mean that everything we perceive changes us completely, as background changes the chameleon's color, although a few vital experiences in life can bring profound change. Rather I refer to the many perceptions that bring some change, perceptions from which we learn, from which we flinch, from which we have joy and sorrow. It might be more accurate to speak of perceptions "in" which we have these things, rather than perceptions "from" which we have them. I shall return later to the pain of the injury.

Inattention and habit are so great in us that we have relatively few fresh perceptions. When we have them, we often change in the course of the experience, and sometimes the change lasts and grows even after the perception is gone. The senses themselves may change, as, for example, the eye and ear grow keener through looking at art and listening to music or the cadences of verse and prose. Quite commonly, too, the ear is injured by loud noises, like those of artillery, helicopters, and rock bands. A tongue subjected regularly to many strong spices loses its capacity for discriminating, or perhaps even perceiving, delicate tastes. The nature of perception is such that our organs, which may be said to gain or lose something in many perceptions, may also be thought of as constantly changing avenues of perception, made fitter and trained in accurate perception, or assaulted, bruised, and made less fit for accuracy and discrimination. And the act of perception includes the pain of the crashing guns and the hurt of the electronically-amplified music. Thus it is with the injured epidermis of the encounter with a lighted match: the perceiver affects the percept and the percept affects the perceiver, even to leaving scars.

What is true of pain as a perceived quality is also true of pleasure. We don't experience pleasure; we talk about it, perhaps too much. We experience particular pleasures, each somewhat unique, as perceived qualities. I have already referred to the phenomenon of a delicious sauce, which is experienced not just as piquant or sweet, but as delicious. Here descriptive words are inadequate because one delicious taste may be very different from another delicious taste. But the delicious quality of the sauce is no less perceived than its sweetness. Indeed, one may find some kinds of sweetness disagreeable, while others are delicious, and because they are delicious, he may want to repeat the experience.

Let me explore one of the paradoxes of hedonism, which is revealing in this context. When one has pleasure in an experience, it has been argued, the pleasure is a by-product of the experience, or perhaps a subjective response to it. The

The Experience of Value

closer the attention to the stimulus, or percept, the greater the pleasure. The paradox, then, is this: if one concentrates attention on the pleasure, he loses it. That is because he has minimized the stimulus, or expunged it from his experience, and in consequence no longer has the response. This argument is a good and valuable one, although misleading, because it is usually stated (as above) without attention to the nature of perception and the nature of experience, and so is misstated. Sexual activity is an obvious example of the argument, for if one forgets the beloved and focuses on derived pleasure, the pleasure is at least diminished. But there are many other examples. Listening to music is a good one.

When one hears a piece of music he likes, he may feel a growing emotional state as the music continues and develops. He becomes more and still more aware of what he is hearing and, as in a properly continuing and sequential experience, what he is aware of at each moment is more than what he would hear if he had heard nothing before. Each note, chord, sound is heard in relation to what was heard before it. If this were not true, we would never hear a melody, but only a succession of discrete notes. The emotional state is in part an experience of an event continuing through time (not of a discontinuous series of temporal events, but of a single, continuing event), and in part the ripening of human organs and psyche so they are ready to perceive the next moment in the event as a part of the temporal flow of the entire event. The analogy to sexual activity seems clear; the advantage of the musical over the sexual example is that the unity of the experience has been somewhat predetermined by the composer. The full experience of the music includes each momentary perception and an "emotional state"* which is the perception of the whole over time, not itself ever grasped at one moment, except perhaps as an idea, but moving, changing, growing as the music continues, and reaching a conclusion with the final notes. We may be suffused with a warm glow when the music ends, and recapture some of the emotional state as we recall parts of the

---

* I have no better name for it.

music, but the emotional state as a special kind of perception ends when the music ends.

The emotional state is, on the whole, a particular kind of pleasure, which contains other elements as well, dramatic, lyrical, exalted, upsetting, even despairing, because those elements are, after all, in the music. The hedonistic paradox, when applied to experience described in this fashion, says that if one concentrates his attention on the emotional state, he loses it. That is because in minimizing, or expunging from his experience, the auditory perception of the more or less discrete sounds, he destroys the temporal perception of the developing whole, which contains memory, emotion, and a growth in sense readiness. That perception of a continuing event depends on strict attention to the discrete moments that make it up and get their shape and meaning from the whole. The great value of the hedonistic paradox is that it tells us to listen, see, hear, and touch with careful attention in a continuing experience, or we will destroy the experience.

Pleasure is experienced in both the moments of musical perception and the experience of the temporal whole. The lovely tone of an instrument is one kind of simple and direct pleasure, as the delicious taste of a sauce is another. But in the temporal sequence of a more or less unified experience the great pleasure comes from the development and structure of the experience. This does not exclude the momentary experiences that make up the event. On the contrary, the pleasures and excitements are chiefly in momentary experiences, when those experiences emerge in their relation to the other momentary experiences of the event. A moment is perceived as a climax when it is not perceived as only a moment, but as an experience to which we are led by what went before. This is equally true in music, drama, and sex. What follows, I think, is that the discreteness of the momentary perception is submerged (not lost, because one still hears the instrument's lovely tone), as it is shaped and given meaning by the emotional state that is the experience of the developing whole.

The word "pleasure" is often used in a special, aesthetic

The Experience of Value

way. All aesthetic experience is then said to give pleasure. A few philosophers, like Bosanquet, treat aesthetic pleasure as different from other pleasure, but for most philosophers the pleasure we take in art is left undifferentiated, or is thought to be similar to other kinds of pleasure. Whether the work we experience is as tragic as *King Lear,* as mournful as *Death and the Maiden,* or as gay as *Twelfth Night,* we presumably derive pleasure from it. The best defense of this thesis, I think, is that art transforms the pain we experience in some parts of a work into an experience that is not painful *per se,* but affords certain satisfactions. Many elements enter the transformation, psychic distance, meaning relations, and so forth, but that is not a matter to be pursued here. Art, though, may be regarded as not anaesthetizing pain, but transforming it.

It is still the case that pain, outside the context of art, is felt when there is an injury, and felt long after the event in which the injury occurred. That is the common experience of men and animals. There is also pain without external injury. Does the high incidence of pain in the absence of external perception refute the idea that pain is perceived? I think not. What it does show is that pain is often kinaesthetic, and kinaesthesis is also perception, but internal, not external perception. It is another common experience of mankind that when one is in pain he seeks the aid of a physician, who assumes that pain is a "symptom" (that is his language) of organic, and sometimes psychic, injury or disorder. And what is a symptom? In medicine, it is an indicator or sign of illness, sometimes thought of as a result or effect of illness, because when the illness disappears, so does the symptom.

For our purpose, the significance of this standard explanation of pain as a symptom is that it eliminates the idea that one just feels pain, which is unconnected with anything else. The same thing is true of the old biological insight that pain is warning, for a warning must be a warning about something, presumably danger. I think the language of perception is much clearer about these matters. Pains of the sort for which medicine prescribes are perceptions of particular injury, illness, and danger. The pain of the burn after the match is extinguished is still agonizing, and may be more agonizing than at the moment of original contact, because one now perceives the burn, not the match. In the same way, the feeling of pain when there has been no external injury is a perception of a bodily state, or a part of that perception. There may be more than that to pain, such as aftereffects when an injury is healed, but such things occur in external perception, too, as in negative afterimages.

Pleasure, as well as pain, has a kinaesthetic, or internally perceived, dimension. In addition to the "emotional state" already discussed, we perceive the pleasant qualities of a full, but not too full, stomach, of a sweet drowsiness after strenuous activity, of exhilaration after some success. A healthy man rarely perceives sheer well-being, because he is used to it and so is inattentive, but a recent invalid may delight in the perception. Yet pleasure and pain are not distinguished from all other perceptions in this regard, although they (especially pain) may be the most extreme instances of kinaesthetic perception.

Bernard Berenson made much of the internal aspects of external perception, and although his interest was the perception of art, most of the things he said about that are equally true of other perceptions. As we watch a bird in flight, we may feel as though our arms move to the beat of his wings and have some sensation of soaring. As for art, we may have a muscular response to the stance of Michelangelo's *David*, feel the arms spread in a *Crucifixion*, or perceive the dead body's limpness as our own in a *Deposition*. I suspect that this sympathetic kinaesthesia is experienced only by the most sympathetic observers, at least in a full and conscious way. It is perhaps most obviously experienced in the empathy we more easily have with a character in fiction or drama, perceiving his perceptions, both internal and external. This empathy, rather than voyeurism, may be the reason for the enduring popularity of pornography.

Much of what I have argued may be resisted by people whose mental picture of things is drawn by science, or rather a philosophical or popular notion of what science is.

The Experience of Value

As a result, they may have neglected experience, and with it that intense interest in experience we find in art.

It is our enormous concern with science, I think, that leads us to a sharp distinction between fact and value. What Hume took pains to argue is now casually taught to students in elementary discussions of method. Yet in experience there is no distinction between fact and value: we see a beautiful woman, a graceful movement, a balanced construction; we even smell a delightful fragrance but cannot put a name to it. The quality of value in an experience is sometimes its dominant characteristic, perhaps because it leads to attitude and action. To discriminate the fact from the value in an experience is eventually to repress part of the experience and perceive only the rest. Extremely insensitive people may be able to do that naturally; most scientists have to be trained to do it. And they do what is relevant to the scientific enterprise. If perception of a color tests a hypothesis, as the color of litmus paper is a test of whether a liquid solution is acid or alkaline, then the color itself and not its value qualities, or other qualities of the paper, like its shape, is what must be perceived correctly, and is all that need be perceived.

In analysis, we may then make a distinction between fact (the color of the litmus paper) and value (the vibrance, brilliance, dullness of the color), although they are one in experience. In analysis, too, we find a value to be a quality of, not in, other qualities, and we speak that way, saying, for example, that a motion is graceful and not that gracefulness is a motion. Such locutions give an undeserved priority to "facts." Yet we do not speak as we do because "facts" always have priority in experience, since they do not. We say a motion is graceful because gracefulness may be attributed equally well to figures in repose. The word for a value normally has wider reference than the word for a fact. We perceive brilliant colors and brilliant tones and we use the adjective metaphorically for minds.

Yet the distinction between fact and value seems so obvious to so many people that it is worth asking why it does, for the distinction is more obsolete than absolute. "Fact," of course, has many meanings; when it is distinguished from value it is rarely clear which meaning of "fact" is intended. "It is a fact that ..." is sometimes used as an equivalent of "It is true that ..." When fact as truth is dintinguished from value, what is intended may be that propositions are true or false but values cannot be either. The difficulty with this distinction is that relational elements exist in all propositions and that a perceived thing is not in itself true or false, but a statement about it, containing a relation, may be. A value, like a perceived thing, cannot be either true or false, so to distinguish a relational statement about perceived things from a bare value, taken alone, is not to compare like, but unlike, matters, ideas with horseshoes. To be sure, a proposition about perceived things may be true or false while a value may not be either, but may not a proposition about values be true or false?

"The first object is higher in the visual field than the second" (a factual statement) is not basically different in form or in the way its truth-value is tested than "The first color is more vivid than the second" (a value statement). And although "That figure is square" is a much simpler statement than "That action is good" I am not sure we can maintain that one but not the other of them has truth-value, if in both statements we know what we mean and are clear about context.

Perceived things are sometimes regarded as facts, but not as true, although descriptions of them may be true. Since our perceptions contain values as fully as they contain figures and colors, perceived things *per se* cannot be distinguished from the values in them. One crucial meaning of "fact," as it is distinguished from value, is "evidential," as in the color of the litmus paper. When we are asked for the facts in the case we are being requested to show evidence that some assertion or denial is true or false. "The facts in the case" are those phenomena and those alone, or their descriptions, which constitute such evidence. "Facts" have been chosen from the flux of experience because they are relevant to the truth-value of a proposition and may therefore be used as evidence.

The Experience of Value

But may we not choose values as relevant to a proposition's truth-value? Of course; it all depends on what the proposition states; but the entire argument above is modeled on an idea of science in which any proposition to be confirmed or disconfirmed by "facts" is one to which only the non-evaluative aspects of perceived things are relevant. The "facts" offered as evidence turn out to be, not phenomena, but qualities of phenomena washed of their values and then regarded as the phenomena themselves. At this point a distinction between fact and value can be made easily, of course, but it is on the one hand a tautology and on the other illegitimate, because when the non-value qualities of a phenomenon are regarded as the entire phenomenon, the value qualities must be assumed to be not qualities at all or, if qualities, then not in the phenomenon but in human response to it, projected somehow (how projected is a mystery we have created) onto the phenomenon by mind or senses. Yet once we start to play that game, then, as I have argued, the phenomenon itself dissolves into human responses to unperceived stimuli, like wave motion or corpuscular motion. For color, too, is a response to unperceived wave motion and is projected onto the surface of things, solidity is a function of resistance, and so on. All perceived things, not just value qualities, become human responses. To distinguish value from fact in terms of response is to bifurcate experience in order to support an unwarranted claim.

Permit me to restate some of this quarrel about fact and value in the way many contemporary philosophers do. The usual fact-value distinction is made in the assertion that value propositions are not derivable from factual propositions or, as noncognitivists sometimes put it, that normative principles are not derivable from factual generalizations. Thus to say "All men eat," meaning that men eat when they want to, if they can, does not allow the conclusion "There is value in eating," or "It is good, or valuable, for men to eat." We could make the derivation, to be sure, by adding to the premise a value-proposition, such as "It is better to live than to die," although perhaps not always, under any circumstances, plus the factual proposition "People do not live unless they eat." The first additional proposition, though, cannot be established factually, even with its qualifications, i.e., there are presumably no observations that will verify it, as there are observations that will verify the second proposition. Thus there is no point in adding a value-proposition to the premise in order to support the deduction of the value-proposition "There is value in eating," because the value-proposition in the premise would need another value-proposition to bolster it, and so on in an infinite regress of value-propositions, each of which is unverifiable.

I would distinguish the statement "There is value in eating" from "It is valuable to eat," and I would prefer the former to be "There are values in eating," which is true, and which can be verified in experience. In the last paragraph, the argument was on the level of generalization, and experience entered only as observation, in order to verify or refute. Perhaps observation is too often thought of as visual. Noise is read in decibels, heat in temperature, weight in pounds or kilos, but they are all read. The substitution of vision for the other senses in many acts of observation may lead to a subtle deprecation of those senses. The concern with particular qualities, such as noise level, eliminates all other qualities from consideration at that time, and it makes no difference whether the sound whose loudness registers as so many decibels is Vivaldi or a machine gun.

Scientific observation is a poor tool for verifying value propositions because it encompasses fewer qualities than ordinary experience and it almost excludes value qualities. There is nothing wrong with that in the conduct of science, but there may be something wrong with the idea that truth is a predicate of factual propositions, but not of value propositions. For the truth of factual propositions is supposed to be established scientifically, and ultimately by scientific observation, while the truth of value propositions cannot be established in the same way. Of course not; the very assertion may be tautological. Yet most propositions uttered by human lips, whether we call them factual propositions or value propositions, are not confirmed or disconfirmed by scientific observation, but by ordinary experience. What we

The Experience of Value

know in life is what we have gathered from life; we do not ask science, natural or social, if it is true. And what we learn in life is both factual and evaluative; often the two are one.

There may be something persuasive on the level of generality when we say that normative principles are not derivable from factual generalizations, perhaps because principles seem different from generalizations and it is not immediately clear how one establishes a principle. "Normative generalizations" might be a better term. And the mere statement that norms cannot be derived from facts may give the impression that some people think they can and that it is most significant that they cannot.

Yet if we leave generalizations and attend to human experiences, let us say the experience of eating when hungry, things are at once different. We experience the pain and weakness of hunger, the fatigue and growing need for sleep, and the deadening of appetite, so that after a long fast we can eat little. Then we experience the qualities of eating: the tastes, the abatement of hunger pangs, the replenishment of strength, and a new vitality. These are values of eating, and some are perceived as we eat and others after we have eaten. Eating is a value-laden activity and we may eat, when we can, *because* of the values in eating. To say that we cannot derive "There are values in eating" from "All men eat," may be true, but surely it is irrelevant to the problems of values. Also, it assumes that eating is a mechanical ingesting of food, which is not eating at all, but only one part of it. And it is then a denial that we can derive *logically* from the fact of that mechanical ingesting of food the *experienced* values that have been omitted from it. Finally, the fact-value distinction usually means more than it says, for it is used regularly to argue that values cannot really be justified, because justification would consist in showing them to be true, and true propositions are factual propositions or propositions logically derived from them.

The chief presupposition of all this, usually accepted without examination or even recognition that there might be something to examine, is that values are not found in experience, but are norms, preferences, attitudes, or some such thing. Because values, conceived in this way, are always thought of as general, never particular, there is no realization that some values are facts, like other facts, and so can be the basis for generalization. There are both value-facts and value-generalizations.

Value-generalizations, often implicit, are necessary for intelligent and purposive action, which they guide. But ordinary empirical propositions, particular and general, and just as often implicit, are also necessary, because they describe the situation in which we act and so, to some extent, dictate the value-generalizations that are to be applied.

Even if we distinguish the valued from the valuable, meaning by "valuable" the values we accept after reflection, we start with the values we experience; we do not start with a list of intellectual possibilities. Ethical and aesthetic values are found, initially, as qualities or characters of things or situations. They are not found as simple values, but are based on them. The value of a rich, dark green, the green of midsummer in temperate zones, is real enough and so is the sound of a lovely word (Poe, for example, loved words with v's, like "violet"), but a painting is more than a color and a poem more than a word. Art requires more elements than one, plus relations between them, or rather related elements. But when green is wanted in a painting, the value of the green is all-important, and a word in a poem should be the right word, in sound as well as sense. Similarly, an ethical value is more than the bright feel in the mouth, almost without taste, of cold, fresh water. That, too, is a value, as a midsummer green is, but it is not an ethical value, as providing drink for the thirsty is.

Yet ethical and aesthetic values are found in things and situations; aesthetic values in natural beauty as well as in artifacts, and ethical values in what we approve, not just in what we like or prefer. Approval rests on reason; liking and preference do not. To be sure, there is what we call cultivated taste and one can give reasons for liking Manet, or preferring him to Pisarro, but that is what I mean by approval; it is very different from simple liking and preference. Simple liking is of simple values: one just likes chocolate and may

The Experience of Value

prefer it to vanilla. A quality of chocolate is singled out and emphasized because that quality (taste, perhaps with the addition of odor) is the value in chocolate that presents itself to us.

If I like chocolate and prefer it to vanilla I may approve a host or hostess who offers it to me, and I may also approve production and distribution of chocolate, especially at a low price. My reasons are that I like chocolate and want opportunities to have it. But when I reflect on the consequences to my health of eating chocolate or of putting into its production and distribution the time, manpower, and money that may be used for other commodities, when I ask what priorities in production are of greatest benefit to society at this time, and when I inquire into what principle of production and consumption under the social conditions of the moment can best be applied to the making, selling, and eating of chocolate, I have moved to the level of ethical values. On this level, approval or disapproval becomes ethical and bears on conduct insofar as it is relevant to value and dysvalue. I may approve a man who tries to live up to his avowed values or a man whose avowed values arouse my admiration. I may approve a situation because it demands choice or because it minimizes irrationality or mindless violence. My approval and disapproval have moved, through reflection, from that which gratifies or frustrates my simple values to that which is justified or condemned by my ethical values. This is an analogue of my approval of the paintings of Manet, which is based on my aesthetic values. And in both cases, the ethical and the aesthetic, values are internalized and can become a second nature. We ordinarily perceive what we approve differently than what we disapprove.

Science has had such an attraction for modern philosophy that art has not had a proper hearing. Its relation to knowledge has been almost unexplored, and its relation to value neglected. Yet the value-element in ordinary experience, shunned by science, is the especial concern of art. That concern leads to a reordering of experience to make art, and art explores and emphasizes value. A new experience is presented by the artist with value-elements revealed and understood. The vibrancy of a blue is presented with technique and care, and its value is qualified by its relation to other colors, including other blues. The meaning of cowardice emerges as it is pursued through a variety of situations (e.g., in *Lord Jim*) and as it is hidden or unfolded under pressure. The tragedy and comedy and seeming folly of a good man in a bad world are explored (e.g., in *Don Quixote*) with a detail and precision that mock expository statement.

The moral philosopher has, then, two sources for understanding value, for bringing critical reflection to bear, ordinary experience and art. To neglect art is, for him, to neglect the most profound expression of value. That neglect wipes out all the ranges of experience beyond his own and limits him to contemplation of what he can experience and imagine in isolation. It thus deprives him of knowing what many things are like, what it is like, or feels like, for example, to be a coward, or to be a good man in a bad world, unless he is one or the other of those. Yet these are things the moral philosopher must know if he is to think about man, society, and values as his culture (and other cultures he may know) has explored them, and not merely make abstract pronouncements about the good, the true, and the beautiful or spend his time analyzing the way value-words are used.

What men value has been treated recently as that which interests them or that which they cherish or prefer. In concentrating on these characteristics of value, philosophers have often overlooked the boundaries of value, yet the world of value is bordered by a series of opposites, good-evil, truth-falsehood, beauty-ugliness, consistency-chaos, brilliance-dullness, love-hate, and so on. Values themselves are on a scale between, and including, these extremes. Things are more and less good, more and less brilliant, more and less consistent. The neglect of the *realm* of value is witnessed by the near lack of a word for the opposite of the valued, for that we do not cherish but disdain, that we do not prefer, but for which we feel antipathy or loathing. I have used the word "dysvalue."

Dysvalues, like values, have their origins in experience.

The Experience of Value

There are ugly people, dull colors and sounds, false witnesses, awkward movements, chaotic thoughts. And there are gradations of these, too, as in values. Ugly people are more or less ugly, movements are more or less awkward, reaching the sickening, colors are more or less muddy, dull, without life. Dysvalues, too, are qualities in and of other qualities. They are generally opposed to values, as evil is to good, but each pair is of the same kind, as evil and good are both of an ethical kind. The words we use for values and dysvalues are general terms whose instances are in experience. A dysvalue is not simply without value, leaving us indifferent, as darkness is sometimes defined as the absence of light; it is anti-value, and we may feel stronger about it than we feel about value, hating tyranny more than we love freedom.

It is apparent that values and dysvalues are closely bound to our concerns, needs, and interests. They are to be sought or avoided, to be held or eliminated, to be used. Their very closeness to us makes for less agreement about them as qualities than for others which are more remote from life's passions. Still, we do find them initially, not invent them, and when we name them we are prepared to reflect on them.

15

EDUCATING THE PERSON
James L. Jarrett

ALTHOUGH HERBERT SCHNEIDER'S VERY FIRST PUBLISHED article was entitled "Dualism in Modern Theories of Moral Education," very few of his subsequent writings have been overtly and explicitly on education. However, when he said that "from most of Dewey's writings, one gets the impression that all things 'are carried on for the sake of education' "[1], he was not far from describing his own case too. Indeed, one imagines Schneider's not quarreling overmuch with Dewey's famous and provocative assertion that "Philosophy may even be defined as the general theory of education," especially if one also remembers the typically neglected first part of the sentence: "If we are willing to conceive education as the process of forming fundamental dispositions, intellectual and emotional, toward nature and fellow men. ..."[2] That is, when one thinks of it, quite a conditional: how many of us are daring enough to think of education that deeply? Or of philosophy, either — for that crucial Dewey passage continues:

---

1. Herbert W. Schneider, *A History of American Philosophy* (New York: Columbia University Press, 1946), p. 569.
2. John Dewey, *Democracy and Education* (New York: The Macmillan Company, 1916), p. 383.

Educating the Person

Unless a philosophy is to remain symbolic — or verbal — or a sentimental indulgence for a few, or else mere arbitrary dogma, its auditing of past experience and its program of values must take effect in conduct. Public agitation, propaganda, legislative and administrative action are effective in producing the change of dispositions which a philosophy indicates as desirable, but only in the degree in which they are educative — that is to say, in the degree in which they modify mental and moral attitudes.

Schneider let Dewey have the last word in *A History of American Philosophy,* and that word was a virtual identification of "democracy" and "education." "Democracy is belief in the ability of human experience to generate the aims and methods by which further experience will grow in ordered richness. . . . If one asks what is meant by experience in this connection, my reply is that it is that free interaction of individual human beings with surrounding conditions, especially the human surroundings, which develops and satisfies need and desire by increasing knowledge of things as they are." The purpose is continually to "open the way into the unexplored and unattained future."[3]

So conceived, philosophy is too "relevant" to be identified with the lucubrations of most philosophers, education too important to be left to educationists or, for that matter, educators; democracy, tired old, battered democracy, acquires a new shine and appeal; and experience struggles up out of its hedonic sty to become saturated with significance: only the splashy parts of the stream of consciousness deserve the honorary name "experience." Compare now Schneider speaking in his own behalf: "I shall use the term 'experience' as the process of learning by operating."[4] It is one of those little sentences that may slide right by unnoticed, but it has a time fuse: its explosion ought to be unsettling. What a lot of weight to put on a word that seems in most contexts to signify passivity, almost somnolence: whatever happens

---

3. Schneider, *op. cit.,* p. 571 from Dewey, "Creative Democracy — the Task before Us," in *The Philosopher of the Common Man* (New York: 1940), p. 227.

4. Schneider, *Ways of Being* (New York: Columbia University Press, 1962), pp. 46-7.

James L. Jarrett

to you. Schneider and Dewey are activist philosophers, future-oriented philosophers, philosophers of education.

Really to *have* experiences is to learn, to get educated. To teach, then, must be to facilitate the having of experience in others. And such *having* entails action, conscious process, operation. Schneider was intensely conscious of the prevalence of another kind of teaching, educating, and "getting educated," falsely so-called. "An educative school," he wrote, "where learning is the primary aim and reflective thinking the method, is a different type of institution from what today we call a school."[5] Most of what we call learning remains foreign, a matter of indifference, "... not appropriated to a person; it is not really *in the mind*."[6]

Schneider says that in his own experience he had found students easier to teach outside of school than in, teaching far more effective when one teaches, as Buber has said, as though one taught not. It might be thought sad, by some, that one who has had a remarkably long life of teaching should confess to a growing scepticism of the efficacy of most teaching; but Schneider is never one for despair, nor even pessimism. He would say, rather, teaching and learning *do* happen: let us learn how and go forth to do likewise. John Dewey, for instance, was, on Schneider's account, a teacher. Not by any means a flashy lecturer, nor one who self-consciously used pedagogical techniques: "The courses which he offered were constructed not in terms of supposed student interest or needs, but in terms of inquiries with which he happened to be preoccupied. ... His lectures were continuous with his study, always laboratory exercises. ... Usually he himself did all the investigating and seemed to forget that anyone might be listening to his labors."[7] (This was of course at the university— presumably even at the graduate— level.) For the less mature, Dewey's method was to expose them "to the privileges and responsibilities of reciprocity,

---

5. Schneider, "Schooling, Learning, and Education," *The Educational Forum* (November, 1964), p. 34.

6. *Loc. cit.*

7. Schneider, "John Dewey as My Teacher," *Progressive Education* (October, 1952), p. 11.

that is, of the kind of give-and-take society which makes it possible and practical for adults to be democratic."[8] But then as if in answer to today's political radicals and their "alternative schools," Schneider added, in Dewey's behalf: "If schools become merely introductions to low politics, politics must necessarily remain an exploitation of nonadult minds."[9]

But do not today's schools sometimes succeed on their own terms? Indeed they do: then we have the "learned person." Although "such disembodied minds have a modest function in a culture," a certain utility, like encyclopedias and computers, they are essentially lifeless. The learned person "exhibits his learning as an excuse for *not being a personality*."[10] Here, stated negatively, is Schneider's finest point. The great aim of education is becoming a person, a person among persons of course, for man is indeed a social animal, but a distinctive person, a functioning person, a personality.

> The task of appropriating the operational complex of the cultural matrix is the central problem of education, for education fails if it fails to produce a mind. ... A person 'is' a mind which an individual acquires and owns as 'his' mind. I am using 'mind' here in perhaps too broad a sense, to signify the personality structure. To make out of the world as it is one's 'own' world, or to transform a piece of the world into one's 'own' environment is the primary task in the formation of a person, and it is a task for his mind primarily. When this is achieved the world has perspective, 'his' perspective and he can recognize his point of view.[11]

This difficult process of achieving "own-ness" of mind, personality, environment, culture,* progresses, according to Schneider, by means of four essential kinds of acts: "the

---

8. *Ibid.,* p. 12.
9. *Ibid.,* p. 13.
10. "Schooling, Learning, and Education," p. 35.
11. *Ways of Being,* pp. 48-9.

* Albert Hofstadter has been reaching for a new profundity in the development of this concept of own-ness in his recent work. See especially *Agony and Epitaph* (New York: George Braziller, 1970), *passim.*

funding of memory, the vesting of interest, the organizing of ideas, and the vitality of imagination."[12] Memory is funded to the extent that one is able to draw upon personal and racial experience to inform present decision, a meaningful use of history that is today often rejected as sterile *because* historical. Interests must be more than capricious excrescences of the individual: they must be grounded in the institutions a society provides in order that they have means of implementation. Also interests must be conceptualized and organized, generalized and "transpersonalized"; that is, they must generate ideas if they are not to remain froth. And finally these interests and ideas need continually to be refreshed by the springs of imagination. "Imagination", Schneider writes, in one of his most deep-cutting sentences, "is a form of energy and not a dreaming."[13] What an educational goal *that* makes: the inspiring, the cultivating, the nourishing, the harvesting of imagination, seen as an energizing of the self as a cultural being.

To become a person. It is again before us as a legitimate, almost a necessary goal. I say "again," because there was a time of contraction of educational ends. We had been led down the primrose path by the progressivists: such was the moan of the fifties. Excellence! Excellence! became the rallying cry. And that meant knowledge, meant basic skills, meant hard work, studying and achievement — as measured by standardized tests, of course. It meant competition; it meant an end to leveling and once again "honors" for the deserving — I had almost said "for the honorable." It is all very well to talk about "the whole child," but the school is inevitably limited in time and resources. Let it stop trying to do everything and do what it *can* do. Let it return to "basics," and go on from there to the transmittal of knowledge. And if for some the rationale of this was the production of better scientists and engineers in the interest of our winning the space race and the cold war, fairness requires the admission of other rationales too. In any case, the counter-re-

---

12. *Ibid.*, p. 51.
13. *Ibid.*, p. 53.

form was a celebration of intellect and effort, and a denunciation of "softness," egalitarianism, and the ascendancy of such ends as "mental health," "citizenship," and "better social living."

We cannot here take the space to detail the (remarkably fast) collapse of this way of thinking, but it is commonplace now to speak of a return of progressivism, though no longer under that name. Yet our hope would be that what we are beginning to see now is not a return but an upward sweep of the dialectic process, with "progressivism" and "excellence" *aufgehoben* into — but what, indeed, shall the new name be, the name of the synthesis struggling to be born? Integrationism?

But we are thinking now not primarily of racial integration or the integration of economic classes in the schools. Rather of integration of the self, the achievement of the person in ways continuous, perhaps, with the lines laid down by Schneider in the fifties.

Can we *imagine* a person? It is not easy, if we mean by "imagine" something that transcends a string of praisewords. We don't even *have* to imagine less-than-persons: they are all around us. (Perhaps, dread thought, they are ourselves.) Furthermore, they are around us in Academe, a nettling fact. The mood can come over us when we say, "Such huge amounts of education for such trifling results!"[20] Here is a learned professor and he is a prig. There is a headpiece stuffed with knowledge atop a graceless tub of guts. There is a walking library that couldn't say boo to a goose. Behold this humorless savant, that scholarly bigot, and this other brilliant mind shrouded in inner misery! No, *of course* this is not the whole story: we all know far better specimens of *homo academicus;* but the question insidiously nudges one from the blind side: is the relationship between being learned and being a person better than accidental?

But this is still too easy, this cynicism, this scorn. We still have the harder job before us, to say what it is like to be a person. Fortunately, some help is available. Indeed, it is more than a little interesting that in recent years a number of psychologists have begun turning from disease to health,

James L. Jarrett

from neurosis to effectiveness, from blockage to creativity, from pathology to humanism. They have looked at effective persons, men and women who have stood out from the crowd as successful in their work, effective in their personal relations, and happy. They have used such expressions as "fully functioning," "self-actualized," and "individuated." (Notice the eclipse of "well-adjusted" as an ideal.) Some existential philosophers have left off talking about dread, *angst,* and forlornness to speak of I-Thou, of care, of authenticity. The words "beautiful" and "love" have probably never before had such heavy usage.

There begins to take shape in my mind's eye a person who seems to have exceptionally strong values, to have many likes and to care about certain things, and more especially certain people, very much, to be generally well-disposed to others, inclined to trust and respect them; to be open to new experience, other opinions, even to the possibility of reversal of his own position, to have a sense of adventure, a willingness to run risks for possible attainments; to be spontaneous and original, to have a taste for novelty, to have retained some of the playfulness we associate with children; to be natural, unaffected, genuine, committed; to respond with humor to many situations and to have compassion for those in distress; to be marked in manner by grace and style; to like and respect himself; to be happy. I imagine that he feels himself as energetic, confident, capable, resilient, graceful, autonomous, and unified or integrated. Persons like this, according to Maslow, are no strangers to "peak experiences." Also, they seem to have personalities that collapse such familiar distinctions as intellectual/emotional, abstract/concrete, selfish/unselfish.

I can imagine a number of responses to this description. Some latter-day E. A. Robinson may wryly predict that my paragon will go home and put a bullet through his head. Others may express disappointment that the account is still abstract. Others may cry out that I have forgotten the most important trait of all, or that a person might have most of these traits and still be neither admirable nor enviable. Nevertheless, I will for now rest content with that description and go on to point out one extremely obvious thing about it. We don't know what if anything our person does for a living, what his religious or political preferences are, how his finances are, what his sex life amounts to, what he looks like, how old he is, whether he be male or female, what his nationality or race, or how much and what kind of education he has had. One might make a guess at each of these latter classifications — that is, indicate his belief that there is a chance better than 50-50 on, say, his not being impoverished, not over 100 years old, and not a kindergarten dropout — but apart from such extremes, the game is very risky. Or put it the other way around: a real person *might* be found almost anywhere, in almost any circumstance, even, in Dostoevsky's famous instance, alone on a one-foot ledge high above the sea, exposed to the weather, and with no hope of escape.

Yet one resists the temptation of believing that he is entirely a sport, a freak of circumstance; or just the fortunate possessor of an uncannily favorable biological program. Are there ways of educating for, conducing to, encouraging, facilitating growth toward — Personhood? Why do I think there must be, when I cannot make more than the most tentative, hesitant, almost bashful guesses about what such education would consist in? Because, I suppose, I share the prevalent belief of our time that education has magical efficacy.

In at least two respects I am old-fashioned about educational matters. I still believe in schools; I cannot see the least value in Ivan Illych's de-schooling movement. This is not at all because I think schools as they are have very great value, but only because in our kind of society I think education has to be institutionalized, and very specifically so, if it is not simply to become so dilute and cursory as to be almost wholly ineffective. My evidence for this is drawn mainly from my observations of *homes*. I know many parents who could teach their children far more, in far less time, than they learn in schools. But they don't. It is too much of a job, in addition to what they are already doing. Teaching has to continue to be professionally assigned. But that is my second old-fashioned belief: in teachers — though less as they are than as they can be. I mean that I don't see much good

James L. Jarrett

coming out of teachers' fading into the woodwork, so as not to upstage the hardware. Students, young or old, left largely to themselves will largely amuse themselves with relatively slight educational increment. This is true, too, I think, with the vast majority of college-age students. I have had students take a year off to read Hegel, think, and in general straighten out their heads. When they came back, it was because they were sick of television. Being a self-starter, capable of independently devised and conducted programs of learning, inner-directed, self-motivated: these are the ideals. They are very hard won, though, and I am not yet any more impressed with laissez-faire in these than I am in economic affairs. Teachers are valuable, principally, to the extent that they are ingenious and assiduous motivators; and as models — though not necessarily ideals—as people who *show* effective ways of acting in selected situations.

But, by and large, students care more about their student companions than they do about their teachers, which most teachers, if they believe it, resent. Better to acknowledge it as probably inevitable and go on from there. The single best encouragement for listening to Beethoven is for an esteemed friend to say, "I *love* Beethoven." Whitehead said that at Cambridge the only lectures he ever heard were on mathematics; but he learned philosophy, history, literature, and politics from his friends, and from the books he had to read in order to hold up his end in arguments at dinner and over sherry late at night. I know that it is terribly hard to take advantage of this fact, if it is a fact, but to fail to do so is probably to continue to have schools that affect their pupils ever so little.

I suspect that it would do more good than harm for students to be aware of the personality traits associated with Personhood — to know what at least some people believe they ought to build toward, in themselves. However, I am confident that a good part of the progress will be made by a glancing, rather than a head-on, attack. Beyond a certain point, attention to oneself becomes both boring and self-defeating. We probably come to know ourselves mainly by concentrating upon things outside ourselves, as long as we come back from time to time with the question: What does this tell me about me? One does need to take stock. Buber said that the best question in the Bible was (appropriately) God's: Adam, where art thou? But it is a question we hope Adam learned to ask himself.

But at this point, I can easily imagine Herbert Schneider interrupting, a trifle impatiently (for such a remarkably good-natured man): But this is too individualistic. Put your pupil back into society — you seem almost to have yanked him out of it. Which would make me remember his contrast between William James and Thomas Jefferson:

> James was preoccupied with the individual consciousness, its emotions, its continual flow, its bondage to the will, its sense of the divine presence, its solitude, its pathology, etc. The social and public aspects of human experience were practically ignored. ... The more spontaneous, personal, and private an experience was, the more it interested William James.[14]

This, Schneider says, was one kind of influential idealism in America. But the other kind was the republicanism of Jefferson, the sense of public service.

> A champion of both natural and civil rights, he conceived liberty to be definable in terms of these rights or "liberties." To safeguard them he relied in part on Montesquieu's device of the separation of powers in the government, particularly on the Supreme Court; but he relied even more on what Montesquieu called *l'esprit des lois,* which in the case of republican government implied a constant discipline of the whole body of citizens in "civic virtue" or public spirit. This would be the primary aim of compulsory public education, which he advocated strenuously and which implied the exercise of good judgment by the whole body of citizens, and not merely by their representatives in the government. He based his high hopes for such a republic not on a naive faith in the equality of "good sense" among all men, but in the creation, through education, moral discipline, and practical experience, of public-spirited communities.[15]

---

14. Schneider, *Sources of Contemporary Philosophical Realism in America* (Indianapolis: The Bobbs-Merrill Company, Inc. 1964), p. xv.

15. *Ibid.,* pp. xiii-xiv.

James L. Jarrett

And we do indeed need to remember this more social kind of idealism as we build, yet once again, though still in our imaginations, a better school, a better education, in the interest of better, more human, persons and a more personalized and humanized society.

16

ADVICE TO THE NEW PHILOSOPHY TEACHER
Lewis E. Hahn

IN HIS PRESIDENTIAL ADDRESS ON "METAPHYSICAL VISION" before the Eastern Division of the American Philosophical Association which appeared in the *Philosophical Review* for September, 1949 (58, 399-411) Herbert W. Schneider in characteristic fashion stressed philosophical insights rather than insight and, speaking metaphorically, noted that though the traditional monocular mental vision has its uses, a binocular vision may supplement and add depth to it. He wisely emphasized the value of multidimensional analysis and suggested that philosophy needs something more than a single-eyed or single-minded approach. If vision is what we seek, it would be too bad to limit ourselves to a single insight, a single perspective, or a single approach. Accordingly, we may have more to gain from our differences than we have sometimes suspected. At any rate, Herbert Schneider's type of philosophic vision seems to me to express itself in practical judgment, penetrating criticism, and poetic imagination and to have the very great virtue of being able to identify distinctive strengths in many diverse approaches and points of view. It is a vision which helps us make the most of a perspective without suggesting that it is the only one. It helps us recognize in the life of the critical imagination the cross-eyed, nearsighted, farsighted, and astigmatic without denying the positive contributions these forms may make.

Hence it seems to me that this general type of approach provides welcome light for many problematic areas; and if the following comments on certain problems encountered by philosophy teachers were found to be in keeping with the spirit of Schneider's kind of philosophic vision, I should be most happy.

There are three features of the philosophical profession which create certain problems and set the framework within which we work with other philosophers, teachers in other fields, administrators, students, and the general public. In the first place, when philosophy is considered as to method, it is frequently equated with criticism, and the philosopher's critical inquiry is fairly likely to lead him into sensitive areas. The philosopher is likely to be in the forefront in criticism of society, the government, the school, the administration, and so on. His concern with presuppositions and implications of a view or position and his search for the significance of a field or a project may lead him to see discrepancies and contradictions more readily than may be true of some other fields. At any rate, from Socrates to, say, my esteemed colleague, Professor Paul A. Schilpp, philosophers have been critics, and I see no reason to expect that there will be any fundamental change in this regard with reference to our younger philosophers. Critics, however, create a certain amount of uneasiness or alarm on the part of the defenders of the criticized positions, views, or practices; and the philosopher, accordingly, is not uncommonly regarded as a danger to established religious beliefs, social practices, and institutions. The more important the area, the more surely can one count on the philosopher to subject it to critical scrutiny.

In the second place, there is a conspicuous lack of agreement among philosophers, and their professional meetings, as Professor Schneider has suggested, afford occasions for them to do battle more or less gloriously with other philosophers and exhibit oppositions holding among them. In few fields, if any, would one find greater diversity of outlook than is the case with philosophy. There are significant differences as between different schools or movements of philosophy as to accepted methods, acceptable conclusions, and significant fields of emphasis. A logical empiricist and an existential philosopher may differ widely on all these matters. The difference between a linguistic analyst and a traditional idealist may be such as to lead one to maintain that the other is not even doing philosophy but something else. Nor is this solely a matter of differences between schools. The logician may have some reservations about the activities and methods of the metaphysician; the epistemologist may have his doubts concerning the procedures of the aesthetician or the philosopher of religion. The ethical theorist may be dubious of the activities and general approach of the legal or social philosopher; and in each case the one thus evaluated is likely to return the compliment.

From one graduate school generation to the next there may be significant differences in dominant philosophical style, thought, and method. One such generation may emphasize heavily one area within the field and one set of methods, and a somewhat later generation a significantly different set. Since there may be several generations of graduate school products active at one time, this helps add to the diversity. Over somewhat longer periods of time — say, a twenty- or thirty-year period — one may find somewhat more stable patterns; but these have a way of recurring over longer periods of time, with earlier emphases once more coming to the fore but usually in a different form. The Logical Positivist of the 1930's blasted Metaphysics, much of Ethics, and Philosophy of Religion, and then in the 1950's and 60's some of these same individuals wrote books on these topics but with significant differences in their mode of treatment of the subjects. There is a sense in which the philosopher never fully shucks off his past but always at any given time requires a fairly heavy portion of it to make clear his present task. Even if he makes use of the history of philosophy only as a device to show what we must avoid or how much better his new way is, there is still much greater emphasis on a longer span of the past for the philosopher than for the natural scientist. Different philosophers, however, make use of somewhat different portions of our past.

This lack of agreement among philosophers most philosophers have learned to live with, if not to enjoy, but it creates great difficulties for philosophers with publishers and with administrators in regard to matters of appointment, promotion, and the like. Since most publishers have a policy of sending a proposed book-length monograph out to two or more readers in the field before deciding whether they will publish it or not, you can see what the characteristic differences among our group may mean for the publication of a book. Various of my friends among the publishers tell me that getting agreement from a set of referees in philosophy on a manuscript is much more difficult than in other fields unless one picks his referees with exceeding care. You may maintain either that we have been saved from a great many manuscripts better unpublished anyway or that we have suffered the loss of not having available some significant monographs; but in any event our differences place a considerable load on the publisher.

The lack of agreement among philosophers also creates great difficulties for us with administrators. On major appointments it is routine to make some check with nationally recognized experts within the field, and their differing evaluations may be the occasion for still more checking or for deciding that perhaps the major appointment had better be in another field than philosophy. Promotions to tenure ranks also normally involve some check with philosophers outside the department. The dean may wish to supplement the references given by the department with some of his own, these latter being selected sometimes in terms of the kind of philosophy he was taught as a student or at least with experts of the sort esteemed by some of his own teachers of philosophy. Significant unexplained differences are fairly sure to block a promotion. In general a negative reaction from one or more individuals may block an appointment or promotion, but it may take a great deal heavier measure of agreement to get any appointment made. Not infrequently

Advice to The New Teacher

I have seen departments kept relatively small because of the dean's distrust of divided recommendations even though there was heavy demand for more philosophy courses on the part of the students.

In the third place, philosophy takes for its province a very broad range or scope in at least three senses. (a) There is the traditional concern for making comprehensive sense of the total range of experience or facts or getting an over-all view of some whole or totality. The philosopher historically has been the scholar concerned with formulating or giving expression to the inveterate human tendency to try to see where we fit into some larger scheme of things, what our place is or may be in one setting or another. For the metaphysician this has meant attempting to provide an intellectual map of the cosmos; and both some philosophers and many outside of philosophy have been dubious of the presumptuous sweep thus claimed. (b) Within the subject matter of philosophy itself there is a broad range of disciplines: Metaphysics, Epistemology, Ethics, Logic, Aesthetics, Philosophy of Science, Social and Political Philosophy, Philosophy of Religion, and various others. Such fields as Philosophy of Education have developed into more or less distinct disciplines of their own. At any rate, the range is so great that it is practically impossible for one to be equally expert in all branches of the field. (c) In terms of levels of teaching the range is from high school (not very common in this country) to graduate work. There is significant work to be done at all levels, and one who may be quite successful at one of these levels may be much less so at another. For example, a scholar who is excellent with graduate students may find difficulty in communicating with freshmen or sophomore students.

In view of the tremendous range within our field able outsiders not infrequently are inclined to raise some question about the depth or superficiality of the treatment philosophers can afford for these levels, subfields, or attempts at comprehensive vision.

These characteristics of philosophy may create special difficulties for the new philosophy teacher, not to mention the ones who have been around for some time. These problems obviously may be approached from a number of vantage points, and I debated whether to set up my observations within the framework of the ethics of our profession or whether to center upon the philosopher as a political animal who needs to take account of certain political facts within the academic domain. I have probably leaned more in the direction of the latter approach though I think most of the advice I have to offer has an ethical as well as a political base. My observations very frequently at least are of a piece with Benjamin Franklin's maxim: "He who spits into the wind spits in his own face." At any rate, there should be some way of helping the new teacher avoid certain rather common mistakes some of us older ones have made and of helping him make use so far as is appropriate of some of the things some of us have learned through hard experience about dealing with these problems. In my own case this has been reinforced by my work as a consultant for various departments and programs which have got into considerable difficulty because of their neglect of certain ethical principles or political maxims.

Assuming, then, that one wishes to further the cause of philosophy and provide opportunity for fruitful personal development as a philosopher-teacher and bearing in mind the problems created by the three characteristics of philosophy I mentioned before, what are some of the things the new philosophy teacher might want to keep an eye out for?

Perhaps our further observations might be grouped under a few general headings, bearing in mind the fact that there will be some overlapping between them: namely, (1) the relation between the philosophy teacher and his field; (2) his relation to other philosophy teachers and to his department; (3) his relation to teachers in other fields; (4) his relation to his department chairman and dean or president; (5) his relation to his students; and (6) his relation to the community or general public. In terms of these relationships I shall try to comment on the three features of the philosophical profession with which I began this discussion.

In terms of our relationship to our field it may be well, in

Advice to The New Teacher

the first place, to remember that it takes more than a Ph.D. and a year or two of teaching experience to qualify one as an expert; and our critical comments may be made with appropriate concern for our own limitations. Lacking omniscience, there is the possibility that in a given case I may be wrong. In the second place, we may remember that criticism involves both positive and negative points; and if our criticism always seems to stress the negative phases to the neglect of the positive, we may be doing an injustice both to ourselves and to our field. In most instances, moreover, balanced criticism is more likely to carry weight with a discriminating listener. Although strictly negative criticism sometimes performs a necessary function, in general we do well to try to use our critical tools with a constructive end in view or with due concern for alternative possibilities. Or stating a portion of this in positive terms, we should carry out our critical tasks in such fashion as to reflect creditably on our field. It goes without saying that we need to master our critical tools so as to develop our field.

With reference to the lack of agreement within our field we should remember that in our diversity is one of our greatest strengths. Unanimity of opinion is not always desirable if, as has sometimes been the case in the course of history, the opinion is an incorrect or ill-founded one. Our very diversity of method, outlook, and emphasis may make possible greater development in our field. In our subject the kinds of things on which one can get unanimity of opinion are rarely the most important ones for us as philosophers.

So far as the broad scope or range claimed for our field is concerned, we need to develop as clear and as deep a knowledge of our field as possible. Digging in on some aspect of our field and achieving a degree of mastery of it will make it possible for us to make greater contributions to philosophy. Since our field is broad we need as much help as we can get from our associates, and it may be well to remember that the portion of the field in which we are most expert needs the supplementation which comes from the work of other scholars in the field. The training and interests of philosophers are likely to fit them particularly well for general education programs. Our tendency to try to see things in context or in perspective and our practice of trying to get a view of a broad range of experiences as a group or set will prove especially valuable here. The philosopher can frequently shed additional light on broad programs in the Humanities, the Social Sciences, or the Natural Sciences, depending, of course, on one's special background and interests. One's long-term contribution to both general education and the field of philosophy is likely to be enhanced by the fact that one has dug in more than superficially in some aspect of philosophy.

Turning to the relation of the philosophy teacher to other philosophy teachers and the department, if the reports coming to me are to be trusted, many philosophy departments of this country are torn by dissension and conflict to such an extent as to make it difficult for the department to carry out its function. In the case of one major Ivy League school this reached such a point some years back that two distinguished members of its department of philosophy communicated with each other on departmental matters only through the president. I think it is safe to say that none of the philosophers involved in this situation gained in stature from this performance.

Some differences in philosophical outlook are to be expected, and critical evaluation of principles held by various members of the department may bring forth a wholesome dialogue. Matters of departmental policy should be discussed within the department rather than in general faculty meetings or public sessions of some sort. If we have serious reservations concerning the methods or approach of a colleague and feel impelled to say something about them, we should do well to explore the whole matter in private with the colleague. If later we wish to make a public statement, this should be done in a framework which makes clear our respect for the colleague as a person and as a philosopher. It is just possible, of course, that he, rather than I, may be correct. Even if he is not fully correct, there is the possibility that both students and colleagues may learn something from his vigorous advocacy of his position.

In addition to tolerance for opposing points of view, it is

Advice to The New Teacher

well to remember in our criticism that various positions may be defended with varying degrees of adequacy, and it is quite possible that one of our colleagues who espouses a position we regard as highly dubious might none the less do this with consummate skill. Competence as a philosopher is not limited to doing well only precisely the kinds of things any one of us sets as his task. For example, during one of the great periods of the Department of Philosophy at the University of Chicago, Carnap used to say of an occasional student's performance that he did quite well the sort of thing that Hartshorne does, and Carnap would accordingly move to pass the student on an oral examination or whatever. Fortunately, agreement as to method, approach, or emphasis is not necessary for fruitful cooperation; but willingness to grant the legitimacy and value of these divergent positions is essential. And for my own part, I can say that I have never had a colleague who did not have certain points of strength and something to contribute both to my knowledge and to our field.

With reference to the range or scope of our field, it seems clear that there is more than enough for all of us to do; and we should be grateful for the fact that we have some colleagues to help us do the job. Certainly no one of us can do it alone.

In our relations with teachers in other fields some of the same considerations apply. The form our criticism takes is frequently very important. Any criticism we may make of the methods or subject matter of another field will have a much better reception if we show some recognition of the strength involved and some appreciation for the efforts practitioners of this field have made to take care of their difficulties. Quite frequently it will turn out to be the case that there are some differences among them on some crucial matters of philosophical significance, and some familiarity with what these positions have to offer is a useful thing to have before criticizing them.

It is well to remember also that we have much to learn from other disciplines, and carrying out our philosophical task is in some instances dependent upon the results attained by workers in other fields. For example, part of what

Kant has to say about space turns about developments in geometry or what he knew of them.

In many instances we can do a better job for our students if suitable courses are available for them in other fields; and we in turn can contribute to the education or training of students in such other fields as English Literature, Economics, Psychology, Sociology, Anthropology, Physics, Biology, Law, Business, Agriculture, Engineering, Home Economics, or Journalism.

If on occasion we have some reservations about the interpretation of philosophy offered by our colleagues in the field, we may from time to time have even greater reservations about the interpretation of philosophy held by colleagues in other fields; and a certain amount of friendly informal discussion with them may help improve their understanding and appreciation of our field. Frequently what they know of philosophy they gained some time back from instructors who may no longer fit the current accepted cycle of philosophizing; but a disparaging attitude toward their views or those of their teachers is likely to cast doubt in their minds on philosophy as a whole and on the critic in particular as a philosopher. Spending some time with them in discussing some of these matters may be quite profitable both in terms of improved mutual understanding of our respective fields and in terms of the advice they may give their students as to whether to take philosophy or not.

In terms of the relation between the philosophy teacher and the department chairman and other administrative officials, perhaps the basic word of advice is to go through channels. In general you have more to lose than to gain from trying to go around your chairman or dean. Most good administrators will welcome constructive criticism, but it is a rare official who welcomes the criticism of himself implied by your going around him or above him to present your case. Going around your chairman weakens him in the eyes of his superiors and therefore tends to lessen the weight of any recommendations he may make for you. If the chairman or senior colleague is one who had a hand in bringing you to the institution in the first place, you have at least that much evi-

Advice to The New Teacher

dence concerning the soundness of his judgment. At least part of what the dean or president thinks about you is probably based on your chairman's earlier recommendation, and to the extent that you shake his confidence in the chairman, you weaken both your own standing and that of the department as well as the field of philosophy.

There are probably no perfect officials, and there is no more point to expecting such perfection of them than there would be of any one of us as scholar-teachers. Very frequently the chairman has reasons as well as difficulties due to higher administrative decision or school regulations which may not be known to you. Before criticizing him adversely it may be well to investigate some of these matters and to confer in friendly fashion with him. It may be salutary when you are inclined to criticize him to reflect, "There but for the grace of God or the Dean go I!" If you expect your chairman to do his best by you, you should provide him with information concerning your achievements — publications, honors, activities, or the like — so that he will have suitable ammunition to present to the appropriate officials. It may be well to remember also that in most instances the chairman has other people and/or problems to deal with and can not devote himself exclusively to you.

Where you feel that you must present criticism of your chairman or a colleague, do this in such fashion as to reflect creditably on our field. Tearing down another person rarely serves any very useful purpose. Most people who have been around for awhile will have something useful to contribute, and it would be strange if we newcomers could not learn something from them. Our negative criticism needs to be accompanied by evidence of our appreciation of some of the strong points of the individual criticized.

On matters of departmental policy it is well to try to reach an agreement with colleagues before making recommendations to deans and administrative officials. In unity there is strength. If we cannot agree among ourselves on a recommendation, we make it that much easier for higher administrative officials to do nothing for our department since any recommendation involving funds probably involves competition with other departments with ideas on how the money could be used more effectively. For some years the department of philosophy at one large university had great difficulty in agreeing on anything, and the department remained relatively small in spite of the expanding enrollment of the university. With a logical empiricist, a Hegelian, a philosopher of religion, and an ethical theorist with a passion for various social causes and movements, they were so frequently at odds on their recommendations that it was hard to get anything done. The departmental chairmanship rotated, and whoever was chairman had the brunt of vigorous criticism from all the others, this criticism being passed on to his superiors. Three of them finally discovered, however, that virtually anything all of them agreed on could be pushed through, and they agreed to fire the ethical theorist, who was a professor with tenure, and almost brought this off. The Board, discovering that the professor could not be fired, came within one vote of abolishing the department to get rid of him and had to wait for his retirement shortly afterwards; but thereafter the development of the unified department in terms of staff additions and departmental benefits was striking. It became a power to be reckoned with in university affairs generally.

In terms of relations between the philosophy teacher and his students, we need to help our students master the tools of criticism; and in our criticism of the views of our colleagues we need to avoid personalities and stress principles. Part of the vitality of our subject, as the students are likely to be quick to see, stems from our differences. We should help our students to see that there are values in these differences. It goes without saying that we should not place students in the position of having to choose whether to study with one member of the department to the exclusion of all others. In some philosophy departments a situation has developed within which a student who does his thesis or dissertation with one individual can expect no help from any of the others, and a type of jealousy prevails which causes the professor to view with suspicion the activities of a student who signs up for courses with such and such other members of the department. This is a ridiculous situation, harmful to all concerned. We owe our students the best we have to offer, but conceivably the best we have might appropriately be supplemented by the ideas and contributions of others.

We need to encourage our students to develop their own creative syntheses, methods, or outlook rather than simply to follow our own brand of philosophy or philosophizing.

Finally, in considering the relation of the philosophy teacher to the community or the general public, we owe our community our best critical efforts. Community projects can profit from our critical skills; and there is greater danger from a lack of criticism than from extreme criticism. If, indeed, as one of our distinguished predecessors has it, the unexamined life is not worth living, most major policies and practices are likely to be the better for searching constructive criticism. The community, moreover, stands to gain from our differences. If we seek light, the possibilities of illumination are greatly increased if we have various ways of getting at it. Covering up or glossing over an issue or blurring fundamental differences is probably not in the public interest. Providing the public with somewhat clearer alternatives is an important service. What we lose in social solidarity, we may gain in light.

The community stands to gain also from the range of disciplines included within our field, and these contributions may come at various levels from high school through the graduate school. There is a possible public gain also from our efforts at syntheses, at getting a balanced view of various activities, seeing things in perspective, or developing a world view of some sort; and the history of philosophy makes clear that there is more than one good way of going about this.

Obviously much that needs to be said on these topics remains unsaid, but perhaps these comments on philosophy as criticism, upon the lack of agreement among philosophers, and the broad range or scope of our subject in terms of the relations of the teacher to his field, other philosophy teachers, teachers in other fields, administrative officials, stu-

Lewis E. Hahn

dents, and the community or general public will direct attention to some important topics and pave the way for a more fruitful discussion of them.

17

THE MORAL RESPONSIBILITIES OF TEACHERS OF PHILOSOPHY*

J. Glenn Gray

THIS TOPIC IS A RATHER PERILOUS ONE FOR ME. IN PREPARing for it, I was tempted to be rather cynical and consequently witty in the currently fashionable way. At the opposite extreme was the temptation to preach, that is, to exhort you and myself on the special duties we *professors* of philosophy have in these times. Both temptations seem to be implicit in this theme. To avoid them I have tried to adopt a tone of lighthearted seriousness, avoiding what the Germans call *tierischer Ernst* (animal-like earnestness) on the one hand, and a mocking irreverence on the other.

To state my position in summary at the outset: I believe that teachers of philosophy should be men first and teachers afterwards. They should be as involved as possible in the affairs and problems of their time: citizens, householders, parents, friends and lovers. By preference they should know foreign countries and languages, a good deal about other modes of earning a living and non-academic types and clas-

---

* For a Symposium of the Mountain-Plains Philosophy Conference, October 16, 1971, at Boulder, Colorado.

ses of any population. In Hegel's phrase, they should have a life *and* opinions, not merely one or the other. In my view philosophical thinking grows first from experience, as action precedes reflection. *Praxis* and *theoria,* to use the wider Greek terms, fertilize and enrich one another in the classrooms and outside it, but practice enjoys a priority over thought. Hence the need of the philosophy teacher to bring a good deal of extra-philosophical experience to his study and exposition of the subject matter of our discipline.

The longer I teach the more loyal I become to what seems to have been the position of Socrates on the question of the moral responsibility of the teacher. I do mean Socrates as distinct from Plato, with whom I have many a lover's quarrel. Socrates was concerned to clarify his own ideas by ever repeated inquiry in dialogue. He professed no doctrines of his own and claimed the teacher's function to be that of a midwife, helping others to bring their ideas to birth. If a philosophy teacher in our time develops a distinctive system or doctrines of his own on the basic problems of philosophy, he should put these doctrines into books or articles and, in my opinion, not use them in the classroom. In my understanding of it, philosophy has no claim to be edifying or doctrinal. Its primary mission is to inquire into the way things are, and the teacher's mission, like Socrates', is to get his own thinking as straight as he can. I am not convinced that an original thinker is a better teacher than one who has no distinctive philosophy. He may be but only if he sternly represses the temptation to indoctrinate his students with his views. If he has his mind made up on most important issues, he is likely to make only disciples and followers, not students of philosophy.

Such teachers commit what Socrates believed to be the original sin of philosophy, namely, to think we know what we do not know. Among other evils, this sin results in intellectual pride, to my mind a more ineradicable evil than pride of birth, of wealth, of race or sex. Though intellectual pride is not restricted to philosophy teachers, rather is endemic among intellectuals, it is perhaps more likely to be found in us. Not all college teachers are intellectuals by any means, but most philosophy teachers are. As the spiritual father of our discipline, Socrates was keenly aware of this perennial peril. "It is no virtue to be ignorant", Herbert Schneider has remarked, "but it is a virtue to know one's ignorance and it is piety to confess it."* Those teachers who make disciples of students are morally irresponsible, for they transform the essence of philosophy into something alien.

Another conviction of Socrates I have come to adopt is his insistence in the *Apology* on the necessity of a private station in life as the only one suited for a teacher of philosophy. He was sure that he would not have lived very long or done his fellow citizens any good, had he been a public official. Nor would any other man, he boldly asserted. "The true champion of justice, if he intends to survive even for a short time, must necessarily confine himself to private life and leave politics alone." (*Apology* 32a)

On first reflection this statement seems paradoxical, for we think of him rightly as a public figure, indeed notoriously so. In fact, Socrates challenged anyone during his trial to assert that he had ever learned or heard anything from him privately which was not open to everybody. It is clear that he was intimately involved in the affairs of his state and even held public office on occasion. But on those occasions he acted as an individual, not as a representative of the people. As an elected member of the ruling Council, he defied their unconstitutional resolves, as he later disobeyed a direct command of the Thirty Tyrants. In office he acted as a private citizen, not as an official. Remaining his own man at the risk of his life he took personal responsibility for his public actions on the state's behalf.

This insistence of Socrates on the inherently private nature of philosophy has been too little remarked, I fear. Yet it seems to be one of his most important emphases. He could hardly have agreed with Plato in *The Republic* that philosophers should be rulers in a good society. On the contrary,

---

* "Whom Ye Ignorantly Worship," *The Iliff Review*, Vol XVI, No. 2, Spring 1959.

J. Glenn Gray

Plato's conviction that those who know the principles of right and justice should be willing to exercise political power stands in stark contrast to Socrates' persuasion of ignorance concerning such principles.

Our situation today seems to be no different. I wish to oppose those who speak in terms of the governance of mind, as some of my friends like to do. I have not been persuaded by their arguments, analogous to Plato's, that governance has any close kinship with teaching. I confess to profound disbelief in the philosopher-king idea. And not only because I fear the pride of the intellectual and not only because I believe that intellectuals are usually, though not always, ineffective in wielding power. My basic reason, rather, is that it is in principle impossible to put oneself in the service of power and in the pursuit of inquiry at the same time, as impossible as it is religiously to serve God and Mammon. In short, I hold that Socrates was right then and is right now that he who pursues philosophy must retain a strictly private position in society.

This does not imply, of course, any more than it did for Socrates, that the philosophy teacher should remain above the battle and apart from involvement in public issues. In the letter recruiting me for my present task, Manuel Davenport, the program chairman, asked whether teachers of philosophy "should remain neutral enough to function as respected critics of those involved in resolving problems of our time." Rightly or wrongly, I have never accepted the idea that philosophy's only function is criticism. I hold even less to the position of certain contemporary philosophers that "... it is not especially the business of philosophers to make value judgments, to tell people how they ought to live." (Ayer, *Revolution in Philosophy,* p. 78). Making value judgments seems to me to have little in common with telling others how they ought to live. With the latter I have as little sympathy as do the positivists. But I would affirm with Socrates that philosophy has everything to do with improving one's own life and judging the better and the worse ways to conduct it. As a practical activity philosophy appears to me not only to be a search for new ideas and new modes of association, but also an attempt to put these ideas and modes into practice.

It is also hard for me not to be irritated by C. D. Broad's position in the Preface to his *Five Types of Ethical Theory*, an otherwise excellent tome, when he writes: "I find it difficult to excite myself over right and wrong in practice.... A healthy appetite for righteousness, kept in due control by good manners, is an excellent thing; but to 'hunger and thirst after' it is often merely a symptom of spiritual diabetes."

It should be clear that my objections to the idea of governance have little in common with these attitudes of Broad and the positivists. My position is, instead, that the teacher of philosophy, while being involved with public issues and constantly educating himself in the difficult matters of *praxis* has a moral duty to keep himself free for his students from any official commitments that tend to make him a spokesman for anyone else. As a thoughtful citizen he should feel free to speak and write his whole mind, and even participate in acts of civil disobedience against social and political injustice.

Nothing, of course, prevents the responsible man from giving up his teaching job for such institutional leadership. Assuming an appropriate time and an appropriate disposition in himself, the teacher may be completely justified in doing so. I at least feel like praising the man who does. But he is mistaken, I believe, if he thinks he can handle political power and the teaching mission of inquiry at one and the same time.

There is still another Socratic conviction of especial relevance to our theme. Shortly before he drank the poison, Socrates is reported by Plato to have said: "To use words wrongly is not only a fault in itself: it also corrupts the soul." (*Phaedo* 115e) This seems an equally astonishing view, though the more one reflects on it the truer it sounds. At first blush not many of us could say why using words wrongly is a moral fault, much less could we convince ourselves or others today that such misuse corrupts the character. Yet when we consider that as teachers we carry out our function almost solely by and through talking, it is possible that our highest moral responsibility is to gain and try to communicate a proper respect for language. There is surely a moral excellence in the purely intellectual struggle to get complex things and relations right in one's thinking and expression. Such a struggle does improve the character or, as Socrates would say, the psyche, which was for him the primary purpose of philosophical discussion and inquiry.

Perhaps the Socratic corollary that this improvement of the psyche is brought about by right thinking and right action is also true. I am not so sure as he was that right thinking and right action are so complementary that if a person achieves the one he necessarily has the other, too. In other words, I am not convinced that virtue *is* knowledge, that a clear perception of what one ought to do will always lead to its doing. We moderns are more impressed than was Socrates with the power of incontinence in human affairs. I happen also to believe in radical evil in addition to moral weakness, as such a force.

Nevertheless, I am persuaded of the lesser Socratic proposition that to use words wrongly is a fault in itself and if persisted in over a period of years can also corrupt the soul. In the classroom one learns after enough experience that if virtue cannot be taught, vice certainly can be. Hospitals were slow in learning that, if unable to cure the maladies of their patients, they had a moral duty at least not to spread disease. Many veteran teachers of philosophy have come, similarly, to breathe a prayer at the end of a course that they have at least not harmed the psyches of their students. Teaching is, as Hoelderlin said of poetry, at once an innocent and a dangerous occupation.

I would certainly like to believe that right thinking and right action are in such complementary relation that possessing the one we would necessarily have the other as well. I suspect, however, that there is no necessity here. Nonetheless, there surely is a relationship. As Aristotle would say, perhaps it is true "for the most part." *Acting rightly* or at least in ways we ourselves deeply approve clarifies our minds and brings about a certain lightness of mood, even when our actions are not approved by society at large. Socrates' cheerfulness at the end of his life has a great deal of philosophical relevance. *Thinking rightly* may not in itself overcome the coward in all of us, but it does have a similar effect in lightening our moods. Thinking rightly is surely, too, a necessary preliminary to any action which has a chance of being effective in the long run. At all events, I wish to conclude that the closer a person can unite in himself the claims of theory and of practice, the more truly will he *realize* (in both senses of the word) his moral responsibility as a teacher of philosophy.

Postscript

The sentence on page two quoted from Herbert Schneider invites a reflection that was not possible to include in the framework of the symposium. The little essay from which it was taken: "Whom Ye Ignorantly Worship" is beautiful and illuminating. What it illuminates, of relevance to my theme, are certain correspondences between Socrates' doctrine of ignorance and later Christian teaching of the unknown God. I have long been haunted by obscure similarities at the root of our Hebraic-Christian and Greek heritages, but never saw them so clearly until I chanced on this compact essay. Nor did I understand the link between meditation and worship.

In his awareness of the negative character of his wisdom, Socrates appears to have been guided by a piety that was truly religious in character. His inability to discover the real definitions of justice, courage, temperance and the like was grounded in an awareness of ignorance of ultimate origin. As Schneider's essay explains, Socrates' devotion to Apollo, the god of wisdom, instilled in him a fidelity or faithfulness which made possible worship "in truth." This was no worshiping out of ignorance nor a confession of faith: I believe because I do not know. "He who believes because he does not know imagines he has a religious substitute for knowledge; he who bows humbly in the awareness of his ignorance is still faithful to knowledge as well as to God." Socrates' piety stirred him to ever renewed inquiry while instilling at the same time an understanding of his limitations concerning the hidden sources of knowledge and truth, the *deus absconditus*.

Perhaps a teacher in our day requires such radical piety, religious as well as philosophical, if he is to allow his students an untrammeled development. In our despairing search for political and social salvation, moral constraints alone often seem inadequate. Socrates' *daimon* was for him a precious surety, whose absence in us is sorely felt. In this regard Socrates is not only the spiritual father of our discipline but its patron saint as well. He seems to have harmonized without dialectical struggle philosophical and religious intuitions. Also without the agony of the cross in Christianity, he achieved serenity in the face of death, a serenity that is perpetual cause for wonder and astonishment. If a teacher is to inspire students with the spirit of philosophy today, I believe he must somewhere seek to worship at the common altar to the unknown God.

18

RELIGION AMONG THE LIBERAL ARTS
John A. Hutchison

ONE OF THE SIGNIFICANT MOVEMENTS IN AMERICAN HIGHer education during the period since World War II has been the large and rapid growth in the scholarly study of religion. New departments of religion (or of "religious studies" as one label has it), have arisen and old ones have been revitalized. Courses dealing with religious subject matters have proliferated in departments of literature, history, philosophy, and the social sciences. Graduate programs offering M.A. and Ph.D. degrees have multiplied in graduate schools throughout the country.

This new movement is the result of many causes, ranging from student interest in religion to faculty and administrative concern that significant bodies of knowledge should be represented in the curriculum, or even at times to the questionable and problematic administrative supposition that religion makes good public relations.

The movement has raised some fundamental issues of educational philosophy which this essay will seek to explore and appraise. Some of these issues are new, while others are old, recurring questions in new form. Looking at both kinds of issues we shall argue that the inclusion of the scholarly study of religion in liberal arts education is a healthy development alike for religion and for education.

John A. Hutchison

Yet as I have made my way over the ground of this discussion, I have come upon a striking historical fact, namely that fully three decades prior to the movement we are describing, one man anticipated most of what is now taking place, and went quietly about the business of including the study of religion in liberal education.

In 1918 Herbert Schneider joined the Philosophy Department of Columbia University. From 1929 until his retirement in 1957 he was professor of religion. During this period in addition to his courses in many aspects of philosophy he taught courses in religion which ranged from world religions to American religion and philosophy. What is pertinent here is that most of the issues which are currently discussed and argued, Herbert Schneider quietly settled by his own exemplary practice.

In all this, I am reminded of a story attributed to William James. James was asked by a student if he believed in adult baptism. "Believe it" he replied, "I have seen it!" Many of us who have been Herbert Schneider's students and friends have had the experience of seeing the scholarly study of religion pursued in full freedom of inquiry and at a high level of excellence. And here as elsewhere a single clear example is worth many pages of exposition and explanation.

Turning now to the contemporary situation in higher education, we must first concern ourselves briefly with definition and delineation of essential terms and assumptions. First of all, "religion" in our title is an ellipsis for the "scholarly study of religion." It may be pointed out that the term "religion" refers to both a pervasive form of human practice and an academic subject matter devoted to the study of this practice. As a form of practice, religion is a generic concern in every human culture of which reliable knowledge exists. Expressed and communicated in the imaginative symbols of myth and ritual, its content is the values or allegiances which give meaning to human life. As a form of study, religion may be characterized as the attempt at understanding or critical appraisal of these central allegiances or evaluations and of their characteristic institutional expressions.

Religion is by no means unique in the academic curriculum in this double relation to theory and practice. Other illustrations range from the fine arts to politics or economics, and obviously each instance presents its own distinctive issues and problems. In the case of religion, the problems are complicated by the fact that in our time many members of the academic community have been so completely estranged from traditional forms of religious practice that they no longer have any dependable knowledge about what either the practice or the study is — and is not. Often these academic opponents (so similar to Schleiermacher's "cultured despisers" of a century and a half ago) confuse religious practice with the scholarly study; and seeking to resist the former, they take stands of adamant opposition to the latter. There is no time and happily no necessity here to enter any of the intriguing issues involved in this confusion, except perhaps to underscore the distinction between religious practice and scholarly study, and to suggest that other academic fields, from art to politics, provide valuable suggestions for coping with some of the current problems in the academic study of religion.

It is the part of realism to begin where we are, that is, with the situation as we find it in the contemporary American academic community and in the wider society of which the academy is a part. With respect to the latter, in American society today we find religious practice, of widely varying quality, spread across a wide spectrum of traditions (mostly Judeo-Christian) together with a small sprinkling of professed unbelievers. Religion has long been popular in contemporary America, and people who question such accepted tenets as God and conventional morality are viewed in contemporary America, as in Athens of Socrates' day, with great hostility.

On this issue the academic community presents a scene approximately one hundred eighty degrees opposite the society of which it is a part. The contemporary American academic establishment continues to be conventionally agnostic in religious outlook, with a minority holding traditional religious affiliations of various sorts, and a slightly larger minority maintaining that ambiguous attitude often called

John A. Hutchison

an "interest in religion." All of these attitudes must for the sake of clarity be distinguished from the scholarly study of religion, which, it must be argued, varies independently of any or all of them.

I mean the term, liberal education, in its simplest, broadest, and commonest meaning. It is, namely, education addressed to man as man. It is that form or kind of contemporary American higher education whose object is to make men more human. As such, it is distinguished from vocational education, which is addressed to man as prospective doctor, lawyer, merchant, or thief, or other vocation.

This broad use of terms deliberately leaves open the question of the content of liberal education, and beyond the all-encompassing aim of humanism, namely, to make us more human, it leaves equally open the questions of objective or goal. Historically the liberal arts have sometimes had a more restricted extension, being limited to those studies traditionally labeled the humanities, hence specifically excluding the natural and social sciences. If we take the broader characterization here suggested, both social and natural science will be included as significant bodies of knowledge which may and often do, in fact, operate humanistically. Thus, for example, physics, as well as Greek literature, may be understood as a liberal or humanistic study, and anthropology as well as Shakespeare is in this broad sense of the word a humanity. Let us in short accept at least for purposes of argument this broad view of liberal or humanistic education, which it might be added is now widely operative in American higher education.

Whatever one's individual opinion on such issues as these, contemporary liberal education shows three traits whose implications for the study of religion must be explored further. One deals with the end or aim of education; and the others have to do with its form and method. The first issue consists of the assertion that the aim of a liberal education is to communicate to an individual the essential features of his whole cultural heritage. While, as we shall presently argue, it is doubtful if liberal education in the twentieth century can be limited to the West, it does mean that the western cultural heritage still must continue to form the core of liberal education in the West.

It is very largely by communicating this liberal heritage to the individual that the humanistic goal of education is achieved. This in turn carries implications concerning the content of liberal education. For example, such makers of the West as Homer, Plato and Shakespeare cannot well be omitted from any education which deserves the appellations, "liberal" or "humane". Nor, as indicated in the previous paragraph, can the fundamental features of natural and social science be omitted. But these remarks about content in turn lead to implications concerning religious features or aspects of this heritage. For if Homer is indispensable, what about the Bible? If Shakespeare, what of Augustine or Aquinas? We shall return to this matter later, but here we note the indispensable and irreducible religious element in the western liberal heritage, and hence in western liberal education. And, conversely, we also note the way in which the western liberal tradition puts a distinctive context around this religious element and the study of it.

Today an additional major complication has been added to this picture. Since World War II America has sought to break out of its provincialism and become acquainted with the non-western world. For liberal education this has meant the task of becoming acquainted with the great Asian civilizations and their respective humane traditions. What this means is that there is not one humanism (what we have called by this name is properly western humanism), but several, each with its own distinctive cluster of humanizing values.

To be liberally educated in our contemporary global world, then, means some awareness of the *Mahabharata* and *Ramayana* as well as the *Iliad* and the *Odyssey,* of Lao-tse and Confucius as well as Aristotle and Plato. Of American education generally it may be said that we are just beginning to take in and understand this wider world. It is interesting to note that Herbert Schneider was again in this respect ahead of his time. In 1932 with Horace Friess he published *Religion in Various Cultures,* and philosophy for

John A. Hutchison

him has consistently meant global philosophy rather than simply western philosophy. In passing also it may be observed that for many American students the most accessible port of entry to the non-western world is through the study of the world's religions.

The other two features of liberal education that lie across our path are its fundamental assumptions of freedom and rationality. In its most immediate application to education, freedom means intellectual freedom, which in turn may be defined as the capacity of the human mind to make and certify judgments on the basis of evidence. Negatively this implies resistance to other means of making or certifying judgments, such, for example, as political or ecclesiastical pressure or authority. Affirmatively, intellectual freedom involves the whole desire and capacity to think, and to submit one's own conclusions to the free criticism of other thinkers. This in turn leads us onward to a fundamental commitment to the whole ongoing process of critical inquiry and appraisal.

Intellectual freedom, as here characterized, is broader and deeper than the usual extension of the term, academic freedom, which might be characterized as the attempt to institutionalize and guard certain specified aspects of intellectual freedom. Yet maximum intellectual freedom, for everyone concerned is clearly a basic moral imperative, implied in all of higher education.

Applied to the scholarly study of religion, intellectual freedom carries several specific implications. One is that this study is free to all who wish to participate, whatever their religious practice or the absence of it, provided only that they agree to play according to the basic approved rules of liberal study.

A good deal of the hostility to the scholarly study of religion centers in this issue. Critics assert or imply that such free study of religion is impossible, for they argue, if a man has a commitment of faith he is to that extent unfree or in bondage. He becomes perforce a propagandist and not a scholar. In reply to such charges it is easy to point to other areas of the curriculum of liberal studies where significant

Religion Among The Liberal Arts

and comparable combinations of the theory and practice of valuation are involved. For example, it is possible for a student of government to be involved in politics and yet to do objective and fairminded study, sometimes even of ideas and movements to which he is opposed. Other instances come to mind from disciplines ranging from economics to literary criticism. In general, it may be argued that intellectual freedom is not the monopoly of any one discipline or any one philosophic or religious viewpoint, of whatever sort. Rather, we must assert, this kind of freedom is where you find it. So, too, is its opposite, namely, intellectual bondage! The conclusion is that judgments concerning intellectual freedom and bondage must be made by competent academic people on the basis of the facts of individual cases and specific situations.

Incidentally, it is possible also for the student of religion to take the offensive on this issue, observing that free and fairminded study is a problem that impinges with equal force on all regions of the curriculum in which important human values are part of the subject matter to be studied. The religion department is by no means the only place where objectivity may give way to advocacy and indoctrination. In many academic departments the teacher's desk is transformed sometimes unconsciously, into a pulpit from which strange gospels are proclaimed.

In the face of all such violations and abuses, the teacher-scholar in the field of religion will continue to strive to maintain his desk as a desk and not a pulpit. It is not a place from which proclamation is made, but a place for critical sifting of evidence and appraisal of issues, with encouragement to students to learn these arts for themselves. For what it may be worth, my own experience of over thirty years in several different colleges and universities leads me to the conclusion that the scholarly study of religion has as good a record in this respect as any other discipline. However, it must also be added that for many reasons, good and bad, the scholarly study of religion continues to be a sensitive area. Many academic people continue to hold misgivings as to its scholarly quality, while groups from outside the university would gladly construe it as a place of indoctrination in traditional values and attitudes. Yet whatever winds of doctrine blow, for those of us who live and work in this area, the best way to gain and maintain acceptance as teachers and scholars is simply to do our best to *be* teachers and scholars.

Talk concerning intellectual freedom leads on to that broader and deeper freedom which is a primary category of the human self and mind. It was Whitehead who once remarked that every self is a bid for freedom. In precisely this vein it is possible to add that the end and goal of liberal education is liberation or freedom. This is to say, its goal is to put a man in charge of himself, or in other words to achieve that kind of human self-determination in which one does his own thinking, and makes his own important choices — in short, lives his own life.

The primary instrument in this process of liberation is human reason or rationality. Like freedom, reason is a multivalued word. Whitehead, again, has spoken aphoristically, of the reason of the foxes and the reason of the gods. The former is rooted in the necessities of animal survival. Perhaps one might say that the reason of the gods emerges when man's fundamental freedom of spirit supervenes upon the animal intelligence of the fox. For then reason ceases to be simply a powerful instrument for animal survival and becomes an intrinsic good, a human power whose exercise is a delight as well as an instrument of human fulfillment. Even conceived as a tool, at this new emergent level, reason's power and scope are enormously increased.

It is tempting to pursue further the theme of still other ingredients or components of humanism or humanistic value in contemporary American education. But it is a temptation which we must resist, both for reasons of space and also for the good reason that here we may simply assume a widely operative consensus in this matter among American educators. Despite disagreements of emphasis and interpretation, the overwhelming majority of American educators agree substantially concerning the content of humanistic values, which is our task to communicate to students.

Religion Among The Liberal Arts

It has been both easy and valid to argue that the freedom and humanism of contemporary liberal education provide an excellent context for the study of religion (as they are for the study of any generic human concern). However, what is not so often recognized is that this same context is, or could be, of comparable value to the practice of religion. Many people of professed piety or faith shrink from encounter with other faiths and philosophies in the context of free inquiry. To all such, let it be said as loudly and as clearly as possible, their shrinking and defensiveness is the measure of their lack of faith. Obvious as this seems, once it has been pointed out, this relationship has not often been seen in its full force and full truth by traditional religion. Often what has been officially denominated as faith has been little more than neurotic anxiety plastered over with pious verbiage. Genuine faith (of whatever kind or lineage) is by contrast not anxious or defensive, but essentially both confident and open in nature. Far from shrinking from encounter with other faiths and philosophies, it seeks them out. The environment of free study sheds a flood of light on this often obscured but all-important distinction between authentic faith and spurious piety.

Liberal study also offers a rational and humane standard by which to measure and judge religion. Like many other generic human concerns, religion is capable of many and variant expressions ranging from snake-handling to the theology of Aquinas or the piety of St. Francis of Assisi or Gandhi. Liberal study offers sharp tools and well-tested standards for distinguishing the best from the worst in man's heritages of faith — together with all the betters and worses lying between these two extremes. It is sometimes argued in reply that rational scholarship clips the wings of the religious spirit, leaving it earthbound and pedestrian. Perceptive students of the history of religion will be able to think of examples where precisely this has taken place. Yet let it be said in response that reason means many things and is used in many ways. As a way of comprehensive sanity and coherence, it can and should at least be a way of standing against incoherence and insanity.

John A. Hutchison

This argument may be advanced more generally in defense of all humanistic scholarship in the field of religion. If in some of its less imaginative formulations it rejects the divine madness along with ordinary insanity; at its best it is a way of standing against the inhuman and dehumanizing influences which threaten the human spirit on so many different fronts today. Speaking in most general and basic terms, religion deals with those central valuations which Tillich called ultimate concerns. In both culture and personality this defines too important an area to go uncriticized. Socrates said that an unexamined faith is not worth holding.

Surely then we may conclude that both the study and practice of religion have much to gain from free study. But is the reverse also true? Does liberal education stand to gain by the inclusion of the scholarly study of religion in the curriculum? It would be possible to argue that religious practice of some sort is a pervasive human concern, and also that its study has been in one way or another a recurring feature of human thought and education in every civilized tradition. Every human society of which reliable records exist show this form of behavior; and therefore like art, science, politics, economics, and other such recurring features of human experience, it demands inclusion in liberal education. It makes this demand in the name of the humanism which holds nothing human alien to its synoptic understanding. To leave it out or to ignore it leaves liberal education, just to that extent, defective or illiberal.

In some ways this essay has been unduly polemical in tone. Doubtless the reader does not need to be informed at this point that it is written out of discussion and argument in which the writer has been an active participant. Yet as we now look at current developments in the field, it is apparent that a new phase of the movement is upon us. No longer is it a question of whether the study of religion will be included among the liberal arts, but of how it will be done, what its aims and objectives will be, what standards of quality will be maintained, what its ground rules will be.

Here again I can make the point I want to make most effectively by invoking the example of Herbert Schneider and his contributions to both teaching and research in this field. I can only hope that those who will work in this field during the next half century will do their work half as well as he has during the past half century.

19

"NEW HEAV'NS, NEW EARTH" — THE LANDSCAPE OF CONTEMPORARY APOCALYPSE*

Nathan A. Scott, Jr.

> And the time shall come when Satan "with his perverted World" shall be dissolved and when there shall be raised
>
> *From the conflagrant mass, purg'd and refin'd,*
> *New Heav'ns, new Earth, Ages of endless date*
> *Founded in righteousness and peace and love,*
> *To bring forth fruits Joy and eternal Bliss.*
>   — John Milton, *Paradise Lost*, Bk. XII

THE *KULTURKAMPF* THAT HAS LAIN SO HEAVILY ON THE American scene since the early 1960s may seem now to situate what is called the New Sensibility at a considerable remove from the dim, gray years of the Eisenhower dispensation. Indeed, those of us who had reached adulthood at

---

* Copyright ©1972 by Nathan A. Scott, Jr.

"New Heav'ns, New Earth"

least by the close of the Second World War will surely feel today a very great difference of tone and atmosphere between that earlier period and the present time. For, then, the intellectual community had already deeply absorbed the lessons that F. O. Matthiessen and Perry Miller and Reinhold Niebuhr and Lionel Trilling and various others had given currency about what was beginning to be called "the American imagination." And it was coming to be assumed that the American mode of imagination was one which found its most natural standpoint in an essentially melodramatic view of human experience. Ours, we had decided, is a tradition whose most deeply ingrained habit it has been — from Jonathan Edwards to Henry James, and from Herman Melville to William Faulkner — to conceive the human story as an affair of great clashing contraries, as an infuriate struggle between the Legions of Light and the Hosts of Darkness. Indeed, remembering (as we had been taught to do by the new specialists in "American Studies") the line of Poe and Hawthorne and Melville and Henry Adams and Mark Twain, we were disposed to locate the place normally indwelt by the American mind not amongst any "temperate zones" but amongst what Emerson called "the extremities and suburbs" of the world. "Do I contradict myself?/Very well then I contradict myself," Whitman had said. And the sanguinity of his admission seemed to make a kind of emblem of a native bias that had persistently been drawn to extravagant oppositions and stark dualities, whether in the form of the Calvinist religion of the New England Puritans or the "Manichaean" radicalism of our most characteristic literature or the oscillations of our politics between nostalgia and utopianism.

By the time of the early 50s, however, we had settled deeply into the straits of our struggle with the powers behind the Iron Curtain, and the bitter dilemmas of that engagement appeared no longer to permit any indulgence of our national penchant for contrariety. Indeed, all counsels of prudence seemed to recommend that the national imagination carefully accommodate its old enchantment with turmoil and conflict to the unprecedented exigencies of the Cold War. For,

Nathan A. Scott, Jr.

in these latter days of our distress, the issues of ambiguity and paradox had suddenly taken on a new moral prestige, and politics thus became a gesture in the direction of "the tragic sense of life."

Van Wyck Brooks — the Brooks of *America's Coming of Age* (1915) — had long since forfeited his earlier eminence, as a result of what was felt to be the essentially retrogressive and sterile piety toward the American past expressed in his great multivolume project on "the literary life in America," *Makers and Finders*. Yet, strangely, it was Brooks's program for dealing with the contradiction and anomaly of American experience that was by way of being generally adopted by intellectuals in this country twenty years ago. For what he had proposed in *America's Coming of Age* was that all the various extremes of thought and feeling endemic to our culture be assuaged by such an "open, skeptical, sympathetic centrality" as would make newly available "a certain focal center" or "national 'point of rest' " wherein the extremities and contradictions could be, if not reconciled, at least so modulated as to make them endurable. And, despite the loss of celebrity that Brooks had suffered in the American forum during the generation that had intervened since the appearance of his brilliant book of 1915, it was something very much like his stoical program of moderation that became a prevailing creed amongst liberal intellectuals in the post-War period of the late 40s and early 50s: the major platform of the time was established by the myth of what Arthur Schlesinger, Jr., called "the vital center."[1]

It was undoubtedly this new "skeptical ... centrality," with its yearning for a "national 'point of rest,' " that prompted the intellectual community in these years to find the public presence of Adlai Stevenson so enormously engaging and attractive. Irving Howe's reconstruction of the matter is wonderfully exact, when he suggests that a large part of Stevenson's appeal for intellectuals at the beginning of the 1950s was rooted in the fact that, though they

---

1. *Vide* Arthur M. Schlesinger, Jr., *The Vital Center: The Politics of Freedom* (Boston: Houghton Mifflin Co., 1949).

had been singed just enough by the alliances with Stalinism in the 30s and 40s to want now to avoid any great crusades, they

> ... still enjoyed a mild idealistic lilt; they were tempted to abandon politics entirely yet felt themselves forced — indeed, trapped — into a lukewarm, gingerly participation; they wished for liberal humaneness but felt that to identify with any social class or group was outmoded, deficient in tone. And here was this remarkable man from Illinois, so charming and cultivated, so witty and so ... well, *somewhat* weary ... come to represent and speak for them.[2]

Which is to say that Stevenson's very distaste for politics (at least as the tone of his public deliverances made it seem) permitted him to appear a kind of "emblem of the intellectual condition,"[3] and thus one to be identified with and admired. He did, of course, command an immense distinction, as an American public man wholly committed to those modes of discourse appropriate to freemen; but his characteristic style — in its air of fastidious ambivalence before the messiness of political actuality — did, indeed, have the effect of confirming a similar ambivalence that had come to be deeply a part of "the liberal imagination." For, as Lionel Trilling was eloquently contending in much of his critical work of this period, after all the expensive disorders of the first half of the twentieth century, the great secret hope of the liberal intelligence was often proving to be a hope "that man's life in politics, which is to say, man's life in history, shall come to an end."[4] And he suggested that the "growing estrangement from history"[5] deserved to be considered a sign of desperation.

Now the idiom and tonality of American cultural life today entail styles that are radically different from those which

---

2. Irving Howe, *Steady Work: Essays in the Politics of Democratic Radicalism* (New York: Harcourt, Brace & World, Inc., 1966), p. 207.
3. *Ibid.*, p. 209.
4. Lionel Trilling, *The Liberal Imagination: Essays on Literature and Society* (New York: Viking Press, 1950), p. 195.
5. *Ibid.*, p. 196.

were prevailing twenty years ago. For the emphasis then on the necessity of achieving flexibility and modulation, of carefully keeping (as Mr. Trilling phrased it) an awareness of "variousness and possibility, ... of complexity and difficulty,"[6] will seem from our present vantage point to have thrown an odd sort of muteness and quiet over cultural life, and to have sponsored such a retreat from social reality as made for a general muffling of any sound of combat. Whereas today, after the jackhammer barrage of the past few years — of psychedelic discothèques and high-decibel Rock, of "multimedia" Events and electronic Happenings, of terrorist assaults on our universities and holocausts in our great cities, and of the endless "offensives" conducted by the choreographers of "confrontation politics" — we have a sense of belonging to the noisiest period of this century; and certainly the clatter and din of the New Sensibility will seem to place it at a great distance from the styles of thought and feeling which were predominant two decades ago. But, beneath all the shrillness and bedlam, it may just be possible to detect a secret hope not unlike that of an earlier time — the hope that we may somehow find a way of releasing ourselves altogether from the duties and contingencies of our life in history. And thus it may well be that ours is a period in which the critical work of a Reinhold Niebuhr or a Lionel Trilling requires not simply to be memorialized but, rather, to be freshly undertaken and done anew.

The visions of the End with which American secular radicalism is drunk today were already being presaged in the 1950s by that great spate of literature which then came to the fore — David Riesman's *The Lonely Crowd,* William H. Whyte's *The Organization Man,* C. Wright Mills' *White Collar,* to mention only the better examples — with its messages about the alienation and loss of personal identity to which we are fated by the dehumanizing collectives of "mass society." The analysis of the modern situation brought forward by "the Orgman-critics" (as Harold Rosenberg nicknamed

---

6. *Ibid.,* p. xv.

them[7]) was, in varying degrees, derivative from the Marx of the *Economic-Philosophical Manuscripts* and from that line of German sociology running from Simmel and Weber and Tönnies to Theodor Adorno and Max Horkheimer. But the American specialists in mass culture were far more simplistic than their German precursors and projected a picture of contemporary society as so deeply involved in the malaise of dehumanization as to leave none of us untouched by the facelessness and anonymity of an "other-directed" culture. "In the muted melodrama" (as Mr. Rosenberg said) of this popular American sociology of the 1950s "the inhuman does not *invade*. It sits in the living room twisting the TV dial or takes the family for a ride in the two-tone hard-top. It is you."[8] For we are, all of us, enveloped within the depersonalizing processes of mass society: we are all doomed, whatever our social class, to be the helpless victims of the Orgworld: there are no privileged persons. "The smiling credit manager you spoke to this morning is a piece of company apparatus like the filing case from which he extracts the card that is you; his human appearance is a disguise and his real name isn't Brown but Agent F-362."[9] It was such a grotesque that appeared to emerge from the account of things we were given by this alarmist school of social criticism. And the telling point that Harold Rosenberg made against it was not that it did not contain elements of empirical truth but, rather, that its representation of life in the modern world as everywhere an affair of the dehumanized collective was calculated only to rob the human reality of any radical implication and to promote a kind of euphoric fatalism. Such a sociology, as he rightly contended, communicates "in atmosphere, if not in stated concept, the sinister overtones of a developing totalitarianism from which there is no escape."[10] And, of course, once the malaise by which we are afflicted is conceived to be so ubiquitous as to leave us

---

7. Harold Rosenberg, "The Orgamerican Phantasy," in *The Tradition of the New* (New York: Horizon Press, 1959), p. 274.
8. *Ibid.*, pp. 272-73.
9. *Ibid.*, p. 274.
10. *Ibid.*, p. 273.

without any melioristic possibilities, then we begin to enter that late stage of things where there is no bang but only a whimper and a sense of the historical process being at an end. Which is to say that we are by way of being seduced by the expensive emotions of Apocalypse. For, when we all bear the sign of the Beast upon our foreheads, the End is near.

Now it is this mode of thought which has lately come to be the great hallmark of that whole insurgency which Theodore Roszak has named the "counter culture."[11] But Mr. Roszak does, somewhat ironically, permit his liking for the spirited phrase to betray his boundless enthusiasm for his subject, for the movement which he has advertised with such great approval is, indeed, in many of its aspects, *against* any true culture, since its most urgently felt commitment would seem to be to some sort of absolute humanity — which is beyond history.

* * * * * *

Ours is not, of course, the first period to be inebriated by the dream of Apocalypse. For the allurements of its *evangelium aeternum* have recurrently bewitched the Western imagination. They were felt by the pauperized hordes who participated in the Crusades, as by the Franciscan Spirituals of the thirteenth century who drew out of the teachings of Joachim of Fiore the material with which to weave a powerful messianic myth around the Emperor Frederick the Second. It was also an essentially apocalyptic image of history that furnished the root-conceptions of the various "heretical" ideologies animating the Brethren of the Free Spirit of the thirteenth and fourteenth centuries. And from the Anabaptist movements of the sixteenth century to the French Enlightenment, and, from the various antinomian radicals of seventeenth-century English Independency ("Diggers" and "Ranters") to the chiliastic zealots of the Third Reich, the notion that the historical drama is to be understood in the light of some great final transformation scene has

---

11. *Vide* Theodore Roszak, *The Making of a Counter Culture* (Garden City, N. Y.: Doubleday and Co., 1969).

proved, again and again, to be a most powerfully influential conception.[12] It is not to be forgotten, however, that this is a pattern of belief which derives, at the very beginning, from certain currents in Judaic speculation of the second century before the birth of Christ. The New Testament's Book of Revelation from St. John the Divine of Patmos does, undoubtedly, present the fullest development of primitive apocalypticism. But perhaps its purest expressions are to be found in various extra-canonical Jewish writings of the last two centuries before Christ (the Books attributed to Enoch, the Testaments of the Twelve Patriarchs, the Book of Zadok) and, most principally, in the Old Testament's Book of Daniel. And it is in the world of thought which this literature reflects that we may perceive most clearly the fundamental motives that distinguish apocalyptic mentality.

The background of the *Sitz im Leben* (or "setting in life") of Jewish apocalypticism is, of course, the repressiveness with which in the second century B.C. the Greek monarch of Syria, Antiochus Epiphanes, undertook to deal with the little state of Judaea. He was eager to weld the various heterogeneous elements of his empire into one culturally organic society; and one measure, therefore, that seemed requisite was the exaction of uniformity of usage in the practice of religion. The Jewish community had by this time been living for a long period under the sway of Hellenistic traditions, and had not been unwilling to make limited use of the Greek language or to adopt such forms and conventions as could be adjusted to its own polity. But it was clear that for the Jewish people to accede to the kind of abnegation of their religious inheritance being now required would be in effect for them to consent to the dissolution of their culture. So they resisted the new edict, and the predictable result of their intransigence was reprisal — which came swiftly, and with a brutality so great as to have provoked, finally (in 168 B.C.), open rebellion under the leadership of a family whose foremost member was the great Judas Maccabaeus.

---

12. Many fascinating phases of this story are brilliantly recounted in Norman Cohn's great book *The Pursuit of the Millennium* (London: Secker & Warburg, 1957).

Nathan A. Scott, Jr.

Now it was in the period of persecution under Antiochus Epiphanes that the genre of apocalyptic emerged as a distinctively new response of the Hebraic imagination to the crises and distempers of history. For, at last, after centuries of disappointment and misfortune, it seemed no longer possible to believe in Yahweh's providential supervision of the historical arena. He had, to be sure, intervened in behalf of His chosen people at many critical points in the past — but now, as it was felt, the world was so lacking in hopefulness that the conclusion had to be that Yahweh had withdrawn from it and that it had fallen under the dominance of evil angels. Indeed, the temporal universe appeared to be irremediably absurd and nothing but a graveyard of the People of God. So the only remaining possibility of regarding history *sub specie aeternitatis* was conceived to lie in a radically futuristic vision of a New Age that Yahweh would eventually inaugurate — when, the evil empires of the heathen being broken like pieces of clay by the "Ancient of Days," they would become "like the chaff of the summer threshing-floors" (Daniel 2:35) and be swept away by the wind, and when the desert would then flower as a garden. Thus it was that, under the pressure of this late, bad time, the answer to the despairing cry "How long, O Lord, how long?" came to be an eschatology set forth by way of the various bizarre "visions" which constitute the source of the elaborate mythological apparatus characteristic of ancient Jewish apocalypse. In short, for the apocalyptists history had so much ceased to be a domain of reality for which one might have any hope that the only significant action to be performed in the historical order appeared to be that of *waiting* — for the End. "Blessed is he that waiteth.... But go thou thy way till the end be: for thou shalt ... stand in thy lot at the end of the days" (Daniel 12:12-13). It is this haunting wistfulness in the closing lines of the Book of Daniel which tended generally to be the sort of culminating note struck by Jewish apocalypticism.

The British scholar H. H. Rowley devotes the concluding chapter of his book *The Relevance of Apocalyptic*— which is one of the most distinguished accounts of its subject in recent literature — to "The Enduring Message of Apocalyptic."[13] And, in this, he represents — allowing for certain notable exceptions, such as those presented by C. H. Dodd[14] and Oscar Cullmann[15] — a frequent tendency of Christian scholars, to try (however desperately) to find in primitive apocalypticism elements of normativeness for Hebraic-Christian faith. But such an all-embracing piety toward the Biblical world was boldly refused by so great a Jewish thinker of our period as Martin Buber, who had no hesitation at all in declaring the apocalyptic movement to be what in fact it would seem to have been — namely, a decadent form of the prophetic tradition.[16]

In the Hebraic line, prophecy and apocalyptic did, to be sure, share certain common features. For both prophets and apocalyptists conceived their vocation to be that of delivering unto their contemporaries the very word of Yahweh Himself. And the context of their deliverances was always that of some urgent historical crisis whose gravity laid upon the people the immediate necessity of discerning anew the will of God. Nor can we fail to be struck by the decidedly eschatological tendency of prophetic thought, as well as of apocalypticism, for the great prophets also looked toward "the day of Yahweh," when the present age would be supplanted by a new dispensation. And thus there was a certain predictive element in prophecy, as in apocalyptic. But, finally, the extraordinary figures belonging to the "classical" period of Hebrew prophecy — Amos and Hosea and Isaiah and Micah and Jeremiah — do, in their central emphasis, represent a way of reckoning with the human situation

---

13. *Vide* H. H. Rowley, *The Relevance of Apocalyptic: A Study of Jewish and Christian Apocalypses from Daniel to the Revelation* (New York: Association Press, 1963; 3rd ed.,), pp. 166-193.

14. *Vide* C. H. Dodd, *The Apostolic Preaching* (New York: Harper & Bros., 1937).

15. *Vide* Oscar Cullmann, *Christ and Time: The Primitive Christian Conception of Time and History,* trans. by Floyd V. Filson (London: S.C.M. Press, 1951).

16. *Vide* Martin Buber, *Pointing the May,* trans. by Maurice Friedman (New York: Harper & Bros., 1957), p. 203.

that differs very sharply from the apocalyptic perspective.

R. B. Y. Scott suggests that apocalyptic be thought of as "a late and specialized form of ... prophecy" which finds its single theme in a vision of "the consummation of history."[17] And, in identifying the theology of *history* as the crucial issue, Professor Scott offers a particularly convenient formulation, for it is indeed just in relation to this theme that the radical divergence between the two modes of thought is to be most clearly seen.

What must in part be striking for a phenomenologist of religion is the virtual absence in the prophetic movement of anything resembling mysticism. "The prophet is a 'public man.' His encounter with God is not private experience withdrawn from contact with workaday things. ... The pressure of public movements and events upon his spirit is the occasion of the encounter with God ... and the truth which the encounter forces upon his mind is public property."[18] Which is to say that, for Hebraic prophetism, history is the *medium* of revelation. Yahweh is not any "unmoved Mover" dwelling in a timeless eternity but a dynamic presence whose righteousness is made manifest in the choices and actions of men. So, for all of His transcendent majesty, He is to be found in the midst of His people, where He is forever directing the course of events toward His own ends. The concrete drama of daily existence, in other words, is His handiwork. And He is to be descried not only in the great original events whereby the Hebrews were elected to their special destiny, not only in the coming climax of history when all things shall be made subject to His reign, but also in every present hour of man's life on earth, for He is "a God at hand ... not a God afar off" (Jeremiah 23:23). Indeed, the prophetic mind was inspired by so profound a sense of Yahweh's immanence in the present that the human future was in effect conceived to be already contained with-

---

17. R. B. Y. Scott, *The Relevance of the Prophets* (New York: Macmillan Co., 1944), p. 4.

18. C. H. Dodd, *The Bible Today* (Cambridge: At the University Press, 1947), p. 100.

in the present. For the overriding issue was man's obligation to respond with obedience to a God whose moral demands were disclosed in the ongoing course of daily events: the character of any tomorrow was felt, in short, to be determined by the response offered Yahweh today: which is why the prophetic oracle is so constantly an affair of "therefore" — " ... yet have ye not returned unto me, saith the Lord. Therefore thus will I do unto thee, O Israel" (Amos 4:11-12).[19] And thus the future which the prophets foretold was always a future that would arise out of the present. Even that last Day, which would bring absolute doom to all the enemies of Yahweh, was not conceived to be discontinuous with the processes of judgment and salvation that had always been a daily reality for the People of God. For though the time will come when, in the presence of Yahweh, "every knee shall bow, [and] every tongue shall swear" (Isaiah 45:23) allegiance, this was not considered to be a time that would be beyond or outside of time: on the contrary, it was expected to be a triumph that Yahweh would achieve *within* history. And it was, therefore, with the events and processes of history that the prophetic imagination was always most deeply engaged, for the perspective of an Amos or a Micah or a Jeremiah was one which understood the horizon of the human reality to be defined by the world of historical experience.

It is, however, quite a different perspective that we meet when we turn to the apocalyptic side of the Hebraic tradition. For, here, what is more striking even than all the bizarre imagery of fantastic beasts and catastrophe being rained down from the heavens is the profound collapse of confidence in the historical order that has been suffered. The world is felt to be so broken and defeated that nothing much can come out of it. The prophets were saying, in effect, again and again, "Return, return, return, Israel, unto the Lord," and, for them, our human drama of moral struggle and decision was of the highest moment, because they conceived it to be the medium on which Yahweh

---

19. *Vide* R. B. Y. Scott, *op. cit.*, p. 151.

Nathan A. Scott, Jr.

Himself was dependent for the realization of His purposes. The relationship between man and God was understood to be an essentially personal relationship in which the human participant was "God's partner in the dialogue of history."[20] And thus our human decisions — either for or against Yahweh — were felt to be of eternal importance, since they were the channels through which Yahweh's will became operative. But, from the apocalyptic standpoint, the world is so hopelessly infected with evil that it is fruitless to address Israel with any appeal to "Return. . . ." Nor does it avail anything even to remember the saving acts of God in the past, so unswervingly is the world careening towards the Abyss. All that matters is the last generation, the last events, the consummatory drama that will mark the End: everything is predetermined, and the world is being swept inexorably toward the final hour. There remains no possibility of history being given a new direction: "all human decisions are only sham struggles,"[21] and about all that remains for men to do is simply to wait to be hurled into the flaming pit. There is, to be sure, a New Age ahead, though it will not arise out of but, rather, break into the present. For the world has grown old, and it cannot of itself any longer bring forth anything that is good.

Such is the view of things that we encounter in the Old Testament's Book of Daniel and in such extra-canonical Jewish writings of the last two centuries before Christ as the *Book of Enoch* and the *Book of Baruch,* the *Book of Jubilees* and the *Testaments of the Twelve Patriarchs.* They, and numerous other similar documents of the period, were, as it has often been said, "tracts for bad times." And so, indeed, they would seem to have been, an expression not merely of a failure of nerve but of a failure of confidence in the capacity of the historical drama to attain any radical significance. For the contingency of our life in time is something utterly intolerable for the apocalyptic mind, and its recourse is,

---

20. Martin Buber, *op. cit.,* p. 198.
21. *Ibid.,* p. 201.

therefore, to some *eschaton* which will usher in a New Age that shall be beyond all the exasperations and uncertainties of history.

*   *   *   *

It is not, however, any merely archaeological datum that we confront in ancient Jewish apocalypticism. For, as Martin Buber was at pains to remind us, whenever and "wherever man shudders before the menace of his own work and longs to flee from the radically demanding historical hour, there he finds himself near to the apocalyptic vision. ...."[22] And, indeed, apocalyptic would seem to be the name and nature of one very powerful impulse lying behind the cultural ferment of the present time that presses in upon us on the American scene.

The apocalypticism which informs so much of our contemporary literature and psychology and art and politics does, of course, in certain respects differ inevitably from its ancient Jewish prototype, for not only does it generally lack any theistic premise but it often tends also to replace the earlier expectancy of cataclysmic destruction with a conception of some less stringent mode of passage from the old aeon into the new. But the sense of the present age as a time of decadence is retained, as is the ancient vision of a great coming renovation. The complex numerology, say, of the Fourth Book of Enoch or of the Book of Daniel has not now the kind of analogue in contemporary idiom that it had in the mythography of William Butler Yeats, but there remains a persisting conviction that we dwell in the Last Days: the night is far spent, and the world has grown old, old enough indeed for the time to have arrived when it is needful for the human spirit to collect itself in preparation for the End and for the New Age that is to come.

It is important also to notice that the sense (traditionally characteristic of apocalyptic mystique) of history as useless, of the world as hopelessly mediocre and sterile — which will

---

22. *Ibid.*, p. 203.

normally now be formulated in the terms of some theory of "alienation" — does, in our own day, very frequently combine with a conviction that the domain of the Real has come to be the pure inwardness of Infinite Subjectivity. For, since everywhere nothing is to be descried but the dilapidation of last tapes and end games and tin drums, it often seems in this late time that the only way of rescuing ourselves from the universal vapidity is to lay claim to that "sanctuary in the heart within"[23] and there to find the locus of whatever truth may gladden and redeem our essential humanity. And this may not at first seem to have been a stratagem anciently a part of the apocalyptic adventure. Yet by way of what else might we account for the predilection so constantly exhibited in primitive Jewish apocalyptic for the symbolism of the Vision? Surely it is the case that the apocalyptists encoded their thought in so elaborate a mythology (of beasts and angels and fallen stars) precisely because, the empirical world having become intolerably threatening and absurd, it had to be radically dissolved — and since the *consummatio* was expected to usher in a transhistorical world beyond all the hazards and casualties of temporal existence, it seems natural that this mentality should have found its most characteristic expression in a kind of atemporal *gnosis* whereby the adept was delivered over to a visionary universe — of infinite subjectivity.

Now it is in just such a "land of unlikeness" that a major soulscape of our own period is to be located. For the belief that the Kingdom of Heaven is to be found "within" begins to be epidemic, as does the assumption that the liberation of "inwardness" offers us an effective release from the bullying of all the vexations of history. On the most strident and most obvious level, it is, of course, the belief which is declared today by the hordes of those young long-haired, jean-clad, pot-smoking bohemians who have entered the world of psy-

---

23. Erich Heller, *The Artist's Journey into the Interior* (New York: Random House, 1965), p. 153. This quoted fragment is drawn from Professor Heller's brilliant discussion of Rilke, in whose poetry — particularly in the *Elegies* — he finds a classic instance of modern apocalyptic.

chedelia. And Leslie Fiedler — whose boundless concern for cultural novelty makes him perhaps our latter-day equivalent of the late Sir Herbert Read — does, undoubtedly, give us an exact designation for this generation of "hipsters, layabouts and ... abstentionists," when he calls them "the new mutants," for they are, indeed, persuaded that something like an absolute mutation in our humanity may now be achievable by way of pharmacology: so, being convinced of the bankruptcy of that whole Western tradition which dedicates the human enterprise to rationality and work and accomplishment, they are aiming at that "post-human future"[24] which is to be found by exploring the spaces of our inwardness with the help of hallucinogens and the various other assorted drugs that may induce ecstatic experience. And it is no wonder, therefore, that the literature in which the Rock generation has found a scriptural power— whether it be William Burroughs' *Naked Lunch* or Ken Kesey's *One Flew Over the Cuckoo's Nest* or Joseph Heller's *Catch-22* or Norman Mailer's *An American Dream* — has been the literature of our period which finds its point of purchase in madness. For some kind of extreme delirium is felt to be the necessary form of poise called forth by the imminent cataclysm.

On a somewhat more genteel level, the seductive power of the gospel of inwardness is discernible in the extraordinary reception recently accorded Charles Reich's book *The Greening of America*[25] by those confused and multitudinous philistines who (like their Buchmanite progenitors of the 1930s) seek out salvation today in the therapy of "encounter" groups. This Yale law professor who heralds a great coming "change of consciousness" presents a typical expression of that unbridled optimism which often marks the apocalyptic mind once it has undergone modern secularization. The present age is for him, to be sure, a time of terror and decadence, for it is the time of advanced technology, of large-

---

24. Leslie A. Fiedler, "The New Mutants," *Partisan Review,* Vol. XXXII, No. 4 (Fall, 1965), p. 508.
25. New York: Random House, 1970.

Nathan A. Scott, Jr.

scale industrialization, and of the "corporate state." In Mr. Reich's account, the prelapsarian period of American history embraces that Edenic time of the country's settlement by the early European immigrants, when by individual initiative and free enterprise small towns were built up in which the primary social form was that of face-to-face relationships; and the mentality which found its ballast in the bourgeois-Protestant virtues of duty and vocation and work he calls "Consciousness I." But this pre-industrial world of free markets and organic communities had finally to yield before the technological revolutions of the nineteenth century and the great concentrations of industrial power which they made inevitable. And, as the nation found itself increasingly battened on by the new breed of "robber barons" who were turning a *laissez-faire* economy to their own account, it began to be apparent that a technocratic culture required planning and scientific management, if the inequities generated by modern industrialization were to be controlled and kept from producing a state of anarchy. Thus it was that "Consciousness II" was born — namely, that commitment to social rationality which was originally intended to mitigate the inhumanity of technocratic civilization but which did itself finally succumb to that inhumanity, in its promotion of an ethos in which the expert (in business cycles and nutrition and sexuality) is conceived to be the repository of all wisdom. But, beyond the present squalor of the corporate state and its dehumanizing rationalism, Mr. Reich sees a New Age of health and happiness whose messianic agents are to be found amongst those who are today offering us "Consciousness III": namely, "the kids."

The world to which Consciousness III gives its suffrage is a world of love and communion, of individual freedom and accountability, of creativity and wholeness. And it is to be had at no great cost, for it awaits not any program of social reform or political revolution but only a general acceptance of that way of reckoning with reality to which "the kids" are beckoning us. In short, transcendence of our fallen condition under the sway of "the corporate state" entails nothing more expensive than the heart's offering its consent to the new table of virtues being handed us by the dropouts and nonparticipants who are once more making visible "the submerged magic of the earth."[26] Which is a prescription for the attainment of Paradise Now that would, indeed, seem to substantiate the claim of one of Mr. Reich's critics, that he is the Norman Vincent Peale of the New Left. For he summons us not to any exacting disciplines of thought and action but only to a certain *metanoia* of "consciousness."

Now the scheme which Charles Reich presents is only a particularly soft and mindless example of what is an easily discernible tendency amongst many of those writers who have become major strategists of advanced thought in the United States today. For his fascination with "consciousness" and his lack of interest in the concrete actuality of the social-political drama make a kind of hallmark of the New Sensibility — if one takes its measure in the black *accusateur* LeRoi Jones, or in the Scots psychologist Ronald Laing, or in the Canadian philosopher of electronic media Marshall McLuhan, or in the Norman Brown of *Life Against Death* and *Love's Body*. Mr. Jones, in his role as spokesman for the anguish of the black multitudes, is, of course, prepared to announce a kind of *eschaton* and to bring down a curtain — on a country and culture which he considers to be utterly rotten. But, though at first he would seem to be a man committed to social reality, what is striking in his social criticism and his works for the theatre is that their screams and blasts are calculated not to open up for his black brethren any viable way into an historical future but, rather, only to stiffen their angers and frustrations into a form of "consciousness" that will itself define their human identity. Such a work, for example, as Mr. Jones's play *The Slave,* far from wanting to alter or redeem an actual condition of men, does, on its lower frequencies, express a profound disengagement from social actuality, since the consciousness which it wants to promote requires the continuance of the *status quo* against which it rages: in short, the real commitment is to "black dada nihilis-

---

26. Theodore Roszak, *op. cit.,* p. 268.

mus,"[27] to the dream of young blacks erupting "like Mt. Vesuvius to crush in hot lava these willful maniacs who call themselves white Americans."[28] And in this, of course, he is endorsed by those mischievous white melodramatists in the liberal community who are eager to propose (along with Genet's Archibald in *Les Nègres*) that "Negroes negrify themselves. . . . to the point of madness. . . ."

Or, again, the psychologist R. D. Laing — who is one of the most revered sages of the New Left — in his slickly fashioned package of psychiatry-cum-existentialism-cum-phenomenology, candidly preaches a gospel of abdication to those who are "only half alive in the fibrillating heartland of a senescent civilization."[29] For, in Dr. Laing's view, modern Western culture, in its basic social forms, is directed toward a rape of the human individual's personhood. What is required, above all else, is conformity to the canonized styles of life and work, and the chief agent of constraint is the family whose job it is, in a society gone mad, to persuade the child to suppress his natural instincts and interests to whatever extent may be entailed by compliance with social norms. The very process of socialization is, in other words, nothing more than institutionalized violence. Which means that the task of therapy must centrally involve the "demystification" of officialized irrationality, and, in the interests of this subversion, Dr. Laing enjoins a rejection of the social world so extreme as to provide, somewhat ironically, a very neat example of the schizophrenia which is a major subject of his technical researches.

Nor does the guru summoning us to "erotic exuberance" in *Life Against Death* and *Love's Body* present any less extreme an instance of disengagement from history, for all of his meditations on its "psychoanalytical meaning." Norman Brown's project began, in his book of 1959 *Life Against*

---

27. *Vide* LeRoi Jones, "BLACK DADA NIHILISMUS," in *The Dead Lecturer* (New York: Grove Press, 1964), p. 61.

28. LeRoi Jones, *Home: Social Essays* (New York: William Morrow & Co., 1966), p. 209.

29. R. D. Laing, *The Politics of Experience* (New York: Ballantine Books, 1968), p. 11.

Death, with the lesson that Freud had laid down in *Civilization and Its Discontents* regarding the repression of man's basic instinctual energies which is exacted by the mechanisms of the social collectivity. Freud, of course, conceived civilization to be an achievement purchased at an immense price: it brings, to be sure, immense dividends, but they are dividends which we can attain only by way of a certain frustration of our natural proclivities, at least in so far as we devise "substitutive gratifications" for impulses essentially directed toward sexual pleasure. Man-in-culture, in other words, is a creature who has chosen to accommodate the "pleasure-principle" to the "reality-principle," in order that, together with his fellows, he may have a world of order and coherence wherewith to confront the hazards of existence. And, though Freud kept a lively sense of what is inclinably tragic in the psychological cost of civilization, he took a largely stoical view of the matter, supposing that the tensions and "discontents" brought by our life in culture, however carefully they may need to be supervised, are a price well paid for the benefits that civilization confers. But, when this professor of classics at Wesleyan University (as Mr. Brown then was) plunged into the canon of Freud's work in the 1950s, he found the lesson of *Civilization and Its Discontents* to be something unbearably shocking, and his conclusion was that, if man "the discontented animal ... is man in history" and if repression generates "historical time,"[30] then man should undertake to live outside historical time, outside the traditional polity of civilization. Mr. Brown was absolutely fearless of what he took to be the final implication of the Freudian kerygma: if man is natively governed by the pleasure-principle and if all the values of civilization — morality and systematic thought and productivity — situate themselves within the person in such a way as to transform the naturally Dionysian ego into an Apollonian ego, then, if man is ultimately to survive, he must somehow

---

30. Norman O. Brown, *Life Against Death: The Psychoanalytical Meaning of History* (Middletown, Conn.: Wesleyan University Press, 1959), p. 93.

summon the courage to put aside Apollonian constraints and to step forward into the essentially Dionysian reality of the human condition, giving up all the repressions of culture for the uninhibited life of polymorphously perverse sexuality. Our life in history may require that we follow the path of sublimation and repression; but, at this moment of history, when "the total obliteration of mankind is at last a practical possibility,"[31] since it is now clear that historical time brings only neurosis and death, it should, therefore, also be apparent that, if man is to prevail, we must bring history to an end — by electing the "unrepressed life" of that "Sabbath of Eternity ... when time no more shall be. ..."[32]

Now, whatever doubt may have lingered regarding the role that the author of *Life Against Death* had chosen, it has surely been dispelled by his more recent book[33] which discloses him to be, indeed, a veritable poet of Apocalypse. For, in *Love's Body,* his "project in psychic archaeology" (as Theodore Roszak calls it) moves toward a rejection of the reality-principle so extreme that schizophrenia itself, finally, is declared to be the happiest human condition. The darkly gnomic apothegms which the book stitches together refuse, of course, to be lined up behind any coherent argument, for that would be only to shore up the repressive world of the superego. So Mr. Brown's basic intentions are somewhat elusive. But, beneath all his artful mystification ("A penis in every convex object and a vagina in every concave one" — "All walking, or wandering, is from mother, to mother, in mother; it gets us nowhere"), he would seem to be wanting to maintain that man's liberation from the stifling restraints of civilization will be by way of the old *coincidentia oppositorum.* All the old barriers and distinctions between Eros and Thanatos, between self and world, between mine and thine, must be broken down, if we are to achieve that androgynous mode of being and that narcis-

---

31. *Ibid.,* p. 307.
32. *Ibid.,* p. 93.
33. *Vide* Norman O. Brown, *Love's Body* (New York: Random House: Vintage Books, 1966).

sistic style of life that the pleasure-principle calls for. And, since it is precisely in schizophrenia that all the repressive boundaries erected by the reality-principle are to be found collapsing, it is, therefore, to a crucifixion of reason and personality, to madness itself, that the human project must be dedicated. This nostrum will no doubt seem expensive, but Mr. Brown considers that we can easily afford it, since, as he tells us — in what is the concluding and perhaps one of the most crucial aphorisms in the book — "everything is only a metaphor. ..." Which is to say — if we pay serious heed to the qualifying adjective "only" — that the world is, at bottom, an affair of phantasm.

Unlike figures so diversely representative of our present moment as LeRoi Jones, Ronald Laing, and Norman Brown, Marshall McLuhan may seem at first to be very far removed indeed from the apocalyptic temper. For here is a man, one will feel, who surely owes his current reputation very largely to the fact that his appetite for the novelties of an electronic age appears to be unsurpassed in our period. Far from conceiving ours to be a time of decadence, the author of *The Gutenberg Galaxy* and *Understanding Media*, it will be said, presents himself as a boundlessly cheerful and buoyant spirit with a great talent for saying "Yea" to the revolutionary "extensions of man" by the most advanced technologies of modern civilization. The culture of "alphabetic man" did, to be sure, breed a richness of spirituality that begins to disappear in an electronic age, for the portable book addresses itself to one reader at a time, and thus the man whose mind is fed by his solitary transactions with the printed page tends thereby to be turned inward upon himself and to be inured in certain habits of self-preoccupation that make for the increase and deepening of the interior life. Which is to say, in Mr. McLuhan's argot, that "typographic" culture was "hot": whereas today things are "cool," for the old ocular culture is being displaced by the new electronic media — whose method is that of the "massage" and the "supersaturated attack," whereby the mind is so "turned on" as to be released from its own hot interiority. But Mr. McLuhan is disinclined to regard the new depthlessness as representing any sort of decline, since he considers it to be simply an inevitable outgrowth of change in the modes of communication about which it would be fruitless to moralize.

Yet, for all of Mr. McLuhan's seeming cheerfulness about the present, his futurism is so radical as to encourage us, nevertheless, to think about the present as though it had precisely the kind of unreality which apocalyptic traditionally attributes to it. That shrewd analyst of fakery, Benjamin DeMott, has noticed how the system works. As he reminds us,[34] if you ask Mr. McLuhan to account for the growth of humanitarian endeavor in the nineteenth century, from the time of Florence Nightingale and Harriet Beecher Stowe onward, his answer will be that the efficient cause was the telegraph. And, since he believes that Hitler's image, had it been projected by television rather than radio, would never have had any mesmerizing effect on the German people, he is prepared to denominate the wireless as the efficient cause of the tragedy suffered by German Jewry under the Third Reich. Or, if he offers any comment on the current racial struggle in this country, it will be some cryptic proposal about the internal-combustion engine being the key factor, since it is "not the expression of moral points of view"[35] but the automobile which is to be counted on to integrate, or to level the differences between, blacks and whites. In short, the strategy involves a great theatricalization of experience that so distances us from the immediacies of historical existence that the world is made to appear (as Mr. DeMott says) a kind of "stunt." Historians, to be sure, may tell us that nineteenth-century philanthropy and the tragedy of German Jewry under Hitler and the racial struggle in America today need to be understood in the light of immensely complicated processes of causation, but the Gospel

---

34. *Vide* Benjamin DeMott, "Understanding M.," in *McLuhan: Hot & Cool*, ed. by Gerald Emanuel Stearn (New York: New American Library: Signet Books, 1969), pp. 240-48.

35. Marshall McLuhan, *Understanding Media: The Extensions of Man* (New York: McGraw-Hill, 1965), p. 221.

"New Heav'ns, New Earth"

According to McLuhan assures us in effect that such counsel will be seen to be only the emptiest pedantry once we have been wafted up into that "Pentecostal condition of universal understanding"[36] which is promised by the coming electrical millennium. For, from that post-historical standpoint, all the exigencies which are a part of our life in historical time will, at worst, appear to signalize only some new shift of technique in the delivery of information — and, at best, will appear to be merely illusory. What is being proposed, in other words, is that we shall begin to be citizens of the New Age, when we give over — to a form of consciousness. And nothing more nicely reveals the radically apocalyptic intention of Mr. McLuhan's myth than his own suggestion that this new form of consciousness — which will "confer a perpetuity of collective harmony and peace" — may be thought of as a kind of "weightlessness."[37]

Now the Negro ideologue LeRoi Jones, the psychiatrist Ronald Laing, the theorist of media Marshall McLuhan, and the philosopher of culture Norman Brown compose what is obviously a very manifold group indeed. Yet each in his own way makes an important kind of gauge of the weather in cultural life of the present time. And what is remarkable is that, despite their many differences of focus and style, they, along with numerous others, are all prompted by the apocalyptic *frisson* to say (with Rimbaud), "Real life is — elsewhere." Nor is this *totaliter aliter* located in any projected rearrangement of concrete historical circumstance: on the contrary, it seems rather to be envisaged as, most essentially, nothing more than a new form of consciousness.

So a certain mystique of inwardness is one leading mark of contemporary apocalyptic. And, given the immense prestige of this persuasion, it should be no cause for wonder that, at the level of concrete morality, a rampant antinomianism is also a conspicuous feature of our period-style. In his provocative book of 1966, *The Triumph of the Therapeutic*, the sociologist Philip Rieff suggests that every culture

---

36. *Ibid.*, p. 80.
37. *Ibid.*

is characterized by a certain pattern of relationship between "the moral demands men make upon themselves" and "the ... remissions by which men release themselves, in some degree, from the strain of conforming" to these demands. He further suggests that, when the relationship between the injunctive and the remissive strains in the life of a people ceases to be genuinely dialectical and "when the releasing or remissive symbolic grows more compelling than the controlling one,"[38] the consequence is cultural revolution. Mr. Rieff wants also to remind us that, in these post-Freudian days of our modern emancipation, in the Age of Psychological Man, our common assumption tends to be that the proper response to the "clinical" fact, whatever it may turn out to be, is "understanding."[39] Which is to say that the wide prevalence today of "the analytic attitude" tends very powerfully to promote a general indifference toward systems of interdiction and commandment, and so indeed it doubtless does. Yet the remissiveness which so emphatically distinguishes the moral tonality of the contemporary scene surely antedates by far the legacy of Freud. For, from Blake to D. H. Lawrence and from Rousseau to André Gide, there is a strong and continuing tendency in modern culture to make normative the recalcitrant idiosyncrasy of the private self and to canonize those primal energies which in *The Marriage of Heaven and Hell* Blake declares to be "one portion of being" and "Prolific." But, of course, in a time when the inclemency of the historical weather leads men to seek the consolations of Apocalypse and when, therefore, the touchstone of the real is to be found in the inwardness of Infinite Subjectivity — in such a time, the antinomian impulse will take on a special imperiousness. For, when inwardness is that which chiefly requires to be nourished and obeyed, the idea of precept, of commandment, of moral imperative, will

---

38. Philip Rieff, *The Triumph of the Therapeutic: Uses of Faith After Freud* (New York: Harper & Row, Inc., 1966), pp. 232-33.
39. *Vide* also Philip Rieff, *Freud: The Mind of the Moralist* (Garden City, N.Y.: Anchor Books, 1961), Chapter X ("The Emergence of Psychological Man").

seem to represent a principle alien to the human spirit, and it will be resisted with the resoluteness which is today encouraged by the cult of everyone doing (as our new patois puts it) his "own thing." Indeed, one feels Irving Howe's estimate to be essentially correct, that no theory of experience is today more seductive than that which he calls *the psychology of unobstructed need* — which says that "men should satisfy those needs which are theirs ... [by learning] to discard or destroy all those obstructions, mostly the result of cultural neurosis, which keep them from satisfying their needs." Nor need costs in this "moral economy ... be entered as a significant item,"[40] since, though my needs may at certain points seem to conflict with yours, in the last analysis, as Norman Brown assures us, "In freedom is fusion"[41] — and, finally, "All flesh shall see it together."[42]

So it is, as Irving Howe suggests, that the psychology of unobstructed need moves us toward a kind of *laissez-faire* economy of the moral life. And one suspects that it is in the light of such an economy that many of our most characteristic cultural styles are now to be understood. If, for example, the *humanum* finds its most essential locus in the infiniteness of subjectivity, then, in the art of painting, it will be assumed that the external world represents a banal gratuitousness which is not worthy of the artist's attention; and thus, instead of painting objects, he will approach his canvas not with an intention "to reproduce, re-design, analyze or 'express' an object, actual or imagined,"[43] but simply with the intention of *doing* something to the canvas itself. In order to keep faith, however, with the pulsations of his own inwardness, such a painter must first bring the history of art to an end, for he wants not only to dispense with everything extrinsic to his own subjectivity but also "with

---

40. Irving Howe, *Decline of the New* (New York: Harcourt, Brace & World, Inc., 1970), p. 253.
41. Norman O. Brown, *op. cit.*, p. 253.
42. *Ibid.*, p. 255.
43. Harold Rosenberg, *The Tradition of the New* (New York: Horizon Press, 1959), p. 25.

drawing, with composition, with color, with texture"[44]: only by radically dismantling in this way the received traditions of art can he take full possession of "the canvas as an arena"[45] in which to explore the limitless interiority of his own existence. The result, of course — in the astonishing work of such artists as Arshile Gorky, Willem de Kooning, Jackson Pollock, Mark Rothko, Clyfford Still, Adolph Gottlieb, and Philip Guston — is the phenomenon that Harold Rosenberg has taught us to speak of as Action Painting, which, despite the various incursions of Pop Art since the early 1960s, is today the reigning American tradition. And what we must perhaps be most struck by in this tradition is the ruthlessness with which it is prepared to dissolve the art work into those "activities of mind [belonging to the painter] that extend beyond the skill involved in ... [the] production"[46] of the work itself. There have been those, of course, who have supposed that, in its extrusion of *things* and its complete abandonment of any representational aim, a composition of de Kooning's or of Barnett Newman's is simply another modern exercise in *l'art pour l'art*. But this is a great misconception, for the Jackson Pollock, say, who hurled paint onto his canvases from a distance had quite given up the old museum conception of art: indeed, in his view, we had reached the end of the history of art, and, in his last years, Pollock in his studio was not so much intending to produce a work of art as to perform an *act*— the result of which, to be sure, would be an artifact but one whose sole purpose would be that of offering some clue to his own turbulent interiority. Which is why Mr. Rosenberg warns us against judging such an art "in terms of schools, styles, form — as if the painter were still concerned with producing a certain kind of object (the work of art), instead of living on the canvas...."[47] The great abstract expressionists of the past twen-

---

44. Harold Rosenberg, *The Anxious Object: Art Today and Its Audience* (New York: Horizon Press, 1964), p. 41.
45. *Ibid.*
46. Harold Rosenberg, *Artworks and Packages* (New York: Horizon Press, 1969), p. 23.
47. Harold Rosenberg, *The Tradition of the New,* p. 28.

ty-five years present us, in other words, with the dazzling paradox of artists to whose work "anything is relevant. ... but art criticism,"[48] since, in the tradition which they have established, the work of art is by way of being dissolved into apocalyptic inwardness: and that inwardness wants to be unobstructed.

But an inwardness wanting to be unobstructed will want also to be released from any such dependence on a *thing* or *object* as characterizes the action painter's relation to his artifact. So it is not surprising that it should have been a young painter, Allan Kaprow, who invented the Happening, when he presented his *18 Happenings in 6 Parts* in October of 1959 at the Reuben Gallery in New York City. Mr. Kaprow and the numerous other young painters and sculptors who joined him in developing this new mode of theatrical extravaganza — Red Grooms, Robert Whitman, Jim Dine, Claes Oldenburg — realized that, though the "action" of an expressionist art is something radically subjective, it does, nevertheless, evolve into an artifact; and they understood that, once that artifact leaves the artist's studio and enters the art market, "the old art game ... [is] going on as usual."[49] So they undertook to sunder the act from the object altogether — and the result was the Happening, whose aesthetic of indeterminacy, when combined with Antonin Artaud's program for a Theatre of Cruelty, found its most celebrated expression in the 1960s in the Living Theatre of Julian Beck and his wife Judith Malina.

The Becks took with the grimmest seriousness Arstaud's polemic against "masterpieces," believing that to submit a troup of actors to a text was to take a stand against "life," whereas they were missionaries in behalf of a "free" theatre whose liberating saturnalia would regenerate both audience and actors through their joint participation in "grope-ins" and "love zaps" and the various other provided revels. So in their most renowned frolic, the spectacle called *Paradise Now*, the last pretense at any sort of disciplined stagecraft

---

48. *Ibid.*
49. Harold Rosenberg, *Artworks and Packages*, p. 224.

was given up, as members of the audience were invited across the footlights to join the actors in peeling off as much of their clothing as the local police would permit and to engage in bacchanalian rites of cosseting and love-play — the whole occasion culminating in exhortations to take all this love and brotherhood "into the streets," to invade the jails, to release the prisoners, to stop the war in Vietnam, and to deliver the cities over into the hands of "the people." And, though the Living Theatre is today a casualty of its own excess, the Dionysiac Happenings arranged by the Becks throughout the 1960s still stand as the largest emblem of that "third theatre" (as Robert Brustein called it[50]) whose apocalyptic drunkenness has so enthralled the radical young in recent years.

The climate which is represented by the anti-art programs of radical painting and radical theatre is, of course, the milieu to which much of recent literature belongs: there, too, as Ihab Hassan's metaphor reminds us,[51] Orpheus is being dismembered, for the styles of contemporary art and literature "are picked up everywhere at the same instant — and shot back and forth ... as items of the total communications package."[52] And this is a package which is chiefly delivering now Apocalypse. That charming scapegrace who is the hero of Saul Bellow's *Herzog* urges us to "get it out of our heads that this is a doomed time, that we are waiting for the end, and the rest of it. ... We love apocalypses too much," he says — "and crisis ethics and florid extremism with its thrilling language." But such counsel, when it has occasionally been voiced over these past years, has not been felt, apparently, by the literary imagination— or at least by those writers who touch the period's deepest passions — to have the potency of Relevance. For none of those who seem to carry the period-style — whether it be William Burroughs or

---

50. *Vide* Robert Brustein, *The Third Theatre* (New York: Alfred A. Knopf, 1969).
51. *Vide* Ihab Hassan, *The Dismemberment of Orpheus: Toward a Postmodern Literature* (New York: Oxford University Press, 1971).
52. Harold Rosenberg, *op. cit.*, p. 13.

"New Heav'ns, New Earth"

Thomas Pynchon or Kurt Vonnegut or Joseph Heller or John Barth or Donald Barthelme or the Norman Mailer of *An American Dream* — strike us as writers who "believe in 'history' as a form of truth."[53] Indeed, theirs is a literature, as one of its apologists has said, which walks "a fine line between...the 'orbiting ecstasy of a true paranoia' and the terrible blankness of the quotidian, between the imagination of disaster and no imagination at all."[54] They want, of course, as John Barth in effect proposes that they should, to deal with ultimacies, "in an age of ultimacies and 'final solutions' — at least *felt* ultimacies, in everything from weaponry to theology, the celebrated dehumanization of society, and the history of the novel...."[55] But it is their very commitment to ultimacies that sometimes has the consequence in their fictions of the solid ground of palpable fact being stripped from beneath our feet, so that we — and they — are left suspended in the void of a nutty and depleted universe which is at the point of being inundated by absolute disaster.

The young protagonist of Heller's *Catch-22,* John Yossarian, who is attached as a bombardier to an American airforce base on an island off the Italian coast during the Second World War, finds himself entrapped in a world where all the effective powers — the German enemy, his own colonel who obdurately sends out his force on increasingly more dangerous missions — seem joined in a conspiracy against him: even the cells of his own body are not to be trusted, for, since each is infectible by some fatal malady, each is "a potential traitor and foe." As first one and then another of Yossarian's friends meet death in various ways, there comes a time when he realizes that "They've got all my pals" and decides, therefore, that, unless he makes a separate peace, he stands no chance of survival. For the catch to the terrible

---

53. The phrase, lifted out of its original context, is Alfred Kazin's: *vide* his "The Literary Sixties, When the World Was Too Much With Us," *The New York Times Book Review,* 21 December 1969, p. 3.

54. Morris Dickstein, "Allen Ginsberg and the 60's," *Commentary,* Vol. 49, No. 1 (January, 1970), p. 68.

55. John Barth, "The Literature of Exhaustion," *The Atlantic,* Vol. 220, No. 2 (August, 1967), p. 30.

joke of life on this "lousy earth" — the great global catch which the novel calls "Catch-22" — is simply that nothing makes any sense, that nowhere is there justice or decency, and that a man is permitted to do anything therefore he can manage to bring off with impunity. So, at the end of the novel, Yossarian deserts this maniacal Armageddon and heads for Sweden, about which he knows nothing except that it is a place where there is no war. "I've been fighting all along to save my country," he says. "Now I'm going to fight a little to save myself."

Or, again, the historical figure of the obscure American poet of the Colonial period, Ebenezer Cooke — whose adventures John Barth fictively chronicles in *The Sot-Weed Factor* — finds the Maryland of his time to be "a motley, mindless world," "a Heraclitean flux," where a man is only a sort of "mayfly flitting down the winds of Chaos." And it is clear that Mr. Barth wants to offer his invented Colonial America as an image of our own time in which a sensitive artist might still make the testimony made by young Cooke, that

> all Things were in such Confusion,
> I thought the World at its Conclusion.

Similarly, the narrator of Thomas Pynchon's *V.* suggests that the veracity of the novel's story is easily to be checked, simply by looking into "any yearly Almanac, under 'Disasters'. ..." And, as we follow Herbert Stencil in his search for the identity of the woman mysteriously referred to in his father's journal as "V," it appears after a time that, indeed, any confirming of the reported facts would be by way of some almanac of disasters. For, as Stencil roams through the "rathouse of history's rags and straws," the world is unveiled as a place so dominated by lunacy and so overshadowed by the imminence of annihilation that the career of humankind can only be construed as a "progression toward inanimateness."

Even a novelist like James Baldwin, whose profoundly ethnic concerns might be expected to guarantee a certain exemption from apocalyptic insobrieties, is to be found in his novel of 1968, *Tell Me How Long the Train's Been Gone*, willfully arranging a climax which projects a great *Sturm und Drang*. The young black militant, Christopher, says (on behalf of his ancestral community) to his friend, the distinguished Negro actor Leo Proudhammer, who is the novel's protagonist, "... you got to agree that we need us some guns" — to which Proudhammer says, "Yes. ... But we're outnumbered, you know." And Christopher's answer — which one takes to be Mr. Baldwin's — is simply "Shit."

The excremental vision is, of course, the controlling vision in the fiction of that high priest of today's Underground, William Burroughs, for to the characters with whom his novels are peopled to be in time is to be in "shit." True, they are figures made special by their entrapment within the blighted underworld of drug addiction. But when one's lunch is indeed "naked" — in, as Mr. Burroughs says, that "frozen moment when everyone sees what is on the end of every fork"[56] — he expects us to behold a universal human reality in the excruciating affliction of the junky. For its "algebra of need" is the algebra of the human condition — absolute hunger, absolute dependence, and thus absolute defenselessness. The horrible exigencies of the drug market — where the addict is totally at the mercy of the junk merchant — are, in other words, only a particular case of the general human experience which is everywhere, as William Burroughs sees it, an affair of men being "turned on," by money and power and violence and sex, of being at the mercy of some "total need" and of being therefore at the mercy of somebody's junk (even if that junk be only the "white junk" of conventional righteousness). So the world, as exhibited in *Naked Lunch* and *The Nova Express* and *The Soft Machine* and *The Ticket that Exploded,* is a seedy and disreputable slum, under the rule of the Pusher, the Mob, the Police — and its pandemic gangsterism is hurtling it ever more surely towards ultimate doom. Which is why it is suggested at a certain point in *Nova Express* that the most appropriate tack

---

56. William S. Burroughs, "Introduction," *Naked Lunch* (New York: Grove Press [Black Cat Edition], 1966), p. xxxvii.

for the artist will be to take "orgasm noises ... and cut them in with torture and accident groans and screams ... and operating-room jokes ... and flicker sex and torture film right with it."

Now such writers as William Burroughs and Joseph Heller and Thomas Pynchon are, of course, being presented here as emblems. Manifestly, they are not, to be sure, representative of the full range of contemporary American literature, and anyone can easily compose his own list of important poets and novelists — people, for example, like Elizabeth Bishop, Richard Wilbur, James Dickey; and Ralph Ellison, Saul Bellow, John Updike — who express other types of commitment and belief. But to speak of Allen Ginsberg and LeRoi Jones, of William Burroughs and Ken Kesey, of Joseph Heller and Thomas Pynchon, of John Barth and Norman Mailer, is to speak of those who, along with many others, variously represent one very powerful movement in our literary life today which distinguishes itself by the zeal with which it is stirring up a great tide of desperate visions of the End which is upon us. And, if any attempt be made at interrogating this literature, if it be suggested (as Lionel Trilling did a few years ago) that art may not "always tell the truth or the best kind of truth and ... [may] not always point out the right way,"[57] there are equally powerful currents in our recent criticism which will insist that a literary formulation of experience is "beyond negation" and that, indeed, to approach it dialectically, as if it might be obliged to prove its case, is only to sponsor (in Susan Sontag's phrase) a "revenge of the intellect upon art."[58]

Despite the remove of a generation at which we now stand from the cultural polemic that accompanied the onset of the Second World War, even the most ardent devotee of *Geistesgeschichte* will surely not have forgotten the mistakes that were made in those years by men like Archibald MacLeish

---

57. Lionel Trilling, *Beyond Culture: Essays on Literature and Learning* (New York: Viking Press, 1965), p. xvii.
58. Susan Sontag, *Against Interpretation* (New York: Farrar, Straus & Giroux, 1966), p. 7.

and Van Wyck Brooks and Bernard DeVoto, who were eager to account for the period's disarray in terms of what they took to be the *trahison des clercs* represented by the intellectual and literary vanguard of *l'entre deux guerres*. As the world began to be overrun by the armies of Hitler at the end of the 30's, these men — Mr. MacLeish in *The Irresponsibles* (1940), Brooks in *The Opinions of Oliver Allston* (1941), and DeVoto in *The Literary Fallacy* (1944) — turned to the principal representatives of modern literary intelligence, in order to determine how steadfastly they had upheld the pieties of democratic culture. Poets like Pound and Eliot and novelists like Joyce and Faulkner and Hemingway were marched into court and were found to be (in Brooks's term) "rattlesnakes," for, as it was charged, in having failed actively to celebrate the democratic spirit, they had in effect betrayed it. So it was with an angry shrewishness that these American critics condemned the whole tradition of modernism, and their claim was that, indeed, this tradition had prepared the way for the onslaught directed by the Nazis on the funded heritage of democratic liberalism.

So vulgar an exercise in scapegoating as was represented by our "democratic humanists" of a generation ago can, of course, at this late date be counted on to disprove itself by the absurdly simplistic demonism of its theory of historical causation. And no proximate account of recent cultural ferment will commend itself. But surely the wrongheadedness of Brooks and MacLeish and DeVoto is not by way of being reinstated, when it is remarked that a significant part in the establishment of a certain mood on the American scene of the present time has been played by such writers and ideologues as have been drawn into this chronicle — by such thinkers and publicists (not all of whom are natives) as Norman Brown, Marshall McLuhan, R. D. Laing, Theodore Roszak, and Charles Reich; and by literary figures like LeRoi Jones and William Burroughs and Allen Ginsberg and Joseph Heller. The mood which finds its major representatives in writers and artists of this sort is a mood of eschatological excitement and anxiety: it is a frame of mind which is ruled by a sense of the present age as a *fin de siècle,* as a time approaching the end-point of its course, when we are at the edge of some great cliff. And, when this attitude is translated into the field of actual politics, the anonymous voice that begins to be heard is very much like that voice which is repeatedly heard in the section of *The Waste Land* called "A Game of Chess," where the Cockneys Bill and Lou and May are forgathered in some London pub the proprietor of which, being eager to close up for the night, keeps saying, "HURRY UP PLEASE ITS TIME". Hurry up, please: it's time — time, that is, for some great leap (past the cliff edge perhaps), for ours is an extreme situation. It is such an urgent and ominous cry as this that we have constantly heard amidst much of the furious political skirmishing that has disrupted the American scene in recent years — hurry up, please: it's time! And though no simple line of causation is to be traced from an Allen Ginsberg or a Norman Brown to the political excesses of the New Left, one may at least remark a certain consistency between the desperately operatic style often characteristic of leftist politics today and the apocalyptic mood which has been so actively promoted by what Mr. Trilling calls the "adversary culture."[59]

Only the blind and the deaf (or the simply wicked) can, of course, be unembarrassed by the squalor that disfigures much of the social and political fabric of American life in our time. The terrible nether-world of the black urban ghettos, the immense and stubbornly self-perpetuating poverty across the land, the stupid inertia and mediocrity of our governmental bureaucracies, the muck and mess and fumes that contaminate our great cities — in all this, and more, any movement of dissent today can easily find its enabling charter. But what is striking about the "mystical militancy" (as Michael Harrington has phrased it[60]) of much recent radical protest is not that it should have pronounced a word of severe judgment but that it should so frequently have adopted what the Negro civil-rights tactician, Bayard Rustin,

---

59. Lionel Trilling, *op. cit.,* pp. xv-xvi.
60. *Vide* Michael Harrington, "The Mystical Militants," *The New Republic,* Vol. 154, No. 8 (19 February 1966), pp. 20-22.

calls "a 'no-win' policy."[61] Since its emergence a little more than a decade ago, the New Left has, to be sure, at many crucial junctures expressed an extraordinarily moving passion for public decency and civic virtue, and we shall not soon forget the generous idealism which it poured into the civil-rights movement in the early 60's or the resolute heroism with which it mobilized opposition to the Vietnam war. But, as it would now seem, the kind of vision that lay behind, for example, the famous *Port Huron Statement* was so radically utopian as to be unable to brook the disappointments inevitably brought by the failure of the millennium quickly to come; and thus, at some point along the way in the 1960s, since "the system" had not collapsed, it began to be decided, under the tutelage of Herbert Marcuse, that the only remaining alternative to "participatory democracy" was a kind of Guevarist "revolution" by way of what has sometimes been called the Permanent Demonstration. For this project the essential technique was conceived to be that of "polarizing" the national community into extremes whose bitterness would have the effect of so paralyzing the established social mechanisms as to permit the new radicals to "organize" the Apocalypse. The whole fantasia was pungently — and typically — expressed by one young man, a student at Rutgers, who declared: "I'm a nihilist! I'm proud of it! I want to fuck this goddam country. Destroy it! No hope, not in fifty years. Tactics? It's too late.... Let's break what we can. Make as many answer as we can. Tear them apart."[62] It is in such tones that the "true believers" address the nation, and they are to be found here and there in the many diverse sects which the New Left has spawned in recent years. Their indulgence in actual violence, though it has occasionally been reckless, has, to be sure, no doubt more often than not only been "theoretic," but it has perhaps, as Irving Howe suggests, been "thereby all the more irresponsible."[63]

---

61. Bayard Rustin, "From Protest to Politics: The Future of the Civil Rights Movement," *Commentary,* Vol. 39, No. 2 (February, 1965), p. 28.
62. Quoted in Dotson Rader, "Princeton Weekend with the SDS," *The New Republic,* Vol. 157, No. 24 (9 December 1967), pp. 15-16.
63. Irving Howe, *Steady Work,* p. 70.

Nathan A. Scott, Jr.

We live, then, it would seem, in a time when many of the most prestigious agencies of our culture would encourage us to slouch — or to dash — toward a New Jerusalem; and a mood which has thus been established finds its correlative, at the level of concrete morality, in a "psychology of unobstructed need" and a "politics of ecstasy." Now in a period when American philosophy, in obedience to its English Nestors in the world of Oxbridge, is doing little more, as it were, than analyzing the structure of sentences, it might well have been supposed that at least the theological community could be counted on to mount a significant debate with the new apocalypticism. Mere querulousness is never, of course, on any occasion an adequate response to cultural reality, and it is not just spleen, therefore, to which one would have expected the religious community to give utterance: indeed, it has tended too frequently in the past toward that sort of irrelevance. On the contrary, in an age when much of cultural and political life is controlled by an impulse "to flee from the radically demanding historical hour" into an apocalyptic world of inwardness and millennialism, it might have been supposed that the religious community would find its mission in part to be that of sustaining a sense of the dignity of our life in the historical order. The Christian imagination certainly will keep a lively sense of the perennial tension between the *civitas terrena* and the *civitas dei,* but, when it is fully in possession of its biblical roots, it will not conceive the distinction between the two cities to be a matter of the difference between terrestrial existence and some "otherworldly" life in "another country." For what Augustine speaks of as the *civitas dei* does, in the New Testament, stand simply for that mode of receiving and acting in "this world" which Jesus of Nazareth brought forward as a new possibility: it represents, in other words, not another *kosmos* but, rather, this present age, this universe already at our disposal, as it will be when the life of man conforms to that mode of being-in the world embodied in Jesus of Nazareth. Which is to say that New Testament eschatology is far "closer to the prophetic than to the apocalyptic tradition,"[64]

---

64. Carl Michalson, *Worldly Theology: The Hermeneutical Focus of an Historical Faith* (New York: Charles Scribner's Sons, 1967), p. 205.

for, when it speaks about the end of the world, it is mainly speaking not about a cosmological event but an historical happening — namely, the radical alteration in the shape of human life that occurs when it submits itself obediently to the will of God, as His will is decisively disclosed in the pattern of life presented by Jesus Christ. And thus, in a period when the hiatus between our hopes for the human City and their fulfillment makes frustration a central human experience — in such a period, it might have been supposed that the theological community, given its commitment to the dignity of our life in the historical order, would be found attempting soberly to confront us with the duties thrust upon us by the present age, and attempting to dissuade us from "allowing ... [our duties] to be defined by either our hopes or our fears."[65]

This is an expectation, however, which has been actualized only very rarely, and what is surely striking about many of our younger theologians is the ardency with which they, too, have joined the "Dionysiac pack." After dancing in the early 60's a strange sort of jig on the grave of God, they want now, many of them, theologies of festivity and play, of fantasy and pentecostalism and the psychedelic experience; and there is perhaps much in these regions of theological inquiry that deserves to claim our sympathy. But, nevertheless, the general abstention of our most gifted younger theologians from any significant debate with the New Sensibility is a notable fact of contemporary theology.[66]

It may well be, however, that the most creative response which the theological imagination might make to the Babel presented by the contemporary scene would be that of urging at least some reappraisal of a central dictum coming down from the greatest apocalyptist in modern literature — namely, the assertion made by that famous aphorism in William Blake's *The Marriage of Heaven and Hell* which says:

---

65. Reinhold Niebuhr, *Discerning the Signs of the Times* (New York: Charles Scribner's Sons, 1946), p. 92.

66. One exception at least is offered by the Roman Catholic thinker Michael Novak: *vide* his "The Volatile Counter-Culture," *Christianity and Crisis,* Vol. XXX, No. 9 (25 May 1970), pp. 107-13.

Nathan A. Scott, Jr.

"The tygers of wrath are wiser than the horses of instruction."

Like many of the focal figures of the Romantic movement, Blake found his central theme in what he took to be the desiccation of the human spirit threatened by the imperialist ambitions of modern rationalism, and his great prayer (as he said on one occasion in a letter to his friend Thomas Butts) was that God might keep us "From Single vision & Newtons sleep." Blake felt that the world of his own time, in its fascination by the legacy of "Bacon & Newton & Locke," was a world about to fall into the grip of a great malignant, dehumanizing power. And that which was about to be trodden down was what he chose to call *Energy*. "Energy," says the IVth Plate of *The Marriage of Heaven and Hell*, "is the only life and is from the Body," and it is declared to be "Eternal Delight" — whose eternal "contrary" is "Reason." Blake says, to be sure, that "Without Contraries [there] is no progression," and, in speaking of Reason as "the bound or outward circumference of Energy," he seems to be implying that it redeems its opposite from chaos; yet his predominant tendency is to represent Reason as a principle of repressiveness. A bird, as it "cuts the airy way," has its flight controlled, he will admit, by "the bound or outward circumference of Energy." But, normally, the life-principle finds its contrary in that imperious "Governor" which is Reason, for no sooner are the primal energies of life contained within this "bound or outward circumference" than they are negated. And since Hell is, indeed, nothing more than the natural vitalities of the world restrained and inhibited, the whole notion of a "marriage" between Heaven and Hell is in part a stroke of irony: Hell is, in other words, Energy restrained, for, once it is restrained, it is destroyed. True, the rationalists and the dogmatists specialize in the restraint of Desire, but they "do so because theirs is weak enough to be restrained": men who are only half-alive perform no great sacrifice when they repress the dynamic impulses for the sake of some specious security. But Heaven is not reserved for the people who have thus triumphed over themselves, for they are those in whom "the Reasoning Power ... Negatives every thing." Prudence, in short, is not one of Blake's cardinal virtues, since, in his perspective, if the human spirit is to be given any kind of chance at all, it must be liberated from all the cages that Reason would devise. "The road of excess leads to the palace of wisdom." So, then, however fearful tigers may be, if they represent untamed Energy and horses domesticated Reason, and if "Prudence is a rich, ugly old maid courted by Incapacity," let us conclude that "The tygers of wrath are wiser than the horses of instruction."

But does the road of excess *always* lead to the palace of wisdom, and are the tigers of wrath *always* wiser than the horses of instruction? No doubt the fury of strife and "the ... siege of contraries" are sometimes a fine thing—but are they *always*? In a letter of March 1819 to his brother and sister-in-law, George and Georgiana, Keats had occasion to remark that "though a quarrel in the Streets is a thing to be hated, the energies displayed in it are fine. ..."[67] But let us make the supposition that Irving Howe invites: Mr. Howe says:

> Suppose that, after reading Mailer's "The White Negro," my "thing" happens to be that, to "dare the unknown" (as Mailer puts it), I want to beat in the brains of an aging candy-store keeper; or after reading LeRoi Jones, I should like to cut up a few Jews, whether or not they keep stores — how is anyone going to argue against the outpouring of my need? .... Acting through violence I will at least have realized myself, for I will have entered (to quote Mailer again) "a new relation with the police" and introduced "a dangerous element" into my life; thereby, too, I will have escaped the cell block of regulation which keeps me from the free air of self-determination.[68]

Yet are we not obliged to raise some question about the energy displayed in such quarrels in the streets? Is it necessarily something fine and splendid simply because it is energy? And do not the energies of our human nature seem

---

67. *The Letters of John Keats,* ed. by Maurice Buxton Forman, 4th ed. (London: Oxford University Press, 1952), p. 316.
68. Irving Howe, *Decline of the New,* pp. 253-54.

Nathan A. Scott, Jr.

to require — at least when we look down into "the foul rag-and-bone shop of the heart" — some "bound or outward circumference"? These are surely questions which cannot easily be suppressed. But they are questions in the answering of which little help comes today from those tigers of wrath into whose hands we have very nearly been delivered. For they are convinced that we are now in the Last Days, when preparation must be made for the New Age which is to come; and they are also convinced that, since the Kingdom of Heaven is to be found in the pure inwardness of Infinite Subjectivity, it is the "unrepressed life" that must be chosen: that is to say, inwardness must be utterly free and unobstructed, if we are to achieve that Pentecostal beatitude which is beyond all the vexatious contingencies of the historical hour. And it seems often to be supposed that, if inwardness is released, if energy is unshackled, "a quarrel in the Streets" may be a very fine thing indeed, may in fact even hurry us along toward that "Sabbath of Eternity ... when time no more shall be." To be sure, one may undertake to challenge such a catechist as Norman Mailer to present some genuine vindication of that ethic which he likes to call "existential" — but then, on finding himself in the dock, one can imagine him, with his marvelously roguish charm, choosing only to say what Norman Brown says, that "everything is only a metaphor."

Now the horses of instruction are doubtless never to be expected to have the bewitching glamor of the tigers of wrath, for they do not scarify us out of the countries of darkness: their function is the humbler one of keeping us on a not too devious track within the established roads of our common journey. They are creatures not very fierce or aggressive, and even the spirited stallion will not seem to represent so well as a tiger that lusty boldness and ferocity which the apocalyptic mind conceives to be necessary for life on the extremest boundaries of the world. But, though the horses of instruction may not command the puissant militancy of the tigers of wrath, they are, in any event, the more effective guardians of that virtue whose loss is precisely what gives rise to the apocalyptic enterprise. And it is the virtue which may most simply be denominated as the strength of endurance.

Apocalyptic, as a distinctive way of managing reality, is, of course, a method which the imagination tends to employ precisely in those moments when the realities of history seem to be quite unmanageable. As it was with ancient Jewish apocalypticism, so it has been with all subsequent outbursts of apocalyptic hysteria, that the convulsive embrace of some vision of the End has been prompted by a sense of the utter intolerableness of historical actuality. Zion has been destroyed, Babylon has been spared: there ensues a great collapse of confidence in the possibility of history taking any new and more hopeful direction: so the apocalyptist, finding the world in its present form to be unendurable, proposes, with a certain heroic gesture, a sort of *amor fati* as the way out. The "radically demanding historical hour" being intolerable, he looks toward the time when time no more shall be, when the world in which the Chosen People are so cruelly disadvantaged will have been replaced by a New Jerusalem; and his resistance to history, his eagerness in fact to get out of it altogether, is his way of dealing with a history which is felt no longer to be manageable. So it is that his testimonies represent "tracts for bad times."

And ours is, to be sure, in many ways an age which is a very bad time indeed. But the times of human life perhaps, viewed under certain perspectives, are always bad. Some of our days fall under the sway of the *demon meridianus,* and others are poisoned by that *taedium vitae* which is brought by the disease of *acedia,* when "the infirm glory of the positive hour" is gone and when "the visionary gleam" is fled. There is, in other words, the boredom — and there is also the horror: as Pascal says, "The last act is tragic, however happy all the rest of the play is; at the last a little earth is thrown upon our head, and that is the end for ever." And antecedent to this last act are all the tests and trials that make up our common lot, of self-doubt and loneliness and the myriad anxieties about health and family and career with which we live from day to day. Brightness is often fallen from the skies; and the nonchalance wherewith in the daily round we are enabled, nevertheless, to get on with the conduct of life is an affair of what Paul Tillich spoke of as "the courage to be."[69]

The horses of instruction, of course, are many and diverse; and they may be expected, therefore, to propose to the moral imagination various forms of courage as normative for the human venture. But, whether we are summoned to the *andreīa* (manliness) of Aristotle or the *apatheia* of the Stoics or the *fortitudo* of the Scholastics or the *Entschlossenheit* (resoluteness) of Heidegger, Tillich is surely right in his insistence that the question of courage is, at bottom, a theological question. For since courage is, as he says (in his distinctly Germanic fashion), "the self-affirmation of being in spite of the fact of nonbeing," any explication of the possibility of courage must involve an exploration of how — despite "the nonbeing which is experienced in the anxiety of fate and death" — it is yet possible for one to be "rooted in a power of being that is greater than the power of oneself and the power of one's world."[70]

Here, indeed, it would seem, is the ultimately decisive issue with which we must always be confronted by any apocalyptic insurgency. For what it betokens, essentially, is a failure of courage, of the kind of courage that permits us to endure and to reckon with the conditioned and imperfect reality of ourselves and the world to which we are committed by the logic of our history. And thus the challenge with which we are presented by our present moment in American culture is one which invites us to seek again for the ultimate grounds on which we may repose some confidence in the possibility of our finding the world, unsatisfactory as it is, a place wherein, nevertheless, we may undertake to do battle with Moloch and whomever or whatever else it may be that threatens our commitment to the human enterprise, of dwelling in historical time.

---

69. *Vide* Paul Tillich, *The Courage to Be* (New Haven: Yale University Press, 1952).

70. *Ibid.*, p. 155.

"New Heav'ns, New Earth"

This is, of course, a challenge which calls for a very large philosophical and theological effort, and it is to be hoped that such an effort will increasingly claim our best systematic thinkers in the coming years. For, otherwise, one suspects that we may not reckon well with "an iron time of doubts, disputes, distractions, fears."

20

THE AMERICAN ESTABLISHMENT, THE CIVILIZING ARTS, AND PHILOSOPHY
Herbert W. Schneider

A REMARK BY HENRY THOREAU FROM THE SHORES OF WALden Pond, made over a century ago, has been haunting me. I shall use it as a text for the following sermon. He observed that "highly improved machines were being run by unimproved men." If such a state of affairs could be observed in the New England of Thoreau, how much more conspicuous it is today! The most wonderful machinery, intricate and powerful beyond the dreams of the nineteenth century, accompanied by their highly expert technicians, are being employed today for the most destructive and atrocious deeds. Barbarous violence, clearly uncivilized behavior, have become common traits of what we dare to call our "culture." For a few years it seemed to be the very existence of mankind that was threatened; today, unless I am too optimistic, it is not human existence, but civilization that is in danger. The unimproved state of our behavior leads us to fear our magnified power, for we are gradually becoming highly developed savages. The kind of human relations that we still label as "negotiation" and as techniques of "bargaining" or "business," the political strategies that a few decades ago were called "pressure politics," have developed such atrocious forms of intimidation and cruelty that we must face them honestly as beastly brutality, less worthy of human beings than our so-called primitive cultures. It is surely evident that if mankind is to achieve anything resembling a humane civilization, our unimproved characters and policies must be drastically improved. If we were unconscious of our desperate situation, if we did not know that we have abundant resources for happiness, our state of affairs would be less tragic. But this apparent inability to do what we know we have the power to do is the incredible tragedy that stares us in the face.

We possess well-established institutions and traditions on which we have traditionally relied as civilizing arts. Among our varied establishments, good and bad, we have been accustomed to respect a few as having the greatest responsibility for improving us as human beings. These establishments are the institutions of: domestication, education, devotion, science, and fine arts. Other establishments, such as the institutions of entertainment, recreation, sport, are less essentially civilizing arts. However, by their character we can most readily judge the level of civilization that we have attained. Government and Industry, too, are, according to our traditions, responsible primarily for making us secure and prosperous, rather than civilized and happy. They are essentially insurance for peace and security. Unfortunately our investment in this insurance is not yielding the intended benefits; instead, we have collective insecurity. It is our families, our schools, our churches, our institutes of research and fine arts, on which the heaviest and primary responsibility rests for improving us as human beings. We are therefore obliged to turn to them and to ask them seriously: What are you doing for civilization?

Our American establishment is fortunate: none of our institutions is more firmly grounded than our schools — both elementary and advanced. These are not easily destroyed. Those inexperienced and impractical revolutionaries who

The American Establishment

trusted the theory that American capitalism could best be destroyed by attacking our colleges and universities, which, according to their theory, are "soft" and which could readily be remade from "scratch," have learned by this time, I trust, that they miscalculated badly. Neither our private nor our public colleges and universities are nearly as vulnerable as the American dollar. Like everything, they are in financial trouble; but they are the most deeply established, morally grounded, of our institutions. The students know very well that, though these establishments are responsible to their students, they cannot be run by students, until the students have been sufficiently "improved." By the time they are graduated, students begin to be competent to help the next generation; but then it is usually too late. If anything is well established in our culture, it is not only our faith in education but also our awareness that education is a difficult art, in fact the basic process whereby both children and adults become civilized. No matter how many mistakes we may make in educational art and theory, we are more determined than ever to maintain systematized education as our basic hope and ultimate resource. Of this there can be no reasonable doubt.

Our families are more vulnerable. I need not explain, for the facts and the problems are only too familiar. When both parents are "gainfully" employed, or as they now say "liberated," much of the civilizing work of the family is thrown upon the schools. The hard-pressed schools, therefore, must engage in so much moral education, esthetic education, physical education, civic education, and even religious education, that they must often beg the parents to teach reading, writing, and arithmetic. The baby-sitters might help in this emergency, if they were competent, and if they did not have so much "home work" to do for their schooling. Under such circumstances there are many educators, even at the college level, who believe that they must emphasize what they call "basic" education rather than "higher" education; and if "basic" here means "basic for civilization," we are lucky, for the chances are against it.

Herbert W. Schneider

This pressure becomes most acute for the universities. In addition to their traditional functions as centers of research and fine arts, they must assume many, more elementary, burdens. Most serious is the fact that there are few professional students and today teachers that are less professional. The so-called students honestly have much more pressing problems than their studies; they must find peace before they can concentrate on education. When students are escapees from both families and politics, the colleges and universities are in danger of becoming, at best, monasteries and at worst, centers for the prolongation of immaturity.

Even older than civilization itself are religious institutions. These have a long and bitter experience in what it takes to become civilized. At present, many of them lack both the educational resources and the financial means to take a leading part in civilizing themselves and in improving human beings. There is a thriving abundance of uncivilized religion that is an educational liability as well as a disgrace to a great tradition and to an inspired gospel. But the notion that currently circulates within the so-called "intelligentsia" that it would improve civilization if religion were abolished is singularly unenlightened and hopelessly impractical. For better or for worse, religion, too, is deeply grounded in our culture and more deeply the more it becomes disestablished. There is sufficient evidence of religious reform and improvement today, as in the past, to convince any reasonable person that it has great vitality and also that it can be an important agency of civilization. Religions have always been at their best and most useful on the parish level. It is the neighborhood and the congregation that are the normal center of civilized devotion and devotions. Therefore, the destruction of neighborliness and neighborhoods by our great cities has created very serious problems for our religious institutions. It is this circumstance that makes the civilizing functions of religious bodies at once very important and very difficult. Public communion is and should be a civilizing part of a community spirit and center. To maintain and perfect the

The American Establishment

public arts of communion is still a powerful privilege and public responsibility of our religious bodies. It seems to me foolish, under present circumstances, that churches should aim at being and having schools. They should be educational institutions, to be sure, but they have their own powerful and beautiful arts to contribute to civilization, without transforming themselves into schools. Communion is not classroom discussion, preaching is not teaching (though it may be a kind of editorializing), and in general, the coming together as a congregation into the public presence of God — these are all significant forms of neighborly sociability and decency quite different from schools. The need for such devotions and services is only too evident. Whatever may happen to theology, religion is certainly well established and useful in our present crisis. But the task of exercising spiritual, educational, civilized leadership today is very difficult. Nobody knows this better than the clergy.

Under all these discouraging circumstances, we are apt to complain to the government and to expect government to be a clearinghouse for all public problems — a kind of universal service station. Unfortunately governments have the financial resources and moral willingness to undertake all kinds of "services" for which they are neither competent nor in fact responsible. After all, government is politics, and our party-politics is low enough on the scale of fine arts to be evidently in no position to shoulder such enormous and such civilized responsibilities. Politicians become the scapegoats for the whole misery of the establishment. This is not fair to them, nor prudent for us.

The responsibility and the privilege of making us more civilized falls more directly on our so-called *cultural* institutions, than on our political, legal, and commercial systems. Somehow, I know not how or when, these traditional institutions must learn to appropriate and employ for civilizing ends the new media and machines with which our inventors have endowed us. They cannot afford to put on a superior air, to draw away in disdain behind academic or ecclesiastical or domestic walls in order not to be polluted by politics, journalism, television, movies, autos, computers, bohemians and the rest of our recently improved machinery. It would be a tragic mistake to follow the example of Thoreau. In order to improve himself he abandoned all improved machinery, and relying on a borrowed axe and a few books lived under a crude shelter in the woods of Walden Pond. There he satirized the railroad and the poor "unimproved" laborers that were laying the tracks. Such high barbism and lofty isolation solves no problems. It is hard on both the improved machines and the unimproved men, even though it states the problem dramatically. And on the other hand to assume a laissez-faire policy toward the new improvements on the assumption that in time they will civilize themselves if let alone is a now discredited and fallacious theory that has proven disastrous. The present clash between the new and the old elements of our culture is bound to be temporary, but their integration into a genuine progress is not an automatic process, either in nature or culture; it involves serious work and intelligence. It is quite possible for both elements to become more decadent than they are.

But enough of this dreary detail and superfluous sermon! It does not require philosophy to feel the burden of our present predicament. I turn now to my colleagues in philosophy and ask: How can we be useful? It is certainly not the responsibility of philosophers to save us. On the other hand, it is no virtue in a philosopher to be irresponsible. For what can we reasonably be held responsible?

Philosophy has never been institutionalized and probably never will be. Thinking philosophically is an individual chore for an independent mind. By tradition and profession philosophers are supposed to raise and clarify problems, not to solve them. Clarification is not cure, as it is supposed to be in some cases of psychoanalysis. To diagnose our troubles as a physician can, with the expectation of restoring us to health, is not within the competence of philosophers. For practical help we should be able to turn to the civilized arts and the behavioral sciences; they are gradually admitting their responsibilities and even their shortcomings. Philosophers have the more modest task of trying to expose confusion, fallacies, non-sense, and evils. Their criticism is supposed to be enlightening and disconcerting. Such clarification is supposed to be a form of critical honesty, frankness, sincerity — calling a spade a spade. There is a genuine utility in such clarification; it may make us better aware of where our troubles are located, may improve our perspective and our orientation, but it does not cure our troubles. If our trouble were only confusion, philosophy might have restorative powers. But clarification of our general unimproved status is a complicated task, involving more than reason, and raising the passions. It is painful. Ever since Socrates philosophers have been accused of being mere gadflies, biting, carping, hurting, making the trouble worse.

Academic philosophers and teachers of philosophy have to a large extent renounced this traditional responsibility, and claim to be only highly improved technicians in the very precise clarification of reason and technical language. Their aim is to be skilled, like mathematicians, in making language precise and making thinking formally correct. They are already on friendly terms with the computers. There is no denying that speech needs clarification, but many of our clarifiers limit their critique to an analysis of correct form and take no thought for the content of what is said. They say that a criticism of the subject matter of speech and reason is beyond their competence. To criticize the beliefs and opinions of men for their factual validity or material truth would imply a command of scientific information. This may be honest enough, and conscientious, but it does not meet the needs for which men are accustomed to turn to philosophy. Love of wisdom and search for enlightenment imply a serious concern and responsibility for civilized human affairs more generally. Specialists prefer not to profess such philosophy despite the range of the academic curricula. This may keep them out of troubles which philosophers have raised traditionally, and it decreases their acknowledged responsibilities.

It may be that institutions of higher learning in general

will find it prudent to follow this example of the teachers of philosophy. They might transform our public institutions of higher learning or universities into something analogous to the monasteries during the cruel, dark centuries of incessant strife. They become fortified centers of refuge, escape mechanisms, where sequestered arts were cultivated in a holy unconcern for the uncivilized external world. This would be a tragic development, for although such monastic fortification might preserve a bit of civilization as in a freezer, the public task of building a civilized world for an improved humanity would be hopelessly lost. In a state of terror such a policy might be a strong temptation and line of least resistance, but it would be treason to the public trust-and-task of our educational institutions.

For these reasons it seems to me that philosophers, even more than educators in general, must be on their guard. They may ruin themselves as critics and renounce their civic responsibilities if they fail to face the common world and help in the urgent clarification of our general cultural problems. Philosophy is still important among human affairs and should carry on as best it can in this environment. Henry Thoreau was already much improved as a philosopher before he went into exile. In the woods he soon became more interested in the beetles and birds around him than in the heavy Oriental tomes which he had carried with him from Concord and transcendentalism. He became a better naturalist, but as a moralist he was more effective during the night he spent in prison.

We might excuse ourselves by saying, Let the social scientists take care of society. The social sciences in fact are busy with technical, methodological improvements in their theories, and the specialists are profiting by these improvements. But this technical jargon among the behavioral scientists when added to the technical jargons among philosophers, is intelligible only to specialists; to laymen it is either meaningless or confusing. Why be perfectly clear, but completely unintelligible? We scientific laymen owe it to our fellow citizens who are also laymen to communicate with them in some kind of common usage. As it

The American Establishment

is we engage with our academic specialists in endless controversies that fail to yield general clarification. Here a real clarification *in public* is an urgent need. If the philosophers can mediate between the scientific specialists and the troubled public, they would serve well. This is especially important now that the theologians are even more technical than the sociologists; they insist in talking only to God, though they are beginning to suspect, on good grounds, that He may not be listening. There must be some nonexperts here who can come to the rescue of the public and perform a service of real enlightenment and clarification in public terms. I realize that this is a thankless task, for the mediators are exposed to fire from both fronts. Thus philosophers are led to seek security by hiding behind a very learned enlightenment of their own making.

Let me now take the risk of being specific by calling attention to a few of the urgent needs for philosophical clarification. I take a few examples from political confusion. We have all been educated to use such terms as democracy, rights, socialism, bureaucracy, capitalism, communism, conservatism, and liberalism as though they designated well-known aspects of our public concerns. In fact, however, the chief function of such terms is to raise misunderstandings and controversies which seldom reach genuine, concrete issues. These terms, in their present applications, obviously cut across and confuse basic distinctions that we have been taught to make sharply, such as: government and business, private and public interests, political and economic affairs, policies and principles, etc. To philosophers it should be clear by this time, as it is to political scientists, that such language creates general confusion and is full of ambiguities. It reflects discriminations that at one time or other and in particular circumstances were clear and useful. However, today we know quite well that business and government are not distinct. We know that individualism and collectivism are misleading abstractions. In short, we know that our categories in matters and discussions of public concern and theory are part of a heritage that has become confusing rather than clarifying.

Herbert W. Schneider

At the time of the American and French Revolutions the faith in Liberty-Equality-Fraternity was conceived as a faith in a secular trinity — in the essential unity of the three ideals. The precise nature of this unity was left unexplained. In as much as the particular ways in which this trinity functioned in various commonwealths differed considerably, no general analysis was attempted. However, the Tricolor, the Red-White-Blue, was used as the emblem of the trinity. Napoleon carried this emblem all over feudal Europe, where the doctrine was hailed as the general liberation from feudal institutions and as the general substance of commonwealth philosophy. In our Constitution, too, the Federal Republic was hailed as an embodiment of the unity of the Three. But during the nineteenth century, in all nations this unity was lost. Devotees of Liberty began quarreling with devotees of Equality, and both with patriots of Fraternity. This disintegration of the moral and political faith of the Enlightenment has become a familiar theme for historians and politicians, but the philosophical damage done has never been clarified. By the French Revolutionaries this secular trinity was openly worshiped as a militant substitute for the Christian Trinity. The mysteries of both trinities ran into increasing opposition during the nineteenth century, and men began to take for granted that both were nothing but mysteries. However, the mystery of the secular faith has needed increasingly a genuine clarification, for the separation of the Three has caused such evil consequences that we have abundant practical experience of the need for reunification. But the theoretical clarification is still lacking; I recommend it as a timely task for philosophical analysis.

As it is, the philosophers have made matters worse, by veiling the mystery in their learned unenlightenment. Anyone who visits the University of Tübingen in the German *Schwarzwald* will be shown a room with three large desks where Hegel, Schelling, and Hölderlin once worked side by side but not together. Each went mad in a different direction. Today, Martin Heidegger, in his nearby retreat, has been studying all three, and, according to latest reports, is

The American Establishment

in danger of a poetic madness from his persistent effort to make sense of all three. I shall restrict myself to Hegel and to his ingenious invention of a dialectic that, in defiance of Immanuel Kant, he called a phenomenology of the Spirit. As an enthusiastic young Lutheran convert to the Trinity of the French Revolution he conceived history to be the systematic, dialectical development of rational freedom or Liberty. He also managed to reconcile this historical dialectic with the Christian Trinity. He understood dialectical movement to be more than enlightenment *(Aufklärung)* and pictured it as a creative work of the Holy Spirit in redeeming mankind by a process of Transfiguration *(Verklärung)*. According to this philosophy historical progress is also spiritual redemption, and the freedom thus achieved is both Liberty and Salvation. Hegel's student, Karl Marx, then got the bright idea of taking the Christian Gospel out of historical dialectic, conceiving dialectic not as the growth of reason but as a material class struggle, and preaching the good news that this theory of evolution was at the same time a science of the inevitability of the emancipation of the Proletariat, and the physical actualization of Liberty. Both Hegel and Marx thus established two powerful new faiths by which men are still living. But neither founder of a faith would have welcomed their historical mission as such; each thought he had explained the mystery of the Trinity. Meanwhile, in and around St. Louis, Missouri, a group of "Speculative Philosophers," as they preferred to call themselves, under the inspiration of Hegel's dialectical logic, during the 1860s and 1870s used this philosophy to explain and rationalize the war between Southern Liberty and Northern Fraternity. The leader of this group, William Torrey Harris, who became the first United States Commissioner of Education, confessed to friends on his death-bed that he regarded himself as a philosophical failure because he was unable to convince anyone of the truth of his interpretation of The Trinity.

There are other such pathetic stories that could be told of the many ways in which philosophers have muddied the waters of speculation instead of clarifying actual issues.

Herbert W. Schneider

Our bad habit of using Greek and Latin when we try to be technically clear and distinct is one of the reasons why we have not made better progress in clarification. Here the Greeks had the advantage over us: they could speak only Greek. When we substituted a Greek word like "dialectic" for "clarification" and "enlightenment" we got into more trouble than the Greek was worth.

There are other sources, too, for our blundering in philosophy. For centuries we have been celebrating for the edification of students the problems of mind and body, person and organism, knowing and feeling, waking and dreaming, the internal and the external world. Until relatively recently these distinctions raised genuine problems for science as well as for philosophy. But now the sciences have solved the basic problems for us, and we have abundant evidence for what we need to know in these matters. We know now how mind and body are related. We know how knowing and feeling are related, how personality emerges in experience, how waking and dreaming take turns, how conscious beings differ from unconscious. There are constantly new technical discoveries that continue to be exciting, but they are far from the worries and ignorance that used to trouble men in general and particularly philosophers. It is an important part of our intellectual heritage to know how these problems were solved. But to rehearse all the old arguments as though they were still problems is a waste of our time and an imposition on students. Such exercises in cleverness for torturing innocent students are not decent education. If we wish to make epistemology, cosmology, metaphysics, and our other Greek mysteries worth studying, we must not use these unimproved tests on improved students. If we could substitute for phenomenology, epistemology, axiology, metaethics, and some of the other fanciwork in our college curricula, some critical attempts to clarify subjects of public concern like: love, honesty, right, peace, decency, and happiness, we would be more reasonable and useful. When there is so much urgent work to be done by both professors and students, we have an obligation to focus our critical abilities on the art of really clarifying real problems. Here an extensive house-cleaning is in order, especially in colleges. In universities and among real graduate students, more technical problems and terminologies have a place, but first things should come first and ultimate things come last.

In general, I am suggesting that philosophers have much hard work at hand in moral science and fine art. In these fields neither we nor our machines are much improved. Many of our devices both in thinking and in educating are antiquated or worse. Such work, when genuinely improved, should lead to constructive contributions in the arts of improving human beings and their behavior. It is especially urgent that philosophers who have educational responsibilities be civilized citizens and useful co-workers in the great reconstruction which confronts us all.

21

RADICAL EMPIRICISM AND RELIGION*
Herbert W. Schneider

I

THERE ARE AT LEAST THREE COMMON APPROACHES TO THE scientific study of religion: the theological or philosophical, which undertakes a critique of religious beliefs in the interest of reconstructing them into a body of knowledge consistent with the approved science of the day; the historical or genetic method, which aims to discover the origins of religion and the causes governing its evolutions and varieties; and the empirical or psychological method, which analyzes the motivations and functions of religion in human experience. This last method is at present in the hands of either academic or therapeutic psychologists, who are notoriously interested in the sentimental aspects or the fantastic forms of religion. The sociologists and anthropologists, on the other hand, who approach the subject more objectively, are still too largely pre-occupied with theories of the origin of religion to give us an empirical account of the significance of our own religious institutions and behavior. Presumably their accounts of so-called primitive religion are empirical, but the mere fact that they are pre-

---

*Reprinted by permission of Holt, Rinehart and Winston, Inc. From *Essays in Honor of John Dewey on The Occasion of His Seventieth Birthday,* edited by John Coss ©1929.

occupied with primitive peoples and the mere fact that they call them "primitive" bears witness to the genetic or historical motivations of their science. Primitive man still bears the burden of being forced to testify for general social theories, which cannot be substantiated by an appeal to modern cultures directly. Certainly there is a practical advantage in starting the empirical account of religion with our own religious institutions and traditions instead of with our more ancient and "primitive" contemporaries, where distance lends enchantment and ignorance lends learning.

There is, of course, much talk of a radically empirical, social, and behavioristic psychology of religion, but a little perusal of the literature in this field is sufficient to convince an innocent amateur that only a small area of religious experience really interests these professed empiricists. William James, the most religiously empirical of them all, was catholic in his sympathies precisely because he was protestant in his interests. Having himself achieved an irreligious "healthy-mindedness" after years of struggle, he was free to extend the broadest sympathy to "sick souls." His *Varieties of Religious Experience* is therefore not an objective account of religion, but a clinical diagnosis of religious diseases. The sicker the soul the better it suited him, for such cases admirably illustrated his philosophy of consciousness. *Varieties of consciousness* were his real interest. James was quite aware of this fact, and would have been the last to claim that his psychology of religion was intended as an empirical account of religion in general; it was material for the psychological laboratory taken from the field of religion. Hence, James, as a psychologist, was interested in the immediate and private aspects of religious experience, and ignored the social and institutional aspects. His protestant background and environment led him in the same direction: the most conspicuous factors of religion in New England were those connected with conversion, salvation, revivals, theological controversy, and similar fundamentals in evangelical and sentimental religion. Pre-occupation with this kind of subject-matter has continued to characterize the psychology of religion since James. The psychoanalysts have, of course, simply exaggerated this tendency.

There is, to be sure, no sense in complaining because psychology is psychology and not everything else. But the preponderance of the psychological interest in religion is really symptomatic of a puritan distaste for the other aspects of religion and ought therefore to put us on our guard. A whole philosophy of religion is presupposed by these psychological "empiricists." For example, James says quite frankly: "I speak not now of your ordinary religious believer, who follows the conventional observances of his country .... His religion has been made for him by others, communicated to him by tradition, determined to fixed forms by imitation, and retained by habit. It would profit us little to study this secondhand religious life."[1] "In one sense at least the personal religion will prove itself more fundamental than either theology or ecclesiasticism. Churches, when once established, live at second-hand upon tradition; but the *founders* of every church owed their power originally to the fact of their direct personal communion with the divine."[2] Here James commits himself definitely to the naïve protestant belief that religions are really founded by their "founders" and that institutional religion is "second-hand." Even if this should be granted from the psychological point of view (though more recent psychology would certainly not grant this), from the historical point of view it is certainly not true. For "founders" are themselves ecclesiastical creations, reared in institutional imagination and erected for social functions. Jesus was obviously not a Christian and as Christ, the "founder," he was created by his church. Furthermore, is it intelligible to abstract Jesus' personal religious experience from its environment, to regard it as primary, and to call the traditions of Hellenistic-Judaism in which he lived "second-hand"? In Lecture XIX on "Other Characteristics," James assigns churches to their proper place: he regards them as satisfying those people whom naked truth does not satisfy and who demand

---

1. *Varieties of Religious Experience*, p. 6.
2. *Varieties of Religious Experience*, p. 30.

aesthetic "richness." His treatment of the aesthetic aspects of religion is clearly ironical, if not sarcastic. The same might be said of his treatment of religious acts and forms — sacrifice, confession, and prayer. Though he admits that prayer "is the very soul and essence of religion,"[3] he dismisses prayer and other religious practices with a few courteous, perfunctory remarks. On the inner emotional side he maintains that only experiences of "solemnity" and "enthusiasm" can be properly called religious. All this reflects James's own philosophical temperament, his individualism, his spontaneity, his hatred of the conventional, and his radical Protestantism.

What is more surprising in James's treatment of religious experience is the cursory way in which he dismisses what he calls "medical materialism" and with it the whole problem of the physical basis and motivation of religion. He discounts the importance of sex and the analysis of physiological functions in general. He does not deny the physical basis, but he regards it as a truism and as insignificant for an interpretation and evaluation of religious experience. More recent psychology has changed all this and has centered its attention on the external motivation rather than the inner content of emotional states. As a result even the science of personal religious experience has been revolutionized since James delivered his Gifford lectures.

There is a significant and neglected passage, however, in which James himself points out a quite different approach to the whole subject-matter of religious experience. I quote it in full:

> The moment we are willing to treat the term "religious sentiment" as a collective name for the many sentiments which religious objects may arouse in alternation, we see that it probably contains nothing whatever of a psychologically specific nature. There is religious fear, religious love, religious awe, religious joy, and so forth. But religious love is only man's natural emotion of love directed to a religious object; religious fear is only the ordinary fear of commerce, so to speak, the

---

3. P. 464.

common quaking of the human breast, in so far as the notion of divine retribution may arouse it; religious awe is the same organic thrill which we feel in a forest at twilight, or in a mountain gorge; only this time it comes over us at the thought of our supernatural relations; and similarly of all the various sentiments which may be called into play in the lives of religious persons. As concrete states of mind, made up a feeling *plus* a specific sort of object, religious emotions of course are psychic entities distinguishable from other concrete emotions; but there is no ground for assuming a simple abstract "religious emotion" to exist as a distinct elementary mental affection by itself, present in every religious experience without exception.

As there thus seems to be no one elementary religious emotion, but only a common storehouse of emotions upon which religious objects may draw, so there might conceivably also prove to be no one specific and essential kind of religious object, and no one specific and essential kind of religious act.[4]

Here James definitely applies the term "religious" to *objects* of experience, not to any immediate content; but he leaves us with only the vaguest notions of what constitutes a religious object. He talks vaguely about "supernatural relations" and he evidently is thinking of God, but he does not even attempt to analyze the meaning of "religious" when applied to an object and not to an emotional state. My thesis, in brief, is that James is right in asserting that religion contains "nothing whatever of a psychologically specific nature," but that what James here called "religious objects" turn out to be, on analysis, specific techniques or social patterns by means of which almost any experience may find expression and in terms of which religion may be distinguished and defined.

Such an approach to the study of religion received its first theoretical formulation in the writings of William James. In his famous essay, "Reflex Action and Theism," he developed the thesis that the intellectual and theological aspect of religion represents an intermediate phase of experience and that it can be understood only in terms of its non-intellectual antecedents and consequences. This

---

4. *Varieties of Religious Experience*, pp. 27-28.

analysis was characteristically couched in physiological terms — in terms of the reflex-arc concept, of stimulus and response — which have since become the commonplaces of psychological methodology. Nevertheless it was with the intermediate, conscious, cognitive phase of experience that James was primarily concerned and hence he regarded the task of making an empirical analysis of the other phases as not a psychologist's business. Since then, psychology has become much more empirical: it takes the whole of human experience and all forms of human behavior into consideration. It is needless to mention the significance of Dewey's writings in giving us a better understanding of the biological and social setting of conscious experience; and it is impossible to mention the various schools of psychology which have contributed in recent years to our concrete knowledge of why we behave as we do. But I can select a few sentences from James's "Reflex Action and Theism" to serve as a text for what more recently psychology has illustrated abundantly.

> God may be called the normal object of the mind's belief. Whether over and above this he be really the living truth is another question ... The conceiving or theorizing faculty — the mind's middle department — functions *exclusively for the sake of ends* that do not exist at all in the world of impressions we receive by way of our senses, but are set by our emotional and practical subjectivity altogether. It is a transformer of the world of our impressions into a totally different world — the world of our conception; and the transformation is effected in the interests of our volitional nature, and for no other purpose whatsoever ... The theological does no more. And the reflex doctrine of the mind's structure, though all theology should as yet have failed of its endeavor, could but confess that the endeavor itself at least obeyed in form the mind's most necessary law ... Man's chief difference from the brutes lies in the exuberant excess of his subjective propensities ... and in the fantastic and unnecessary character of his wants, physical, moral, aesthetic, and intellectual ... And from the consciousness of this he should draw the lesson that his wants are to be trusted; that even when their gratification seems farthest off, the uneasiness they occasion is still the best guide of his life.

Herbert W. Schneider

By putting together these scattered bits of the essay, I have given a different direction to the argument than James did. He developed the argument along Kantian lines. I have purposely selected certain passages which point away from Kant, and towards Dewey; and I aim in the present essay merely to call attention to certain empirical aspects of religion, implied in the foregoing citation from James, but neglected by him and other empiricists.

II

To an irreligious observer the most obvious characteristic of a religious person must be the fact that he engages in certain practices in which others do not: he goes to church or prays or sacrifices or reads sacred scriptures; in short, he performs acts which are known to everyone as religious. Just what acts are regarded as religious depends upon the particular culture and religion of the people; what is religious to some is not to others, but within any culture there is usually a fairly distinct and generally recognized group of religious activities. Engaging in these activities, unless they are practised perfunctorily or for some ulterior motive, marks a person as religious. Merely to have certain beliefs is obviously not enough. Theological beliefs are religious only in so far as they lead to the above-named practices.

Even the devil believes in God, but he does not fall on his knees. And, vice versa, even atheism is often a religious cult. No doubt beliefs of one sort or another function in religious practices, but there is no specific belief which brands the believer as either religious or irreligious apart from the acts with which that belief is associated. Nor is there any one set of acts which is universally characteristic of all religions. Religion can be defined only relatively; relatively, that is, to the culture of which it is a part. But within any given culture certain acts are conventionally known as religious. In order to engage in these practices, a person is forced more or less to participate in a social institution and in conventional forms and symbols. To be sure, there may be privacy in religion, but a purely private religion is a physical impossibility. At least a few of the elements of a socially recognized cult are necessary: the prayers may be private and unconventional, but prayer is conventional; the particular god may be an innovation, but to have a god is conventional; or, in case there is neither prayer nor god, there is always some other conventional form or symbol (meditation, meeting, sermon, celebration, or what not). Without these a religion would be unrecognizable. Nor can each man have his own religion; there must be a minimum of discipleship, communion, or sharing of common rites and ideas. A religion, like a language or a dance, even in its private aspects, employs social patterns. It is, therefore, something which can be studied objectively, like any other cultural institution.

Such an objective study naturally begins with the question, why people engage in these practices; that is to say, not what the historical origin of these practices is, nor what reason people give when asked why they engage in them, but what they actually get out of them. For the discovery that these practices are established by custom and performed by habit may be true enough, but it does not answer our question. We want to know what satisfactions or burdens such customs entail now. A habit is not based on habit, but on some continuous function or motive which it serves. Of course, the *original* function or motive may long have been lost; but the question we are now raising is not historical, but psychological: what does the participant get out of it here and now? To say that he prays because his ancestors practised magic makes sense only to an historian. On the other hand, it will not do to ask him who prays and take for granted that his answer is correct; he may not know and may merely repeat a conventional answer to the question. It is plainly a case for experimental observation such as any natural science must employ.

Of the many answers which may be given to this question we list a few — enough to serve as illustrations of the variety of facts and inquiries which are relevant to an empirical study of religion. First of all, we might mention that religion serves as a means of expression. It is a kind of language or art whereby we can give social and intelligible expression to our ideas, feelings, needs and hopes. A community of farmers, for example, is in the midst of a drought; the crops are burning and every one thinks only of rain. They come together and pray for rain, or they publicly assert their confidence in Providence, or they fast, or in some other conventional and mutually intelligible way they give vent to their common anxiety. There are, of course, non-religious ways of doing this; and in the long run, the religious methods must compete with the secular on the basis of their effectiveness as mediums of expression. From this point of view rain-rituals are essentially art-techniques. Of course, they may in addition be devices for securing rain; but that is another question. Let us suppose, for the present, that the farmers know all about the causes of the weather. Nevertheless they continue to pray for rain, not all of them, perhaps, not so industriously perhaps, but nevertheless the need of rain prompts prayers for rain. The way in which this is done will naturally reflect the tension and the tastes of the community; it may be a simple "Lord have mercy upon us!" or it may be an elaborate fast or a dance or an imitation shower. In China, I believe, there was an ancient custom prescribing more and more elaborate sacrifices until the rain came; and when it finally *did* come, it was a religious duty to stand still and be drenched — theoretically, in order not to offend the rain; psychologically, no doubt, in order to enjoy the longed-for drenching. I have chosen a simple, elemental religious rite to illustrate the way religion gives expression to needs and desires. The reader can easily supply his own illustrations for the expression of sorrow, rejoicing, love, fear, rest, remorse, hope, loyalty, victory, truth, error — practically anything that enters the human mind and heart. Whatever else it is, then, religion is at least an art of expression, a form of celebration, an established technique for symbolizing and publishing human experience.

But it goes beyond this function of expression to one of sheer imaginative creation. Compensation phenomena and techniques for escaping from reality into a world of the imagination are found in all the arts — from drinking to painting. The religious techniques of this sort are not so much new and distinctive as they are a synthesis of various secular devices. Classic rituals of salvation have embodied in one form or another, in one combination or another, ecstatic dancing, drunkenness, visions, hysteria, myth, poetry, music, hypnotism, etc. Indeed one chief reason why religion is so powerful is because it compounds the powers of these various devices into an unusually effective stimulant. Few utopias can vie with the classic religious heavens; few dramas have the power of the cosmic tragedy of sin and salvation; few orgies are so ravishing as a wholehearted revival camp-meeting; few romances equal that of St. Catherine, the bride of Christ. Though this type of imaginative stimulation is enjoyable, it is not necessarily pleasurable. Man freely tortures himself and others and gets certain satisfactions in the tragedy. Both penance and salvation have their intrinsic values and the cross is as powerful as the crown in commanding affection and obedience.

Another function which religion commonly serves is that of offering the opportunity for participation in the life of a public group. Membership in a family or in a corporation is not enough to lift an ordinary private person to an active sense of his membership in the public, and the opportunities for political action are too circumscribed even in a democracy. But public worship immediately conveys to the participant the sense of his social dignity and the feeling of membership with "the Lord's people." The communion may be silent, the process of sharing may not be articulate, but the effect is achieved in spite of, perhaps even because of, the fact that it operates sub-consciously. In addition to conducting public worship, the churches, of course, carry on any number of other social activities which may or may not be recognized as religious; but it may be doubted whether the so-called social work of the churches is half as social, either in motivation or in effect, as is their public worship. But this is a matter of taste. Some prefer religious sociability to the more subtle and imaginative forms of public worship. They deliver sermons to *their* worshipers, or they chat genially after church or in Sunday School. Even prayer tends to become a conversation; and many evidently prefer communication with the saints to the communion of the saints. The way in which religion satisfies this conversational need is best illustrated in spiritualism, where a simple and effective device has been invented for enabling the bereaved to talk with their departed, and lovers to meet with their "spirit-mates"; where all sorts and conditions of men (mostly women) who seek concrete and practical guidance, but are deprived of trustworthy friends, can get "spiritual" advice for all their daily troubles, their business deals, their health, and their future.

The mention of one more function of religion must suffice for the present: a religion provides a faith. Having a creed or a faith is not like having beliefs; it is, as St. Paul said, more like fighting a good fight. A creed is the analogue of a flag or banner; its literal value may be negligible, but as a symbol of one's willingness to fight, it is invaluable. Most creeds which are actually in operation, irrespective of their origins, are not formulations of beliefs actually held, nor even of beliefs which it is thought ought to be held; they are sanctified slogans. They serve as badges by which the faithful are known and as banners under which the faithful fight. They represent the "secret doctrine" of the initiate, the esoteric wisdom of the elect. To have such symbols, to be one of the faithful, is a luxury with which few persons can dispense. To "keep the faith," to believe *in* God, is quite different from believing *that* God exists; it is to be convinced that in pursuing one's interests one is also fighting for ideals. It puts a halo on the drab routine of life; it lends "spiritual significance" to what might else be merely a struggle for existence. It fortifies one against doubt, keeps one on the alert for enemies, and comforts one in defeat. Faith is by nature indomitable. Faith is not necessarily religious, witness salesmen and senators; but it tends to become religious if it meets sufficient obstacles. Certainly religion is notoriously faithful.

III

It would be an endless and thankless task to continue to map out the domain of religion in human experience in all its detail; we proceed, therefore, to the theoretical points which the foregoing considerations raise.

(1) Religion is an institutionalized form of behavior rather than a kind of experience. Or, to put it in other words, it is not the inner contents, but the social forms, which determine whether an experience is religious or not. The few illustrations given above were intended to suggest that any conceivable emotion or idea can be put into a religious form. Religion, apart from the limitations of any particular religion, is as broad as human experience. The whole gamut of needs, aspirations, pleasures, sorrows, loves, and hates may receive religious treatment, just as it may receive musical or dramatic treatment. Or, if I may be permitted to use another analogy, so-called religious experience is logically on the same plane with cognitive, linguistic, or aesthetic experience, and must be defined in terms of its formal structure, not in terms of its possible content. Almost anything may be known, said, or put to music; even more, if possible, may be expressed religiously.

Epistemology is gradually freeing itself from the question: what can I know? and attempting to answer the question: how do I know? But the would-be sciences of aesthetics and religion, for motives which the reader may suspect, are still engaged in the desperate task of locating their distinctive realms of experience. Such terms as the "numinous," the sacred, the holy, the supernatural, and "the religious thrill" are supposed to describe a concrete inner content of a particular kind of experience. In reality, I suspect, their popularity is due to the fact that they have given metaphysical apologists a fresh category to exploit; they are convenient methodological devices and are not really descriptive of any empirical content whatsoever— except that perhaps these terms roughly indicate the state of mind in which scientists now approach religion, a state, so to speak, of taking off their intellectual shoes when they touch "holy" ground. But supposing for the present that the psychologist can find this "numinous" quality in experience, we can readily infer from the above illustrations, if not from our own experience, that such a quality must play a compara-

Herbert W. Schneider

tively minor role in religion. For, unless we take an ultra-puritanical and narrow view of religious experience, the behavior which is known as religious reflects all the varying moods of the seasons and fortunes of mankind. And this is true not only of the ecclesiastical rites, but of the more private devotions of mystics. Any good mystic can get more varieties of religious experience than a "numinous" psychologist can talk about.

If we abandon all this attempt to locate *the* religious experience, and turn to the distinctive *forms* or techniques of religion, we are confronted with a limited number of readily observable and socially conventional patterns, the discovery of which is neither difficult nor profound. We are confronted with a number of institutions, theologies, and customs, functioning as integral parts of a culture, whose features they reflect and whose fortunes they share. But here again scientists have spoiled the picture by pretending to find a single, essential *social function* for religion. Most famous, perhaps, is the theory of the Positivists who assign to religion the essential task of maintaining social 'solidarity'. More recently, Malinowski has proclaimed a somewhat similar theory to the effect that the essential function of religion is to impress the individual with the power and value of tradition. Freud's theory that religion is essentially a sublimation of the sex-complexes arising out of family life is another variant of the same general attempt to find *the* social function of religion. That these are all over-simplifications becomes quite evident when one faces the bewildering variety of cults, each with its own variety of functions. Religion may unite or it may divide a society; it may maintain conventional standards or it may break them; it may keep the masses under or it may incite them to revolt. Religion can serve God or Mammon or both. And who are we to decide which is *true* religion!

For the functions of religion must not be confused with its values. Whether or not it is good that religion should do the things it does is another question entirely. The present account is purely descriptive. But obviously the question of value is not apt to make much progress until there is more light on the question of empirical functions.

(2) Religion is an art, not an inquiry. This is really but a corollary of what has just been said. Since religion is identified by its techniques or forms, it is obvious that these must vary with the material and intellectual cultures of which they are a part. They must express local needs and varying tastes. The functions and values of religious techniques must therefore be estimated in their interactions with the other arts of a particular culture; their scientific status or naked truth is irrelevant. A negro "spiritual" loses its spirituality in a night-club and God loses his religious value in the hands of an epistemologist. Puritanism is unintelligible apart from its historical and geographical locus; Shintoism could not be a religion in Germany; a crucifix is not sacred to a Latter-day Saint, nor is the Book of Mormon sacred to a Catholic priest. There are a few religions which enjoy a specious universality, like Christianity, but the universal name really conceals many different cults. Christianity in Haiti is hardly to be identified with Christianity in Havana, nor, for that matter, in Palm Beach. This social relativity of religion makes it possible to criticize it intelligibly. Were religion a search for the Absolute, one might throw stones at it or pity it; but since it is a human art, expressive of human themes in terms of standardized artistic techniques, it is subject to the same canons of criticism that apply to any other art. There is no excuse for it, if it is not done well. It can be cultivated, not as an intellectual necessity or a moral obligation, but as an opportunity for creative, imaginative art.

This applies not only to religion as an art of expression, but to its other functions as well. The arts of salvation, comfort, anaesthesia, loyalty, conflict, celebration, and contemplation, to mention only a few at random, are all subject to the ordinary canons of criticism. And what is more, as secular arts performing these same functions increase in power and in perfection of technique, the corresponding religious arts feel the keen competition. There was a time when religion had almost a monopoly in this field. At present, however, almost all the great religions are decadent, lamely hobbling along with outworn techniques, vulgar standards, and mediocre talents. It remains to be seen whether or not they can bear up under the competition. If not, it is more probable that new cults will take their places than that the secular arts will crowd out religion entirely.

(3) Theology is not primarily a science, but a religious technique. We are now back where we started — back with James and his thesis that theology is an intermediate phase of experience. But the social interpretation of this pragmatic thesis, I hope, throws it into a different light. It suggests that God is not the *object* of religious experience, but a part of its *apparatus*. Whatever use scientists and metaphysicians may be able to put theology to, the religious use it serves is that of a mythology. To insist that theology is a mythology would seem to be a celebration of the commonplace, were the fact not so generally overlooked. Philosophers especially seem to dread mythology — (probably a defence mechanism). But in religion mythology is very useful; in fact, without a mythology a religion could hardly operate. For the materials taken from mythology are usually the most effective instruments of religious expression. The biblical stories of the creation and the fall of man, of the Mosaic legislation, of the divine government of the world and the day of judgement; the doctrine of the Trinity, the lives of the saints, and the love of God — all this religious material forms the very heart of the practical devices by which the Christian religion operates. Take away the use of the mythology and you take away the religion. Take away the *belief* in the truth of mythology, and you begin to understand the religion for what it really is. The theological ideas are neither the cause nor end of religion — they are means. By them faith is symbolized, hopes are dramatized, needs are made explicit, and joys are celebrated. Religion is not merely a system of magic, nor is theology mere rationalization; theology is a religious instrument in the imaginative representation of the fruits of experience.

To illustrate: when a man prays, the reason for his prayer

is not found in the object to which he prays. He may be a monotheist or a polytheist, he may practise idolatry or he may believe in the guidance of the Holy Spirit; he may light a candle, use a rug, tell beads, or lock himself in his closet. All these factors are technical or formal. The efficient cause of stimulus of his praying is to be found in *what he prays for;* the prayer is a device for making his wants explicit. Take the farmers we spoke of before, who gather to pray for rain. It is the need of rain that is uppermost in their minds; acts of prayer, church, God, and all the rest are so much ready technique or apparatus for expressing this need. Probably they have no option as to how and to whom they pray; they must use the forms and objects of prayer which happen to be available in their community. As part of the act of prayer, to be sure, it is important to address God, but the conception of God, the hearer of prayer, is a means, not a cause of prayer. The cause is to be sought in the contents of the petition. Now, to complicate matters, let us suppose that our farmers pray not merely because they seek an outlet for their anxiety, but because they believe that by praying they might possibly get rain sooner than otherwise. In this case, the premium is put on praying as well as possible, or, as they would put it, making their prayers acceptable to the Lord. This would call into play their standards of worship, of propriety, and in general of the best way to behave under the circumstances. How to pray effectively would be the uppermost question. Now, to change the case, let us suppose that they realize that it makes no practical difference whether they pray or not, and that hence if they pray they do so in order thus to express their need for rain. In this case, they would use or devise whatever techniques most adequately expressed their needs. This would put their conventional religious practices to the test. In either case (whether prayer is believed to have magical efficacy or not), the problem on which the worshiper focuses his attention tends to shift from the original problem of the drought to the technical problem of *how* to pray well. This sublimation of the anxiety for rain into an aesthetic problem of expression is presumably the cause for the relief from tension which prayer may be, the logical point is that the practical preoccupation with technique in the act of prayer, misleads both the worshiper and the observer into believing that he prays in order to worship God when as a matter of fact the motive which drove him to prayer was his anxiety over the drought. Such a misplacement of means and end is but another illustration of a common fallacy in the analysis of experience, to which the writings of Dewey have called our attention.

Now, to return to the farmer, if the technique of prayer should be completely standardized for him by a fixed and satisfactory ritual, and hence no technical problem be presented by his engaging in prayer, his mind remains focused on the anxiety for rain which the ritual expresses, but the form or technique of the ritual transforms that anxiety into a calm dignified feeling of dependence or into a hilarious excitement, according to the nature of the ritual. Here we have a case where the intellectual and moral structure of the experience remains true to its original intent; means and end are not confused. Perhaps an analogy may be useful to clear up the logical point at issue here. The act of prayer may be likened unto an automobile ride. The driver may become so pre-occupied with his engine that he actually drives for the sake of running his engine, whereas his original intention was probably either to enjoy the scenery or get somewhere or both. Traditional theology, being the product of religious conflicts, is so pre-occupied with the technique of prayer that it forgets its empirical occasions and foundations: God, the technical object of prayer, is transformed by the theologian into the psychological object or goal of prayer. A more disinterested observer of religious experience is able to see the techniques of religion in their proper, empirical functions and perspectives.

The foregoing analysis applies to what might be called primary, naïve, or unreflective religious behavior. It obviously does not apply to the theologian, to whom God is an end and not a means. To infer from this that theologians are irreligious, would be a *reductio ad absurdum* of the whole argument, though many an illustrious theologue might lend support to such a conclusion by his personal habits, if not by his sermons. The aim of the argument is rather to put theology in its proper religious setting. Gods exist for the reasons we have given, but once created, God may be consciously sought as the object of a real need. St. Augustine and St. Anselm, to say nothing of the mystics, are notoriously seekers after God. But this type of religious experience is derivative, not primary. It may be generated by inner conflict, doubt, and confusion, or by the rivalry of Gods for the kingdoms of this world. Under such circumstances the search for "the True God" or for the infallible proof for God may become a direct need of the human soul expressing itself in theology. This need, however, is not the origin of religion, but one of its incidental products. It is introspective, introverted, and, in extreme cases, inversive religion. It is not necessarily pathological, but it is always a secondary, reflective form of religious experience produced by conflicts within a religious order. If space permitted, it would be easy to prove by historical illustration that theology thrives in an atmosphere of contention, not in what is usually known as a religious atmosphere; and that, in other words, attention is centered on God, when conventional religion ceases to satisfy. Men consciously believe in God only after they have begun to doubt him. Theology is the beginning of the end for any religion. The prophet of God imagines he is doing his Lord a service by defending him in the face of his enemies, but eventually a God who relies on prophets is doomed.

Whether or not this introverted form of religion is better than the more overt forms, is, of course, a matter of religious taste which this essay does not presume to discuss. Religion may find its euthanasia in giving birth to theology, and the love of God may be higher than the earthly loves out of which it grows. It is enough for the present argument that the empirical relationship between the two be established; that the search of the soul for God, when it is definitely religious and not merely a scientific or metaphysical enquiry, be understood in terms of those more primary forms of religion which take sacred beings for granted and use them in the expression or satisfaction of the varieties of human experience. Images and symbols are religiously useful and may also be beautiful, but when some professional priest exploits the symbolism, he transforms religion into idolatry. And theism is but artless idolatry.

In one sense idolatry is harmless, and there is sufficient room in the world for a variety of things, even for theology. Morally and intellectually, too, the search for God is not necessarily fruitless. The chief harm done by theology is neither to science nor to society, but to religion. It robs religion of its spontaneity and humaneness. The so-called "minister" or priest, like his secular analogue, the "servant-of-the-people," is too apt to forget his servitude and sincerely imagines that he and his symbols are the crown of all culture. Thus religion becomes self-centered and forgets its dependence on that mother-sea of human experience whom it must serve in order to survive. By dint of increasing hardships, theology itself is now half-heartedly recognizing these obligations and resigning itself to its instrumental functions. The theologian is turning from his quarrel with science to learn something about civilized life and how it can be served by religious art. If I may paraphrase Professor Whitehead, who says "religion is tending to degenerate into a decent formula wherewith to embellish a comfortable life,"[5] I could sum up my contentions by saying, if religion ever again becomes a decent formula wherewith to embellish a comfortable life, it will cease to be degenerate.

IV

Now, to return from this critical digression to religion itself. In the long run religious institutions and practices adapt themselves to the actual needs and satisfactions of the participants. I know that generation after generation may take up its religious cross and bear its religious burden

---

5. *Science and the Modern World*, p. 262.

out of a sheer sense of duty or a tenacious faith in its literal efficacy, but even the bearing of this burden has an intrinsic tragic fascination which makes it seem plausible and empirical. Sooner or later, however, the merely obligatory and the pseudo-utilitarian aspects of a religion are sloughed off, though theology may not discover the change until much later.

A closer examination of living rituals and rites would demonstrate, I believe, that few practices maintain themselves out of sheer social inertia, or sheer theological belief in their utility. They have in them something intrinsically enjoyable. Also, I think it would be found that few theological ideas live or die because of their truth or falsity; their religious vitality depends on their usefulness in religious practices, and religious practices follow the wanderings of human experience, not the dialectics of theology. To take an illustration: there is among spiritualists today a definite demand for more specific and concrete guidance than the traditional forms of prayer offer and consequently they patronize "message services," mediums, and other devices for connecting them with spirits who know them intimately. In this sort of religious technique the spirits displace God in practice. And in their theology, though God still presides over the spiritual world, he is definitely receding into the background. He is still called in whenever ultimate metaphysical explanations of the structure and machinery of the spirit world are needed, but He is of practically no value in the actual operation of the cult. If the practices continue to be popular, the theology will probably revert to a frank spiritism such as our "primitive" neighbors employ. The Great God, meanwhile is passing from religion to metaphysics. In general, metaphysics might be pictured as picking up religious discards — but that is another story.

To conceive religion in terms of social techniques may seem like conceiving art in terms of paints and brushes. And in a sense the analogy is just. It is academic nonsense to pretend that art can be explained by "aesthetic impulses"; and it is a false empiricism that bases religion on *religious* experience. The method of departmentalizing experience is too easy to be informative. Civilization consists of particular ways of achieving particular ends, but no particular instrument of civilization can monopolize a particular realm of human nature. Business, sport, art, religion, and science are not distinguished by the wants they satisfy, but by their *methods* of satisfying wants. A radical empiricism will, therefore, insist on judging particular cults, practices, and beliefs by their effectiveness as specialized instruments in the service of whatever varieties of human experience may care to use them.

Of course, civilization does not exist independently of civilized human beings; nor can religion be divorced from the individuals who practise it. The thesis that religion and other institutions are instrumental would be meaningless if one overlooked the persons whom they serve. An empiricist can ill afford to forget experience. But neither can he afford to regard the institutions of society as "second-hand." Society is but a name for certain ways in which individuals behave and does not exist as an independent reality. To be understood, a social institution must be seen at work, living in persons.

Hence religion, though social, is none the less personal and vital. Music is not less intimate because it needs physical instruments nor is thought less personal because it is expressed in social symbols. Human wants, hopes, emotions, and ideals are not robbed of their power nor of their sincerity by being religiously expressed and cultivated. But particular religions may petrify and particular gods may die. They become not only "second-hand," but useless. They may linger to haunt the living, but their forms are empty and their strength gone. With them we have no quarrel; they have had their day. In general, as empiricists, we have no quarrel with religion, nor with any particular religion; we are, however, provided with a method of analysis which enables us to understand how religion works or fails to work, and to separate the living from the dead.

22

PHILOSOPHY WILL NEVER BE A SCIENCE*
Herbert W. Schneider

I DO NOT INTEND TO INSIST, AS A CLASSICIST MIGHT, THAT philosophy *should be* the love of wisdom because that is what it was originally and that all departures from this original conception of philosophy's essence are signs of degeneracy. My concern is not with an ideal for philosophy, but merely with the fact that philosophy as it is being carried on today shows traits which distinguish it from science or from whatever one may choose to name the co-operative and systematic search for experimental evidence. Any historian of philosophy knows that philosophers have usually imagined themselves to be scientists and have represented themselves as seekers or finders of one or more objective truths. A philosophy is usually cast by its author into the form of a systematic demonstration of propositions that purport to be true. And yet, no philosophy as a whole must be characterized by other predicates, not by true and false. Why is this so?

Let us suppose, in order to simplify our task, that truth,

---

* Published in *Philosophical Essays,* No. 2 (Edizioni di "Filosofia", Torino), pp. 3-7; reprinted by permission of the author and publisher.

beauty, and justice are divine, eternal, transcendent ideals, to which men of all ages and cultures have aspired, but which remain far above their various imperfect manifestations. In other words, let us here be Platonists in admitting that men love certain goods which they can behold only with the eyes of the mind. Though they can express to each other through language what it is that they love, and though they can suggest to those who do not share their love, by the use of analogies and symbols, some of the attributes of what they seek, still in their fullness these objects elude men's grasp and lead them on and up. And let us also admit with Plato that the language of philosophy is a language of love. Shall we say that wisdom, or whatever it is that philosophers love, is one of these ideals? I wish to suggest that however lovely wisdom may be, philosophical love is not like the love of truth, beauty, and justice; and that just as Socrates in Plato's *Symposium* dethroned love from its divine honors, so the object of philosophical love is not one of these divine objects. Or, in other words, philosophers' love is not Platonic.

All serious love idealizes. Photographs of the beloved are notoriously unsatisfactory; portraits, if painted by a lover, may be better, since they are at least expressions of love. But love is never content with knowledge, unless it be Platonic love. There is always an element of longing in its enjoyments and of trust in its possessions. This is especially evident when there is life in the object loved, and when there is a reciprocity in love. It is from this point of view that I wish to contrast the pursuit of truth as it is found in science with philosophy as it is exhibited in philosophical literature and in philosophical persons. Truth may be quite cold and its pursuit may be more like a life of devotion than like a life of love; whereas there is a kind of living warmth in wisdom, which makes philosophers appear to be engaged in a kind of reciprocity or participation. The life of reason is not necessarily a form of desire, whereas the life of philosophy is essentially a love-life and philosophical dialogue is more than logical dialectic.

By those who are not directly acquainted with the philosophical life a philosopher is often represented as a sagé; he is put on a pedestal, given statuesque virtues, and conceived

Herbert W. Schneider

as if he were looking down on human affairs from some height, like a Lucretius or a god. But in fact, as Socrates pointed out, philosophers are not wise men. They neither follow a star nor point a way. Lucretius, more than Epicurus, was at heart a natural scientist, who felt close enough to omniscience to associate with gods rather than men. But his laughter at human follies was poetic, and in his poetry more than in his science he betrayed the fact that he was human after all, and more of a philosopher than a sage. Spinoza, too, in spite of his youth, began to imagine himself wise, having escaped "human bondage." And Herbert Spencer, after he had worked out his Synthetic Philosophy, was observed to smile constantly; he explained that there are two kinds of philosophers, those who seek the truth and those who have found it, and he alone had found it. In contrast to such complacent, satisfied, semi-scientists, the philosopher is a Socratic man, wisely seeking truth among men. Philosophical truth is found only in the context of human life and hence the philosophical mind must have a genuine love for human affairs and a readiness to remain in human fellowship. Both the pursuit of truth and the pursuit of wisdom may be endless, but they are endless in different ways. Truth remains eventual; it comes at the end. But wisdom is more analogous to happiness; the pursuit of wisdom and happiness requires that these goals be conceived not as end-products, but as qualifications of the pursuit, exhibiting themselves along the way. Wisdom and happiness are not objects; they are ways of being human.

Now, to descend from these generalities to a more factual analysis of philosophy as it exists actually, let me point to three familiar traits of philosophy which serve to distinguish it from science and relate it to the pursuit of happiness. First, philosophy is more personal than science. It is the philosopher and his philosophising that constitutes the primary being of philosophy. No philosophical system is wholly impersonal either in form or content. We do well to label a philosophy by the name of its author, for it always reflects the love of an individual. Attempts have been made by philosophical associations, schools, federations, to give philosophy a more corporate, co-operative and collective existence, but without success. Much more than in science each philosopher works out his ideas into a system which is significantly his own. He may borrow ideas, he may belong to a school or tendency, he may seek to form a movement or "circle" or a community; but always he remains the center of his thought. "*Penso io*" is more philosophical than the mere *cogito*. Like poetry and the other arts, philosophy is a personal creation and expression even in its aim at universality. Aristotle, Spinoza Leibniz, Kant, Cassirer, and Wittgenstein — men who admired the objectivity of technical expression, studied the available sciences, and cultivated impersonal symbolical forms — have all of them given their names and personalities to their systems. Thomas Aquinas, perhaps the least personal among the philosophers, might have been content to be a "summator" rather than an author, an encyclopedia of truth rather than a lover of wisdom. And the Roman Church has attempted to make his thought even more impersonal, an official doctrine rather than a Thomist philosophy. But this orthodoxy will always bear the name of Thomas, and there are frequent deviationists whose "neo-Thomism" always has something quite personal in it.

Accordingly, the history of philosophy is still the story of philosophers. To reduce it to the history of ideas is to take the philosophical life out of it, unless the ideas are presented as somebody's ideas. Hegel's attempt to transform the history of philosophy into a philosophy of universal dialectic illustrates this point. To construct some such historical mythology as a stage for their own system is the ambition of most philosophers; for though not many publish their self interpretations, each conceives of his ideas as the logical outcome of all previous thought. Philosophers make poor historians. The history of philosophy is not really cumulative as is the history of science. Scientists look with amusement at the history of science, as a history of errors, but philosophers of all ages must take each other seriously, as though all were engaged in a common dialogue and shared a single pursuit. Such study is more then the study of history; it is a human fellowship of experience and reflection, a communion among lovers — and not without jealousy.

Herbert W. Schneider

The second circumstance to which I call attention is the fact that no philosophy is complete without a moral philosophy. "*Sagesse*" in any language connotes more than animal intelligence; it stands for the continuity between ordinary reasonableness and a sense of values. A philosophy which does not cultivate *sagesse* and provide criteria for evaluation is truly no philosophy. If this be admitted, it follows that any philosophy is not only personally created but also culturally conditioned and oriented. The life-span of a philosophy must be measured culturally and historically in terms of the philosophy's relevance to a particular moral environment. We are accustomed, for example, to refer as a matter of course to "Eastern" and "Western" philosophies, not because we believe, as some do, that "East" and "West" designate philosophical differences, but merely in order to designate vaguely the cultural fields of operation in which a particular philosophy has its existence and meaning. Similarly we speak of ancient and modern, French and German, pagan and Christian philosophies not in order to define them but in order to locate them existentially. Such discriminations are decidedly accidental for science, but for philosophy they are necessary. Who would dare discuss Platonic ethics without distinguishing the various epochs and cultures in which Platonism has lived its varied career? And who would venture to expound the philosophical significance of Sankara's system without referring to the social and religious system in which it has functioned? Any philosophy is located in a moral world and dated historically, whether it be *philosophia perennis* or some obviously *ad hoc* ideology. Whatever be the validity of a transcendental system, its value depends on circumstances. And no philosopher can afford to admit that the value of his ideas is not for him an essential consideration, for if he be indifferent to values he cannot pretend to have a philosophy.

Thirdly, almost all philosophers put their philosophy into book form. Without literary embodiment and expression a philosophy is practically powerless. Philosophical writings are very different from laboratory reports; they are usually intended to be read and enjoyed. If they are used for reference or as classroom texts, such uses are not their primary intention. However technical their language may be, they are not technology. They may be clumsy as literature and dull as entertainment, but they are nevertheless substantial reading matter. Consequently the idioms, nuances, and limitations of vernaculars are much more serious for philosophical understanding than they are for scientific research. The problems of translation here are not merely linguistic; they are peculiarly subtle, because one senses at once how inadequate even the most faithful translation may be to communicate the "spirit" of a philosophy to a person of another culture. The most ardent disagreements within a culture are less baffling and less discouraging than the cross-cultural indifferences. In our international philosophical organizations we are especially aware of this difficulty. What philosopher will admit that he is understood, if he is not taken seriously? And how can anyone take seriously something that is quite foreign? Is not this circumstance clear testimony to the historical nature and cultural limitations of philosophical thinking?

This question of *importance* is central for philosophy. We fail to understand a philosopher if we fail to understand why he thinks that what he says is important. We may be able to debate the truth or falsity of many of the propositions that are put to us, but there is no love of wisdom shown and no communication of such love unless somehow we can convey to each other what importance our doctrines have not only for us, but in general for the pursuit of happiness. All philosophies by their very nature have the responsibility of being humane, and their humanity can neither be conceived in terms of subject matter alone nor be reported coldly to a community of research. Thus a philosophical tradition is kept alive only when its ideas become important to a new generation and when this importance can be systematized and communicated in such a way that the philosophy acquires a new cultural embodiment. A philosophical tradition does not flourish from generation to generation in the same soil, like an old tree; it can live only by being transplanted with each generation to new soil, gaining a fresh hold on new human beings. For wisdom, even if it be cast into proverbial maxims, is not a static system of prudence and can never achieve finality so long as human beings continue to live and to reflect on their lives. Wisdom, humanly speaking and pragmatically conceived, lives not among the Platonic immortals but among persons who love it and who exhibit it in their lives. Wisdom is not learned or taught; it is enjoyed by those who can discover for themselves what is worth learning and teaching. It is only after the *study* of philosophy has yielded to a new love for what cannot be studied that a person becomes a philosopher and philosophy becomes a living being.

23

"REASONABLE RATIONALISM: THE HERITAGE OF THE ENLIGHTENMENT"[1]

Herbert W. Schneider

THIS YEAR IS A CENTENNIAL OF UNUSUAL SERIOUSNESS. Seventy-five years ago, when this University was founded, 1848 was merely a famous date, the year of revolution, and revolutions were then largely of historic interest. In 1848 began our present political era. The institutions and ideas that were then revolutionary are today the cornerstone of our politics and the commonplaces of our social ideals. But now that a century has elapsed, 1848 haunts us as a year that is more than monumental, for there is now a general apprehensiveness if not anxiety, lest 1948 be the end of an era. We feel this anxiety almost too intimately for speech, and each inarticulately asks his own conscience: Is this too a revolution? Are we starting something new in 1948? For better or for worse? Under these circumstances it is not only appropriate that we celebrate 1848, but that we reflect earnestly on the whole century which closed in that year, the century of the enlightenment. The century that lies between us and 1848 tells the story of

---

1. Paper delivered at the Humanities Institute of the University of Toledo and the Toledo Museum of Art on March 6, 1948. Published as *The Age of Enlightenment* (Toledo, 1948).

Herbert W. Schneider

our troubles. The century before 1848 may well serve to throw light on those troubles, and to guide us in the difficult days ahead. For at the end of a stormy, adventuresome, romantic era of struggle and discovery, it may pay us to seek enlightenment from an era when it was revolutionary to be reasonable. Thus our contemporary agony and fear causes us to turn today half in envy, half in hope, to an age which proclaimed clearly and effectively its boundless faith in reason.

The bubble of progress has burst, and beneath all our thinking and striving lurks a basic uneasiness. The sense of security is gone. The dawn of the age of reason, which the eighteenth-century prophets announced, and the glowing confidence in human perfectibility which animated the early nineteenth century, are gone.

Sensing this intellectual and social anxiety, the traditional churches have regained their nerve and reasserted what they call their faith, but what might better be called their despair. The predicaments and failures of liberalism have been exploited by them to preach a return to authoritarianism, dogmatism, intolerance, fanaticism, and all the other religious vices from which the Enlightenment was supposed to have freed us. Religious liberalism, being essentially a mediator, has thus been caught between two fires. It is neither firmly rooted in historical Christianity and Judaism nor well-grounded in natural science and secular art. The one-time rebellious liberals have become prosperous parsons, and their fashionable gospel of brotherhood, peace, and God's Kingdom on earth already has the hollow sound of an ecclesiastical creed that is recited but not believed, asserted but not obeyed. A hard-shell Calvinist was once overheard to remark that the doctrine of total depravity is good doctrine if it were only lived up to. Similarly in the case of the social gospel of liberalism, though it continues to be preached as a gospel, its adherents really feel a bit homesick for sin and damnation. A smug liberalism is far from enlightenment. For what James called "the religion of healthy-mindedness" seems inappropriate to an obviously sick society, and, as James himself said, only "the sick soul" or "twice-born man" escapes religious superficiality. Today liberalism is too "healthy-minded"; in the eighteenth century it implied radical conversion and social revolution. So, taking advantage of liberalism's weaknesses, the perennial prophets of doom have blamed science, education and democracy for all the failures everywhere, for in these the enlightenment had put their trust.

In these various ways the reaction has grown against our rationalist heritage. It is not merely a revolt against the incidental aspects of liberalism. It is not merely *laissez faire* and parliamentary government and human equality and individualism that are being challenged. It is the whole Enlightenment, the whole faith of the French Revolution that is being challenged. And this challenge is of particular significance to Americans, since in no other country have the basic ideas and institutions of national life been so directly and thoroughly conceived in this faith.

It is a common fallacy to infer from this challenge to the French Revolutionary ideology that we must return to the *ancien régime*, that we are even headed toward a new medievalism — social feudalism, political imperialism, and religious Catholicism. It is assumed that the work of the Enlightenment can literally be undone and that we may possibly return to a civilization in which its traces will be wiped out and everything be as if the period of rationalism had not been. In view of such careless habits of thought, I wish to call your attention to those achievements of rationalism that are not seriously threatened and that may well be regarded as enduring contributions to the civilization of mankind.

First, I should mention the triumph of natural knowledge and of faith in it. Faith in reason does not imply the belief that science is God, omnipotent. Science is a worthy object of faith because it does not demand worship; it comes to us as a *reliable* technique of gathering and ordering information, invention and knowledge. Its spirit is that of a public servant, not of a universal savior. The specific beliefs and methods adopted by scientists have varied enormously from time to time, but the cumulative insight into nature, society,

Herbert W. Schneider

history, and mind achieved by the sciences becomes daily more impressive. One characteristic of the Enlightenment was its faith that no limits could be put to science, and *this* faith is more firm now than ever. There was a time when theology, morals, psychology, and politics (to mention only a few of the most important domains of thought) were regarded as by their nature either beyond science or at least independent of each other as sciences. Remnants of this attitude persist today, and zealots occasionally defend the so-called independence of theology, or of the field of values, or of the soul, from the other sciences. On the whole, however, the interdependence of all the sciences is being recognized increasingly, and no one has been able to say effectively to the sciences: here, in this field, you shall not enter, for this field has independent sources of information. At the same time, one after another of science's rivals have fallen by the wayside, or at least are falling into comparative disrepute as methods of getting information. Revelation, authority, vision, intuition, mystic experience, miracles, spiritualism, and the rest of the substitutes that flourished in the nineteenth century are making little headway, and when compared with the brilliant conquests of genuine science are really pitiable.

The extent to which even theology has become a matter of ordinary science is little appreciated outside the ranks of the theologians themselves. They prefer to keep the matter quiet, for as long as the old terms and symbols appear in theological literature, casual readers get the impression that the fundamentals are safe and sound. But anyone who takes the trouble to examine the kind of arguments used and the actual meaning of the terms employed will be amazed at the revolution in modern theology since the Enlightenment. Not only the rationalist and historical schools of theology, both of them now out of fashion, but even the neo-orthodoxies and new-mysticisms are decidedly dominated by science. For though many of the doctrines, that is, the conclusions reached, are orthodox, the methods by which they have been reached are very *neo*. And though I do not wish to hold a brief for the so-called science of theology, I think it is only fair and highly significant to note that reputable modern theologians at least *try* to be scientific, and scientific in the sense of *natural* science. For example, there is now a *science* of mysticism, as there formerly was of psychical research. Modern students of mystic experience and theology pride themselves on their scientific technique in describing and analyzing the mystics. Their defenses of mysticism are not based on mysticism, but on empirical science. Similarly the neo-Thomism of the Catholics, which is blessed even less with a sense of humor than neo-mysticism, is going to no end of trouble to prove that the doctrines of the Angelic Doctor are compatible with the best modern science. What greater tribute could science desire than the fact that the beliefs in immortality, in revelation, and in dogma are being subjected *by their own believers* to scientific methods of inquiry?

Even more significant than the growth of scientific theology is the growth of scientific psychology. The detailed knowledge gained during the last century concerning the physical basis and mechanisms of the human mind and emotions is so great that even the most supernaturally minded soul-saver can not afford to ignore it. Never was the physical basis of the soul so evident as now; and never was the belief in an immortal soul or immaterial substance (in its conventional sense) less plausible. There are many schools of psychology and many conflicting theories of the structure and life of the mind, but they are all based on the careful observation of man's physical organism and behavior. I know that captious journalists and malicious theologians find both glee and comfort in the recent revolt against mechanism. They chortle when they read such statements as the following from a brilliant little book by Tillich, *The Religious Situation*. "The psychical in general and the individual soul in particular are primary creative structures which can be apprehended in their unity and vitality only by means of intuition. But wherever the creative character of a reality is intuited there the way to the original, creative ground has been opened. The emancipation of psychology from domination by physiology has been particularly important for this development." But in their religious zeal they do not read the next two sentences, or at least never quote them: "No one can seriously doubt the dependence of the psychical upon the physical. But the real problem is how this dependence is to be explained." This means that whatever the detailed explanation may turn out to be, "no one can seriously doubt" the major propositions for which the materialism of the Enlightenment had to fight. Materialism, in the sense in which it is opposed to spiritualism, was never on surer ground than it is today.

In general, those who delight in chanting funeral dirges over materialism are a bit premature in their enthusiasm. I know that the scientific theories of the structure and nature of matter have undergone revolutionary changes; and I am aware of the fact that the old-fashioned conception of mechanism has been generally discarded. But the new theories of the physical world are far from undermining materialism in the general sense of that term. The belief that all energies are fundamentally interacting, and that all life is based on these energies and functions only through material organisms (and, surely, this is the kernel of materialism), is more firmly entrenched than ever.

Historical materialism and the economic interpretation of history are, I admit, less certain than formerly, but these doctrines are post-Enlightenment and their weaknesses really support the older materialism. For the attempt to identify the material side of life with purely economic activities or with class struggles implies that the so-called spiritual sides of life have no solid matter to stand on. The problems of the body, so the argument runs, are fundamental to the problems of the soul. The force of this argument depends entirely on one's ability to separate the body and soul. Once grant, as scientific materialism does, that the life of the mind is just as much a part of the body as the life of the stomach or the heart, there is at least no *a priori* reason for believing that food (or lack of food) generates ideas, but that ideas are sterile.

In general, it is certainly true that the basic principles

and aims of materialism, for which the philosophers of the Enlightenment were compelled to fight, can now be taken for granted, even though the philosophies of science and the knowledge of matter have changed enormously since that time.

A second great contribution of the Enlightenment to modern culture is secularism. This term is even more difficult to define than materialism, but the facts for which it stands are so familiar that I need not attempt to give a precise meaning to something that is really vague. What I refer to is the general attempt to think and act in terms of the happiness and interests of actual men in the real world, not in terms of immortal souls in a future world. I have already spoken of the social gospel which liberal Christianity professes. This gospel is merely a first step in a revolutionary change that is coming over religion. It is an initial confession of the bankruptcy of the un-social gospel, of the literal version of the traditional gospel of redemption, resurrection, last judgment and eternal bliss or punishment. When we recall how bitterly rationalists of the past were attacked for repudiating the literal interpretation of this gospel and condemning the ecclesiastical exploitations thereof, the victory of humanitarian and social religion is no small tribute to the success of their cause. But once this leaven of secular, social reason has begun to work in religion, there is no telling how far it will go. Certainly it can not stop where it is, and even more certainly religion can not return to its former shell once that has been cast off.

This fact is frequently overlooked. It may be that the smug liberalism of yesterday is being repudiated today, but its work can never be wholly destroyed. The reconstruction has been too radical. The sophisticated revivals among contemporary theologians of the doctrines of St. Paul, St. Augustine, St. Thomas, St. Francis, Calvin, and other ancient champions of the gospel of sin and damnation, which the liberals had politely ignored, and which have a fresh power in every recurrence of human crisis and despair, are by no means mere revivals. They are radical reinterpretations based, for the most part, on contemporary experience and modern social philosophy. The doctrine of sin and redemption may be revived to give theological symbols to the confession of the failure of liberalism in our crisis and the need for some more powerful "redeemer," but the conscious use of theological mythology to express secular truth is by no means identical with the habit the classic theologians had of using secular history to prove sacred truth. Here again, the careful student will find in theology as in the sciences that the current attacks on rationalism are at the same time tributes to its success.

For rationalism is never as broad as the reason it worships. The temples it builds to reason are ornate with passing superstition, and frequently enshrine what it hopes to demolish. Therefore rationalism, of all faiths, must be most eager to remodel its temples. The temples we build today may prove too flimsy to endure reason long, but future temples must for that very reason be built on surer foundations, not on those which were inadequate even for us and which we have torn down. Reason, like time, is a quiet corrosive and works most effectively when it is least noticed. The boring from within which it has carried on in religion has ruined supernatural faith permanently. Future reconstruction may conceal the damage done, but it can not undo it. In the long run, the faith of rationalism is least damaged by reason. Of course, much that passes for reason in religion turns out to be merely another superstition, but reason itself makes these discoveries. This is the most beautiful trait of reason; it is a self-corrective. It is the best judge of its own shortcomings. Its failures of today make easier its work tomorrow. And though it may not discover eternal truth, it nevertheless goes on eternally discovering, uncovering, throwing new light on unexpected places.

It would be foolhardy, therefore, to venture to predict what reason may do to religion in the future. Suffice it to point out that it has already done wonders. The current tendencies are sufficient to prove my point that there are no set bounds to the secularization of religion, and that the rigid separation of modern secular culture and national politics from the traditional churches may prove to be but a temporary expedient in a more radical reconstruction of religion.

Whether or not secularism invades the very heart of religion, as I have suggested it may, the fact remains that it has already freed morality, law and politics from many of the arbitrary ideals and burdens imposed upon them by irrational forms of religion. And this work of liberation can not easily be undone. Anyone who doubts the effectiveness and pervasiveness of secular morality has but to pick up a typical textbook on ethics of a century ago and compare it with one of today. Those of today are, on the whole, less readable, less explicit, less certain and less systematic than those of the eighteenth century, but they are certainly less dogmatic and less hortatory. One of the most popular eighteenth-century texts was *The Whole Duty of Man*. Few modern moralists would have the temerity to write "The Whole Duty of Man," even though some of them talk as if they knew it.

In the face of this growing secularism and in the face of the fact that secularism is already generating its own religious features and fanaticisms, the claim made by some of the churches, notably the Catholic, that Christianity is more than a religion, that it is a type of civilization, even if it were true, is a confession that religion is at the service of civilization, and not civilization at the service of religion. That Christendom was at one time dominated by Christianity I do not doubt, and that in the future there may be a Christian civilization is possible, though not probable. But that Christianity, especially Catholicism, should aim at being an adequate and inclusive culture, embracing the whole of life in a unified pattern, competent to direct the intellectual, moral, economic and political life of man, is simply Christian secularism. Christianity is now a religion at best, an independent institution among others. Far from showing any capacity to dominate our civilization, it is itself increasingly dominated by secular institutions and ideals. Under these circumstances it is possible that church and state, religion and secular culture, may at some fairly

Herbert W. Schneider

distant time be reunited, and that this future culture may be called Christian, but it would undoubtedly not be recognized as such by any present Christian church, least of all by the Catholic. The very ideal of building a Christian civilization is now being preached in the name of humanity and humanitarian reform.

A third heritage from the Enlightenment is Republicanism. In its historic meaning republicanism stands not for a type of government but for a type of character. A republican in the eighteenth century was an anti-monarchist by accident; as in the United States today he is anti-democrat by accident. It was because monarchs had become tyrants that faithful servants of the commonwealth turned against monarchy, and called themselves neither nobles, nor lords, nor proprietors, nor tenants, nor peasants, but citizens — public servants. In classical theory both a true monarch and a true subject are equally republican, in the sense that their political station demands of them public spirit, devotion to the commonwealth.

The genuine *republicanism* of the Enlightenment consisted in its concern for the *res publica*, for matters of state, for the common interests of men as citizens. No one knew just what the *res publica* actually was; it served as an ideal for political faith. But whatever it might turn out to be in reality, it was by definition the opposite of the *res privata*. It embraced the interests shared by all as distinct from those which each pursued as his own personal business. There were many theories during the eighteenth century as to how the *res publica* might best be promoted, whether by enlightened self-interest or by service to the common will. But republicanism itself, the pursuit of the public weal or the greatest happiness of the greatest number is eminently and evidently a rationalistic moral ideal. It is the platform of plain reason in the field of social morality. The democratic type of government is merely one way of pursuing this ideal, and a rather romantic way, more credible during the nineteenth century than during the eighteenth century. In any case, the *value* of democracy must be tested, rationally speaking, by its ability to promote the *res publica.* Therefore, to condemn utilitarian morality or republican morality because of the shortcomings of democratic government is quite arbitrary. And in general to assume that the democratic dogmas are essentials of the rationalist faith betrays an all too superficial acquaintance with rational habits of thought. Had eighteenth-century rationalism been allowed to develop republicanism rationally instead of romantically, had it followed the lead of Montesquieu instead of Rousseau, or of Thomas Jefferson instead of Andrew Jackson, we might be much nearer the greatest happiness of the greatest number than we are.

Another article in the faith of the Enlightenment was the belief in universal progress, the perfectibility of man. This doctrine too suffered romantic corruption. It became a doctrine of natural evolution. Had rationalism followed the line of criticism taken by the Enlightenment, it would have insisted that progress is a human art, not natural history. As it was, however, the nineteenth century exaggerated the objectivity of reason. It deified and worshiped the laws of nature. Laws of evolution were identified by the theologians of science with inevitable progress. The theories of objective progress expounded by Hegel and Spencer are now revealed as the tawdriest nature-faking and theologizing. Naturally rationalism gets much of the blame for imposing such frauds on the human mind. Had it washed its hands in the beginning of such vacuous romanticism, and remained true to its eighteenth-century humanitarianism, it might be a better guide for us today.

I have now briefly surveyed the four chief articles of the rationalist faith, which have come down to us no longer as objects of faith but as commonplaces of common sense, namely, 1) the use of scientific method, 2) the hope of finding salvation in *this* world rather than in another, 3) the ideal of serving the common weal, and 4) the humanitarian zeal for the progress of all mankind. Though these articles of faith have been corrupted, confused, ridiculed and repudiated, they have survived a century of abuse and can still command the decent respect of reasonable men. There is nothing cold or forbidding about true enlightenment; its ideals naturally appeal to men as true ideals, however impractical they may seem as programs. And in our darkest hours they come with the sweetest comfort.

Let me close with a single illustration. Let me try out on you as a test case a typical expression of enlightened idealism. Does it appeal to you as it does to me?

A certain group of German liberals, the "Colony of the Friends of Nature," in 1791 used the following poem as a canticle for their conventicles. Mozart put the words to music. Though I cannot reproduce here Mozart's celestial music, nor the rhythm of the German words, the spirit of the hymn is nevertheless present even in a prosaic reading:

> Ye who honor this boundless world's creator,
> Who call him God, Tien or Brahma,
> Hear ye these words from the trumpet of the universal sovereign
> Resounding through earth, moons and suns.
> Hear him ye, too, my fellow-men!
> "Love me in my works, love order,
> Equity and peace;
> Love yourselves and your brothers.
> Let strength and beauty adorn your bodies
> And count him a nobleman whose mind is clear.
> Clasp hands in friendship's security, for
> Only madness has so long estranged you.
> Truth never will estrange.
> Break this mad bondage,
> Tear the veil of prejudice,
> Cast off sectarian robes,
> Forge reapers' sickles from iron that
> Hitherto has spilt your blood.
> Blast mountains with the black dust
> That has been driving lead into your brothers' hearts.
> Do not imagine that true evil can endure on earth,
> For what is called evil is but beneficent instruction
> When it spurs you to better deeds.
> It is you in the blindness of your folly who create evil when
> You use for retreat the spur that is intended to urge you forward.
> Be wise, be strong, be brothers
> And you will have my benediction.
> Your tears will be of joy

And your *Miserere* become a hymn of praise.
Deserts will be transformed into Edens;
All nature will rejoice for you,
And true happiness will at last be achieved."[2]

There is a sweet reasonableness in this faith that must make it admirable always among enlightened minds. Such a gospel must appeal to you as it does to me, not merely with the enchantment of distance, nor the grace of an antique, but as a genuine expression of human hope and an eternal revelation of reason.

To sum up, let me make a plea for a new Enlightenment. Reason is not something to be worshiped but to be used; and no greater blow could have been aimed at true rationalism than this attempt to make Reason a God. It is an active faith in reasoning, a *reliance on* rather than a *devotion to* reason, a willingness to be reasonable. The danger to rationalism comes not from freethinking but from loose thinking. Therefore let me recommend the example of the great rationalists of the seventeenth and eighteenth centuries. The real question for us is not: Does Reason govern the Universe? nor even: Is the world intelligible? but solely: Are *we* reasonable? Is what we think and say intelligible? *Good* thinking is in the long run the *freest*, and to be reasonable will always remain the chief glory of man, no matter what kind of a world it is we live in.

---

2. K.619. Composed in 1791. It is, of course, very similar to his compositions celebrating Freemasonry.

24

COMMUNITY, COMMUNICATION, AND COMMUNION*
Herbert W. Schneider

IT HAS BEEN CUSTOMARY AMONG SOCIOLOGISTS TO ANALYZE the forms of society into pairs of polar opposites. Such are the distinctions between natural and artificial society, civil and political, private and public, folk and urban, open and closed, *Gemeinschaft* and *Gesellschaft,* etc. To Herbert Spencer, James T. Shotwell, and Howard Becker (to mention a few representatives of a large group) it appears that human history is the gradual secularization of social relations — the passage from social solidarity (expressed by various forms of communion, divine right, or covenant) to social individualism and to purely practical or "industrial" forms of association. In the majority of these systems, religious communion has been associated with the more intimate, spontaneous, friendly types of society; and politics has become associated increasingly (both in theory and in fact) with the more businesslike forms of society. The problem central to all these traditional contrasts when applied to present-day

*Reprinted with permission from *NOMOS II: Community,* ed. Carl J. Friedrich (New York: The Liberal Arts Press, 1959), pp. 216-224.

institutions concerns the interpretation of the structure of a typical modern, industrial community. Such a society is not a face-to-face community or neighborhood in the classical sense; it does not rest on friendship or on common values. But neither is it merely a network of associations or a particular business among businesses. If a community is interpreted as *Gemeinschaft,* and *Gemeinschaft* is associated with intimacy or communion, it is clear that the traditional concepts and definitions no longer apply, for certainly a modern urban community is not a communion.

Reacting against the individualistic tendencies in Kierkegaard's, Bergson's, and Heidegger's theories of communion, Georges Gurvitch has attempted to locate community and communion as "degrees of sociality." According to him, in social "masses" there is a minimum of "personal interpenetration," and in communion such interpenetration is at a maximum, whereas in community there is an "average" or intermediate intensity of the "we." The general effect of communion is not universality (as in Bergson's theory) but social particularism and exclusiveness, sectarianism. When the "most intense degree of union or of 'we' is attained ... when minds open out as widely as possible and the least accessible depths of the 'I' are integrated in this fusion (which presupposes states of collective ecstasy) sociality is communion."[1] Hence the "opening out" of minds is toward each other, not toward God, and culminates in intimacy rather than in moral universality.

Max Weber attempted a more complicated classification of social forms by distinguishing four types of society: traditional (based on custom or communion); affectional (based on natural gregariousness or emotional bonds); rational (based on common values); and rational (based on common purposes or functions). But such a classification was not intended to define communities, since they embrace all four types. Similarly Talcott Parsons' "components" of the structure of social action are not types of societies but elements in any social organization.

---

1. Georges Gurvitch, "Mass, Community, Communion," in *Journal of Philosophy* (1941), pp. 485-96. Quotation on p. 487.

Herbert W. Schneider

In order to clarify the relation between community and communion, let me propose a fourfold classification of societies that is closely related to Max Weber's distinctions. Consider first the traditional polarities mentioned above as indicative of one axis of social relations: natural vs. utilitarian society; comradeship vs. business partnership; the intimate, friendly society of personal ties vs. the calculating, businesslike associations or co-operatives. A typical modern community does not fit into any pole of this axis, nor does it lie on any intermediate point between the poles. Such opposites do not mix; they remain complementary. Likewise, modern forms of religious communion cannot be located along this axis. But if we conceive another axis, crossing this one, with community at one pole and communion at the other, we have four types of society whose relations can be studied. They are based on two types of contrast, two axes.

At the intersection of these two axes let us place the art of communication through language and symbolism, for in this art they all share. We can then note four different directions along which language develops as it adapts itself to four different types of interpersonal relations. In the intimacies of private life, such as friendships and families, which constitute the primary reference in Tönnies' theory of community *(Gemeinschaft),* language must be expressive, more or less emotional and sentimental. It must center around the relations of natural gregariousness, the ties of natural groups, or what we usually call the more personal relationships. Opposite to such language is the language of public affairs and special interests — a colder language, better defined terms, concepts appropriate to the more "rational" associations. This polarity between home and office, family and factory, is as familiar as it is basic; and the types of communication appropriate to each are also well known.

Perpendicular to these two is the axis on which we have located communion and community. A community might still be called a neighborhood in a technical sense, but the modern way of being neighbors, whether urban or international, is very different from village neighborliness; the geographical huddling is less essential and personal bonds are less conspicuous. Members need not be friends and may have

Community, Communication, Communion

no emotional ties whatsoever. They may seldom meet and may not know who is "next door." They communicate not as persons who are directly important to each other, but as members who recognize each other's rights and duties. Community language is the language of morality and of equitable reciprocity. Neither are these modern neighbors business associates: their associational interests and labors may carry them in very different directions and may be based on conflicting values. What constitutes the core of the community is the organization of a public. A public administers a neighborhood's common needs, necessities, and conveniences. The community is held together physically at the bottom, rather than morally at the top. The co-operation implied in a community's public concerns is confined to instrumental goods or utilities rather than to the "common good" of idealist philosophy. The members communicate in order to establish and administer the general conditions under which each natural group and each particular business may go its own way in peace and freedom. Such moral concerns demand primarily a clear definition and distribution of responsibilities, and the more complicated the community becomes, the more the language of responsibility approaches the specialized, technical language of judicial procedure. Communication among members of such a community culminates in the law.

Basic to this public art of communication is the transformation of signs into symbols. The importance of the difference between signs and symbols is easily overlooked. Signs are essentially expressive mechanisms and become communicative of ideas by a slow process of standardization. But a symbol is a standard from the start. Symbols are the basic form of common property. It takes one to make a gesture, two to use signs, and a convention to establish a symbol. A symbol is nobody's private possession; its essence is communal, implying acceptance, agreement, convention, transaction. It is therefore not only an instrument of communication, it is a constitutive element in community. Without this minimum of common property a genuine community is inconceivable. For a community is more than a clan, more than a geographical neighborhood, and more than a *de facto* division of labor. It formalizes the division of labor and institutionalizes communication. It provides public recognition of specific agreements and such recognition presupposes more than custom; it presupposes articulate, accurate, public statements. By sharing the use of symbols a neighborhood acquires a public, and its habits become general propositions. A symbol, more than an oath, insures public recognition of a contract and lays the foundations for public intervention when needed. Being itself a form of obligation and responsibility, symbolical communication becomes a primary instrument in making other forms of responsibility possible. It is difficult to *hold* others responsible unless the act of holding can be made formal and public. Without standardized responses our attitudes toward each other would remain expressions of likes and dislikes and would fail to have the force of public praise and blame. But once expressed formally, our stated attitudes of praise and blame elicit responsible responses. In short, a community becomes operative only when a network of generalized responsibilities symbolically formulated is supported by standardized observance of the obligations stated.[2]

If this is so, it follows that the art of communication is a public service in a community to the extent that it promotes responsible expression and recognition of conventions. Public opinion, to be genuine, must be a responsible response to a public issue. It is not an aggregate or calculus of private expression in public symbols. There is this much truth in Rousseau's myth of the General Will. A community need not have a will at all; it need not have common objectives. But it must have a commonweal, that is, a system more or less explicit of recognized responsibilities. In this system the respect for symbols is itself a basic duty.

It is usual to interpret such a system of stated obligations

---

2. Cf. Jerome Hall, "Law and Religion," in *The Christian Leader* (October, 1950), p. 346: "Knowledge of the law ... means knowledge of certain precisely articulated moral ideas and of their daily operation in legal institutions."

as communal self-government. But prior to its function as government such a system is self-expression made public. Social concepts are social bonds, and the awareness of these bonds of reciprocity constitutes a kind of general acceptance or social contract prior to and fundamental to government. Even as government, however, the legal system represents a culmination both for morals and for communication. Formulation leads naturally to regulation, and norms generated in the context of agreements become norms for the settling of conflicts.

This legalistic perfection of communication is paralleled by the mathematical precision achieved in the sciences. Both bodies of symbolism, law and science, aim at clarity and coherence, but their functions and fields are different. Though the scientific languages are ideal in much the same sense that the legal language is, they are less directly made for communication. They are primarily tools of research and are spoken only in laboratories and classrooms. Of course, the scientists form a community of their own, and for their special community the languages of technology are essential as means of communication. But I am ignoring the community of science in the present analysis.

The antithesis of legal language is not scientific language but rather the language of communion. Here symbolism takes a very different course. It is seldom that a community is also a communion, though most communities sense the need for having communions in them. Occasionally, in festival, or crisis, a community may engage in what Gurvitch calls "collective ecstasy," in an intense expression of inner "sociality" or solidarity, but even such communal religiosity is not typical of modern religious communions. A communion is not based on mutual concern as is a community.[3] A communion is a social body, but not a community. It is held together not by a public or commonweal, but by a common

---

3. Cf. T. Foster Lindley, "The Church as Community," in *The Iliff Review* (1952), pp. 50-55. He conceives the church as a function of "community concern" and writes: "Those groupings which are doing the most to enhance values of the group through mutual concern are at the same time the groups that best characterize the community."

Herbert W. Schneider

expression of individual trust and faith. Its members meet not to commune with each other but to commune with God or with whatever object of supreme devotion brings them together. They may speak of *serving* God and of attending church *services*, but this is a misleading use of the term "service." A gathering for communion is a meeting in public, but it is not, or is not supposed to be, a social occasion. Of course, churches, being social institutions, engage in many activities besides communion; they may engage in mutual improvement, in social service, in community suppers, in plastic arts, in almost anything. But few churches regard communion as a minor concern, and by communion they mean communion with God, not social intimacy. During communion the members of a community divest themselves of their community relations and appear each alone before God or before an absolute judge and lord, to confess, petition, praise, sacrifice, or perform whatever other actions may be involved in the act of communion. Communion is an intensely personal or individual act, even when performed in public.

Hence, communion and community make very different demands on the art of symbolism. Symbols are conspicuous in communion, but not as instruments of communication. Their meaning is sacramental, hallowed but vague, sentimental but expressive of faith. The function of the symbols is to carry minds and imaginations away from the daily concerns, away from social affairs, until each communicant feels himself to be in the presence of God. The relation of devotee to Lord is not that of communication. The Lord is addressed, but there is no conversation. There may be what the religious call an "encounter," a genuine meeting, but this is not a meeting of minds. The language of communion is not designed for communication either with God or with neighbor; it is an expression of fellowship-in-communion, whose symbols are a public expression of a personal devotion.

Communion may, of course, be private, and some believe that the private life with God is primary to public communion. I am inclined to believe the opposite. The private devotions are an extension of the public use of symbols. The "com" in "communion" is essential. A fully aware communi-

Community, Communication, Communion

ty needs communion in public, not because God is to be met only in God's house, but because persons need to get out of their houses, factories, offices, gardens, into a special environment and unworldly atmosphere. As in the case of a hospital, so a church edifice is a public building used for individual treatments. The public display of the special symbols and arts of communion is as much a culmination of the arts of devotion as a hospital well equipped is the culmination of the medical arts. Communion renders the community a service, but in its operation it is intended neither as community nor as communication.

Communion is the culmination of the expressive use of symbols. Expressive language is at once the most primitive and the most sublime form of gesture, and the development of symbolism as a public institution would be incomplete if there were no opportunity for members of the community to express themselves publicly on matters of deepest concern. In their acts of communion men attempt to make their needs and faiths objective, though they may be unable to formulate them clearly either to themselves or to God. This predicament of human awareness, this explicit inarticulateness, this knowledge of human ignorance, leads those who have felt the limitations of communication to feel as one of their basic needs the opportunity to commune.

Thus law and communion supplement each other. One makes agreements explicit, the other makes concerns eloquent. One serves the cause of responsibility and peace, the other serves loyalty and devotion. Both are forms of concord, but in very different senses. Both are symbolical systems, but they use symbols in opposite ways. In law there is a persistent concern for the integrity of the symbols; in communion there is a public avowal of the symbols of integrity. Taken as independent systems, these two appear to be incompatible, but taken as developments in high cultures from a common matrix they appear to supply each other's deficiencies. A well-formed community needs both these dimensions of concord, and it does well to keep them apart, for when mixed they corrupt each other: law becomes a fetish and communion degenerates into a community center.

HERBERT WALLACE SCHNEIDER
A Bibliography

BOOKS

1. *Science and Social Progress: A Philosophical Introduction to Moral Science,* (Archives of Philosophy, No. 12, 1920.) New York: Columbia University Press, 1920.
2. *Making the Fascist State.* Oxford: Oxford University Press, 1928; Reprint, 1968, Fertig.
3. *Bibliography of John Dewey* (with M. H. Thomas). New York: Columbia University Press, 1929; Oxford University Press, 1930.
4. *Making Fascists* (with S. B. Clough), (University of Chicago, Studies in the Making of Citizens, No. 5). Chicago: University of Chicago Press, 1929.
5. *Samuel Johnson, President of King's College: His Career and Writings,* Edited by HWS and Carol Schneider with a foreword by Nicholas Murray Butler. New York: Columbia University Press, 1929.
6. *Puritan Mind* (Studies in Religion and Culture, American Religion series, No. 1). New York: Holt, 1930; Reprint, Constable, 1931; Reprint, University of Michigan Press, Ann Arbor paperback, 1958.
7. *Religion in Various Cultures* (with Horace Freiss), (Studies in Religion and Culture). New York: Holt, 1932; Reprint, Johnson, 1966.
8. *Fascist Government of Italy,* (Governments of Modern Europe series). Van Nostrand, 1936.
9. *Source Book on European Governments* (Section III edited by H.W.S.:) *Documents on the Fascist Government of Italy,* pages III-1 through III-113. Van Nostrand, 1937.
10. *Meditations in Season: On the Elements of Christian Philosophy.* Oxford: Oxford University Press, 1938.
11. *A Bibliography of John Dewey, 1882-1939,* Second edition revised and enlarged by M. H. Thomas, with an introduction by HWS. New York: Columbia University Press, 1939.

Bibliography

12. *Fountainheads of Freedom: The Growth of the Democratic Idea,* HWS and Irwin Edman. Reynal, 1941.
13. *Landmarks in Philosophy,* HWS and Irwin Edman, eds. Reynal, 1941; Reprint, *Landmarks for Beginners in Philosophy* (ed. with assistance of E. N. Garbar and others), Reynal, 1941.
14. *Prophet and a Pilgrim,* being the incredible history of Thomas Lake Harris and Laurence Oliphant, their sexual mysticisms and utopian communities amply documented to confound the skeptic, by George Lawton, ed. by HWS (Columbia Studies in American Culture, No. 11). New York, Columbia University Press, 1942.
15. *In Commemoration of William James, 1842-1942,* ed. by HWS and Brand Blanshard. New York: Columbia University Press, 1942.
16. *History of American Philosophy,* (Columbia Studies in American Culture, No. 18). New York: Columbia University Press, 1946; 2nd edition, Columbia University Press, 1963.
17. *Adam Smith: Moral and Political Philosophy,* ed. with Introduction by HWS. New York: Hafner Publishing Company, 1948; Reprint, Harper Torchbooks, 1970.
18. *Dante Alighieri: On World Government or De Monarchia,* Trans. by HWS, Introduction by D. Bigongiari. New York: Liberal Arts Press, 1949; 2nd revised edition, 1957.
19. *Historia de la Filosofia Norteamericana,* Trans. of 16, by Egenio Imaz. Mexico: Fondo de Cultura Economica, 1950.
20. *Religion in 20th Century America,* (Library of Congress Series in American Civilization). Cambridge: Harvard University Press, 1952; Reprint, Oxford, 1953; Revised Edition, Atheneum Publishers, 1964.
21. *Histoire de la philosophie américaine,* Trans. of 16 by Cl. Simonnet.
22. *Three Dimensions of Public Morality* (Indiana University, Mahlon Powell Foundation Lectures). Bloomington: Indiana University Press, 1954.
23. *Geschichte der amerikanischen Philosophie,* Trans. of 16 by Peter Krausser. Hamburg: Meiner, 1957.
24. *A History of American Philosophy,* paper edition. New York: Liberal Arts Press, 1957.
25. *Hobbes: Leviathan, Parts 1 and 2,* Edited with introduction by HWS. New York: Liberal Arts Press, 1958.
26. *Dialogue on John Dewey,* ed. Corliss Lamont; HWS as a participant. New York: Horizon Press, 1959.
27. *Morals for Mankind,* (University of Missouri, Paul Anthony Brick Lectures, Inaugural Series, 1960). Columbia, Missouri: University of Missouri Press, 1960.
28. *Viš Sataker America-y tharma,* (Bengali) Trans.of 20 by Sanatan Gosvami. Calcutta: Parichay Publishers, 1961.
29. *Visavya Satakantil Amerike-madhala Dharma,* (Marathi) Trans. of 20 by C. V. Bavdekar. Bombay: Vora and Company, 1961.
30. *Visbhi sadina America-ma tharmanus sthan,* (Gujarati) Trans. of 20 by Mannbhai Maheta. Bombay: Vora and Company, 1961.

Bibliography

31. *20va satabdi America lo matamu,* (Telugu) Trans. of 20 by Tirumala Ramachandra. Rajahmundry: Addepalli and Company, [1961?].
32. *Storia della filosofia Americana,* Trans. of 16 by Vittoria Fercatini and Paolo Valerio. Il Mulino, 1963.
33. *Dharma da svarup adhunik America men,* (Hindi) Trans. of 20 by [?]. Allahabad: Bharati Bhander, 1962.
34. *Ways of Being: Elements of Analytic Ontology,* (Columbia University Woodbridge Lectures, No. 7). New York: Columbia University Press, 1962; Reprint, Columbia University Press, 1964. Reprint, Greenwood Press, 1974.
35. *Sources of Contemporary Philosophical Realism in America.* Indianapolis and New York: Bobbs-Merrill, 1964.
36. *Moral Para a Humanidad,* (Portuguese) Trans. of 27 by Aydono Arruda. Sao Paulo: Ibrasa, 1964.
37. *Civilized Religion: An Historical and Philosophical Analysis.* New York: Exposition Press, 1972.

PAMPHLETS

38. *Italy Incorporated: The Guild Organization of the Italian People* (Pamphlet No. 3). New York: Italian Historical Society, 113 West 42 Street, New York, 1928.
39. *Activity and Worship. The Colgate-Rochester Divinity School Bulletin,* October, 1937.
40. *Natural Religion. The Harvard Divinity School Bulletin,* No. 36, 1939, 26 pages.
41. *Pan, the Logos and John Dewey: A Legend of the Green Mountains,* (Including *The Realism of Jane Adams,* by John Dewey). Philadelphia: Philadelphia Woman's International League for Peace and Freedom; Reprint, J. Dewey-J. Adams Centennial, 1959-60. Originally published as pp. 122-134 of HWS's essay, "The Prospect for Empirical Philosophy", in *John Dewey: The Man and His Philosophy.* Addresses Delivered in New York in Celebration of His Seventieth Birthday (Cambridge, Mass.: Harvard University Press, 1930). See item #127 below.

ARTICLES

42. "Dualism in Modern Theories of Moral Education," *Educational Review,* LII (November, 1916), 372-384.
43. "The Theory of Values," *Journal of Philosophy,* XIV (1917), 141-154.
44. "Values of Pragmatic Theory: A Rejoinder to Professor Urban," *Journal of Philosophy,* XIV (1917), 706-714.
45. "Instrumental Instrumentalism," *Journal of Philosophy,* XVIII (1921), 113-117.
46. "John Dewey and His Influence," *The New Era,* 2, no. 5, (January, 1921), 136-140.
47. "Faith," *Journal of Philosophy,* XXI (1924), 36-40.

Bibliography

48. "The 24th Annual Meeting of the Eastern Division of the American Philosophical Association," *Journal of Philosophy,* XXII (1925), 42-48.
49. "Intelligence and Morals," *Journal of Philosophy,* XXIII (1926), 213-220.
50. "Note on the Samuel Johnson Papers," *American Historical Review,* XXXI (July, 1926), 724-726.
51. "Italy's New Syndicalist Constitution," *Political Science Quarterly,* XLII (June, 1927), 161-202.
52. "Giovinezza," *Century,* CXV (December, 1927), 185-194.
53. "An International Congress of Higher Critics," *Journal of Philosophy,* XXIV (1927), 447-448.
54. "Phases of Fascism," *Historical Outlook,* XIX, no. 1 (January, 1928), 7-12.
55. "Holy Commonwealth in America," *International Journal of Ethics,* XXXIX, no. 1 (October, 1928), 50-60.
56. "Ways of Being," *Journal of Philosophy,* XXI (1928), 365-378.
57. "He Modernized Our Schools," (on occasion of John Dewey's 70th birthday), *New York Herald Tribune* (October 13, 1929), 8, 28, 29.
58. "Jonathan Edwards," *Nation,* CXXXI (November 26, 1930), 584.
59. "Post-War Protestantism," *Church History,* Vol. IV., No. 2 (June, 1935), 87-102.
60. "Religious Celebration in the Home," *Child Study,* XIII (February, 1936), 137-139.
61. "The Divorce of American Philosophy and Psychology since James," (Abstract) *Journal of Philosophy,* XXXIII (1936), 686-687.
62. "Laird's Inquiry into Moral Notions," *Journal of Philosophy,* XXXIV (April 15, 1937), 210-216.
63. "Theology and Science in Contemporary Platonic Idealism," *Review of Religion,* II (1938), 166-174.
64. "High and Low Road to Peace," *International Journal of Ethics,* LXVIII (January, 1938), 214-220.
65. "Note on Dewey's Theory of Valuation," *Journal of Philosophy,* XXXVI (August 31, 1939), 490-495.
66. "Moral Obligation," *Ethics,* L (October, 1939), 45-56.
67. "William James as a Moralist," (Abstract) *Journal of Philosophy,* XXXVIII (December 4, 1941), 674-675.
68. "Enlightenment in Thomas Jefferson," *Ethics,* LIII, no. 4 (July, 1943), 246-254.
69. "Sin and Society," *Review of Religion,* VI (May, 1943), 407-413.
70. "Enlightenment in Thomas Jefferson," *Ethics,* LIII, no. 4 (July, 1943), 246-254.
71. "Queries on Natural Law, Human Rights, and Human Nature," *Journal of Philosophy,* XL (September 16, 1943), 515-516.
72. "Influence of Darwin and Spencer on American Philosophical Theology," *Journal of the History of Ideas,* VI (January, 1945), 3-18.
73. "Liberal Theology: A Comment," *Journal of Religion,* XXVI (January, 1946), 49-50.

Bibliography

74. "Symposium: The Distinctive Contribution of Philosophy to the Issues of the Peace," with Glenn Morrow and Ralph Barton Perry, (Abstract) *Journal of Philosophy*, XLIII (1946), 72-74.
75. "Philosophy in the Fight and at Work," *Ethics*, LVI (July, 1946), 267-272.
76. "Religion in America," *Review of Religion*, III (March, 1947), 307-310.
77. "Century of Romantic Imagination in America," *Philosophical Review*, LVI (July, 1947), 351-356.
78. "International Congresses and the International Federation of Philosophical Studies," *Journal of Philosophy*, XLVIII (1948), 636-642.
79. "Reasonable Rationalism: The Heritage of the Enlightenment," *The Age of Enlightenment:* Proceedings of the Humanities Institute (March 6-7, 1948). Toledo: The University of Toledo, 1948, 5-13.
80. "Religion: Its Functions in Human Life. A Study of Religion from the Point of View of Psychology," *Review of Religion*, XII (March, 1948), 531-534.
81. "Metaphysical Vision," *Philosophical Review*, LVIII (September, 1949), 399-411. (Presidential Address to the American Philosophical Association, December, 1948).
82. "Wilhelm Kosch's Deutsches Literatur-Lexikon: Biographisches und Bibliographisches Handbuch," *German Review*, XXV (1950), 67-69.
83. "On Defining Ideals," *Standard*, XXXVII (October, 1950), 19-24.
84. "A Symposium on Philosophic Thought in France and the United States," with Roy Wood Sellars, *Philosophy and Phenomenological Research*, XI (1951), 376-400.
85. "La Pensée de George Santayana," Par Jacques Duron; discussion by HWS, *Journal of Philosophy*, XLVIII (1951), 251-261.
86. "Natural Thought and the World of Religion," *Journal of Philosophy*, XLVIII (February 1, 1951), 66-74.
87. "La Pensée Philosophique en France et aux États-Unis," *Les Études Philosophiques*, VII (1952), 16-29.
88. "John Dewey as My Teacher," *Progressive Education*, XXX (October, 1952), 11-13.
89. "Note on a Not-So Vicious Intellectualism," *Journal of Philosophy*, XLIX (February 14, 1972), 121-122.
90. "Santayana and Realistic Conceptions of Authority," *Journal of Philosophy*, XLIX (March 27, 1952), 214-220.
91. "Utilitarianism and Moral Obligation: Obligations and the Pursuit of Happiness," *Philosophical Review*, LXI (July, 1952), 312-319.
92. "Comment," *Ethics*, LXIV (October, 1953), 50-51.
93. "The Old Theory and the New Practice of Religious Loyalty," *American Quarterly*, V (Winter, 1953), 291-300.
94. "Idealism East and West," *Philosophy East and West*, IV (1954), 265-269.
95. "Commentaire américaine sur le dualisme européen," *Revue COMPRENDRE*, Nos. 10-11 (1954), 1-3.
96. "Natural and Cultural Processes," *Madras University Journal*, 1955, 241-245.

Bibliography

97. "Ontologik und amerikanische 'process philosophy'," *Zeitschrift für Philosophische Forschung,* IX (1955), 306-312.
98. "René Le Senne et la Communication des Consciences," *Les Études Philosophiques,* X (1955), 418-419.
99. "Dialogue and Dialectic," (A review of the conference held in Athens, May 2-6, 1955, auspices of the International Institute of Philosophy), by Gilbert Varet, trans. by HWS, *Journal of Philosophy,* LII (1955), 533-539.
100. "La Liberté, la loi et les droits," *Révue Liberale,* XII (1955), 122-126.
101. "III. Convegno dei Lettori di Filosofia," *Studi Francescani,* 52 (1955), 139-140.
102. "On Reading Heschel's *God in Search of Man;* A Review Article," *Review of Religion,* XXI (November, 1956), 31-38.
103. "Realité et Éxistence dans la Philosophie," *La Table Ronde,* no. 105 (1956), 67-72.
104. "American Traits and Principles," contribution to Prelim. Report on 3rd East-West Philosophers' Conference, *Philosophy East and West,* IX (April-July, 1959), 52-53.
105. "Western Philosophy and Practical Affairs," contribution to Prelim. Report on 3rd East-West Philosophers' Conference, *Philosophy East and West,* IX (April-July, 1959), 11-12.
106. "Whom Ye Ignorantly Worship," *The Iliff Review,* XVI, no. 2 (Spring, 1959), 49-52.
107. "The Developments in Protestantism during the Nineteenth Century Throughout the World," *Cahiers d'Histoire Mondiale,* VI (1960-61), 97-121.
108. "A emigracão das idéias para a America," *Revista Brasileira de Filosofia,* X, no. 4 (October-December, 1960), 519-522.
109. "Historical Construction and Reconstruction," *Eranos-Jahrbuch,* XXIX (1960), 243-264.
110. "Gaston Berger," *Études Philosophiques,* XVI (1961), 413-415.
111. "The Humanist Faith — Perennial and Universal," *The Humanist,* Vol. 23, No. 1 (January-February, 1963), 2-4.
112. "Schooling, Learning, and Education," The Hullfish Tribute Lecture, November 1, 1963, College of Education, University of Cincinnati; published in *The Educational Forum* (November, 1964), 31-38.
113. "La Philosophie de l'Histoire aux États-Unis," *Études Philosophiques,* XIX (1964), 255-264.
114. " 'Chevalier' Ramsay's Critique of Spinoza," *Journal of the History of Philosophy* III (1965), 91-96.
115. "The Democracy of Hawthorne," *The Emory University Quarterly,* Vol. XXII, No. 2 (Summer, 1966), 123-132.
116. "Addenda of George Santayana," *Journal of the History of Philosophy,* VI (July, 1968), 285-287.
117. "Moral Strategy and Religious Humanism," *Religious Humanism,* II, (Winter, 1968), 23-24.

Bibliography

118. "Piety as a Public Utility," *Religious Humanism,* II (Spring, 1968), 65-69.
119. "Religion in the Service of Modern Society," *Buffalo Studies,* Vol. IV, No. 5 (December, 1968), 27-41.
120. "Needs and Values," *Zygon,* Vol. 4, No. 3 (September, 1969), 291-292.
121. "Crisis in Santayana's Life and Mind," *Southern Journal of Philosophy,* Vol. 10, No. 2 (October, 1972), 109-113.
122. "Philosophy Will Never Be a Science," *Philosophical Essays,* II (Torino: Edizioni di 'Filosofia', [n.d.]), 3-7.
123. Note on Beth Singer's *The Rational Society: A Critical Study of Santayana's Social Thought,* in *The Philosophy Forum,* vol. 12, nos. 3-4 (Dec., 1972), 333-336.

ARTICLES IN BOOKS

124. "Reflective Thinking in Law," in *An Introduction to Reflective Thinking,* by Columbia Associates in Philosophy (Boston: Houghton Mifflin Company, 1923, Chapter XI), 265-300.
125. "Political Implications of Recent Philosophical Movements," in *A History of Political Theories: Recent Times,* edited by Charles Merriam and Harry Elmer Barnes (New York: Macmillan and Company, 1924, Chapter VIII), 313-356.
126. "Radical Empiricism and Religion," *Essays in Honor of John Dewey by his Students and Associates,* (on occasion of his 70th birthday). (New York: Holt, 1929), 336-353.
127. "The Prospect for Empirical Philosophy," in *John Dewey — The Man and His Philosophy* (Cambridge: Harvard University Press, 1930), 106-134. ("Pan, the Logos and John Dewey," listed above as item #41 was first published as pages 122-134 of this article.)
128. "The Significance of Benjamin Franklin's Moral Philosophy," *Studies in the History of Ideas,* II (New York: Columbia University Press, 1932), 291-312.
129. "Mill's Methods and Formal Logic," *Studies in the History of Ideas,* III (New York: Columbia University Press, 1935), 407-426.
130. "Political Morality," in *American Philosophy Today and Tomorrow,* edited by H. M. Kallen and S. Hook (New York: Furman, Inc., 1935).
131. "Documents on the Fascist Government of Italy," in *Source Book on European Governments* (Van Nostrand, 1937).
132. "Philosophical Difference Between the Constitution and the Bill of Rights," in American Historical Association's *The Constitution Reconsidered,* edited by Conyers Read (New York: Columbia University Press, 1938), 143-156.
133. "William James as a Moralist," in *In Commemoration of William James,* edited by Horace Kallen (New York: Columbia University Press, 1942), 127-139. (An earlier version of this paper appears as item #67 above.)

Bibliography

134. "Power of Free Religion," in *Conference on the Scientific Spirit and Democratic Faith,* First Symposium (New York: King's Crown Press, 1944), 87-92.
135. "Unnatural," in *Naturalism and the Human Spirit,* edited by Y. H. Kirkorian (New York: Columbia University Press, 1944), 121-132.
136. "Laurens Persens Hickok: American Philosopher," *Laurens Persens Hickok* [Union Worthies, no. 2] (Schenectady: Union College, 1947), 11-16.
137. "The Puritan Tradition," in *Wellsprings of the American Spirit,* edited by F. E. Johnson (New York: Institute for Religious and Social Studies, Harper, 1948), 1-13.
138. "Social Ideals of American Naturalism," in *Proceedings of the 10th International Congress of Philosophy,* Amsterdam, August 11-18, 1948, edited by E. W. Beth, H. J. Pas and J. H. Hollak (Amsterdam: North Holland Publishing Company, 1949), 1003-1006.
139. "Permanent Committee on Bibliography," in *Proceedings and Addresses of the American Philosophical Association,* Vol. 23 (1949-50) (Yellow Springs, Ohio, 1950), 69-70.
140. "Laity and Prelacy in American Democracy," in *John Dewey: Philosopher of Science and Freedom,* edited by S. Hook (New York: Dial Press, 1950), 170-183.
141. "Fourthness," in *Studies in the Philosophy of Charles Sanders Peirce,* edited by P. P. Weiner and F. H. Young (Cambridge: Harvard University Press, 1952-1964), 209-214.
142. "John Dewey, (1859-1952)," *Yearbook of The American Philosophical Society,* 1952, 311-315.
143. "Humanism and Ontology," in *Actes de XIe Congres International de Philosophie: Tome III, Métaphysique et Ontologie,* held 1953 in Bruxelles (Amsterdam: North Holland Publishing Company, 1953), 40-43.
144. "Reformation and National Churches; Protestant Revolt," by HWS and Harry Elmer Barnes in *Chapters in Western Civilization,* 1954, Vol. I, p. 234-250; 258-70 [original edition, 1948] selected and edited by the Contemporary Civilization staff of Columbia College (New York: Columbia University Press, 1948).
145. "Pouvoir et devoir," in *Le Pouvoir,* Tome II, *Théorie,* Par G. Davy, J. Maritain, HWS, H. B. Acton, et al., (Annales de philosophie politique, 2), Institute de Philosophie politique (Paris: Presses Universitaires de France, 1957), 57-67.
146. "Christian Theocracy and Hobbes's 'Mortal God'," *Studies in the History of Religions,* (Supplements to *Numen*), IV: The Sacral Kingship (Leiden: E. J. Brill, 1959), 627-632.
147. "Community, Communication, and Communion," Chapter 13 of C. J. Friedrich, editor, *Nomos II: Community* (New York: Liberal Arts Press, 1959).
148. "Western Philosophy and Practical Affairs," in *Proceedings of the East-West Philosophy Conference,* edited by Charles Moore, [pub. unknown], 1959, 67-80.

Bibliography

149. "Peace as Scientific Problem and as Personal Experience," *Eranos-Jahrbuch*, XXVII, 1959, 333-57.
150. "Nature and Man's World," Vol. II in *Atti del XII Congresso Internazionale di Filosofia* (Venezia 12-18 settembre 1958: L'Uomo e la natura, discorsi della sedutta inaugurale) (Firenze: Sansoni, 1960), 383-387.
151. "Discussioni," with: V. Molodzow, P. Siwek, I. Höllhuber, T. Stepanjan, E. Riverso, S. Moser, S. Krohn, E. Albrecht, R. Schottlaender, V. Ruml, A. Siracky, R. Lazzarini, G. Calogero, K. Momdjian, Z. Adamczewski, Y. Melvil, G. Palumbo, A. Muñoz-Alonso, R. McKeon. Vol. III of *Atti del XII Congresso Internazionale di Filosofia* (Venezia, 12-18 settembre, 1958: Liberta e valore) (Firenze: Sansoni, 1960), 469-508.
152. "Vom Sinn der Symbole in Rechtlicher und religiöser Gemeinschaft," In *Sinn und sein: Ein philosophisches Symposion*, edited by Eichard Wisser (Tübingen: Max Niemeyer Verlag, 1960), 731-42. (German translation of #147).
153. "International Relations and World Religions," *The Radhakrishnan Number: A Souvenir Volume of Appreciations* (Madras: Vyasa Publications, 1962), 179-184.
154. "Global orientation," in *Memorias del XIII Congreso Internacional de Filosofia* (Mexico, D. F., 7-14 de Septiembre de 1962), Vol. I (Mexico: Universidad Nacional Autonoma de Mexico, 1963), 193-213. Reprinted in *Revue COMPRENDRE*, No. 26-27, 1964,1-15 in French translation.
155. "Die geschichtliche Bedeutung der Buberschen Philosophie," in *The Philosophy of Martin Buber,* edited by P. A. Schilpp and M. Friedman (Stuttgart, 1963), 414-19.
156. "The developments in Protestantism during the nineteenth century throughout the world," in Metraux, Guy S. and Crouzet, François, editors, *The Nineteenth-Century World: Readings from the History of Mankind* (New York: New American Library [Mentor Books], 1963). Reprinted from *Journal of World History,* "The developments in Protestantism during the Nineteenth Century throughout the World," Vol. 6 (1960-61), 97-121.
157. "American Transcendentalism's escape from Phenomenology," in Simon, Myron and Parsons, Thornton H., editors, *Transcendentalism and Its Legacy* (Ann Arbor: University of Michigan Press, 1966).
158. "The Historical Significance of Buber's Philosophy," *The Philosophy of Martin Buber, The Library of Living Philosophers*, Vol. XII (La Salle: Open Court, 1967), 469-475. (English version of #155.)
159. "A Minor Prophet on the American Frontier," *Glaube, Geist, Geschichte: Festschrift für Ernst Benz Zum 60. Gerburtstage am 17. November, 1967* (Leiden: E. J. Brill, 1967), 344-348.
160. "Philosophies and sciences in modern cultures," in *Science, Philosophy and Culture: Essays presented in Honor of Humgyun Kabir's 62nd Birthday,* edited by Frank Moraes (Bombay: Asia Publishing House, 1968).
161. "To Be and Not to Be," in *American Philosophers at Work*, edited by S. Hook (New York: Greenwood Press, 1968), 277-286.

162. "Philosophy," *American Civilization: An Introduction*, edited by A. N. J. den Hollander and Sigmund Skard (London: Longmans, Green and Co., Ltd., 1968), 277-294 (Chapter 9).
163. "A Changing Sense of Sin," *Puritanism in 17th Century Massachusetts*, edited by David D. Hall (New York: Holt, Rinehart and Winston, 1968), 92-99.
164. "High and Higher Education," *Philosophy of Education: 1969. Proceedings of the Philosophy of Education Society, Denver, March 30-April 2, 1969* (Edwardsville: Studies in Philosophy and Education, 1969), 64-73.
165. "Dewey's Ethics: Part I," *Guide to the Works of John Dewey*, edited by J. A. Boydston (Carbondale, Illinois: Southern Illinois University Press, 1970), 99-111.
166. "Dewey's Psychology," *Guide to the Works of John Dewey*, edited by J. A. Boydston (Carbondale, Illinois: Southern Illinois University Press, 1970), 1-14.
167. "Barriers to Communication between Theology and Religion," Conference on Science, Philosophy and Religion, 5th Symposium [n.d.], 665-676.
168. "Declaration, Theory and Existence of Human Rights," *Festschrift for Paul Arthur Schilpp*, edited by Eugene Freeman (Glencoe: The Open Court Press, forthcoming).

ARTICLES IN ENCYCLOPEDIAS

169. "Bradford, William," in *Encyclopaedia of the Social Sciences*, Macmillan, 1930, Vol. 2, 671-672.
170. "Brownson, Orestes Augustus," in *Encyclopaedia of the Social Sciences*, Macmillan, 1930, Vol. 3, 16-17.
171. "Christian Science," in *Encyclopaedia of the Social Sciences*, Macmillan, 1930, Vol. 2, 446-449.
172. "Cotton, John," in *Encyclopaedia of the Social Sciences*, Macmillan, 1930, Vol. 4, 493-494.
173. "Eddy, Mary Baker," in *Encyclopaedia of the Social Sciences*, Macmillan, 1930, Vol. 5, 395-396.
174. "Edwards, Jonathan," in *Encyclopaedia of the Social Sciences*, Macmillan, 1930, Vol. 5, 436-437.
175. "Ethical Culture Movement," in *Encyclopaedia of the Social Sciences*, Macmillan, 1930, Vol. 5, 600-602.
176. "Italy under Fascism," in *Encyclopaedia of the Social Sciences*, Macmillan, 1930, Vol. 1, 277-279.
177. "Revivals, Religious," in *Encyclopaedia of the Social Sciences*, Macmillan, 1930, Vol. 13, 363-366.
178. "Transcendentalism," in *Encyclopaedia of the Social Sciences*, Macmillan, 1930, Vol. 15, 75-77.
179. "Philosophy," *The American Annual: Events of 1949*, The Americana Corporation, 1950, 543-544.

NOTES ON CONTRIBUTORS

JOHN P. ANTON is Fuller E. Callaway Professor of Philosophy and chairman of the Department of Philosophy at Emory University; he has served on the faculties of S.U.N.Y. at Buffalo, Columbia University, Ohio Wesleyan University, University of Nebraska and the University of New Mexico, and has written or edited a number of books, including *Aristotle's Theory of Contrarieties, Naturalism and Historical Understanding, Philosophical Essays* and *Essays in Ancient Greek Philosophy.*

JOSEPH BLAU took his A. B. (1931), A.M. (1933) and Ph.D. (Philosophy, 1945) at Columbia University, where he has taught since 1946 in the Department of Religion. He has held a number of research fellowships, and has been visiting professor at several American colleges and universities. Among his writings are *The Christian Interpretation of the Cabala in the Renaissance* (1945, 1966); *Men and Movements in American Philosophy* (1952); and *The Story of Jewish Philosophy* (1964).

WHITAKER T. DEININGER (B. A. Amherst College, 1944; Ph.D. Columbia University, 1952) teaches Humanities and Philosophy at the California State University, San Jose. Concerned with the value areas of philosophical analysis, he has published essays on philosophy of history and social thought, and *Problems in Social and Political Thought* (Macmillan, 1965).

MAX H. FISCH (B. A. Butler University, 1924; Ph.D. Cornell, 1930) is Professor Emeritus at University of Illinois, has taught at many universities here and abroad (including Italy, India and Japan) and has served as officer of a number of learned societies. His many articles and books include *Philosophy in America from the Puritans to James* (with Paul R. Anderson), *Classic American Philosophers, The Autobiography of Giambattista Vico* and *The New Science of Giambattista Vico* (both translated and edited with Thomas G. Bergin).

J. GLENN GRAY is Professor of Philosophy at Colorado College in Color-

Biographical Notes

ado Springs; he received his doctorate at Columbia University where Herbert Schneider was his teacher, and since then a good friend. Author of *Hegel and Greek Thought, The Warriors: Reflections on Men in Battle, The Promise of Wisdom: A Philosophical Theory of Education.* Gray has been for the last eight years the general editor for translating Martin Heidegger's writings into English.

LEWIS E. HAHN is Research Professor of Philosophy, Southern Illinois University at Carbondale. Author of *A Contextualistic Theory of Perception,* co-author of *Value: A Cooperative Inquiry, Guide to the Works of John Dewey* and *Evolution-Revolution,* he has taught at the University of Missouri, Princeton and Washington University. He has served as President of the Southwestern Philosophical Society and the Southern Society for Philosophy and Psychology, and has held various posts in the American Philosophical Association.

JOHN A. HUTCHISON received his Ph.D. at Columbia University with a dissertation under Herbert Schneider's direction, and has since taught philosophy and religion at the College of Wooster, Williams College, Columbia University and now at the Claremont Graduate School where once more Herbert Schneider is mentor, colleague and friend.

JAMES L. JARRETT studied at UCLA, University of Utah, and the University of Michigan (Ph.D., 1948), and has taught at Utah, Columbia, Michigan, Western Washington (President, 1959-1964), and Colorado College. Professor of Philosophy of Education at U. of C., Berkeley since 1964, presently with UC London Office (1972-1974). Among his writings are *Quest for Beauty, Language and Informal Logic, Educational Theories of the Sophists* and *The Humanities and Humanistic Education.*

GEORGE L. KLINE is Professor of Philosophy at Bryn Mawr College, and has taught at Columbia, the University of Chicago and elsewhere. His first formal course work in metaphysics was with Herbert Schneider (Columbia summer session, 1947), and Schneider was a member (with James Gutmann and John H. Randall) of Kline's dissertation committee (published as *Spinoza in Soviet Philosophy).* Kline's latest book is *Religious and Anti-Religious Thought in Russia.*

PAUL KURTZ is Professor of Philosophy at S.U.N.Y. at Buffalo, and is the author of *Decision and the Condition of Man,* as well as editor of *American Thought Before 1900* and *American Philosophy in the Twentieth Century;* he is also editor of *The Humanist.*

BERTRAM MORRIS has his A.B. from Princeton (1930) and his Ph.D. from Cornell University (1934). He has taught at the University of Wyoming and at Northwestern University prior to assuming his present position at the University of Colorado. In addition to visiting professorships and grants, he is the author of a number of articles and books, including *The Aesthetic Process* (1943), *Philosophical Aspects of Culture* (1961) and *Institutions of Intelligence* (1969).

RICHARD H. POPKIN took his A.B. (1943), A.M. (1945) and Ph.D. (1950) at Columbia University. Recipient of a number of research fellowships for study in France and Holland, he has taught at several universities,

Biographical Notes

including University of California, San Diego and (presently) Washington University. In addition to a number of visiting professorships, he is the author of many articles and of *The History of Scepticism from Erasmus to Descartes* (1960, 1964), translator of Pierre Bayle's *Historical and Critical Dictionary* (1965), co-editor of *David Hume: Philosophical Historian* (1965), and is editor of the *Journal of the History of Philosophy.*

RALPH ROSS is Hartley Burr Alexander Professor of Humanities and Professor of Philosophy at Scripps College, and author of *Obligation: A Social Theory,* and *Symbols and Civilization,* among others. He has edited books by William James, George Santayana, Samuel Alexander, F. H. Bradley and Bernard Bosanquet, and has contributed to encyclopaedias, anthologies and periodicals.

DARNELL RUCKER is Professor of Philosophy at Skidmore College, and author of *The Chicago Pragmatists,* as well as articles on American philosophy, ethics and education. He has taught at the University College of the University of Chicago, and at Colorado College. His B.E.E. is from Georgia Institute of Technology, A.M. and Ph.D. from the University of Chicago; he has held fellowships from the Carnegie Program for Internships in General Education and from the American Council of Learned Societies.

NATHAN A. SCOTT, JR. has his A.B. from the University of Michigan (1944), B.D. from Union Theological Seminary (1946) and Ph.D. from Columbia University (1949); since 1955 he has taught at the University of Chicago where he presently serves as Shailer Mathews Professor of Theology and Literature in the University's Divinity School and Department of English. Among his books are *The Wild Prayer of Longing: Poetry and the Sacred, Negative Capability: Studies in the New Literature and the Religious Situation* and *The Unquiet Vision: Mirrors of Man in Existentialism.* He is also Canon Theologian of the Cathedral of St. James, Chicago.

VICTORINO TEJERA is Professor of Philosophy at S.U.N.Y. at Stony Brook. From Venezuela, he was Herbert Schneider's student in American Philosophy, and his assistant at the Second Inter-American Congress of Philosophy (Columbia, 1947). His books include *Art and Human Intelligence, Aristotle's Analytics, Aristotle's Poetics and Rhetoric, Modes of Greek Thought* and (nearing completion) *Satire, Structure and Allegory in Plato's Dialogues.*

GIORGIO TONELLI is Professor of Philosophy at S.U.N.Y. at Binghamton. Educated in Pisa, Basel, the Sorbonne, Frankfurt and Naples, he holds the Libera Docenza in History of Philosophy and in German Language and Literature. He has taught at Pisa and Columbia Universities, and has lectured and held research positions in many countries, as well as serving on several scholarly editorial boards. Among his many books and articles are *Kant, dall 'estitica metafisica all' estetica psicoempirica* (Torino, 1955), and "Qu'estce que l'histoire de la philosophia?" (in *Rév. philos. de la France et de l'étranger).*

THEODORE WALDMAN is Professor of Philosophy at Harvey Mudd Col-

Biographical Notes

lege, with an A.M. from Washington University and U. of C., Berkeley, Ph.D. from Berkeley. His publications are in political philosophy, the history of ideas, and on Locke, Rousseau and Hobbes.

CRAIG WALTON was introduced to philosophy by Herbert Schneider at Pomona College in the Fall of 1959, later wrote the dissertation under the direction of Schneider, Popkin and Philip Merlan (published as *De la Recherche du Bien: A Study of Malebranche's Science of Ethics*) at the Claremont Graduate School. He has taught at the University of Southern California, Northern Illinois University, Emory University and (presently) at the University of Nevada, Las Vegas, and has published primarily in the history of philosophy.

HARVARD UNIVERSITY
http://lib.harvard.edu

If the item is recalled, the borrower will be notified of the need for an earlier return.

WIDENER SEP 1 0 2015	

Thank you for helping us to preserve our collection!